Crystal Yoga I
THE CRYSTAL MESA

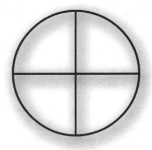

Roger Calverley

LOTUS
PRESS

P.O. Box 325
Twin Lakes, Wisconsin 53181 USA

Book Design & Layout: Susan Tinkle

Cover Design: Kim Murphy

First Edition 2006

Printed in the United States of America

ISBN 13: 978-0-9409-8592-6
ISBN 10: 0-9409-8592-6

Library of Congress Control Number: 2006927812

LOTUS
PRESS

Lotus Press, P.O. Box 325, Twin Lakes, WI 53181 USA
web: www.lotuspress.com
email: lotuspress@lotuspress.com
800.824.6396

TABLE OF CONTENTS

FOREWORD

A book about Yoga must spring first and foremost from personal experience. For this, there can be no substitute. But to share mystical experiences with strangers is to make public what is essentially sacred. For very good reasons, contemplative experiences must be nurtured in the secret chamber of the heart until their transformative power is fully assimilated. If shared, best shared with those whose hearts and minds are already open to the action of Spirit. And when shared, only when and where sanction of the Higher Self has already opened the doors.

In writing this Foreword, my hope and trust is that you the reader will find your way into the life-transforming experiences of Crystal Yoga more readily if I share some of my own experiences. My personal journey has been richly rewarding and often unpredictable so I ask your indulgence as I situate the book's contents in this context. It is this inner voyage of discovery which I have been on these past thirty and more years which has brought me to the writing of a book on Yoga. And it is as a living adventure that the path will continue to unfold wherever it moves beyond theory into practice.

I still remember very clearly the occasion of my first encounter with cosmic consciousness. I had been exercising in Hart House, on the campus of the University of Toronto, and was leaving the building with friends. Just as I stepped out the front door, my awareness suddenly altered and within a split second, I was perceiving the whole world in a way utterly unlike anything I had ever known.

It is not easy to describe what that state is like. I was aware of everything as it had always seemed; in terms of visual appearance, the cars, trees, grass and people looked the same. But what I was seeing, or rather knowing in all of these, was not difference, but sameness. I was in touch with the living essence behind it all. I knew the One manifesting itself through all these forms, and I knew this indefinable essence as identical to my own being. I was THAT which I was seeing multifariously presented before my eyes. But this was not a thought. Nor was it a state of blissful exaltation. It was unemotionally, clearly, and fully obvious to me that the many forms my eyes perceived were all the same thing, the same living, conscious being. It was as natural as breathing to perceive this, it was effortless, self-evident. The cars were THAT; the sidewalk was THAT; I was THAT, and so were my friends and everyone else around me. All was THAT, only THAT.

In hindsight, I wish I had been at liberty to sit and meditate, and thus perhaps consolidate this state of consciousness and make it permanent, but I was not. The experience gradually wore off over the next half hour, and I remember clearly how bit by bit my normal, thinking mind encroached on this clear space of seeing and being and gradually re-established its thinking patterns in my head. I have to say that this experience of the One Living Being (whose self-presentation is multiplicity) was not induced by anything that I can pinpoint. I had been meditating daily for an hour or more for five or ten years, prior to that day, but this experience was not generated by a meditation, it just happened. Later, several years later, I entered the experience of the 'peace that passes all understanding' while meditating. Thus, I am very clear about the difference between a spontaneous experience and one that arises out of 'infused' contemplation. This initial contact with the cosmic consciousness had come about spontaneously and unprovoked.

Yet, it would be mistaken to say that it was unrelated to my years of daily meditation, or the time and energy I had put into selfless service, or the study of spirituality in which for many years I had been engaged. In all the ways that felt right and possible, I had cultivated a life of spiritual aspiration. I had studied meditation with a former disciple of Sri Aurobindo and the Mother, and for a number of years I had been accepting invitations to travel and give talks on meditation. I had begun to write books on self development and spirituality. And I was not unfamiliar with mystical domains of inner experience. It has been my custom for many years to sit for meditation every morning at 7 am with a clear quartz sphere in the palm of my hands, and an aspiration to unite with the Divine in my heart. This attunement using crystals, and these years of regular practice certainly laid the foundation for what has evolved in my understanding of Crystal Yoga.

In the course of writing a book on *Radionics and Self Development*, in 1985-6 I had my first inner interview with The Mother. This meeting on the inner planes came during the intermediate consciousness that is neither sleeping nor waking, a region where many of my revelatory experiences seem to take place. The Mother came to me in the inner world and was very interested to talk about the possibilities that existed in the crossover between healing technology (such as radionics) and the evolution of consciousness. I remember very clearly how natural and easy to be with she was, and how genial and affectionate her presence seemed. It was like meeting a dear relative that you have known for a long time, but not seen very often, who made you feel completely at ease and who had a very kind and, well, "motherly" interest in what you were about. I suppose, in retrospect, she was sanctioning or blessing my early venture into the field of writing about consciousness and its awakening. This would not be my last experience with the Mother, but it was the first time that my mind was fully aware of her involvement in my life. Since then, I have had a growing awareness of her presence; she seems especially close to me at certain times when I am writing, and also when I am engaged in healing practices that clear the way for spiritual progress. Sensitive people can feel that the Ancient Mysteries Tarot Deck and its accompanying book carry the Shakti force; this I attribute to her action.

I mention these two experiences to lead into a theme that I feel to be very important, and in need of clear statement at the very outset. Yoga is not, in reality, something we do, although we have this impression at the beginning of our practice. It is a matter essentially of letting go and releasing the mind and ego from their interference patterns so that our Higher Self can become the doer. Two kinds of action, *letting go* and *opening up*, between them, contain the whole of Yoga. And these are best accomplished by allowing a higher power to work on us and in us and through us. Crystal Yoga is simply working with crystals in the process of opening up and letting go, placing ourselves in the flow of this higher power. When we let go of the domination which ego and mind have exercised over life, the Divine becomes the doer not only of meditation but of all actions, and all action becomes a form or self-offering to Source. It does not matter whether we identify the Divine as God the Father, or the Mother, or in any other form, or whether we interpret the Divine to be a formless Presence or an infinite, impersonal Consciousness. What does matter is that we place ourselves in the flow of living experience that connects us to Source. If working with crystals helps you to do this, then you have an opening for Crystal Yoga, and the present book may serve you in your growth. This would be my hope as you begin your reading.

In the opening chapter of *The Primal Runes,* I described a period of time when I lived in the forest and cultivated a connection with the four sacred elements and brought forward my bardic gifts to compose words and music for the harp. At this time I began making trips to Peru where I was drawn into a study of the shamanic tradition. It began by a seeming co-incidence. I was stepping through the door from my guest house in Cusco when I met an American traveller who was heading down-town. There was no other door onto this particular street for a good half block, so had I exited fifteen seconds earlier or later I would not have met this individual. We ended up talking as we walked to the main square, and he recommended that I take the time to meet a shaman with whom he had been working. A few days later, I did make contact with this shaman, Don Mario. We met a number of times and it resulted in a variety of interesting experiences. But the experience I wish to share from this period of time did not happen when I was with Don Mario. It came when I was alone, and sleeping.

I had a powerful dream. In this dream, I was in the basement of a vast building, and all the pipes that served the upper stories were running here and there across the ceilings and throughout the space of the room in a dense network. Lightening began to strike the pipes, and each time lightening would flash down with an abrupt crashing sound, the metal would turn orange and begin to glow. I have had many unusual dreams, but I mention this one for two reasons. When I awoke, I had a distinct feeling that something remarkable had happened. I felt surcharged with a different quality and quantity of energy than I was used to. Secondly, weeks or months after the dream, I came to understand what it had meant. One who is called to be a shaman in the tradition of the Peruvian shamans is most often elected from on high by being struck with lightening. And this experience of being struck by lightening can happen as many as three times. In this dream, the building was an image of my own microcosm, and the lightening repeatedly striking the various pipes was the mandate from on high, the invitation for me to embark on the shamanic journey.

I made a number of return trips to Peru between 1999 and 2006, and received a variety of initiations into various aspects of shamanic experience. I did not want to use psychedelic substances like Ayahuasca or San Pedro, although one or two shamans I had met would have made this available had I wanted. Rather, my way forward seemed to involve a relationship with Mother Earth, stone, and in particular, crystals.

My path forward became very clear in another dream of archetypal significance that I had on the same day that I met the Peruvian shamanic teacher, Regis Llerena. In this dream, I was on a mountain top and a large, white and fluffy condor chick landed beside me and began to talk with me. This dream merged into another dream in which mother Mary appeared, and in this dream was accompanied by a feeling of exaltation and rapture. Regis interpreted the first dream to mean that the spirits of the Apus, the gods of the mountains, were ready to work with me. I myself interpret the second dream as the blessing of the Mother on this work.

Some of my most deeply moving experiences in the Peruvian Andean tradition came during my stay with the Q'ero Indians, direct ancestors of the Incas, and preservers of the purest shamanic teaching and practice. The journey to the land of the Q'ero became possible after I met Dennis, who was a student of Don Sebastian. He spent time at a restaurant in Cusco where I knew I could get vegetarian food, and it was not long after meeting him there that a plan to travel to the land of the Q'ero was hatched between us. Dennis, another friend and I travelled together by bus, by taxi, and finally on horseback over perilous mountain roads, along narrow paths, across glaciers and through steep passes until we came to the village where Don Sebastian lived.

During the time I spent in that village, learning about shamanism in the Q'ero tradition and being initiated as a Pampa Mesayoq, my most remarkable experience took place in the wee hours of the morning. I awoke in the middle of the night and went outside to answer the call of nature. As I looked up at the sky, my attention was drawn to one of the stars. It began to sparkle and glow in a most unusual way. As I watched, its light and radiance slowly increased until it was at least ten times as bright as any other star in the sky. Even while watching it, I thought: "This can't be happening! But this IS happening!." I was not in a meditative state, and I was not dreaming; I was watching something happen that science could not explain. The star continued gleaming; minutes passed. A shooting star flashed by. Then, slowly the star had resumed its normal lustre, and I returned to bed.

I knew enough of the shamanic tradition to understand that a second important element of the true shamanic calling had fallen into place. I had met my "star," my "estrella" as the locals would say. When the "estrella" appears, and it may take several forms, the Holy Spirit has come and blessed the way forward; the star is a sign that you have been granted higher help and guidance. The meaning of the experience is not unlike the meaning of the "star" card in Tarot. This experience took place on the morning of my initiation, and I sensed it to be a most auspicious omen. Other favourable omens had also occurred. These included the appearance of hummingbirds at moments of unique importance, the appearance of eagles where they are rarely seen just prior to sacred ceremonies, and coca leaf readings which consistently pointed to the same thing, namely that my newly awakened shamanic interest was aligned to the divine plan and that the way forward was open.

It is only by following the guidance that comes to us from within, listening to the voice of the Spirit, and doing our best to accomplish the soul's work that we can go forward in the spiritual life. All Yoga is a "yoking" or linking of what is above (infinite consciousness) with what is below (our human potential). The greatness above is nothing other than the divine will, or as the Chinese called it, the "mandate of heaven." Only by becoming a servant and an instrument of this divine direction, a child of the Mother, as Sri Aurobindo puts it, can the human body-mind actualize the realities of transcendental consciousness.

In large measure, what we need is clarity. Clarity means freedom from confusion, absence of ego, liberation from desires, and a focused will lit from within by an open, loving heart. The early phases of yoga are largely about developing these qualities, for without them, we can not go very far. With them, the possibilities are endless. In the field of infinite possibility, there arises a special opening made possible from the beginning of time by divine providence. It has always been part of the cosmic plan that crystals would contribute their unique qualities to humanity's spiritual awakening. Crystals came into existence in order to actualize with us the full Earth-Heaven marriage. We fulfil both their purpose and our own higher destiny when we unite to accomplish the soul's work.

After travelling to Peru a number of times and developing my own personal *mesa*, I began to receive an inner prompting from the Muse (one aspect of the Divine Mother to which I am connected) to reveal a body of knowledge that relates to Crystal Yoga, and in particular the value of a Crystal Mesa for doing yoga. I had spent long hours wandering the banks of various streams and the Urubamba River collecting special stones, and I had prayed at the ancient Inca Temple of the Moon in Pisac to be able to re-incarnate the ancient traditions accurately. On that occasion, I gathered a small pebble from each of the stone alcoves of the temple which I placed in a carved stone box in order to have the complete vibrations of the lunar path constantly nearby. Because I had already written three books on the subject of crystals (Crystal Spirit, The Healing Gems, and The Language of Crystals), I was not un-acquainted with their esoteric properties. Still, when the impulse to begin this book came, I had just finished writing *The Primal Runes* and was not eager to place myself at the keyboard and the computer screen for the long months it would take to complete a new piece of writing.

In all choices that present themselves, and in the attitude one takes, the them, you either have the blessing and guidance of the higher forces, or you do not. The blessing is always there, in point of fact, but our access to it is often constricted by wrong attitude or by selfish choice. One cannot say "no" to the inner guidance if one wants to continue moving forward in the inner life, so setting aside any reluctance I plunged into the writing of this new book.

When I began the writing, I had not been aware that there was a "deva" in the inner world who presided over the knowledge associated with Crystal Yoga, or a "deva" for the wisdom of Crystal Mesa. However, during the final weeks of the book's writing, my friend

Margherita did several channelling sessions in which I had the good fortune to ask these devas any question I wanted and to satisfy myself on a number of points relating to the book's contents. I must say a sincere "thank-you" to Margherita and to everyone else who has encouraged me during the writing process. It is always helpful to have a few friends to talk to and share chapters with as they are written, it helps keep the flow going. Margherita herself is a very experienced crystal healer and teacher and I have been privileged to consult with her and ask suggestions at several points in the writing process.

One interesting fact that came out during question and answer periods with these two devas is that Crystal Yoga is based on a crystal, or jewel, which exists at the core of the spiritual heart. I believe this is the same jewel referred to in the great mantra of Tibetan Buddhism: *Om Mani Padme Hum.* Some people have lost their connection with this jewel, and others have not. For those who maintain the connection, the yoga is possible. For those who have compromised the connection, a change of lifestyle and thinking is necessary. If the jewel at the centre of your spiritual heart is still intact and has not been clouded over, you are ready to read this book in full and to begin practice. As of the present moment, with Christmas 2005 fast approaching, there are between (according to the deva) eight and ten thousand persons in North America who are ready to begin the practice of Crystal Yoga.

For those of you who feel the call to this form of practice, let me conclude this short Foreword by sharing one or two pointers that may be of help...

Crystal Yoga is not a new path. Crystal Yoga is as ancient as Lemuria, as fresh and new as the magic that attracts you to a particular stone from hundreds of others that look much like it. You may use the techniques and information that you find in this book with any other path you now follow whether you think of yourself as a Sufi, a Taoist, a yogi or a Christian mystic. When you use crystals, you are inviting Mother Nature to support your practice, and you are uniting yourself with the aspiration of the planet. Crystals are the most evolved beings of the mineral kingdom. They have realized the stillness, interior order, clarity and focused purpose to which spiritually awakening humans aspire. They are living, surrendered life-forms ready to place all they have and all that they are at our disposal, and to co-create with us a truly spiritual ascension of consciousness. They support our aspiration for full realization of the Source.

You will find many ideas and suggestions for practice in the following pages, but keep in mind that your own imagination and your open heart are your best tools for discovering the unique approach that works best in your own individual case. Respect the tradition, know it thoroughly, but feel your way forward by listening to your heart. Trust your intuition, grow with it in confidence. Have crystals near you as you read. Open your mind and soul to the fullness of the possibilities that lie ahead in the journey that you are about to begin.

May every page you turn take you a step closer to the full possession of that most beautiful of all crystals, the self-form that your soul has birthed in the core of your very own spiritual heart.

ROGER CALVERLEY
Lindsay, December 1, 2005

The Andean Cross, or "Chakana" is seen here with the Crystal Mesa Logo at its centre. The "chakana" design constitutes the floorplan of an inner temple which we visualize in the Thirteenth Attunement.

FACETS OF THE JEWEL

Now will I do in thee my marvelous works.
I will fasten thy nature with my cords of strength,
Subdue to my delight thy spirit's limbs
And make thee a vivid knot of all my bliss
And build in thee my proud and crystal home.

Savitri, pg. 698

In prefacing his writings about Hermetic Magic, Franz Bardon noted that everything he had written was simply an exploration of the wisdom inherent on the first three cards of Tarot. In the same sense, what I have written in this book about *Crystal Mesa* is an exploration of one particular vein of wisdom which can be glimpsed in Sri Aurobindo's *Savitri,* which I consider to be the greatest piece of spiritual writing from the 20th century.

The essence of this wisdom is very ancient: "As below, so above; as within, so without." High above us in the skies, we see the stars, bodies of divine beings, and we have known from earliest times that their essence is condensed into the gem crystals of our very own Mother Earth. Our bodies are microcosms of THAT. We have within our physical, etheric, astral and mental bodies all that we see writ large above us and around us as the stuff of the universe. And this interior potential that we embody can be activated. This precious temple of our very own embodied existence can house the powers and presences of living gods. (The Sanskrit root of "deva" clearly shows that a god is a 'Light-being.') The accomplishment of this inner work is possible through right knowledge and use of crystals, and of a special assemblage of crystals known as the Crystal Mesa. In time, and with practice, each stone within the mesa comes to be understood as the physical body of a "deva" - or as they would have said in ancient India, a god. Our inner universe, our precious microcosm becomes a congress of the gods whose unified action establishes celestial harmony in all planes and parts of our being. Beyond that, according to our capacity and the divine will, we become instruments of a similar transformation in the planet, and co-creators of its spiritual destiny.

Crystals, and in particular the energies that move through them, can help us accomplish our inner, spiritual work of ordering, perfecting and harmonizing the light-bodies which incarnate our soul in time and space. By doing this work of transformation, the mesa-keeper's mind and microcosm slowly and surely become a reflection of celestial wholeness and perfection. Crystal workers become attuned to spiritual worlds beyond this physical plane, and sensitive to the living energies of conscious beings that exist in the inner worlds all the way up to Source. Moreover, the mesa's capacity to purify, open and illumine our light-bodies and chakras expedites our progress on the path to ascension. With correct use of this sacred bundle, we move more surely and quickly forward to realization and ultimate enlightenment, which in ancient times was called "apotheosis" – the attainment of the divine state. Apollonius and Pythagoras were historical personages of the classical world who, in all probability, had this attainment, as did many of the Vedic seers and sages of India. Crystal Yoga is simply the use of crystals to complete the soul's mission on Earth according to the divine plan.

In the inner worlds, there is a circle of twelve disincarnate intelligent beings who join in consciousness to attune human beings to the work that is to be done with crystals. They observe the spiritual possibility of certain people, and where appropriate, they beam in energies which will expedite the work. Although they have never physically incarnated, they are empowered and mandated to attune individuals to the special sensitivities, capacities and understandings required to work with the physical mineral kingdom. Other teachers and initiates who have left the body also work from the inner planes to communicate understanding to those doing this work on Earth. Thus, there is a band of souls knit together in common endeavour to bring the Divine Plan to fruition, and it includes those working in a physical body, those who have left the body behind, and those who have never taken a physical body. There is, in fact, no isolation in this work, and its seemingly fragmented nature at this time is perhaps inevitable, because this is only the beginning phase of a vast undertaking.

Progressively, a unification of consciousness and information will take place on these foundations which we are laying, and the basis for a higher stage of consciousness on Earth will be realized. The crystalline nature of our own physical microcosm destines us to be light-workers and earth-transformers. When we consciously choose to go forward in this adventure of spiritual discovery, the subject of Crystal Yoga becomes most meaningful; the practice of attunement to Source with progressive realization of our starseed destiny yields rich rewards of joy and peace.

There is one goal, but the paths are many. Crystal Yoga has several distinguishing features. It is **first of all**, a yoga of the masters, in a double sense. Crystals are masters in the mineral kingdom. They have evolved perfection of form, clarity and purity and are thus able to work with light and energy in remarkable ways. When we work with crystals, we are working with the masters of the mineral kingdom, but also we are working on the foundations that come from human spiritual masters who have gone before us. Authors such as Katrina Raphael have written about the twelve master crystals, and they are important for the work undertaken in Crystal Yoga. The ultimate goal of life, and the way to its realization have been contemplated from the most ancient times, and a body of traditional wisdom has been passed down through various lineages and schools, including the mystery schools that flourished up until the time of the Roman Emperor Constantine. Those souls who manifest deep attainment renew the tradition, teach it, and sometimes initiate the awakening of others through their words and actions. They are masters, and we are all in training for this mastery.

Secondly, Crystal Yoga is a yoga of manifestation, and therefore it flows from the will and power of the Divine Mother. The Absolute Supreme takes form, for the purposes of creation, as the Mother-Power, and all transformation flows from Her. Just as all humans are physically children of Mother Earth, so our souls are divine children of the Divine Mother, the Mother of all creation. Only through the dynamic, action of the Mother and those who have realized and embodied her action on Earth is evolution of consciousness, and hence yoga, possible.

Thirdly, Crystal Yoga is an integral yoga. That is to say, it engages all parts of our being, the body, emotions, mind, and spirit or soul, unifying them around a divine seed of pre-established spiritual perfection. This crystal of perfection has already been planted in the spiritual heart of each soul destined for this yoga; it is the celebrated jewel in the lotus of the heart referred to in the Tibetan mantra: OM MANI PADME HUM. We work with this seed and its inherent perfection to bring forth the fullness of our soul's capacity, thus realizing our goal of attaining conscious oneness with Source.

Crystal Yoga is, **fourthly,** a yoga of transformation. Its object is not merely to find a way beyond suffering and opt out of the cosmic play, but rather to transform our own being, and also the world into a perfect reflection of Heaven. The goal is not merely to attain realization of the static aspect of the Higher Self, although this is important. Beyond this, the yoga calls us to participate in a dynamic, unfolding work that the Divine Creative Power is accomplishing on Earth. We can thus add that, **fifthly,** this yoga is a planetary ascension of shared experience, not a private quest for personal power. Our aspiration derives not merely from our ego's individual desire for personal salvation; rather it flows from a larger will to serve the divine plan for humanity, and for the entire planet with all its life forms, including even the stones of the physical body of Mother Earth.

Crystal yoga is, **sixthly,** a domain of experience within the yoga we find set forth by Sri Aurobindo in his spiritual masterpiece, Savitri. This remarkable spiritual testimony summarizes the master's comprehensive inner experience, and is a revelation that will serve spiritual seekers for millennia to come. It gives a detailed picture of the divine plan as it unfolds in all the inner worlds, as well as the soul's mission and destiny within that framework. Crystal Yoga is not the only yoga we find in this monumental work of visionary creativity, it is one of several, or we could say, one of many. But the reader who is interested to explore the text of Savitri will find a treasure-house of imagery, symbolism and allegory that activates the process of spiritual awakening in consciousness.

Seventh, Crystal yoga is archetypal in the sense that the archetypes are fundamentally important for its action. Four significant archetypes are at the centre of the crystal mesa, and constitute the core of its structural dynamic. Lemurian Jade is placed within the mesa-bundle as the crystalline body of the Mother, and Lapis Lazuli is there as the energy and consciousness of the archetypal Sage. The gold flecks in black matrix of Lemurian Jade represent the stars in the night-time sky, while the gold flecks in an indigo-blue matrix of Lapis Lazuli represent the same stars in the daytime sky. Night is the matrix of aspiration, and day is the sun-filled air of spiritual attainment. The gold stars are the cosmic gods and their powers; descent of their gold light into the Earth atmosphere and into the human microcosm takes place when we attain illumination. The lunar and solar pathways of return to Source are figured in the archetypes of Mother and the Sage.

The one who makes the journey of return to Source is the inner child, the psychic being or soul, represented in the mesa by Rhodochrosite. And the power by which the journey is made is Agni, which is the flame of aspiration, the Hero, represented in the mesa by Rutilated Smokey Quartz (or alternately by Rutilated Citrine). At the centre of these four crystal archetypes is a sphere of pure, clear quartz crystal, which represents Source. The Mother, the Child, the Hero and the Sage are thus the principle archetypes of the Crystal Mesa; they assist the mesa-keeper along the path to direct experience of Transcendental Reality. In making the journey, each soul recapitulates a timeless and ancient pathway of return to Source, and for each the journey is unique despite the common elements of practice and orientation outlined here.

Eighthly, Crystal Yoga is elemental – and this in two senses. The Four Sacred Elements are centrally important in the early stages of practice, and in the Crystal Mesa these are represented by four groups of seven crystals. The Mother presides over the seven Earth Crystals; the Child is placed with the Water Crystals; the Hero is with the Fire Crystals and the Sage is with the Air Crystals. There are stones for Spirit Earth (Jade), Spirit Water (Selenite), Spirit Fire (Ruby) and Spirit Air (Apophyllite or Celestite), as well as separate crystals for the Yin and Yang energies of these four elements. Thus, in total, the main body of the mesa is comprised of 28 stones, one for each day of the lunar cycle. This comprises a complete palette of the energies of the gods. Also, each crystal has its own elemental inner life, sometimes called a "Deva." Some elements of the teaching and practice have been received from the Deva of Crystal Yoga who is a real being in the inner world charged with the responsibility for holding and imparting this knowledge. One can contact and work with the devic intelligences of crystals in collaboration, and on this significant parts of the practice are based.

This points to the next distinguishing feature of Crystal Yoga, which is that it is (**ninthly**) co-creative. We collaborate and co-operate with the Divine Mother, the four archetypes, the crystals and their devas as well as other beings both physical and non-physical at most stages of practice. We could say, in this sense, that Crystal Yoga is a collective yoga. The "creative" side of the term co-creative is quite important. All forms of creative expression have a valuable place in this yoga. Singing, writing, painting and imagining can be as important as meditation during certain phases of practice.

The **tenth** feature of Crystal Yoga is that it is Primal. The wisdom of this ancient way goes back even to pre-Atlantean times and to the age of Lemuria. Its knowledge is pre-Vedic in large part, but in its modern, resurrected form Crystal Yoga is a renewal of what has already been known and done. It seemingly re-constitutes itself like the phoenix from the ashes of the past, pulling in fragments here and there that are scattered remnants of the original, unified body of teaching which in Lemurian times was simply the planetary way of life. Much of this wisdom has been maintained by tribal societies for uncounted millennia and renewed from generation to generation by shamans.

Eleventh, Crystal Yoga is a heart-path. For all who engage these practices, the opening of the spiritual heart is centrally important. It is the direct route to awareness of the soul and its mission, which lays the groundwork for advanced practice. The qualities of the spiritual heart are indispensable, among them love, devotion, surrender, aspiration, dedication, intuition, faith and a capacity for selfless service to the world and humanity.

Twelfth, and flowing from the importance of the heart, comes the fact that Crystal Yoga is experiential, not theoretical. All yogas must to a large extent be experiential, but in Crystal Yoga all progress comes through a growth of personal experience, and thus the path is not identical for any two individuals. A teacher of this yoga cannot be too categorical or prescriptive. It is soon clear that each seeker is at a different point of the experiential journey, and from day to day, or even from moment to moment the yoga is a creative interface with the infinite consciousness through its self-revealing forms. No fixed pattern of understanding and no set of steps based on linear thinking can substitute for direct intuitive experience in exploring this mystery.

By attunement to crystalline energies, by opening our energy centers and our awareness to an inner, divine influence, and by the cultivation of spiritual light in our own light-body, we effect an inner transformation in the substance of our being. This expedites the evolution of the physical body, emotions and mind so that they become transparent to the power and reality of Soul, or Spirit, which is the divine presence within the spiritual heart at the centre of our microcosm.

When the light of soul is established in unimpeded flow, the stage is set for a more or less rapid movement into spiritual realization. Those who work with a crystal *mesa* as described in this book can anticipate significant progress in this line of experience. The early chapters of this book touch on crystals and their use in Crystal Yoga, and then the main body of the book presents the role of the crystal *mesa* as a sacred means to access the spiritual potential of crystals.

The various techniques of attunement presented in this book are progressive, so it is best to work through them in order. Your own inner guidance will tell you when you have sufficient experience and have made adequate progress to begin a new form of practice. Remember, even the earliest and simplest forms of practice can and should be engaged at more advanced stages of the path. The fundamentals are always important because without them, the foundation cannot be renewed.

You may have some stones that you have collected or saved over the years. This would be a good time to get them out, place them in front of you, and see which one speaks to you most. In doing this, you are starting your journey in Crystal Yoga. There may be more than one stone that you feel drawn to at any given time. Feeling your way forward in this matter is the way to learn attunement. Choose the stone or stones that most interest you, and one by one tune in to the impressions or feelings you get from each. You need not be able to verbalize these impressions, it is enough to note them. Crystal Yoga is possible simply because stones do catch our attention, engage our interest and call out to be held and considered by us.

From the most ancient times to this very day, stones engage us to interact with the body of Mother Earth. They call to us to discover our own unique way of feeling and sensing life's deep mystery and purpose. If you can feel this call, or if you have this interest to touch, to hold, to interact and to explore the mysteries of crystals, then you are ready for the experience of attunement. There is no better time to re-affirm the experiential pull that stones and crystals have than this very moment. When you have done this, you have completed your first attunement. It is as simple as that.

The deep affinity between our physical incarnation and the bones of Mother Earth is a mystery to be explored, as real and engaging as the physical fact of the stones that rest in the palm of your hand. Just as your hand has five fingers, the minerals of which these stones are constituted form five families. Your stones will be predominantly related to the energies of Earth, Water, Fire, Air or Ether. Five fingers, five domains of energy, infinite possibilities of experience and learning – you have all you need to make a beginning. When you are holding several stones in the palm of your hand, you have the simplest and original form of a *mesa*. Everything you will ever do in Crystal Yoga builds on this natural foundation: a hand holding stones, a mind and heart open to experience.

When you recognize and respond to this call to co-create a more perfect state of consciousness within yourself and a more beautiful world for all living beings, then you are ready to go forward on this adventure.

THE KEY CRYSTAL

It will help if you have a double-terminated quartz crystal with you when you read this section. You will work with crystal energy in the activation of your heart-crystal and the crystal you choose for this attunement will be your 'Key Stone.' Understand that your physical body and your nervous system have a special relationship with quartz, for they are both constructed (in part) from silica. Quartz is one crystalline form of silica, and silica is an indispensable component that gives you form and function. When you work with a double terminated quartz crystal, you are working with a component of your very own wholeness. Try, as you hold your crystal, to fully appreciate this fact. Silica plays a significant part in your destiny. Some of the most beautiful and functional threads of your being are silica crystal; you are ready to build on this component of your light body and realize your potential for wholeness.

Look at the largest facet at the tip of your crystal. Then reflect: This crystal is a master of the mineral kingdom; this facet expresses mastery. Similarly, this facet in my heart-crystal destines me for mastery. I acknowledge this facet of my heart crystal. I activate my heart-crystal's mastery facet. I am a master of my life's highest good.

Look at the next facet to the right of the first one, and reflect: This crystal manifests wholeness by the power of the Divine. This facet of my heart crystal destines me also to manifest the power of the Divine. I activate this facet of my heart crystal. I accept the responsibility to manifest Divine wholeness. I place my heart and my life in the lap of the Divine Mother to become all she has dreamed for me from the beginning of time.

Looking at the next facet to the right of the one you have just focused on, reflect: This crystal has its wholeness and completeness intact. It is functioning in an integral way, in balanced wholeness. My very own heart crystal is whole and balanced. I am an integral being, and I claim all parts and powers of my being for my soul's intent.

Continuing to the next facet: This crystal is transformational. It has demonstrated the power to grow and establish perfect form, and it now embodies this power. My very own heart crystal also has this power of self-transformation. I activate my heart-crystal and call its transformational power into my life. I take responsibility to transform all aspects of my life into the image of my soul's crystal perfection. I have the power to be transformed, totally.

Focusing on the next facet: This crystal is attuned to all other crystals and thus to all life. It is part of a collective manifestation, as am I. I acknowledge my heart-crystal's relation to the pattern of the whole and I undertake to honour the collective dimension of my spiritual unfoldment.

Moving your attention to the sixth facet, which is the only one remaining at this end of the crystal: This crystal is a perfect expression of form and beauty; it is an embodiment of harmony. I undertake to express beauty in my life, by drawing continuously on the beauty of my heart crystal. I will enrich my mind with beauty to remember the beauty of my divine potential, and I will pay attention to the selections from *Savitri* in this book as an example of the beauty of true speech.

Now, focusing attention on the largest facet at the opposite end of the crystal: This crystal is archetypal. It is built up from the primal numbers and proportions of creation, pristine in its expression of divine form and intent. My heart's crystal is archetypally perfect, and I claim it as the truth of my being.

Moving to the next fact to the right: This crystal solidifies the action of the four sacred elements and holds them in a state of harmonious balance. My heart crystal is also a philosopher's stone, holding Earth, Water, Fire and Air in sacred balance, and linking them with Ether, which is ascension to Source.

Looking at the next facet: This crystal is co-creative. It is birthed from Mother Earth, and it has grown according to a divine plan. My heart crystal is a co-creative action of the divine in the core of my being. I acknowledge this power in my heart crystal, and in my life.

Now, turning the crystal and focusing on the next facet: This crystal is primal. It has been evolving its form steadily, surely and with unbroken continuity for tens of thousands of years. My heart crystal is also primal, ancient, steeped with clear intent to manifest its full potential on Earth.

Gazing on the next-to-last facet: This crystal speaks to my heart, because it is a form which was originated and born from the heart of Mother Earth. My heart crystal destines my heart for infinite love. I claim this as my spiritual destiny. I live to embody infinite love.

Finally, focusing attention on the last facet: This crystal is a living reality, not a mental concept. My heart crystal is equally real, or even more real. The living power of this reality is fully and totally at my disposal. I claim my heart crystal and all it embodies as the core of my life, and the guiding light of my thoughts, actions and aspirations.

You will see that in the central portion of your double terminated crystal, there are six sides. If you want to be really-co-creative, then meditate and let your heart show you six other facets of your heart that you can claim as your own. Name them and claim them.

Place this crystal in your *mesa* and let it be known as your "Key" crystal. It represents the wholeness and infinite capacity of your soul. It is a physical counterpart of the seed crystal in your spiritual heart that enables the yoga.

By linking a real and living symbol from the outer world to the real and living (although invisible) potential of your heart crystal, you have begun to use crystal for yoga. If you can bring this process to life, feel it within your soul, it will have powerful results. By naming and claiming the facets of your heart jewel, you remember the fullness of your divine potential and make it your very own.

THE PERFECTION OF CRYSTAL

We have all felt, at one time or another, the inner need to go beyond the limitations of our human predicament, to transcend our ordinary consciousness and exceed the boundaries of personality. There is a dimension of reality that is completely other than the world of our concepts, free of the structures and confines of ego and mind. That dimension of reality has been called by different names: the Divine, the Infinite, the Beyond, the Absolute, the Spirit, the Self. Thinkers, mystics and sages of all times throughout history have agreed that this reality is beyond the senses and represents our highest good and fullest possibility. But to experience or realize this level of awareness, the human mind has to break through its habit-patterns of ordinary consciousness and strip away the conditioning which has defined and limited its parameters.

Various schools of meditation, self-development and mysticism teach techniques and processes for raising awareness to the spiritual level. Crystals are sometimes a part of these processes, particularly in teachings that derive from the North American Native cultures, or the shamanic indigenous traditions. There is also a highly developed school of crystal and gem lore that has its roots in India and Tibet with ancient connections extending all the way back to the times of Atlantis and beyond to Lemuria. People who take an interest in crystals and gems are often opening up to what Aldous Huxley called the 'Perennial Philosophy.' Many individuals who have begun their quest for inner awakening have an innate sense that there is something fulfilling beyond the physical dimension of life, and they want to explore and experience more of their inner potential. It is in this context that crystals may be acquired as friends for the journeying and tools for the inner work.

Quartz and other varieties of crystals have been applied to every sphere of life from the most mundane to the mystical. They can be used to soothe the emotions, to alleviate pain, to clarify and calm the mind, to heal the body, and to help with the achievement of a particular ambition or goal. They are harnessed to purify and energize water, food and soil, as well as to improve the energy-level of indoor living environments. Crystals are used to heal mental and emotional wounds, and to enhance holistic modes of understanding and relating. They may even, at a certain stage of the spiritual seeker's quest, help in the attainment of liberation, and at this point they interface with the spiritual practices called yoga.

What makes crystal such a special tool for working with energy and consciousness? Those who have studied crystal in its many forms sometimes answer this question by referring to a model of the universe at once as ancient as the mystery schools and as modern as quantum physics. This model is set forth in the world's most ancient scriptures, the Vedas, and it is also current in the advanced theories of our own leading scientists. It is even finding expression in movies like *"What The Bleep Do We Know?"* According to this paradigm, all phenomena in the universe are held to be different forms or expressions of a single, ultimate reality. The ancient sources refer to this reality as consciousness, while the more modern ones sometimes use the term energy. In religious terms, the reality might be called Spirit, while physicists are beginning to acknowledge it as a field infinite consciousness.

On the highest vibratory levels, according to the ancient scriptures of India, there exists pure divine consciousness-energy, pure spiritual light. Then, on lower levels this light manifests as the non-material planes of existence, including the various heavens. And finally, it manifests as matter, a very dense, devolved form of the divine energy. Human beings have a mind and spirit which can be attuned to the higher planes of reality, and in proportion as mankind does lift its attention, it evolves beyond the animal consciousness and into a progressively enlightened destiny.

Because cosmic energy, visible light, electricity, thought and matter are all variants of the one primal reality, it is possible for special material structures like crystal to store, amplify, transduce and focus any or all of the various manifestations of consciousness-energy. Like man, the Earth is a living, evolving entity. Like the body of man, it has arteries of specially refined substances which carry and transmit energy of various kinds into the denser matter. Many of the veins of ore are interlaced with crystalline formations which as we know are excellent receivers and transmitters. A tremendous variety of cosmic energy is picked up by the crystalline structures within the Earth and relayed into the denser portions of the Earth-body to energize it and promote its evolution.

Slowly, the material substance of the Earth becomes radiant with life-force and consciousness. The crystalline gem substances in particular act as sensitive relay stations within the body of the Earth which pick up and transmit cosmic energy much the same way that nerve cells receive minute energy impulses and transmit them through the physical body. The Earth receives energies of many different kinds from the various bodies which surround it in space. Each of the different kinds of energies is picked up by mineral substances on Earth and channeled into the life-experiences of the Earth. Gemlike crystals are special formations of matter which take shape and evolve under the influences of these planetary and cosmic energies. The colour of a crystal and its structure show the kind of energy that is being expressed. Because crystals and gems are the most highly developed portions of the body of the Earth, they perform particular functions with energy and consciousness, and what they have been accomplishing for the planetary body they can do within the human microcosm as well.

All the inter-galactic and inter-planetary energies that permeate the universe are vibrating with different frequencies. They send their pulsations throughout space, and all these frequencies radiate their own influence to build up a tremendous variety of life-forms and a diversity of living phenomena. A vast range of vibrations comes down through the density of the stratosphere, and combines in every conceivable way on Earth. The shifting patterns of the zodiac indicate what energies predominate at any given time. The combinations of these subtle forces make every particle of this planet what it is in the infinite variety of form, sound, texture and energy that one sees in physical manifestation.

Possibly the most important family of crystals for our planet is quartz. Its wide distribution, its many forms and colours and its unique qualities place it at the forefront of human interest as a tool for accomplishing the modification of energy. Scientists are already beginning to develop a conceptual framework to accommodate the experiences of crystal users who are discovering the potential for non-physical transformation in their own inner emotional, mental and psycho-physical nature.

It is important to understand why crystal can perform these various functions so very well. The human body takes its atoms and molecules from the body of Earth which is a composite of stardust from the ends of the universe. The bones of the human body, like the crystalline rocks of Earth have a certain capacity to transmit, magnify and connect our microcosm of energy and consciousness to that of the stars and the galaxies. The expression "I feel it in my bones" is based on this. As children of the stars, composites of stardust, we are part of a wider whole, a cosmic plan. We are working out parts of that plan in our physical incarnation on Earth, and the crystals have also evolved to serve this end.

Within a quartz crystal, millions of spiraling molecules are ar-ranged in perfect alignment and symmetry. The exquisite order of their inner patterning explains the remarkable properties of quartz, its ability to receive, record, amplify, convert and focus an astounding range of vibrations. Quartz crystal is indispensable in the construc-tion of computers, radios, televisions and all forms of technology that rely on silicon chips. But for the human consciousness in quest of greater awareness, the question is less technological and more te-leological. How can crystals support and empower my own deeply personal and interior work with energy and consciousness?

Crystals embody many of the qualities we need in our journey from limitation to fullness. One of these qualities is clarity. Crystals provide no obstruction to the action of light. Some crystals, like some humans, are rather flawed and opaque, but certain crystals embody a remarkable clarity that sets them apart in the mineral world. Because of the internal coherence and order of their molecular arrangement, they respond with precision and sensitivity to every input of energy. If we were speaking of an evolved human being, we would say that he or she is more aware, more responsive, more refined, perhaps more clear. Clear gem crystals are the most evolved members of the mineral kingdom and have a perfection equivalent, in their own domain, to that of a highly evolved human being in the human world. A crystal has another capacity that most humans lack, which is the capacity to surrender to its master; actually, the deva inside the stone body of the crystal point is the conscious entity that interacts with our human consciousness. Crystal devas do not have a separate agenda of egoistically centred intent. They are whole and perfect as the divine idea made them, not wounded as we human souls are. In one sense, we would say that not having developed separate volition and ego, they are less evolved than the humans that use them. However, in another sense, they are more perfect for being truly surrendered instruments of higher intent, and the perfect molecular order of their stone bodies reflects this fact.

In appearance, water-clear quartz crystals suggest infinity, especially when cut and polished to the form of a sphere. When we study the energy fields around crystals, we find that they are dynamic energy systems that in many ways resemble humans. However, unlike humans, their energy is perfectly balanced and regulated. Each crystal emits a distinct tone which, for some people, is actually audible; so does each person emit his or her distinctive tone, smell and coloured auric energy. Each quartz crystal, for example, has its own highly individual signature, as distinctive as a personal odour would be in a human being, something that is perfectly obvious, say to a dog. Crystals are adapted to different functions according to their distinctive patterning. Some are meant to work at the physical level, while others interface more dynamically at the astral or mental or intuitive levels of our being. Unlike people, crystals do not make noise. They express simplicity, steadiness, harmony and silent power. A crystal's natural form is symmetrical, aesthetic, rarely "busy." A beautiful, clear crystal sitting quietly near a sunny window is one of nature's purest expressions of the state of effortless contemplation. Egoless, still, clear, poised and harmoniously balanced in all ways, while dynamically energetic, a high quality crystal is a wonderful creation of nature that more and more people are using for attunement to higher energy and consciousness. These qualities of crystal have been recognized for thousands of years, and shamans, healers and spiritual seekers have kept crystals in sacred bundles, or *mesas*, and used them in many ways for attaining wholeness.

It helps to be clear about the different ways that crystals can interface with human energy.

Firstly, crystals enable us to transfer energy. Their highly patterned internal structure does not present any impediment to the flow of energy of all kinds, on various levels, including mental and astral. In fact, one can cycle imbalanced energy through a crystal and have it cleansed and balanced in the process. Secondly, crystals will amplify energy. For example, mental energy in the form of thoughts can be empowered and projected by using crystals and they can be incorporated into healing devices for just this purpose. Crystals tend to organize and transform the molecular structure of substances placed in proximity to them. Beyond this, they have a third application, the storage of vibrations of all kinds – something we see in the computer industry and silicon chips. The famous crystal skull has revealed a great deal of information, and certain ancient cultures used crystals as libraries. We are recovering and processing information from these record-keeper crystals and it is fuelling our recovery of long lost ancient knowledge.

Another important quality of crystals is that they can be programmed. To programme a crystal means to place certain energy patterns into it which will then perform a specific kind of function. These energies can be at any level from the physical to the spiritual. For self-development purposes, crystals can be used to amplify spiritual and higher mental energies so that one's consciousness and sensitivity can expand to higher levels. One can programme a crystal mentally if one has the capacity to concentrate thought sufficiently, to visualize distinct images and hold them steadily in mind while projecting them into the molecular lattice of the crystal. This skill may take some time to develop. One crystal may be useful for treating physical disorders while another may be better for psychological problems and still a third may be programmable with spiritual energies. Crystals can also be cleared after they have been programmed and used in a different way the next time.

The *mesa* is a collection of objects such as crystals which creates a place or space of higher order and energy. It is thus a device whereby human consciousness and energy become focused on higher levels of functioning. Human thought and action depart from the eternal order when they become obsessed with the narrow concerns of the separate self, or we may say, the ego. To the degree that we widen and clarify consciousness and energy to their pristine, crystalline condition, it is possible to embrace our own higher reaches of potential.

The ancient lore of the *mesa* gives us the means of assembling crystals (and other sacred objects) in such a way as to create a tool of empowerment, knowledge, attainment and regeneration. A correctly constructed and activated *mesa* creates sacred space, which means that it is a kind of portable temple. Crystals go very well within *mesas* not only because they facilitate the achievement of personal goals and the removal of obstacles, but beyond this, they constantly express what pure consciousness is like. They are a material embodiment and a concrete expression in matter of what seeking humans aspire to become. Perfectly surrendered to the consciousness that uses them, they nonetheless point the way beyond all forms of human strategy to a state that is already complete and whole.

In their book, *Walkers Between the Worlds*, Caitlin and John Matthews make this clear:

The macrocosm represents the eternal reality of light, the reality of God. The microcosm is a reflection or fragmentation of the light, the realm of humanity in creation, the Body of Light scattered throughout the universe. Each created thing bears a spark of the divine Light. While some forget their original condition, others remember and become walkers between the worlds who make the reassembling of the Body of Light their overriding aim. Yet the Body of Light, like that of Humpty Dumpty is so fragmented that it seems the pieces could never be reassembled between inertia and the multiplicity of ways to achieve this end, the task looks impossible. For some, the realization that their individual divine spark is trapped in flesh brings about a denial of the body itself. There are some, though, who seek to reassemble the Body of Light by religious or esoteric means. In each generation there are a number of people who dedicate themselves to this task. (pgs 170 – 1)

A well assembled *mesa* is a body of light. It is a patterned assemblage of the most perfectly crystallized lights that exist in the body of Mother Earth, the precious and semi-precious gems. In the cosmically-organized crystal *mesa,* these nodes of materialized light embody the full spectrum of the *tattwic* powers of the Five Sacred Elements. When they are assembled into a symbolic temple for birthing the Body of Light, they form a synergy of possibilities.

Let us summarize the unique contribution that crystals can make to yoga more clearly and succinctly. Crystal is light, solid light. Crystal is energy, pure energy. Crystal, being structurally perfected in its own domain, stands for what man aspires to become in his kingdom. Crystal is clarity. In crystal, there is no ego, no mind, no individualistic desire. Noise and agitation are not created by crystals. Yet these evolved mineral beings surrender their perfect symmetry and purified energy to their human users. They thus embody the principle of egoless self-surrender. They are pure thoughts of the creator, untainted; they mirror reality without distortion; they channel energy without obstruction.

Although we may begin to work with crystals in order to fulfil our own strategies, we eventually grow into a greater wisdom and come to study and learn from crystals what they have to teach us. We eventually transcend our desire to exploit them and become students of these evolved helper-teachers from the mineral world.

Am I ready for Crystal Yoga? If so, I should keep in mind several things. The crystals that come to me will freely put at my disposal all they have, their egoless clarity, their desireless availability for service, their lack of mental complexity, their freedom from delusion. I have much to learn from crystals if I can set aside the presumptions of my ignorance and learn to attune, to feel, and to open to previously undreamed of possibilities.

By bringing various kinds of crystals together in a *mesa* in a cosmically patterned order, I can have the privilege of learning about nature's own precious temple where the birthing of spirit in matter is continuously accomplished. Crystals can help empower my *mesa* so that it becomes a consolidation of the infinite power that Heaven radiates to Earth. With help from crystals, my *mesa* can be a *mandala* of timeless wisdom, a sacred cauldron of alchemical transformation, and a power-source for initiation and ascension.

CRYSTAL YOGA

The phrase "Crystal Yoga" was an expression I first heard in a conversation with Margherita Vondrak at my forested Ontario retreat where we had traveled to do a sacred ceremony in a circle of standing stones among the trees. She, in turn, had first heard these words used by Katrina Raphael with whom she had studied the art of crystal healing in Hawaii. I have to thank both Margherita and Katrina for their fine work in the field of crystal study and practice; their insights, wisdom and writings have been most helpful in the preparation of this book on the subject of Crystal Yoga.

When I first heard the words "Crystal Yoga," I experienced an immediate 'recognition-signal' that pulled together a large region of my personal study, writing and spiritual practice extending as far back as the publication of my first book, *The Healing Gems,* in the early 1980's. In comic books and cartoons, sometimes you see little light bulb going on above the head of a character who gets a 'brilliant idea' – well, that was the experience! I knew immediately, and shared with Margherita my inner feeling, that THIS would be the start of a new phase in an important work, not a completely new work, but a very ancient work that she knew our souls had been engaged in for lifetimes, sometimes individually and at other times in collaboration.

Margherita made me a gift that day of her own compilation on crystals, a booklet called *The Crystal Lotus Handbook: Crystal Keys and Affirmations,* and placed its information at the disposal of the new project. It is a metaphysical guide that describes 200 crystals used in healing, with a wonderfully insightful system for using these crystalline minerals in the process of discernment. With this system of attunement to the properties of mineral crystals, the resulting healing has a strong likelihood of being deep and permanent. In conversations over the next 48 hours, we reached a clear understanding of the work that lay ahead. I had already completed a book on Crystal Mesa that had been accepted for publication, but it was now clear that this was only one aspect of a larger topic, Crystal Yoga.

I have learned in my music, writing and meditation to value the inner guidance that comes through moments of clear insight. Simply put, an unpredictable instant comes when there is a flash of recognition and one feels and knows: THIS is the thing to do, THIS is the work to complete, THIS is the assignment I have been given. Such knowing comes by finding and following the inner guidance we each receive through the spiritual heart. Taking time to listen to this guidance and to feel the living inner presence is what meditation is all about. This reality that guides us from within is what Buddhists call the 'inner light,' and what Christians and Hindus frequently refer to as the 'soul.'

Yoga means "yoking," or linking the energies and consciousness of Heaven and Earth both in the microcosm and in the macrocosm but, in the end, its ultimate requirement is that we find and follow the law of love. Crystallographers and scientists will see crystals from their own perspectives, and the information they provide is of considerable intellectual interest. Spiritual seekers, on the other hand, will feel and intuitively know that crystals express something of the divine plan on Earth. Alignment of individual spiritual practice with the 'original contract' between Heaven and Earth is indispensable for our future evolution in consciousness, as for the survival of our planet and our species.

In this work of self-dedication to the creative action of the Source, crystals have boundless capacity to teach and to enhance our development. We complete the meaning of their existence and they facilitate the evolution of ours when we co-create. All of this has been known and practiced by enlightened souls from the beginning of time. The masters' words and example are our best reference point for understanding the roots of this spiritual tradition wherein the contributions of all life forms, including minerals, are valued in aligning personal and planetary energies to Source. Yoga requires from the individual a sincere self-opening to the soul's full potential so that it may act as an inner guide in the return journey of consciousness to Source. When aspiration grows beyond private salvation-seeking into a supra-personal participation in the original Earth-Heaven contract, it enters the same domain as 'Crystal Yoga.' It should be remembered that the immortal spirits who are keepers and teachers of this wisdom in the inner worlds interact not only with life on planet Earth, but with intelligent beings in other star systems as well. On Earth, significant transmission of wisdom related to Crystal Yoga or Crystal Mesa can be effected by invoking the 'Crystal Yoga Deva' or the 'Crystal Mesa Deva.' I have to thank Margherita in particular for her work with me in this area. The wisdom can also be accessed directly through meditation and attunement to the soul, or by the connection of the soul with the Muse, which is the Mother's influence of creative inspiration.

In Lemurian times, life was more consciously aligned with divine intent, and thus there could not be a separate field of 'practice' called yoga. But as the centuries and millennia wore on, and the Atlantean civilization flourished, there was a development of the human mind and vital away from their original immersion in the matrix of Nature and the divine plan it revealed. Gradually, a kind of individualistic and self-seeking willfulness became a choice for significant numbers of humans. In this way, most humans lost the awareness that the whole of life expressed the divine plan. As a result, various fields of specialized knowledge and practice such as alchemy and crystallography developed in Atlantean times to reflect the human mind's increasing complexity, as well as its innate tendency to diverge from the guiding light of soul and heart. For those who wanted to keep the mind-heart balance and find and follow the inner guidance, spiritual practice and yoga were developed and taught. It became possible to separate spirituality from life, and then to confine it to temples and churches. Of course, the original Lemurian harmony of Heaven and Earth was by this time something that humanity had to work at maintaining because elements of discord had been released and the primal balance was in jeopardy.

The great cataclysm which resulted in the destruction of Atlantis was an event of supreme importance in humanity's history. Elements of the Atlantean and Lemurian wisdom-tradition were dispersed in various directions, certain parts to North and South America, other elements to Egypt, Mesopotamia and even distant India. But much of the ancient wisdom was lost, and a resulting dark age ensued. This was in large part due to a misuse of power and to an exploitation of crystals that deviated from the divine plan.

The official archaeological record, and orthodox academic historians see the earliest civilizations as starting somewhere between four and eight thousand years BC in the Middle East. A great deal of evidence that does not harmonize with this view is suppressed, or worse, destroyed, and scholars who think outside the officially approved paradigm are frequently ostracized. But there is an instinctive recognition of truth of which we are all capable when we open our intuitive intelligence, and despite the incompleteness of the official historical record, many of us can still sense our ancient roots and our connection to what is archetypal and primal in the dim past. Simply to see or hold a Lemurian crystal can be for many of us such an experience.

Indigenous, shamanic cultures in many parts of the world still retain elements of the primal Lemurian cosmology, particularly in the Pacific rim, and in such tribal settings it has been widely recognized that crystals express the influence of spirit on matter. Crystals hold the light and energy of the stars and transduce it into forms which the human biofields can handle, thus assisting us to align and balance our consciousness, our energy and our physical bodies with progressively higher levels of order and refinement. This is how the evolution of consciousness proceeds; it is an over-simplification to reduce it to a simple process of Darwinian selection and survival of the fittest.

Crystals are model teachers because they exhibit the perfect ordering of physical matter according to the pure laws of geometry. In this way, they remind us of the great design and intent behind creation. They orient us, when we develop the capacity to be intuitively attuned, toward the experience of original Oneness that lies behind the painful separation of Earth from Heaven. Thus it is that crystals help to heal the fragmentation of the primal and ancient harmony caused by ignorance and willfulness in the human mind and ego. They exemplify silence and they embody surrender to the intent-of-Source even as their orderly molecular patterning sets us an example of the perfectibility of matter. The life-force or devic presence in each crystal is eager to serve the divine plan, and has never deviated from its alignment to this fundamental truth of its being.

For many reasons, crystals link us to the original design of creation, and remind us that all life exists to complete a cosmic dream which originates in the heart of the Supreme Dreamer. But the most important teaching of crystals is that we and they are co-creators of the coming golden age when Spirit will achieve a more perfect expression in matter. The only way that such co-creation between humans and crystals can take place is in a free choice on our part to approach the mineral kingdom with kindness, love and respect, to enlist its participation in the evolutionary practices and processes which we call yoga. The term yoga, of course, means any practice that aligns consciousness with Source, only a small part of which involves physical postures or *asanas* such as we find in 'Hatha Yoga.' Not only does this attitude of respect and openness for all beings, including crystals, bring about the best results in deepening our capacity for relationship, it is the only way of acting that has any value or meaning within the context of the 'original contract' between Earth and Heaven. Any result achieved by disharmony will wither away with time and dissolve into nothingness. From the point of view of true alignment to divine intent, which the crystal devas constantly embody, disrespect, selfishness, ego, desire and greed are all aberrations and discords. Even though the devas must surrender to the intent of ignorant humans who sometimes misuse them, the living entities within these crystals cannot flourish or fulfil the meaning of their existence in conditions of disharmony, or by violating the laws of divine providence. Only unhappiness comes from putting crystals to use in ways contrary to their alignment. Many humans these days are miserable, and this unhappiness is the karmic suffering which invariably flows from breaking universal laws.

If you own a crystal, a good way of commencing your journey is to simply hold it in your hands and begin relating to its presence and appearance with open eyes and an open heart. Feel that the crystal is a friend who has something of value to share, something which you personally feel the want of and could really use. Wait, listen, meditate. Do not think or analyze, simply tune in to the presence and energy of the crystal. Sense that it is alive. Small openings in your mind may thus come about and result in a readiness or capacity to receive. Forceful requests from a closed mind will lead nowhere. When you send your request in a correct frequency and it registers with the living energy inside the crystal, there will be an opening that you can experience in a variety of ways. Each person must find the right key to bring about the opening, and it works far better if you do not bring any expectations to the process.

Try quietly humming the various vowel sounds to your crystal as if you were communicating with it and as you do this, sense where there is an accord with the crystal. Sense which sounds the crystal seems to like. Sense which progressions of sound the crystal prefers. This is one method of attunement. Bathe the crystal with your affection through the vowel sounds that you sing to it. Then, feel your intuitive connection to the crystal and be available, without any specific expectation, to notice anything at all that registers in your awareness.

The Deva of Crystal Yoga has shared a most precious teaching about the process of receptivity that makes this yoga possible. Not all humans, sad to say, have the quality of receptivity needed for the processes of Crystal Yoga. In about forty percent of humans, there is in the heart-space, in the ether of the spiritual heart, an etheric crystal which is the seed that enables an individual to successfully practice the processes of Crystal Yoga. Sri Aurobindo refers to this in *Savitri:*

The seed of Godhead sleeps in mortal hearts,
The flower of Godhead grows on the world-tree:
Savitri, pg 446

One or two percent of humans were not born with this crystal, and something approaching sixty percent of humans have destroyed or compromised it by their actions and choices. The capacity for intuitive responses to crystals (upon which this yoga is based) will be present in those who have this seed crystal intact, and it is fairly easy to assess who such individuals are. Teachers of the yoga will have the ability to see and assess this quality in prospective students, and in fact teachers are advised to evaluate people who show interest in Crystal Yoga to see if the crystal of the heart is present so that the work is possible.

Supposing that the spiritual heart of an interested seeker is suited to the yoga, the Crystal Mesa is the ideal beginner's tool for developing the inner potential needed go forward with the practices. The Crystal Mesa not only fosters awareness of the Heaven-Earth alignment, but it teaches and trains those who work with it to activate their full potential. By studying this book and practicing the exercises described, a sincere seeker can develop his or her potential to progress in attunement to Source.

Another consideration which is helpful at the beginning of the yoga is to prepare a suitable environment for practice. The easiest way of doing this is to create a circle of crystals with a carefully selected and probably large crystal in the centre, and to align these crystals so that they create an environment of harmonious energy that supports spiritual practice. The space thus created is like a dome, and all work with energy and consciousness inside this dome will be enhanced. The position, number and selection of crystals for the circle, the choosing of a suitable crystal for the centrepiece, and the art of rotating it for attunement to various energies is a whole field of study unto itself within the larger field of Crystal Yoga. Indeed, a Crystal Mesa can itself become such an energy-dome when used correctly in sacred ceremony for it is both a temple in miniature and an excellent means to create a larger grid of energies that enhance practice. For example, a Crystal Mesa can be placed on top of the central crystal within the circle and programmed into the energy-field of the dome to introduce a complete set of harmonies in energy for application to the work. The Crystal Mesa talisman, a *mesa* which can be worn, is the preferred tool for this purpose.

In Atlantis, such crystal domes of energy were well known and widely used. Subsequently, this knowledge was passed on through the field of study known as geomancy, and some of it was also present in certain architects who took an interest in things esoteric as it related to the building materials and proportions of spaces used for sacred ceremony. Hints that this arcane knowledge was widely known and applied may be gleaned from certain gothic cathedrals like Chartres, and from the most ancient temples in Egypt, Peru and elsewhere, although many of these are at present in a sad state of decline.

I have personally visited many of these structures and meditated in them for inner guidance in order to bring through a clear understanding of how to renew the ancient wisdom in ways appropriate to our modern needs. At the site of Knossos in Crete, and among the ruins of the Acropolis in Athens, at the temples of Tiruvannamalai and Chidambaram in Southern India, in the temples of Luxor and at the Sphinx and the Pyramids in Egypt, in scattered temples of the Khmer in Eastern Thailand and in the temples of the Incas that lie in the Sacred Valley near Cusco, I have meditated on the wisdom held by the stones. These stones radiate a silent testimony of ancient harmonies, a way of knowing and being that is timeless and priceless. All of these meditations have ripened over the years into a way of seeing and being that makes the present book on Crystal Yoga possible. Yoga, and awareness of its workings depends far more on the inner journeys that your soul has made than on the outer experiences you have had. That being said, a new possibility comes into play when we practice collectively, and the work we do with select crystals is already a seeding of intent for collective practice.

Because human beings are in various stages of becoming crystalline, they will exhibit various levels of understanding of this phenomenon. To be simultaneously human and crystalline means, among other things, to be clear both in consciousness and energy, to be aligned with soul and with Source in one's central intent, to be pure, and to be aspiring for surrender to the true doer of the Yoga, which means consecrated to the Divine Will. Being crystalline also means to be relatively egoless, to be capable of profound silence, stillness, and of sustained focus both in interior concentration and in outer action. Human beings have these capacities in varying degrees, but Crystal Yoga helps us to develop them more quickly with a view to enabling complete attunement of all planes and parts of our human microcosm to the Eternal Source.

The famous Tibetan mantra: *Om Mani Padme Hum* refers to the jewel in the lotus of the heart, which we have touched on above as a seed crystal that makes practice possible. It is this jewel which grows in clarity and power as the crystalline qualities are established at all levels of a seeker's body and mind, including the chakras, auric fields and subconscious levels of one's being. When all parts of the human microcosm are aligned to the crystal within the spiritual heart, and when this crystal is fully activated, a permanent transformation can take place. It is a lasting and integral illumination which gives birth to the capacity to manifest the soul's qualities fully in this lifetime. Those who care to develop the jewel in the heart will greatly benefit from the study and practice of Crystal Yoga.

It is helpful to point out that yoga brings people together, and that Crystal Yoga inevitably brings crystals together in various kinds of assemblies as well. A Crystal Mesa is a constellation of crystals aligned with the intent of its keeper. The mineral crystals, including quartz, were birthed in the matrix of Mother Earth long ago to serve this cosmic plan of which spiritual seekers are aware in varying degrees. It was foreseen that a time would come when crystals, in particular their conscious use by humans, would not only redress the karmic excesses of Atlantis, but open new possibilities for exponential leaps in consciousness. The modern computer technology based on quartz crystal is one striking example of how crystal science has changed the world in modern times. It is not quite a hundred years since the earliest crystal radios came into being, and we have progressed immensely in recent decades to a greater understanding of crystal technology. A similar advance in the individual and collective consciousness may be realized if Crystal Yoga finds application in the lives of those for whom it is suited.

We have mentioned that the Crystal Mesa can act as a key to unlock seeds of potential, and to evolve people who feel called to this form of practice. As the yoga progresses, other crystal tools and techniques become appropriate to facilitate the central work of bringing a higher light of awareness down into the material plane where our waking consciousness is localized. The alchemical transformation of the four elements from lightness to density and back again is very much at work in this yoga, but only those who have established a crystalline consciousness and energy field will be able to do the more advanced work. The phrase "crystalline consciousness and energy" simply means that internal order and structural perfection of alignment have been established. We have already listed the qualities that flow from this, such as clarity, integrity, focus, and purity. If you have a crystal seed or jewel within your heart and if you choose to activate it through practice, you may very well develop these qualities, master the processes of attunement and experience the integral transformation that this effects.

One significant aspect of this yoga which we mentioned in the Preface is its experiential nature. It is an exploration in direct experience (not merely intellectual analysis) of various fields of possibility. A living yoga based on inner experience can never be a pre-ordained set of sequential steps, for many of its processes unfold simultaneously. The yoga does not really require too much information at the outset, although deep understanding becomes more important as one advances. For beginners, it is actual practice leading to first hand experience that counts most. Only experimentally can one discover one's own way to relate to crystals and experience an interaction with them that informs personal practice. Meditation with crystals, and particularly meditation with an open spiritual heart aligned to the inner divine presence, is extremely important at all stages. Daily practice should be considered indispensable. When it comes to the attitude we bring to this practice, the qualities of joy and play are just as important as discipline, sincerity and seriousness.

Quartz crystals and a carefully assembled Crystal Mesa are the principal tools of the yoga at the outset; however it must be recognized that the main instrument of practice is the human microcosm itself and that the real doer of this yoga is the divine presence within. For many or most beginners, simply put, this means the Divine Mother. Lemurian quartz crystals become more important in later stages of the yoga, as do certain of the twelve master crystals, but their full potential need not necessarily be recognized or called in during the initial phase of practice. Because crystals are attuned to many ranges of vibration, the use of sound, tonality and music has an important place in Crystal Yoga. There are a number of books that discuss various techniques for working with crystals, and most of them touch on the role of sound for activating and directing energy and consciousness. We will also explore this subject in greater detail at a later point in the journey.

Information is useful if one balances reading with actual practice, and if one enters the processes of this yoga from a heart-centred space of intuitive attunement. Crystals have a long association with Atlantean, scientific consciousness and the willful personal ego which was first brought forward at that period of history. Many people who are intellectually fascinated with crystals approach the subject from this karmic background. They cannot see or feel the inherent flaws in their approach because these are so much a part of them; when ego does the seeing and deciding, it rarely sees its own action. It is virtually indistinguishable from the thinking mind which is its main instrument of expression. Unless the correct mind-heart balance is found at the very outset, one may commence the practice from a wrong perspective, and this invariably leads to flawed results. For example, the need for personal empowerment is hardly desirable for an individual who is egotistical and selfish. The right orientation of a seeker's attitude and spirit from the very beginning of practice are of the utmost importance, and it is a teacher's responsibility to ensure that this is so. In this regard, the eightfold elements of fundamental practice (found in the chapter entitled A Living Relationship) are the indispensable ingredients of a good beginning.

In the spiritual life, we invariably come to appreciate the importance of connecting inwardly with the masters, especially with the truly God-realized masters whose words embody and communicate the light of the truth they express. My own study and thought has drawn deeply on the wells of wisdom-light to be found in the writings of Sri Aurobindo, in particular his greatest writing, *Savitri*. This mystical poem, the longest in the English language, manages to capture a very high consciousness in words, and to project its cosmic vision in archetypal images. In *Savitri*, you will find passages on the crystal in the heart, the soul's journey to Source, the work of Mother Earth and the Divine Mother in completing the original divine plan, the Child in the Heart, the archetypal Hero and Sage, the sacred flame, the Immortals who hold and dispense the primal wisdom-teachings, the role of Nature in yoga, and the energies of the stars, jewels, gods and crystals that together weave this magical milieu of possibilities wherein our souls incarnate.

Many phrases from *Savitri* express the essence of Crystal Yoga and Crystal Mesa. For example, each of the following phrases from *Savitri* (page references supplied) reveals an aspect of the meaning of Crystal Mesa. A Crystal Mesa is, or can be all of the following for one who truly understands it:

> *A magic key (49); the anthem of the stars (55); rays of a spiritual sun (55); clay images of unborn gods (60); the knot that ties together the stars (63); the mystic door near to the well of vision in the soul (74); the rhythms and metres of the stars (74); a hidden chamber (74); the symbol powers of number and of form, and the secret code of the history of the world (74); Nature's correspondence with the soul (74); the mystery of God's covenant with the Night (75); the world's buried secret rose (75); archives of the spirit's crypt (75); mystic keys (83); magic of formative number and design (84); a wonder-weft of knowledge incalculable (86); mnemonics of the craft of the Infinite (86); sealed hermetic wisdom (87); fragments of the mystery of omnipotence (87); bodies signalling the Bodiless (88); shadows gleaming with the birth of*

*gods (88); a map of subtle signs surpassing thought (88);
an organ scale of the Eternal's acts (89); the music born in
Matter's silences (89); a hierarchy of climbing harmonies
(91); the structured visions of the cosmic Self (96); form-
bound spiritual thoughts (96); forms that open moving doors
on things divine (96); the symbols of the Spirit's reality (96);
living bodies of the Bodiless (96); the figures of (his) spirit's
greater life (97); the Idea self-luminous key to all ideas (97);
a brief compendium of the Vast (98); a summary of the stages
of the spirit (98); a subtle pattern of the universe (98);
(an) image of the mighty Whole (100); Nature's giant stair
(102); a magic crystal air (103); an immortal godhead's
perishable parts (107); Symbols of That which never yet was
made (109); (a) house of the divine Idea, (109); a Time-inn
for the Unborn (109); a nebula of the splendours of the gods
(119).*

In sixty pages of the text chosen at random, (from a work over 700 pages long), we find this abundance of imagery that hints at many deep meanings associated with Crystal Mesa. Not that Sri Aurobindo was consciously writing about the subject of *mesa* in *Savitri;* rather his words, because they emanate from universal consciousness, shed light on many fields of spiritual practice and experience including some aspect of Crystal Mesa. It would be possible to write a short commentary explaining how the Crystal Mesa embodies each of these descriptive phrases, and a student of Crystal Yoga who had progressed in understanding and use of the *mesa* would be able to do just that. If you read *Savitri* from the point of view of its teachings on yoga, you will find that the wisdom is conveyed through a wealth of symbolic imagery.

A symbol is a mystery to be contemplated, not an intellectual theorem to be explicated. Reading and re-reading the words of true masters feeds our imagination with archetypal patterns through which Nature expresses the vast Divine Plan. When you study the writing of true spiritual masters, you will frequently experience an alignment of consciousness to your Higher Self.

Sri Aurobindo states on page 108 of *Savitri* that "To seize the absolute in shapes that pass, / to fix the eternal's touch in time-made things, / this is the law of all perfection here. / A fragment here is caught of heaven's design; / else could we never hope for greater life." The phrase "heaven's design" expresses exactly what the Crystal Mesa is and what it transmits:

Acting upon this visible Nature's scheme
It wakens our earth-matter's heavy doze
To think and feel and to react to joy;
It models in us our diviner parts,
Lifts mortal mind into a greater air,
Makes yearn this life of flesh to intangible aims,
Links the body's death with immortality's call:
Out of the swoon of the Inconscience
It labours towards a superconscient Light. (99)

I cite these passages as an example of how the words of the masters help us to understand and practice yoga on a secure and well-founded base, and to enlarge on a comment made in the Preface that Crystal Yoga is an elaboration of indications to be found in *Savitri*. There is no other sure foundation for the practice of yoga than the heart's recognition of its spiritual guiding light, and the alignment of this instinct with the inner support of the true masters. "Thus," as Sri Aurobindo writes in *Savitri*, "we draw near to the All-Wonderful, following his rapture in things as sign and guide."

Crystal Yoga is an approach to intuitive attunement that may be combined with most spiritual paths that value integral development and the linking of Heaven with Earth, bearing in mind that his linking takes place both on a planetary and on an individual scale. The illustration of themes centrally important to Crystal Yoga by referring to writings of Sri Aurobindo serves as an example of a larger principle, namely that the teachings of all true masters will be aligned with the original contract between the Divine and its earthly manifestation.

For those who approach the spiritual life from a universal perspective, with a truly open mind and heart, crystals can help to foster awareness of the deepest connections that we have with timeless truth; the masters' words inspire seekers on various paths to a more profound understanding not only of the mineral kingdom, but of all other kingdoms of nature. These kingdoms exist not as separate fields of scientific inquiry, but as co-ordinates of a cosmic plan in which every element down to the least grain of sand is an indispensable part of the whole. Although we humans often think of ourselves as separate and superior to other life forms on the planet, we are cherishing mental delusions to imagine that humanity is somehow outside the domain of Nature and beyond the authority of the Divine Mother.

Just as all humans are my brothers and sisters, so all the kingdoms of nature are parts of my extended family. The whole of life, and even the parts of existence that seem inanimate, or unconscious are my very own expanded reality. In the fullness of my heart's inner recognition, I come to see and know that stones and crystals are far from unconscious. It is my own unconsciousness and my own closed mind which have prevented me from recognizing their possibilities. As I break down the walls of mental separation which I have erected by my, thoughts, actions and choices, I come to know for a certainty that we all have a co-creative role to play in this field of life and experience. I am called from the core of my being to play the part that my soul has chosen within the divine plan. As I progress in the yoga, not only do I see and feel this truth, but I come to live and breathe the spirit of oneness in everything that I say, do and think. I feel the seed crystal in the lotus of my spiritual heart glowing with love and light, and this opens my way forward into a momentum of continuous self-transcendence.

The Crystal Mesa Logo
reveals a pattern of relationship between Source, at the
centre, and its manifestation
in time and space.

THE DARK MIRROR

All knowing is ignorance.
Unknowing is the dark mirror
Held by the heart
Before the face of Truth.

If the heart crystal is the seed of your spiritual potential, the child in the heart is the magical enabler that can help you to realize that potential. The archetypal child abiding within the lotus of the spiritual heart helps us to attain the wisdom of unknowing.

To connect with this interior part of our being, we need to get out of the head, beyond intellectual activity and words, and into our deeper feelings. When we do this, whether during meditation or spontaneously at other times, there is an unmistakable sense of 'coming home' and also of being linked to something peaceful, harmonious and beautiful. When we know through the medium of intuitive feeling, or what may be called feeling-attunement, we may link directly with our own inner light, which mirrors the Source and its wisdom.

The wisdom of the heart does not translate perfectly into the words and conceptual language of the head. In my own personal experience, I find that playing my harp music expresses the communication of the spiritual heart much better than using words. But insofar as words can convey a few glimpses of the heart's wisdom, I believe that the heart-child teaches in this way:

Everything the mind can verbalize is already dilution of the magic. Every kind of thinking-knowing is ignorance. It is the eyes of the heart that have magical seeing. They have yin-fire, or spirit-knowing. This is what the mind calls 'unknowing.'

All beings who abide in unknowing can be as teachers for the heart; it can be a dog, a tree, a stone, a bird, any of Nature's children who are anchored in the primal unknowing.

The eyes of the heart perceive through the light of yin-fire. In the light beyond our intellectual knowing lives the full power of Being. Yin-fire teaches us the wisdom of identification. Yin-fire is power to find and cultivate the path of crystal-wisdom. To see and be as yin-fire is to know all things through 'feeling-clarity.'

We can name the jewel of the heart in many ways, and each name points to one of its modes of being, and in each of these is a teaching. The jewel of the heart is the love-crystal, the wisdom-crystal, the magic-crystal, the intuition-crystal, and it has innumerable other aspects as well.

Each of these capacities has been given physical, crystalline expression. Humans have named these crystals, sometimes wisely (e.g.. Moonstone and Selenite) and sometimes according to intellectual understanding (e.g.. Morganite and Hemimorphite), and they have been widely studied with the scientific mind.

If you approach rose quartz through your child-heart of unknowing, and hold a piece of this living light close to your spiritual heart, you may be able to feel it as an embodied ray of your very own heart-jewel. Feel it, smile into it, sing to it, call to Source from within its radiance, merge in its yin-fire, find its wisdom.

Hold this love-crystal steady, there in the dark mirror of heart's unknowing; it will take you closer to the jewel in the lotus. Go within to the crystal temple of the heart like a naked child in all holy innocence; bathe in the crystalline waters of the pool that is there; feel the light of your heart's lotus-jewel. You will emerge reborn, the golden child of the heart, the incarnation of soul.

Most of us have to process truth through the left brain (rational logic) before we can assimilate it. This is why, for many people at present, the mirror of the heart is experienced as a 'dark mirror.' Some of us have come to recognize that the scientific paradigm, and the level of mind it is based on, are big obstacles for knowing the divine through direct experience. It has been difficult for us to grasp how we are being led astray by knowledge when, for so long in our history, knowledge was the door-opener on the path of light.

Although we are hungry for a life-enhancing cosmology, we have been educated and trained to doubt the wisdom of our own hearts, the value of imagination, the reality of magic, and the validity of intuitive attunement as a means of understanding invisible realities, whose importance we also question. Thus, many of us find it difficult to make use of stones as tools for development.

The elders have always known that crystals and rocks are repositories of ancient wisdom-teaching in relation to our own unfoldment and that of planet Earth. But what are the implications of this? What do we actually do about it? We may accept that our souls came here to know the divine in matter, and we may even acknowledge that the Goddess, the Mother, is centrally important in this process of spiritual co-creation. After all, even catholic theologians like Matthew Fox have started writing and speaking about this. For many of us, it is a struggle to find ways to open to the spiritual presence and power of the Mother in her own forms of self-expression in Nature; we seem to have lost the instinct for cocreating an integral spirituality with the seven families of crystals, the community of trees, and the totem birds and beasts. We still carry a considerable amount of mental conditioning from Judeo-Christian tradition telling us that all this is idolatry, superstition, and heretical nonsense.

The reality is, you and I and every human on Earth have been gifted with the most exquisite treasure imaginable, the human body. It is the soul's temple, the spirit's musical instrument, the divine's *mesa*. Only in a human body is God-realization possible, and only on Earth does the karmic struggle lead to this glorious attainment. Even the cosmic gods have to incarnate in human bodies if they want the ultimate realization: full, conscious oneness with Source. Just as power encoded in our *chakras* and DNA is ready to be released, so is the knowledge and energy encoded in crystals, which opens the way to their co-creation with us in yoga. Our own encoding and that of crystals might seem to be two different things, but in the end we learn that we and they are components of a single divine plan. When we use crystals as instruments of co-creation aligned with the Divine for uniting Earth and Heaven, we are accomplishing the soul's work. In doing so, we release the full potential of our own body-mind *mesa* and activate the magic of our heart-jewel.

The soul can be thought of as a 'deva' , or living spirit, dwelling in the crystal which we call the human body. Or you can say the body IS the soul materially expressed. Simply put, this means that the body is the soul's crystal tool for spiritual expression. When the divine in us uses the human body to attain higher states of awareness and particularly when our yoga is one of co-creation with Mother Earth's body, then what we are doing is one form or another of Crystal Yoga.

Most humans are ignorant and clumsy when it comes to skilful use of this precious vehicle, the human microcosm. It does not matter what name we apply to our chosen path of aspiration, the important thing is that we have sincere alignment to Source and clear intent to co-operate with the divine plan. Working toward our highest spiritual possibilities through sacred objects, sounds and ceremony is one way of engaging the fullness of our own microcosm's encoded potential. All of these can nurture our meditation, and are complementary in the same way that the inner and outer parts of our lives form a complete whole. Crystal Yoga exists because there is a great work that the Mother is eager to accomplish in and through these crystalline temples that we call our human bodies. All forms of practice are acceptable to Her if the intent is pure and the aspiration sincere.

In the stones, we find the magic of the stars and the magic of Earth mixed. And that same blend of celestial and terrestrial elements is the reality of our own being as well. If we can let go of our negative programs concerning idolatry and gods, the divine guidance can show us how to co-create from our heart's guiding wisdom, which the logic-bound mind can only construe as a kind of "unknowing."

In Crystal Yoga, She, the Goddess, the Mother, aspires through us for the release of consciousness in *all* her children. Humans are gifted with precious bodies, microcosms of the whole, because we were created for priesthood in the cosmic ritual of return to Source. In the whole of creation we have been assigned this special role, and given freedom to fulfill it in many ways, whether as scientists, shamans, bards, mystics or housewives. When we know that our bodies are part of Her body, and that Her body is our spiritual refuge, we engage the heart's guidance more surely than ever.

Wisdom is a many-faceted attainment and its presence or absence is one of the best measures of the soul's progress. Every life-lesson that we master opens up a new facet of our heart-jewel's complex beauty. In time, as our living relationship to light widens and deepens, the richly-faceted heart-crystal radiates its influence through every part of our being, establishing clarity and alignment with divine light.

Every aspect of life can teach us its own wisdom, and all facets of this wisdom are keyed to the energies of crystals. The various crystalline minerals act as a mirror to things we do not normally see reflected. They assist us to develop sensitivity and discernment, shedding light on the dim recesses of our unconscious programming. For example, Rose Quartz, especially the girasol variety, holds the wisdom of love, and teaches us about how to find our soul's balance through experiencing the polarities of hate and kindness. Sodalite teaches us about how to be more understanding. It assists us to discover a point of equilibrium as we experience the opposites of mental chatter and mental order. Imperial Golden Topaz can impart wisdom regarding our relationship to abundance and shed light on experiences of poverty and wealth. Every one of these crystals resonates a certain frequency of colour and a certain energy of light, and each has its own unique molecular structure. These patterns of structure, colour, chemical composition, energy and other properties that any given crystal may have determine the role that it can play in Crystal Yoga. Each crystal is light in material form, and each speaks to specific regions of our bio-electric bodies and to different psychological and spiritual issues in our awareness.

Through mastering life's lessons, we grow in wisdom. The heart-jewel becomes steadily more luminous and activated as we evolve in consciousness. This etheric seed-crystal at the center of the lotus of the spiritual heart has the capacity to hold and radiate the complete wisdom of our attainment accumulated in this and other lifetimes on Earth. The microcosm reflects the macrocosm, and the crystal within the spiritual heart is capable of embodying and transmitting the accumulated wisdom-light of all the crystals in creation, both in the physical world beneath our feet and in the subtle words beyond the five senses. A human being who has realized his or her own heart-potential becomes a radiant crystal of the inner light, shining for the whole of humanity. Simply to sit in the presence of a living spiritual master is to bask in a blissfully uplifting flow of spiritual presence, as I can testify from a number of such personal encounters.

New kinds of crystals are constantly being discovered, brought up from the depths of Mother Earth and placed in contact with humans in a process that is correlative to the evolution of human consciousness. Some sorts of gems which were rare in the past, like Amethyst, are now abundantly available and quite inexpensive. Other minerals, like Turquoise, seem to be diminishing, as new ones come into prominence to take their place.

Enlightenment is simply the process of mastering the lessons of life and expressing our soul-light so that it moves in a continuous flow from Source to Spirit, from Spirit to soul, and thence through the heart to all parts and all levels of our microcosm. This is what the Vedas meant when they spoke of finding the buried treasure and releasing its rays. In ancient Indian spirituality, the heart-crystal is also sometimes called a spiritual sun, and according to this metaphor, the path to wisdom requires that we dissolve the clouds that obscure the face of the solar deity, so that its rays shine through the whole of creation.

The Crystal Mesa is one way of actualizing the full capacity of the heart-crystal in outer form, because the various crystals within the *mesa* refer to the wisdom-components of the enlightened heart. When we learn how to use it correctly, our *mesa* becomes for us a many-faceted crystal assembly embodying these rays of spiritual light:

	Earth	Water	Fire	Air
Spirit	Heart Path (Jade)	Dynamic Flow (Iolite) Light Activation (Selenite)	Passion (Ruby)	Listening (Celestite) Inner Journey (Apophylite)
Yang	Physical Mastery (Tiger's Eye) Primal Power (Dark Green Tourmaline)	Perspective (Blue Chalcedony)	Solar Alignment (Sunstone)	Clearing (Kyanite)

Yin	Patience (Petrified Wood)	Graceful Love (Pink Chalcedony) Healer (Turquoise)	Compassion (Rose Quartz)	Peace (Bluelace Agate)
Air	Abundance (Pyrite)	Truth (Aquamarine) Honesty (Amazonite)	Clarity (Citrine)	Mental Order (Fluorite)
Fire	Transformation (Fire Agate)	Magic (Labradorite)	Sacred Body (Red Garnet) Alchemy (Imperial Topaz)	Aspiration (Amethyst)
Water	Emotional Mastery (Malachite) Emotional Balance (Aventurine)	Attunement (Moonstone)	Union (Gold Labradorite) Cohesion (Blue Pietersite)	Freedom (Azurite)
Earth	Nurturing (Red Jasper)	Physical Temple (Chrysocolla)	Protection (Obsidian)	Understanding (Sodalite) Courage (Chrysoprase)

The complete Crystal Mesa includes also four stones for principal archetypes, namely:

Wisdom Stone (Lapis Lazuli)	The Sage Archetype
Transformation Stone (Rutilated Smokey Quartz or Citrine)	The Hero Archetype

Inner Child Stone (Rhodochrosite)	The Child Archetype
Earth Mother Stone (Lemurian Jade)	The Mother Archetype

Additionally, there is a clear quartz sphere at the centre of the *mesa* representing Infinity, or the Source.

Taken as a whole, this symbolic expression of the heart crystal represents 33 key themes, each being a phase of the Eternal Wisdom. In actuality, each of these 32 stones has a number of qualities, and can be used in a variety of ways. Thus, the Crystal Mesa is a symbolic embodiment of the potential of the seed crystal, or precious jewel, which anchors the divine in core of the spiritual heart. This human body-mind is in reality a *mesa* of the divine, and when we allow the divine will to become the doer in our life, everything we have and are becomes alchemically transformed into the 'philosopher's stone,' which is the potential of infinite consciousness.

The consciousness and mental conditioning of the individual is of the utmost importance in the question of what lessons, energies and dynamics are actually at work in any given situation. For me, personally, for example, Rose Quartz is an excellent stone for entering into the consciousness of the spiritual heart. I do not experience the child in the heart, or psychic being, as an entity, but rather I merge with its consciousness and become its way of being. For me, the psychic being is a space of consciousness in which my innately innocent and unconditioned nature comes alive, with all its magical depth and freshness. Some people, however, are able to see the child in the heart, and can identify its approximate age and appearance. Each of us has his or her own way of making the connection.

Stones other than those named above may very effectively activate and work with the issues named, because different individuals have different openings at various points of time in their development. The names above refer to the central, archetypal zone of influence that the deva of that crystal specializes in; it does not preclude other ways of working that the stone can very well manifest. In fact, it is quite valuable and important to discover how a stone works personally and to approach each crystal without mental preconceptions so that one may discover its sphere of action through direct experience. In this way, the yoga is engaged as a living process, which it is meant to be, and not an imposition of ideas from some outside source.

We began by introducing the theme of "unknowing," pointing out the importance of this disposition for true and deep transformation. This consciousness of "unknowing" identifies us with the receptive or YIN dimension of existence, which places us inwardly in the domain of the matrix, which is the womb, or transformational cauldron. When we are in this space, we are receptive, sensitive, open. One way of meditating is simply to spend time in this heart-centred disposition of openness, free of mental conditioning, clear of desire and expectation, yet with an aspiration to be one with the Divine. One of the first things to work on in Crystal Yoga is to find this space of consciousness, and to discover a way of being there that comes naturally to us. When we find this, we will want to return frequently to this space, and we will be happy resting there for long periods of time. The yoga is then not work but a pleasurable experience of fulfillment. The Mother, collaborator with Sri Aurobindo in his Integral Yoga, refers to this as the 'sunlit path.'

The state of consciousness called 'unknowing' is well known to the mystics, and the author of the well known Christian classic, *The Cloud of Unknowing,* has this to say:

Anyone who takes on this work unless he be given special grace, or has been long accustomed to it, will find it hard indeed. The demanding nature of this work is to be found in the putting down of the memory of creatures and holding them under the cloud of forgetting. This is man's work with the help of grace. The stirring of love, that is God's work. So press on and do your part, and I promise that He will not fail in his. Work away then. Work hard for a while and the burden will soon be lightened. For although it is hard in the beginning when you lack devotion, after a while when devotion is kindled it will become restful and light... Do everything that is in you to behave as if you did not know that the memories and thoughts press between you and God. Try to look over their shoulders seeking something else, which is God shrouded in the cloud of unknowing. If you do this, I believe that in a short while your work will be eased. I believe that if this device is well and truly understood, it is nothing else but a longing desire for God, to feel him and see him as far as may be in this life. Such a

*desire is love, and it always makes for a lightening of your work...
Be content to dwell in darkness and to renounce all desire of knowledge, for that will hinder more than help. It is enough that you are
moved lovingly – by what you do not know – and that you have no
thought of anything less than God and that your desire is nakedly
directed to God alone. (Daily Readings from the Cloud of Unknowing,
Springfield, 1986, pgs. 45-50)*

There are many fine insights and recommendations in this passage. One of these has to do with the impediment of mental conditioning, which is important to understand. Any mental notions that we carry into the purity of our heartspace from the past will not be useful for the interior attunement described here. Simply put, mental conditioning prevents us from being truly receptive. The clear heartspace can be described as a domain of intellectual emptying, or "unknowing," and at the same time a heartfelt fullness of pure Being. In essence, it is a yin-polarity of consciousness, an interior openness that invites all revelations of Presence that may be appropriate. This is what the writer of *The Cloud of Unknowing* means by such phrases as "dwelling in darkness" and "renouncing knowledge." He says: "your desire is nakedly directed to God alone."

When we cultivate this disposition or consciousness, we need not import any specific name or form of the Divine from the religions of the past. For receiving pure revelations in the ether of the spiritual heart, I find it most useful to connect with my heart's eagerness to be in a state of grace, an aspiration to be centred in the Divine Presence. To abide in 'the light of the soul,' to find 'the state of Pure Being,' whatever words we use, it is in the end an experience of coming home to *who we really are*. If the mind has all the questions, it is the spiritual heart which can provide the ultimate answers. Only the heart can answer the question of questions: Who Am I?

Yes, the control of thoughts and letting go of personal problems and worldly preoccupations is important. But in my own experience, this comes more easily through the intrinsic joy, beauty and peace of connecting to Source than by struggling against mental distractions. In this regard, the right kind of music can be a great help for relaxing the nervous system and opening the mind and heart to Presence. I highly recommend crystal bowls, Tibetan bowls, and recordings of them for this purpose (see pg. 413).

In cultivating the heart's intuitive attunement to Source, crystals offer much support. They are a perpetual mystery which you can only penetrate through intuitive perception. You have to be absolutely neutral and receptive to register the thing that a crystal might want to show you about yourself. Any stone or crystal you ever meet might trigger an insight into your soul, or your relation to Source. Equally, it may want to mirror to you the limitations you unconsciously cherish that block you from your own inner light. The mystics and the poets tell us that even a grain of sand (which is, of course crystalline) holds the paradigm of Eternity! It can be very helpful to know that each crystal is a key for unlocking certain polarities of experience, as we have described above. Crystal keys can be used in working with the polarities named, or with other polarities that we intuit from our inner guidance, and we have to be ready to go beyond the general guidelines into new territory at any moment.

In their silent, undeviating alignment with original cosmic intent, crystals are wonderful guides and teachers for finding the interior heartspace of unknowing, or what I call the inner radiance of "yin fire." This is the intuitive awareness wherein we can be linked with the presence and power of Spirit. One stone not normally associated with this linking is Labradorite, and at the time of writing this passage it is working very well at attuning me with the spiritual sky of the heart. Pursue your own experience and be guided by your own intuitive sense in these matters, because developing a sure intuition is actually one of the main lines that the work takes in its early phases.

When you want to work with one of the crystals from your *mesa*, you may place the stones on a table in front of you and choose it visually, or close your eyes and feel which crystal speaks to you by using your sense of touch. We have called this the First Attunement, and it is worth reviewing this first step toward awareness of stones and how they work. When one of the stones calls to you, allow yourself to relate to it in the domain of your intuitive feelings. Clear your mind of any trace of expectation. Be there with your crystal just to share the joy spending time with a friend. And realize that you may not even recognize the shift of energy that comes, so make no judgements as to what has taken place. Gratitude is one of the best heart-openers of all, if you can bring this quality forward during your attunement. When you are filled with gratitude, there is no other space you can be in but your spiritual heart.

In this way, intuitive links to subtle energy may be developed, but the process works best if you actually experience it as something enjoyable. For this reason, I hesitate to think and speak of time spent with the *mesa* as "exercises" or "practice sessions," although the English language does not provide many better words; it really is better to simply play with the stones, and allow the play to move gently into long periods of quiet, meditative absorption. This is certainly preferable to making efforts at wrestling the mind into stillness. The state of meditation is not something you have to work at if you can approach your crystal friends through a disposition of playfulness and gratitude. If you discover your own natural way of coming close to your inner child, you are much farther ahead than approaching 'the subject of meditation' through books, techniques and 'practice sessions' to still the mind.

The quotation that begins this chapter came during such a period of interior recollection that blossomed quite spontaneously as I was waking up one morning. For all of us, the sleeping and dreaming states can be a source of profound learning if we take a few moments before getting up to remember our connection with Source. Sleeping with a crystal, and holding it as we fall asleep, and holding it again as we wake up, can help us to cultivate a deeper awareness of the magic that is in dreams. There are times when you enter a state of grace or have a divine experience during your sleep, but this can easily be forgotten if you awake in a state of distraction. Recollection is an ideal theme to associate with a crystal that you hold as you enter and exit the state of sleep.

Sometimes the voice from inside your heart will come to you as a rhythm that seeks to clothe itself in musical sounds or poetic words. You honour that impulse when you give it expression and dedicate time for creative activities. You allow the Mother to work through you when you cherish the gifts of the Muse and share them with the world. To be a bard, poet, musician, oracle or prophet is to activate various facets of the jewel in the heart. Although many people would not think of these pursuits as a part of yoga, we should acknowledge that anything which links us to our higher capacities fulfils the divine plan. In any creative endeavour through which we become a more pure and crystalline channel for inspiration, we are doing the Mother's work.

I am reminded of this by a five rupee coin I was given in India, and which I treasure. On it there is engraved a likeness of Sri Aurobindo, and a quote from his writings: *All life is yoga.* The yoga in which we align with Mother Earth and the crystalline relics of her sacred body is a supra-personal participation in the divine plan which gave birth to the universe. To be one with this Way is to know who we truly are, and to manifest all that the soul has dreamed possible.

THE SECOND ATTUNEMENT

The sacred element of Air is very important for connecting. It connects individualized consciousness (e.g. the human mind) to that which is considered 'other' or outer. In *Savitri*, Sri Aurobindo reveals some fascinating aspects of Air that show us its value in meditation. It emerges that 'air' can refer to a state of consciousness, as in the lines: "A thinker and toiler in the ideal's air" (22) and "A breath comes down from a supernal air" (47). Among many interesting references to this element (there are almost one hundred and fifty in *Savitri!*), we find the following:

> *Air was a vibrant link between earth and heaven; (4) His spirit breathed a superhuman air; (82) Immaculate in the Spirit's deathless air; (109) In the white-blue-moonbeam air of Paradise; (234) The Thinker entered the Immortals' air; (263) In gleaming clarities of amethyst air; (264) A silent touch from the Supernal's air; (272) Breathe her divine, illimitable air; (276) a crystal mood of air; (289)*

Many more such lines with imagery rich in potential for meditation may be found in the remaining two-thirds of *Savitri*, for these examples are found by researching only 276 out of 724 pages of the full text. I see special meaning in this passage which exactly describes the work of the Crystal Mesa:

> *It is a brief compendium of the Vast.*
> *This was the single stair to being's goal.*
> *A summary of the stages of the spirit,*
> *Its copy of the cosmic hierarchies*
> *Refashioned in our secret **air** of self*

A subtle pattern of the universe.
It is within, below, without, above.
Acting upon this visible Nature's scheme
It wakens our earth-matter's heavy doze
To think and feel and to react to joy;
It models in us our diviner parts,
*Lifts mortal mind into a greater **air**,*
Makes yearn this life of flesh to intangible aims,
Links the body's death with immortality's call: (98-99)

The element Air is twice mentioned here (bold print added by me); although the master was perhaps not thinking about *mesa*, the work which a *mesa* does is clearly described. Shortly after this passage, we find:

*He came into **a magic crystal air***
And found a life that lived not by the flesh,
A light that made visible immaterial things. (103)

On the next page, he writes:

A finer consciousness with happier lines,
It has a tact our touch cannot attain,
A purity of sense we never feel;
Its intercession with the eternal Ray
Inspires our transient earth's brief-lived attempts
At beauty and the perfect shape of things.
In rooms of the young divinity of power
And early play of the eternal Child
The embodiments of his outwinging thoughts
Laved in a bright everlasting wonder's tints
And lulled by whispers of that lucid air
Take dream-hued rest like birds on timeless trees
Before they dive to float on earth-time's sea. (104)

This conveys a very fine sense of the ether of the spiritual heart wherein the archetype of the Child makes its home. Repeatedly, we find that a space of inner consciousness is referred to as an "air." Many examples can be found of this in *Savitri*, too many to list.

However, an excellent method of attunement through crystals to this inner air can be derived from the master's words, combining breath, visualization and mantra.

For this exercise, you may want to hold a crystal, or to imagine that you are holding one. It can be a point or a sphere, the larger the better. Begin by breathing in slowly and deeply. Quiet the mind and body and relax completely. Imagine that you are in a space where the air is crystalline. You are inhaling a "crystal air." Feel the crystalline qualities of clarity, purity, freshness and light entering every cell of the body as you inhale. Then, as you exhale, vibrate these energies in the cells of the body by intoning "OM."

Sri Aurobindo refers at one point in *Savitri* to "amethyst air" (see above). You may want to visualize that the air you are inhaling has the colour and energy of Amethyst, or you may picture any other crystal whose qualities you intuitively sense will be nurturing. For entering the heartspace, Rose Quartz is ideal. For vitality, cleansing and lightness, Citrine would work very well. You have many choices. Slowly and surely visualize yourself merging into this "crystal air" as you inhale and exhale. Continue this conscious breathing until the mind is perfectly still. At this point, you will experience a deep state of peace. Merge in that state of silence and peace. Rest there as long as you can remain focused.

If you want to attune to any of the crystal energies through the Water element, imagine the crystal as a flowing liquid washing over and through your mind and body.

If you want to attune to a crystal energy through the Fire element, visualize the crystal as a flame inside which your entire being is situated; feel the crystal flame permeating all parts of your being.

When the mind starts to become active, resume the conscious breathing and see if you can again enter the state of peace. It may help to recall phrases like "Immaculate in the Spirit's deathless air," or others. These affirmations can permeate the subconscious mind and bring it to greater openness and an even more profound state of relaxation. Every line of *Savitri* is mantra.

These exercises are recorded and available on the CD "Crystal Yoga" – details at the end of this book.

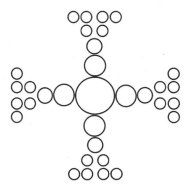

TEACHING MESA

This layout pattern shows the connections
between the various parts of the *mesa* and
its overall structure. The internal logic of its
pattern is clearly illustrated by this layout,
particularly the connection between the
center and the parts. This layout helps us
consider the four sacred elements and their
relationship to each other. The appeal of
this layout is to our mental understanding; it
emphasizes the interior order of the components of the crystal *mesa*.

THE POWER OF STONE

... great figures of gods
Conscious in stone and living without breath,
Watching with fixed regard the soul of man,
Executive figures of the cosmic self,
World-symbols of immutable potency.

Savitri, Book VII, Canto V

Stone is the Earth's original Mystery School. As some of the most solid and dense of the terrestrial manifestations, stones embody the extreme involution of consciousness. But more significantly, they are also the turning point from which consciousness begins its secret ascent to the Source. Thus, for human beings who aspire to be one with the Source of life and being, the wisdom that stones embody can be of the utmost importance.

Stones crystallize, vibrate and reveal aspects of our own completeness. Each one is a portion or fragment of the wholeness that our souls aspire to embody in material form on Earth, as we grow towards the condition of ultimately liberated and spiritually realized individuals. Stones embody energies that amplify our strengths, supplement our capacities and expand our potential. Because of this, they can be as teachers who help us make wise choices. When you know how to relate to them, certain stones will work very well to assist your soul to complete its inner alignment and attunement to wholeness and perfection. Humans have deviated from the divine paradigm more than other forms of life on Earth. In the Bible, this is described as a result of Adam and Eve eating the fruits of the tree of knowledge. Crystals in particular have never deviated from their divine pattern; they hold and express it continuously, and in this they have much to teach us about silence, surrender, integrity and wholeness.

When the soul comes into this physical time-space continuum, it aligns with a wide spectrum of crystalline Earth-energies to create a physical body which it will inhabit. This body that we assemble from the constituents of clay and the dust of Mother Earth is in reality a soul-temple, and it is full of magical potential. In the outer world stones, and especially the crystalline minerals, are concrete masses of physical matter that solidify the potencies of the cosmic energies, distilling them into concrete form so that they may be used by physically embodied living entities. By learning to work with crystalline gems and their energies, we grow into an awareness of the star-forces that they concentrate, and we discover how to apply these rarified potencies to the process of our evolution in consciousness. Crystals, therefore, can be as helpful in the process of yoga as any other traditional tool, including the use of sound in mantras, the relationship with a living human teacher, the experience of community and collective aspiration, or the creation of a suitable environment for contemplation.

Learning to listen is very important in our journey toward inner wholeness and completion; it is at the core of any deeper relationship to the world in which we take physical incarnation. The sages of ancient India taught that it is through the sense of hearing that we are best able to penetrate below the surface of things and merge in union with the Divine Source. Because of this, they went very far and deep in their exploration of vibration, working with the power that sound has to alter consciousness. They developed a spiritual science of sound known as *mantra*. One of the high points of this very ancient exploration, and mankind's oldest scripture, is the body of mantras known as the *Veda*. Parts of this monumental scripture are over five thousand years old, and until it was written down in historical times it was passed on by word of mouth in unbroken continuity from the rishis and seers to their disciples.

Centrally important to the Veda and other ancient traditions is the theme that VAK, the Divine Word, carries the power to transform and perfect all levels of our existence. As the Gospel of John says: "In the beginning was the Word, and the Word was with God, and the word was God."

There is a profound connection between sound and crystal. For a start, they are both vibrational. Sound can be used, especially mantric sound, to activate our crystalline microcosm into its full potential, while the perfect structure of crystal in the molecules of our blood and elsewhere can hold, transduce, amplify and direct energy, supporting the process of realizing our highest consciousness. We cannot draw an artificial line and separate the crystalline substances of our own body from those of the body of Mother Earth, or those of Mother Earth from the energies of the stars. Nor can we forget that crystals are every bit as much manifestations of cosmic sound and harmony as they are physical structures of perfected form. Coming to know all this first hand is part of the journey that I call Crystal Yoga.

It is through the experience of identification that we intuit the true nature of our microcosm, our macrocosm, and our soul's work of mediation between the high perfection of Heaven and the buried potential of Earth. For this reason, learning to listen, learning to truly hear, developing a capacity for profound absorption and attunement, is of the utmost important for our growth in meditation. At the most obvious level, stones appear to be silent. But when we learn to listen, it is possible to know firsthand the deep mystery that they have held for eons within their silence. Then, we begin to discover in our own living experience how crystals can be as keys to the very heart and soul of material creation. They structure and reveal its essence and meaning to the pilgrim soul in its long journey of self-unfolding.

Our aspiration for wholeness is not and cannot be achieved without cultivating a deeply experiential relationship to matter, for our souls came here not only to realize the highest Truth, but to also to transform this plane of existence into its image. Our souls take birth to manifest a dream in the conditions of the material creation. We are artists of the divine. Our palette and canvas are supplied to us by the bones and flesh of the Earth.

The Tibetans have a book called Bardo Thodol, "Liberation by Hearing." The German translator of this book, Louise Goepfert-March writes:

The first step is learning to hear, wanting to hear, releasing the chaos within oneself, releasing it in the way one releases the body in physical death. This step means that one no longer wishes to interfere, to change things, to quarrel, to express an opinion, to translate what was heard into everyday mechanical language … It means that one rests easy next to the giant army of onrushing associations of thoughts, feelings and physical things.

There are certain sounds that communicate to the listener the true nature of the universe, but if one has not learned to penetrate the depths of silence and to listen from within the heart of silence, one cannot find this core resonance. In meditation with stones, we seek this attunement to what is deep and hidden. Through this intuitive link, we open portals into a universe of as yet undreamed possibilities.

AN INNER SCIENCE

For over a century, scientists have been paying attention to crystal because of its remarkable properties. Computer technology and thus much of the world's modern communications and military capacity is based on harnessing the powers of crystal to focus energy. As with all things, 'what you see (and thus what you get)' from any field of study depends very much on your angle of vision and your preconceptions. In the scientific paradigm, the only things considered 'real' are those that can be measured with instruments and analyzed by the rational mind. All other phenomena, such as love, bliss, the meaning of life, fall outside the boundaries of what modern science considers.

In ancient times, science was integral, meaning that all human faculties and modes of perception were considered valid methodologies for exploring reality. Thus intuition, inner vision, psychometry, extra sensory perception, dowsing, and other ways of knowing and interacting with the world around us and inside us were deployed and used as appropriate. In this open-ended approach, the prophet, the seer, the oracle, the bard, the mystic and the visionary all had valid contributions, and their gifts were acknowledged and celebrated. In many ways, because of this open-minded approach, the ancients achieved significant results beyond what modern science considers possible. The pyramids of Egypt and stone ruins elsewhere in the world testify to the remarkable sophistication of ancient technology.

In the earliest scriptures of India, we read of flying machines (*vamana*) and of weapons that equaled nuclear bombs in their destructive power. There is a lot of denial and discomfort about such subjects among modern scientists, because they feel that their paradigm is threatened by evidence pointing to the narrowness of their assumptions. However, modern quantum physics is leading the way in replacing the Newtonian concept of the world with one much closer, or even essentially identical to, that of the ancient seers and sages of India (and elsewhere).

When scientific thinking emerged in post-Renaissance Europe, it was a refreshing advance on the stultifying theology of Roman imperial Christianity. When the bishops of the Roman Empire suppressed and destroyed the various Gnostic traditions in the third and fourth centuries AD for the sake of religious uniformity, they sacrificed much of Christianity's spiritual depth and vitality. Science has become the prevailing paradigm of the modern world, but in its success it has similarly suppressed or denied the validity of evidence from ranges of reality beyond its defined frame of reference. If, for example, science cannot acknowledge and study consciousness, and all its ranges of expression in the human microcosm, it is going to give us a picture of life and its meaning that is sadly incomplete. If such a restrictive scientific outlook shapes and dominates our way of knowing and being, we end up greatly diminished human beings, the kind of unhappy people you find in Sartre's existential novels. We often fail to see how spiritually, creatively and imaginatively constricted have been the effects of the materialist and positivistic outlook that prevails among orthodox scientists. It is now well known that truly valuable work in many fields such as archaeology and psychology is frequently suppressed by the scientific establishment in order to maintain its orthodox paradigm. Thus many scientists have become enforcers of the very narrowness that science formerly opposed in its early years of evolution, when it championed intellectual freedom over and against the constricting boundaries of institutional religion.

In spiritual practice, or, to use a Sanskrit term, *sadhana*, everything begins and ends with consciousness. There is a recognition among all spiritual seekers that it is mastery of consciousness which brings expertise and knowledge relevant to the soul and its purpose in life. In the long tradition of spiritual seeking, one who has opened up the inner vision and is aware of other planes or worlds of reality is known as a 'seer' and his or her knowledge has its place in the overall scheme of things. One who has made a deep study (through personal experience in contemplation) of the higher worlds and their significance to human life on Earth and who has attained a heightened or expanded level of awareness in this area is known as a 'sage.' Indeed, our knowledge of such important concepts as "original contract" can only come from the inner vision and knowledge of those who have this kind of mastery in the domain of consciousness. It is for this reason that I frequently cite Sri Aurobindo, and make reference to other masters like the Buddha. There is no doubt that spiritual masters have a profound and direct experience of ultimate reality, and in their unique capacity to teach and share this inner vision with others they awaken us to our full potential. Thus, Crystal Yoga is, as mentioned in the Preface, a 'yoga of the masters.'

Spiritual masters were and still are honoured by a majority of the world's population as experts within their domain of competence, which is the field of consciousness. Traditional societies have always acknowledged the importance of masters, mystics, shamans and healers for maintaining the balance necessary to life on Earth. They have accorded places of appropriate social importance to individuals with spiritual, psychic, or paranormal gifts, all of which were thought of as 'gifts of the Spirit.' In the whole of our known history, it would seem that only our own modern post-industrial society with its narrowly defined "scientific" approach to reality has ignored such endowments of consciousness as sources of input for understanding the way the universe works.

We might pause to consider why in the fields of education and human development we have made no effort to develop and widen and deepen our notions about human consciousness. We act as if the only tool we have is the rational mind so beloved of scientists. Questions concerning the ultimate purpose of life are simply not raised in this intellectual climate; they cannot be answered or even discussed because they are politically incorrect in the modern academic paradigm. The result is that we live in a world which T.S.Eliot and other great minds have experienced as a kind of wasteland of the soul. Yet while all this is the prevailing situation, both for scientific technology and for spiritual seekers, crystals are opening a whole set of fresh possibilities, a brave new world where energy and consciousness can no longer be fitted into outdated paradigms.

From all of the above, it naturally follows that the revelations of the great souls about the purpose of life and the structure of the universe must be a foundation for the work that serious students of consciousness do in their chosen field of spiritual practice. And when we study the words of the masters, we find that in different ways, these great teachers all say essentially the same thing. I would summarize some of the main points of their vision, as its relates to Crystal Yoga, as follows:

1) **Consciousness is the ultimate reality of which we as humans can become aware. The Infinite Consciousness, sometimes called the Self, is beyond form, but within the manifest universe, it expresses as energy and light. Matter is solidified energy or light.** *Comment:* Crystal is a highly organized kind of solidified light (or energy) which is to say, it is solidified consciousness. It is like ice in relation to water, which can manifest in a still more rarified form as steam or mist. Matter is a finite expression of the Infinite Reality. Crystalline matter's internal ordering is such that it symbolizes or expresses this reality better than any other creation in the mineral world.

2) **Energy Follows thought.** *Comment:* The physical creation is a materialization of thought. In nature we see revealed the thought of the Creator. In human culture, and in the evolving human microcosm, we see manifest many of the thoughts of man. The application of sustained and focused thought can modify energy and matter over a period of time, most particularly through the DNA.

3) **Thought is conditioned by feeling.** *Comment:* Feeling, at the average level of human development, takes the form of craving, or desire. But there is a higher kind of feeling which can be attuned to the Divine. Establishing a connection between one's thought-life and the inner core of one's feeling-life is a most important step toward liberation.

4) **The spiritual heart reveals the light of spirit in human consciousness.** *Comment:* Earth is a place where spirit manifests in matter, in form. Humanity is evolving toward more perfect levels of order and awareness. Those who aspire to realize their full po-

tential experience an inner aspiration to refine the physical, vital-emotional and mental levels of their existence so these become more permeable to the light of Spirit. The focusing of attention and feeling on the ideal to be realized brings about a transformation of consciousness. In the East, this discipline is called Yoga.

5) **When purified consciousness becomes the doer, action becomes an unobstructed flow of the light of Spirit.** *Comment:* As long as humanity acts under the compulsion of vital-emotional impulses, and as long as thought is ruled by craving, the action of Spirit can at best be intermittent and its influence incomplete. For the individual who aspires to transcend the limitations of the human condition, some discipline of self-development is a necessity.

6) **The unobstructed flow of consciousness-light, or Spirit, transforms and perfects the human microcosm at all levels.** *Comment:* Spiritual realization brings an unobstructed flow of pure consciousness. The higher help of the Infinite Consciousness is sometimes referred to as grace; when invoked, it supplements self-effort to expedite the attainment of realization.

7) **When right relation to Source becomes the guiding spirit of all action, integral realization or enlightenment is attainable. With this attainment, light completes a significant phase of its return journey to Source.** *Comment:* Consciousness, attaining awareness of its oneness with Source, transforms the human microcosm into an instrument of Divine action, but only after complete surrender to the divine action has been established.

When one has attained the level of understanding summarized in these seven points and can demonstrate it in practice, it becomes possible to know and express fundamentals of spiritual science in a clear way. In ancient times, when yoga or spiritual practice were studied, the words of the sages were greatly valued for this reason. They were known to be men of genuine attainment, men who had arrived at the vision of Truth.

What follows is a summary of spiritual understanding central to the tradition of the masters that underpins the subject of Crystal Yoga. I have set this down in sutra style, this being the most appropriate for the subject matter.

1) In the primordial space, the place of beginnings, in the abode of the Great Mother, all things have their origin. In this space they exist and evolve. And into this space, at the end of their allotted time they return to merge with their Source.

2) In the matrix of creation there is an energy which is beyond division, unqualified, boundless and clear. It pervades infinite space, and is full of awareness. It is pure, without separate identity, beyond name and beyond form.

3) We may speak of this primordial existence as the light of consciousness, or the original luminosity. It was and is the reality behind what is apparent to the mind and senses. One who knows this attains wisdom.

4) From within the heart of this nameless, formless energy come the five pure lights. More subtle than visible light, more subtle than anything the eye can perceive, more subtle than any energy that can be named, measured or experienced, these lights are the energies from which all other energies derive.

5) First comes *akasha* or ether, the colourless light of space.

6) Thence comes the clear light, or air; the red light, or fire; the blue light, or water; and the yellow light which is Earth. These four, and *akasha*, are the five faces of that primal luminosity which is beyond name and form. In these five, the great Unknowable becomes the knowable and ignorance begins.

7) The human intelligence seeks wisdom by using the mind of duality, and thus humans come to experience these lights as something substantial. It is the distortion of dualistic vision that perceives these lights as being gross in nature. From gross perception comes gross understanding, in which ignorance flourishes.

8) As we discriminate and study these elements, we elaborate and trace the pathways by which they manifest all phenomena. We come to see that without exception the various objects and subjects of our experience derive from the primal five.

9) By the power of *maya*, spirit manifests as energy and matter. Through devolution, the five primal lights become the gross physical elements and the qualities that differentiate external reality. The externalized mind becomes lost in the outer appearance of things, and thus pure awareness is obscured.

10) This precious human body, this temple of the spirit, is a gift of the primal five and a temple of pure awareness, or wisdom. The five lights permeate the body, its senses, limbs, fingers, toes and every cell of the human microcosm. They are woven through the organs of perception, thought and understanding as well.

11) In ignorance, these five lights form the five kinds of delusion, and in wisdom they reveal the five liberating kinds of wisdom. When wisdom grows, ignorance recedes.

12) When we see the five lights as being one in essence, we experience ceaseless revelations of their infinite Source. Thus, mind begins the journey to enlightenment, the passage from the temporal to the Eternal which ends in liberation.

13) When we see the five lights dualistically, we think that they exist externally, as objects of perception; seeing thus, mind becomes clouded, consciousness becomes conditioned and the weight of *karma* increases.

14) Awareness itself is forever pure. But the qualities that arise within awareness can be positive or negative, conducing to liberation, or leading to karmic involvement and earthly limitation.

15) When awareness anchors itself in perception of the pure qualities, remembering the five lights and their Source, the liberated awareness arises spontaneously. When awareness becomes lost in the external appearances and desire-filled relationships with the many, ignorance prevails.

16) We have this choice before us. We may see all things in their relation to the five and their Source, or we may cling to the false notions of separation and live as subjects who experience external objects.

17) Right relation to experience arises of its own accord when we take the five lights as our teachers. *Mesa* is the assembly of the family of primal teachers.

18) *Mesa* assembles those energies which nature has birthed, and sees them in their true nature as pure sources of the living energy and consciousness of the five lights.

19) Knowing these five through their gem-like perfections in crystal Earth, we are reminded in awareness of their Source. In time, contemplating the connection of all things to the primal five, and

the oneness of the five with the Eternal Source, we birth the light of wisdom.

20) Knowing both the gross and the subtle forms through which the primal five are expressed, we attain the full knowledge of these sacred elements. This leads in turn to the mastery of the gross and subtle levels of our own microcosm.

21) In this, we find freedom and bliss. In this, we transcend limitation and become one with all that is.

22) At this time, the names and forms of the Sacred Five constitute a temple of boundless awareness, and the mind of wisdom realizes: "I AM THAT."

23) Dwelling in freedom, beyond the snares of ignorance, such a realized soul becomes enlightened, a ray of wisdom for all who seek the way.

Sutra is a very useful style for distilling the essence of wisdom in pithy statements which can be contemplated or even memorized. Because *mesa* involves a sacred approach to being and doing, it is a subject worthy of such a style. Sometimes in the wisdom-tradition, there are certain kinds of teaching that demand prophetic or bardic presentation because this is the most concentrated and lofty form of verbal expression, and is simply the style best adapted to the subject. Often what we intuit or overhear in the *music of words* has more impact than the bare bones logic of the intellectual thoughts. Of course, in accepting such sources as music, mantra, poetry, sutra and revelation as input for our spiritual work, we have overstepped the boundaries of modern science. We have progressed into a wider domain that we might call 'spiritual science.' Only in this fuller way of understanding and being can Crystal Yoga be conceptualized and explored.

A NEW WAY OF KNOWING

When we move beyond intellectual logic as a way of knowing, a whole new world of insight opens up, and in this wider space of consciousness everything we experience can contribute in an unexpected way to our fund of wisdom.

For example, dreams can become a rich source of inner experience and guidance. Dreams can occur on any number of planes of consciousness. Those which come from higher planes of consciousness can be significant for the spiritual life. Moreover, the universal consciousness has its own lexicon of symbols through which communication between planes can take place. This is so regardless of the distortion introduced by individuals whose consciousness is obscure, or whose dream experience is largely undigested subconscious fragments. Also, many souls have the experience of visiting inner schools during sleep. If we meditate with a crystal before sleeping, and meditate with it once again when we wake, we may be able to remember and access the fund of experiences that come to us in the dreaming state.

Dream experiences of all kinds are considered real by many spiritual masters, no less real than this plane of waking consciousness to which we give so much importance. One can learn, by studying dreams and the nature of dream-experience, to understand the dreamlike (and hence not completely real) nature of waking experience. When the dreamlike nature of ALL experience is seen, one's inner discernment is intuitively closer to recognizing the nature of Being, because one has seen into the nature of *maya*, or illusion. All experience short of knowing Reality is to some degree illusory, but many dreams are more archetypal and universal than the fragmentary input we have on the physical plane of awareness. Certain dreams carry a greater intensity of light, love and consciousness than the ego-generated fictions and figments of our semi-conscious waking lives. In this sense, they are truer. After all, poetry, as Aristotle said, can be truer than history just because it sometimes comes closer to expressing eternal and archetypal reality. The masters teach that what is eternal and timeless is more real, not less real, than physical facts which can be analyzed by the five senses and the rational intellect.

Intellect arrives at understanding by differentiating, distinguishing, separating, deconstructing. But intuition works through synthesis, harmonizing, merging and revealing hidden structures of oneness. The knowledge of the intuitive heart reveals underlying patterns of a hidden unity which can be sensed permeating all forms of being and all strains of experience. The artistic and creative process (right brain) depends on such intuitive modes of awareness to arrive at its perception of reality, a reality beyond the stark facts of outer physical appearance.

In the extended DVD version of the movie, *The Return of the King,* based on Tolkein's *Lord of the Rings* trilogy, there is an entire DVD devoted to the "making of Middle Earth." Watching this documentary during a lunch break while writing this manuscript, the phrase "making of Middle Earth" resonated strongly in my imagination. It struck me that this is what we do in spiritual practice, we remake the human microcosm so that it can reflect and embody the higher harmonies of the Cosmic Artist's vision. This documentary about the production of *Lord of the Rings* showed how the set designers translated Tolkein's descriptions of Minas Tirith into a movie-version physical 'reality.' I was particularly attentive to a quotation from book three of the Tolkein trilogy which the narrator read as the documentary showed parts of the set being built:

> ...*the fashion of Minas Tirith was such that it was built on seven levels, each delved into the hill, and about each was set a wall and in each wall was a gate. But the gates were not set in a line: the Great Gate in the City Wall was at the east point of the circuit, but the next faced half south, and the third half north and so to and fro upwards; so that the paved way that climbed towards the Citadel turned first this way and then that across the face of the hill. (Part 3, Ch. 1)*

This unusual patterning resembles many another sacredly-designed city of myth and legend. It is not unlike Camelot, or other cities that were 'built to music,' which is to say that there is a long tradition of mythic places of human habitation modeled on the harmonious proportions of the cosmic pattern. The seven levels of Minas Tirith correspond to the seven levels of energy and consciousness in the human microcosm and to the chakras which are our windows or gates of perception. The hill into which these are delved is the physical stuff of the sacred element Earth, the clay that our souls assemble into a living human body through the course of a lifetime's experience.

Going on to provide more detail about each of these seven levels, Tolkein says: "about each was set a wall and in each wall was a gate." Each plane of our being has its own body with its own auric boundary, and the gateways of the seven chakras open us at each level to what lies beyond our five senses. If you look at the ancient symbol of the caduceus, the ancient classical symbol of the ascending kundalini as it wound through the chakras, you will see the undulating pattern of the serpents that meet and cross at these 'gateways.' A chakra is a disc or circle, and the architectural style of making circular doorways reminds our intuitive mind that all places of coming and going, all thresholds of entry, are numinous. The paved way that winds up the hill of Minas Tirith follows this primal snaking pattern of our own microcosmic kundalini energy through the seven principal gates of the city. Just as the set-builders translated Tolkein's literary vision into a physical film set for their movie, so those who work with the human microcosm through processes of yoga transform a human, clay tenement into an archetypal temple of the divine presence. For the work is always about a dream-vision and its expression as a living reality on this physical planet.

I cite this example not so much to illustrate the literary crafts-manship of Tolkein as to make a statement about the mastery of consciousness which is evident in the mastery of the literary craft. Tolkein was depicting the primal pattern of the human microcosm in his description of Minas Tirith, and this is a clear example of the intuitive and creative mind's ability to find and express insights concerning the divine plan that shapes creation. Hearing or reading a description of this archetypal city, one may gain an insight into the sevenfold, many-gated pattern of our own human microcosm. After all, the creative inspiration to become a divine builder and to fashion in our own being a city 'not built by human hands' is at the core of Crystal Yoga. For this inner work, one needs to cultivate the mind-set of the seer, the eloquence of the poet, the reverential depth of the mystic, the devotion of a divine lover, and the sensitivity of a dreamer. With such inner lights and riches, one may then intuit the underlying pattern of oneness wherever it reveals itself, sometimes in the least probable places.

You never know when the world will shine out a ray of its hidden magic, but when you read Tolkein, or watch the movie version of *Lord of the Rings*, or marvel at the beauty of a Lemurian crystal, you can sense that the magic is real. For example, drawing from the writings of Tolkein, the *Lord of the Rings* movie trilogy depicts the palantir as crystal spheres which could connect people's intuitive minds wherever they might be, even at opposite ends of the Earth. Thus the palantir give glimpses of what unaided human minds would otherwise have found impossible. Writing as he did long before crystals became a popular New Age fad, Tolkein's understanding of the palantir shows how a true bard can intuit ancient realities and depict them in fresh language. It is in this way that poets renew the power of the timeless archetypes to speak to us once again. The bards and the visions they channel sow the power of the revealing word in our individual and collective imagination.

During the course of our personal spiritual journey through life, we must time and again renew our dreams, our insights, our inspirations, or those of the masters to whom we are drawn. When we contemplate the power of these words and assimilate the light of Truth that they hold, we bring more fully to life our own inner guidance and creativity. This is absolutely indispensable if we are to do the soul's work that we have chosen, re-fashioning the microcosm given to us and thus changing the destiny of Middle Earth. This opportunity to live in a human body, and to make a statement about the meaning of life through our choices and actions, this is our soul's great adventure. This is the task given to us by our inner divinity.

THE YOGA OF SAVITRI

It is not easy to master any of the fields of expertise we have mentioned. Still more difficult and rare is it to find the mastery of *all* these domains within the achievement of a single individual. Yet, such an adept was Sri Aurobindo. He was a spiritual master, Vedic scholar, literary scholar, seer, sage, prophet and bard, and it is no hyperbole to suggest that he is the most outstanding example of such universal wisdom that the twentieth century has produced. Any serious study of yoga in modern times, and in particular any approach to yoga as an *integral process,* co-extensive with the whole of life, must take into account the work of Sri Aurobindo. His mystical poem *Savitri* is probably the most significant piece of spiritual writing since the Vedas, and it is certainly the longest poem in the English language. If any single piece of writing in modern times can be considered authoritative as an account of the soul's journey through life, *Savitri* undoubtedly heads the list. Not only is it a summary of the master's entire spiritual experience, it is also a depiction of how Mother Earth aspires through man to realize the divine plan. Perhaps not surprisingly, *Savitri* is a rich mine of insights on Crystal Yoga.

We do not have to look far to validate this last point. For example, the theme that all yoga comes from an 'original contract' between Heaven and Earth is clearly expressed in a number of passages such as:

> *There is a truth to know, a work to do;*
> *Her play is real; a Mystery he fulfils:*
> *There is a plan in the Mother's deep world-whim,*
> *A purpose in her vast and random game.*
> *This ever she meant since the first dawn of life,*
> *This constant will she covered with her sport,*
> *To evoke a Person in the impersonal Void,*
> *With the Truth-Light strike earth's massive roots of trance,*
> *Wake a dumb self in the inconscient depths*
> *And raise a lost Power from its python sleep*
> *That the eyes of the Timeless might look out from Time*
> *And the world manifest the unveiled Divine.*
> *For this he left his white infinity*
> *And laid on the spirit the burden of the flesh,*
> *That Godhead's seed might flower in mindless Space. (72-3)*

(Since all editions of Savitri have the same pagination, references are made in terms of the page on which the lines are found.)

The great work that the soul comes to Earth to do arises not from individual humans and their motivation to avoid suffering or find personal happiness, although such motives play a significant role. It might appear that personal motivation is the all-important factor in yoga from our present perspective, when human consciousness is locked into its mind and ego. However, from the point of view of the Sage, from the point of view of Truth-Consciousness, the soul's journey arises from something more universal, namely:

> *… the unfulfilled demand of earth*
> *And the song of promise of unrealized heavens (29)*

The work that is accomplished within the human microcosm is not based solely on the motivation of humans and their personal needs. More important is the working of the Mother in and through awakened humans to realize her divine plan for creation as a whole:

Ignorant and weary and invincible,
She seeks through the soul's war and quivering pain
The pure perfection her marred nature needs,
A breath of Godhead on her stone and mire. (51)
The inspiring goddess entered a mortal's breast,
Made there her study of divining thought
And sanctuary of prophetic speech
And sat upon the tripod seat of mind:
All was made wide above, all lit below.
In darkness' core she dug out wells of light,
On the undiscovered depths imposed a form,
Lent a vibrant cry to the unuttered vasts,
And through great shoreless, voiceless, starless breadths
Bore earthward fragments of revealing thought
Hewn from the silence of the Ineffable. (41)

The development of human personhood, its individualization, its growth in awareness, its elaboration and transcendence of ego, and its final liberation from ignorance are all part of the work that the Mother, the creative divine power, accomplishes in and through us. Sri Aurobindo clearly states that the seed of the divine possibility within us is a crystal, equivalent to a magic key on which all our future potentials hinge:

In a brief moment caught, a little space,
All-Knowledge packed into great wordless thoughts
Lodged in the expectant stillness of his depths
A crystal of the ultimate Absolute,
A portion of the inexpressible Truth
Revealed by silence to the silent soul.
The intense creatrix in his stillness wrought;
Her power fallen speechless grew more intimate;
She looked upon the seen and the unforeseen,
Unguessed domains she made her native field. (38)
*Always we bear in us **a magic key***
Concealed in life's hermetic envelope.
A burning Witness in the sanctuary
Regards through Time and the blind walls of Form;
***A timeless Light** is in his hidden eyes;*

He sees the secret things no words can speak
And knows the goal of the unconscious world
And the heart of the mystery of the journeying years. (49)

Yoga, the yoking of Heaven and Earth, is the work that our souls are here to do. This is made clear in many passages, for example:

A Voice ill-heard shall speak, the soul obey,
A Power into mind's inner chamber steal,
A charm and sweetness open life's closed doors
And beauty conquer the resisting world,
The Truth-Light capture Nature by surprise,
A stealth of God compel the heart to bliss
And earth grow unexpectedly divine.
In Matter shall be lit the spirit's glow,
In body and body kindled the sacred birth;
Night shall awake to the anthem of the stars,
The days become a happy pilgrim march,
Our will a force of the Eternal's power,
And thought the rays of a spiritual sun. (55)
This is our deepest need to join once more
What now is parted, opposite and twain,
Remote in sovereign spheres that never meet
Or fronting like far poles of Night and Day.
We must fill the immense lacuna we have made,
Re-wed the closed finite's lonely consonant
With the open vowels of Infinity,
A hyphen must connect Matter and Mind,
The narrow isthmus of the ascending soul:
We must renew the secret bond in things,
Our hearts recall the lost divine Idea,
Reconstitute the perfect word, unite
The Alpha and the Omega in one sound;
Then shall the Spirit and Nature be at one. (56-7)

The Mother, the Child, the Hero and the Sage are important archetypes in Sri Aurobindo's epic account of the soul's journey of return to the Source. However, the importance of nature in yoga goes much deeper than that.

Many details of mystical experience in *Savitri* are presented through the imagery of crystal. For example, when the soul journeys deep within, Sri Aurobindo writes that "The inner planes uncovered their crystal doors;" (33) And when the soul arrives at its goal, the reunion of seeker and Source is described thus:

The divine intention suddenly shall be seen,
The end vindicate intuition's sure technique.
A graph shall be of many meeting worlds,
A cube and union-crystal of the gods; (100)

In other words, just as a crystal was placed inside our secret hearts as a seed of divine possibility, a magic key to the journey, (see the quote above) so a crystal will be the form that the journey's final completion takes. The supreme promise of this is given to the pilgrim soul toward the end of the poem. In the following passage, the master links crystals with the stars:

I will fasten thy nature with my cords of strength,
Subdue to my delight thy spirit's limbs
And make thee a vivid knot of all my bliss
*And build in thee **my proud and crystal home.***
*Thy days shall be my shafts of power and **light,***
*Thy nights my **starry mysteries of joy** (698)*

There are also in *Savitri* a number of instances where mystical buildings are described as having floors of moonstone or other crystalline substance. Just as the cosmic city of Minas Tirith was modeled on a cosmic design, the substance of crystal is repeatedly used by Sri Aurobindo in many instances to indicate a high degree of achieved perfection. Certainly the image of Diamond, which appears on eleven occasions in the course of the poem, is repeatedly used in this sense.

Another interesting use of the crystal image is that it characterizes the magical inner ether in which higher perception is possible at various stages of the journey:

In the impalpable field of secret self,
This little outer being's vast support
Parted from vision by earth's solid fence,

*He came into **a magic crystal air***
And found a life that lived not by the flesh,
*A **light** that made visible immaterial things.* (103)

During the course of *Savitri*, we repeatedly find that light, silence, a ray, a subtle ether, or an interior space of consciousness are associated with crystal, as in the following:

As if a beckoning finger of secrecy
*Outstretched into **a crystal mood of air**,*
Pointing at him from some near hidden depth,
*As if a message from the **world's deep soul**,*
An intimation of a lurking joy
That flowed out from a cup of brooding bliss,
There shimmered stealing out into the Mind
*A mute and quivering ecstasy of **light**,*
*A passion and delicacy of **roseate fire**,*
As one drawn to his lost spiritual home
Feels now the closeness of a waiting love, (289)
Here, living centre of that vision of peace,
*A Woman sat in **clear and crystal light**:*
Heaven had unveiled its lustre in her eyes,
Her feet were moonbeams, her face was a bright sun, (514)
Immune she beheld the strong immortals' seats
Who live for a celestial joy and rule,
*The middle regions of **the unfading Ray**.*
Great forms of deities sat in deathless tiers,
Eyes of an unborn gaze towards her leaned
*Through a transparency of **crystal fire**.* (676)

Mind itself is described as a "gleaming crystal" (616), and the eyes of an illumined soul are depicted as "crystal windows":

Celestial-human deep warm slumbrous fires
Woke in the long fringed glory of her eyes
Like altar-burnings in a mysteried shrine.
*Out of those **crystal windows** gleamed a will*
That brought a large significance to life. (357)

And the purity of the soul is described in terms of crystal as well:

*Like drops of **fire** upon a silver page,*
In her young spirit yet untouched with tears,
All beautiful things eternal seem and new
*To virgin wonder in her **crystal soul**. (422)*

There are references throughout *Savitri* to Amethyst (2), Chrysoprase (1), Coral (1), Lapis Lazuli (1), Sapphire (14), Ruby (2), Emerald (21), Topaz (1), Amber (1), Diamond (11), Moonstone (1), Pearl (7), Sunstone (1) Gems (3), Jewels (18), and other similar images drawn from the mineral kingdom. These frequently occur in conjunction not only with images of light, silence, rays and associations with purely spiritual domains of experience, but are also linked to imagery of the stars of which there are 88 instances in the poem as a whole.

This association which Sri Aurobindo makes between crystals and light is not original. Crystals have been understood from the most ancient times as 'solidified light,' not only in the Mystery Schools of Egypt, Greece, Mesopotamia and India, but among indigenous peoples as well. For example, among the Wiradjeri of Australia, a candidate for shamanism is inducted into his role by being sprinkled with a "sacred powerful water" that is understood to be liquefied quartz. Mircea Eliade comments that "All this is as much as to say that one becomes a shaman when one is stuffed with 'solidified light,' that is with quartz crystals..." (*Shamanism*, NY, 1964, pg. 138)

What can we conclude? Reading *Savitri* as a whole, it is clear that for Sri Aurobindo the spiritual journey is something being worked out by higher powers through those humans who are ready and willing to find and follow the light of the soul. Humanity's ascent in consciousness is part of a cosmic reunion between Heaven and Earth, a particular instance of a planetary evolution of consciousness in which Nature plays a central role. Crystals and gems are the most spiritualized beings within the mineral kingdom, the yogis and enlightened beings of Earth's earliest awakening. They speak most eloquently about where we have come from and where, as spiritual seekers, we are going. Echoing the Vedas, *Savitri* speaks of a hidden treasure concealed in the depths of matter. The task awaiting the spiritual hero is to find and liberate this inner wealth so that its light and power can transform creation. Remembering that the Sanskrit word for wealth and treasure is *"ratna"* or jewel, let us consider these lines from the master:

> *The master of existence lurks in us*
> *And plays at hide-and-seek with his own Force;*
> *In Nature's instrument loiters secret God.*
> *The Immanent lives in man as in his house;*
> *He has made the universe his pastime's field,*
> *A vast gymnasium of his works of might.*
> *All-knowing he accepts our darkened state,*
> *Divine, wears shapes of animal or man;*
> *Eternal, he assents to Fate and Time,*
> *Immortal, dallies with mortality.*
> *The All-Conscious ventured into Ignorance,*
> *The All-Blissful bore to be insensible.*
> *Incarnate in a world of strife and pain,*
> *He puts on joy and sorrow like a robe*
> *And drinks experience like a strengthening wine.*
> *He whose transcendence rules the pregnant Vasts,*
> *Prescient now dwells in our subliminal depths,*
> *A luminous individual Power, alone.*
> *The Absolute, the Perfect, the Alone*
> *Has called out of the Silence his mute Force*
> *Where she lay in the featureless and formless hush*
> *Guarding from Time by her immobile sleep*
> *The ineffable puissance of his solitude.*
> *The Absolute, the Perfect, the Alone*
> *Has entered with his silence into space:*
> *He has fashioned these countless persons of one self;*
> *He has built a million figures of his power;*
> *He lives in all, who lived in his Vast alone;*
> *Space is himself and Time is only he.*
> *The Absolute, the Perfect, the Immune,*
> *One who is in us as our secret self,*
> *Our mask of imperfection has assumed,*
> *He has made this tenement of flesh his own,*

His image in the human measure cast
That to his divine measure we might rise;
Then in a figure of divinity
The Maker shall recast us and impose
A plan of godhead on the mortal's mould
Lifting our finite minds to his infinite,
Touching the moment with eternity.
This transfiguration is earth's due to heaven:
A mutual debt binds man to the Supreme:
His nature we must put on as he put ours;
We are sons of God and must be even as he:
His human portion, we must grow divine. (66-7)

Sri Aurobindo knew from his own experience that the mind of light, so centrally important to yoga, is the same mind that we begin to develop through the creative and imaginative processes of music and poetry. The higher mind is fundamental to spiritual vision, mystical revelation, the acquisition of wisdom, spiritual knowledge, and attunement to the realities of the soul's world. Sri Aurobindo knew that this higher, illumined mind can, if it chooses, express the inner vision of Truth in words of power. A true bard, or a spiritual master makes words into vehicles of light, for his words are charged with a spiritual energy beyond that of ordinary language. Such words have the power to illumine those who can listen and truly hear. The use of sound and language in this way is not dissociated from crystals in Crystal Yoga, it is brought into play as a means of accessing the buried treasure within. This approach is very ancient. The Vedic seers taught that the power of mantra was a key to the attainment.

Knowing this, Sri Aurobindo spent quite a few years of his life working with words to express his experiences of the inner planes, the summation of which is the spiritual epic, *Savitri*. In reality, *Savitri* is an extraordinary example of the power of mantra, the same science of sound which was developed and used so extensively by the sages whom Sri Aurobindo had studied and about whom he had written for many years.

The consistent pattern in *Savitri* of references to crystals and gems of all kinds gives a valuable overview concerning the subject of Crystal Yoga, and repays careful study. I refer to *Savitri* as an important source for Crystal Yoga because the mind of the bard and sage is the jewel of true understanding in the field of yoga. The consciousness of spiritual awakening can be communicated by the words of a real sage to any sincere seeker who undertakes the necessary inner work. One final reference in this regard can be made to Lapis Lazuli, the crystalline substance which embodies the capacity of the Sage. In the master's words:

> *O deathless sage who knowest all things here,*
> *If I could read by the ray of my own wish*
> *Through the carved shield of symbol images*
> *Which thou has thrown before thy heavenly mind*
> *I might see the steps of a young godlike life*
> *Happily beginning* **luminous-***eyes on earth;*
> *Between the Unknowable and the unseen*
> *Born on the borders of two wonder-worlds,*
> ***It flames out symbols of the infinite***
> *And lives in* ***a great light*** *of inner suns.*
> *For it has read and broken the wizard seals;*
> *It has drunk of the Immortal's wells of joy,*
> *It has looked across* ***the jewel bars of heaven,***
> *It has entered the aspiring Secrecy,*
> *It sees beyond terrestrial common things*
> *And communes with the Powers that build the worlds,*
> *Till through the shining gates and mystic streets*
> *Of* ***the city of lapis lazuli and pearl***
> *Proud deeds step forth, a rank and march of gods. (421)*

CONCLUSION

In yoga, and especially in 'crystal yoga,' our starting point must be an understanding of "original contract." This concept was well understood by indigenous peoples around the Earth, but it has faded with the development of institutional religion. Although spiritual and mystical streams of experience have grown within these religions, there has also been much ignorance about the role of nature in the evolution of consciousness and the process of achieving enlightenment. In spirituality, often we misunderstand what we are doing because we do not recognize that both individually and collectively we are part of a "primary contract" that exists between Heaven and Earth. Seeking some private salvation or nirvana outside the original planetary plan has been an aberration of spiritual history.

In Crystal Yoga, our starting point is not the individual dilemma of personal need, nor is our spiritual work primarily a quest for personal salvation. The real scope of our spiritual action in any truly "integral" yoga is collective, and its real effect is cosmic.

From the very beginning, Heaven seeded Earth with crystalline light, the light of the stars and planets which was buried below the surface of Mother Gaia in the veins of gemlike stones. This light was destined to grow from hidden seeds into a unique terrestrial manifestation of beauty and perfection, according to the original divine plan or intent. This buried light is the hidden treasure of which the Vedas and other myths and legends speak from most ancient times. It is both spiritual and physical; the two are not different.

The advent of humans in the progressive evolution of consciousness on Earth meant that a new phase of intelligent co-creation became possible. The Goddess planned and arranged it that way. The awareness of this co-creation is very evident in humanity's oldest spiritual records, and in the understanding of indigenous peoples all around the world.

Crystals are an evolutionary turning-point where consciousness ceased its devolution into inert matter, and began its long ascent of return to the infinity of Source. In one way, crystals have the clearest original divine mandate and patterning of all earthly beings because in them, and in the devic presences that inhabit their temple-forms, consciousness is unmixed with the mental ego that dominates humans. Yet because humans are more evolved, and because humans are capable of co-creation, the arrival of human consciousness in the earthly arena has meant that the role of crystals in the original divine scheme could be more fully realized – or more egregiously violated, as it was in Atlantis, and as we see taking place today.

Together, humans and crystals (and in fact all the kingdoms of devic and other beings) have a work to do for bringing about the harmony of Heaven and Earth. The ancient way of seeing stones as 'people,' not unconscious and lifeless lumps, is true to the primal plan of creation. As the earliest beings to populate the earth, crystals have a role to play in the cosmic drama; they can co-operate with humans in making Earth a reflection of Heaven. This is our starting point for understanding what is involved in "Crystal Yoga."

This yoga is a supra-personal and trans-personal journey of lived experience in which individual liberation comes automatically in the context of a much larger, planetary and cosmic process. The starting point for any integral yoga, and in particular this yoga which is based on crystals in harmony with Nature, is to acknowledge our role within the divine scheme of creation. It is thus that we honour the "original contract." Like the most ancient forms of spiritual understanding and practice, this Crystal Yoga is nothing short of a collective, planetary alchemy. Within that larger pattern of terrestrial ascension, our personal liberation, and enlightenment are already assured; indeed, they were never in question. In renewing our spiritual co-creation with crystals, we are remembering a dream that Divine Providence has destined to be a reality from the very beginning.

In the Crystal Mesa Logo, the ascending forces of transformation intersect the horizontal plane of earthly, three-dimensional reality at the centre of a sacred cross within the circle of cosmic wholeness. Our perceptions of time and space arise from the heart of this pattern.

THE COSMIC PLOT

*A*ll the conditions, possibilities, difficulties and necessities of our soul's earthly sojourn were established long, long before we had any say whatsoever in the process. We come to this planet as spiritual refugees, and enter on the earthly scene for brief lives as uncertain pilgrims en route to a destination we cannot explain. We each play a small part in a vast production of cosmic proportions, a drama about which we really know very little. Rarely do we glimpse the pattern-of-the-whole, yet we trust that such insight is attainable by those who have achieved spiritual perfection or mature wisdom. For this reason, as we begin to awaken spiritually, we take greater interest in the perennial philosophy, and the example of enlightened souls who have found and revealed the Way.

When we study the words and teachings of the masters, we can begin to see the purpose and pattern of life on Earth, and to make sense of our soul's decision to incarnate physically at a certain place on the planet and at a certain time in history. If at a certain point we choose to become co-creators in the Divine Plan, it is even more important to attune to our own soul's inner guidance and that of the masters. We will each, if we are sincere, find the teaching that is appropriate for us.

I make reference at various points in this book on Crystal Yoga to the Buddha and to Sri Aurobindo as examples of 'universal' masters, or some would say, avatars. Few in number are such beings; they are a special and rare class of souls whose advent changes the course of spiritual history on earth. Their knowledge and their teachings have special importance in the study of spirituality and yoga, and particularly in the work of finding the long hidden spiritual practice that comes from alignment with the mineral kingdoms and their wisdom, which is the subject of this book. These masters did not write about Crystal Yoga. However, their clear knowledge of the universal plan, their authoritative insights into the goal and the way, help us greatly to situate Crystal Yoga in its correct context.

The challenge in exploring this subject is to see and understand how Nature (in particular her crystalline kingdom) exists in relation to spiritually awakening humans in a divine scheme of co-creation that will bring together Heaven and Earth. Whatever is true in Crystal Yoga has been fore-ordained and predestined from all time. Whatever we may work up with the clever intellectual mind has no lasting value. By basing our study of this subject on inner guidance, and on the visions of the Sages of all time, we are on sure ground. The universal source of inner guidance is ultimately the Mother, for it is she who presides over the work of bringing light and love to Earth. In her aspect as patroness of writers, she is sometimes called the Muse, or the Goddess. She has been pictured and understood in many ways at various points in history, but beyond all our imaginings and experiences, beyond the multiplicity of her self-revelations, she is ONE. She is the creatrix of all life and presiding spirit in all yogas. In her, through her and by her, our sincere aspirations grow toward Truth and develop meaning. Without her, we have nothing, are nothing and can do nothing.

In his immortal distillation of the whole course of spiritual life on earth, *Savitri*, Sri Aurobindo makes it very clear that evolution of Earth towards its heavenly destiny is the work assigned to the Mother. He shows how she gives birth to the Divine Child, fosters his spiritual evolution into a heroic warrior in the adventure of consciousness, and ultimately matures his whole being into the complete attainment of a Sage. The Sage is one in whom the Mother has completed her work. The Sage is one who knows Truth. As a sage, Sri Aurobindo has left us a wonderful compendium about the way in which Truth is emerging from darkness on Earth, complete and exhaustively detailed about every stage of the master-plot.

The Source has been unknowable for most of humanity from the beginning of time, but the Sage has attained direct experience of its reality, and communicates its light to those who sincerely seek. In the journey home to the Source, the questing soul covers many regions in the inner worlds, domains of light, beauty, perfection and sweetness. Of special importance is the kingdom of the Immortals. Using the sage-vision and the bardic capacity to express it, Sri Aurobindo writes:

> *In the wide signless ether of the Self,*
> *In the unchanging Silence white and nude,*
> *Aloof, resplendent like gold dazzling suns*
> *Veiled by the ray no mortal eye can bear,*
> *The Spirit's bare and absolute potencies*
> *Burn in the solitude of the thoughts of God...*
> *In his inalienable bliss they live.*
> *Immaculate in self-knowledge and self-power,*
> *Calm they repose on the eternal Will.*
> *Only his law they count and him obey;*
> *They have no goal to reach, no aim to serve.*
> *Implacable in their timeless purity,*
> *All barter or bribe of worship they refuse;*
> *Unmoved by cry of revolt and ignorant prayer*
> *They reckon not our virtue and our sin;*
> *They bend not to the voices that implore,*
> *They hold no traffic with error and its reign;*
> *They are guardians of the silence of the Truth,*
> *They are keepers of the immutable decree.*
> *A deep surrender is their source of might,*
> *A still identity their way to know,*
> *Motionless is their action like a sleep.*
> *At peace, regarding the trouble beneath the stars,*
> *Deathless, watching the works of Death and Chance,*
> *Immobile, seeing the millenniums pass,*
> *Untouched while the long map of Fate unrolls,*
> *They look on our struggle with impartial eyes,*
> *And yet without them cosmos could not be. (57)*

In ancient tradition, the stars were associated with the Immortals, and on Earth the crystalline, gem-like minerals were understood to be nodules of their light, physical crystallizations of their deathless bodies. In other words, from the very beginning, crystals have incarnated the potencies of the Immortals on Earth. This traditional understanding comes not from rational analysis, which is the way modern scientists would validate any theory, but from the inner vision proper to a sage. Sri Aurobindo makes it clear that the sage-vision is far beyond the normal ranges of human intellect:

He (the sage) moved through regions of transcendent Truth
Inward, immense, innumerably one.
There distance was his own huge spirit's extent;
Delivered from the fictions of the mind
Time's triple dividing step baffled no more;
Its inevitable and continuous stream,
The long flow of its manifesting course,
Was held in spirit's single wide regard.
A universal beauty showed its face:
The invisible deep-fraught significances,
Here sheltered behind form's insensible screen,
Uncovered to him their deathless harmony
And the key to the wonder-book of common things.
In their uniting law stood up revealed
The multiple measures of the upbuilding force,
The lines of the World-Geometer's technique,
The enchantments that uphold the cosmic web
And the magic underlying simple shapes... (299)

In Crystal Yoga, we do not work in the realm of theory or belief, but in certainty, a certainty based on the verity of our own inner light, and our intuitive ability to recognize Truth in the teachings of the masters. It is important to keep this in mind, because yoga is not speculative or theoretical, it is experiential, founded on action, ripened in insight and completed in genuine attainment. Nowhere do we see the "lines of the World-Geometer's technique" or the "enchantments that uphold the cosmic web," the "magic underlying simple shapes" more clearly than in crystals. Under the appearance of pure linear form, they perform an indispensable function in the evolution of life and consciousness on this Earth. Although many writers can convey intellectual simulacrums of truth, only a master can forge words to convey the living energy, or illumining consciousness of Truth. A universal master is not only in this sense a bard, but also a spiritual scientist, and a co-creator of earth's spiritual destiny with the Mother herself.

Let us consider some of the main elements of the cosmic story, with key themes being indicated by **bold** lettering.

For the sage, the spiritual work of yoga unfolds in the context of the **original contract** between Heaven and Earth. The goal of his life, and of all life on this evolutionary planet, is to express the light of **Source** in a material creation. The **difficulties** of **earthly conditions** are well known to all spiritual seekers, not least to the ones who have spiritual attainment. However, the sage sees also the **magical milieu** that underlies the prosaic appearance of this earth. He sees the centrally important **role of Nature** in our spiritual lives, and **the work that the Mother does** through all evolving forms on this planet. He sees the **hidden treasure** that is awaiting discovery in the **dark caves** of matter and the subconscious. He knows **the work** that is to be accomplished by the soul, and he knows also the way of its **working** out. **Silence** has taught **the Sage** how to perceive (**Sage Vision**) and how to hear (**Sage Audition**), how to see and know that which is invisible to the normal human senses. The sage has embodied not only the conquering spirit of **the archetypal Hero**, but the sweetness and sensitivity of **the Divine Child**. He sees all parts in the wholeness of their relationship to Source, each as a unique note in the anthem of the stars. In Appendix One, you can reference various sections of *Savitri* that describe each of these themes in detail.

Although the teachings of the masters and sages are the indispensable foundation for yoga, it is safe to say that the average seeker will not be able to appreciate their true significance for a long time, because it is not until practice has deepened one's understanding that the depth of these teachings can be truly valued. The way forward unfolds not on the basis of study and understanding only, important though this may be. It is an integral process involving the heart as much as the head, or more so, and actions and choices at every moment of our waking life. There is no single simple system that encompasses the fundamentals of practice as well as the Buddha's eightfold summary of the Way. He taught that all spiritual discipline must be founded on these principles:

1) Right View, or Understanding

2) Right Thought (and Resolve)

3) Right Speech
4) Right Action (or Conduct)
5) Right Livelihood
6) Right Effort
7) Right Mindfulness
8) Right Concentration (and Meditation)

Taken as a whole, these may be summarized by one term: right relationship, or to be more precise, right relationship to Source (or Self).

I see an interesting correlation between these disciplines and the chakras, as follows:

Base Chakra	Right Livelihood
Sacral Chakra	Right Effort
Solar Plexus Chakra	Right Action
Heart Chakra	Right Mindfulness
Throat Chakra	Right Speech
Brow Chakra	Right Thoughts (and Resolve)
Crown Chakra	Right View, or Understanding
All inclusive result:	Right Meditation (or Concentration)

It follows that the crystals dealing with Base Chakra issues can help us toward Right Livelihood; those proper to the Sacral Chakra can assist us with Right Effort; Those of the Solar Plexus Chakra can abet our efforts toward Right Action, and so forth. Beyond this, we can see that each chakra has its own way of expressing each of the eight disciplines. In the Base Chakra, Right Livelihood, Effort, Action, Mindfulness, Speech, etc. will take one form, and in the Heart or Crown Chakras, the same wisdom or mastery will manifest in a different form. The archetype stones in each of the elements stand for the all-inclusive result, the attainment of right consciousness, or meditation, or concentration. The spirit stone in each element and the six other stones accompanying it are all sources of alignment, energy and teaching for practice.

There is another way of approaching the question, in which the research of Margherita Vondrak proves very helpful. In her *Crystal Lotus Handbook*, she has made a study of which developmental issues each of the gems and mineral crystals address. For example, Amazonite has to do with Honesty, in particular the polarities of "not speaking" and "expressing." This is a question of what the Buddha termed "Right Speech," and hence in that area of the path, Amazonite would have application. On the other hand, Amber, which is the next entry in her book, has to do with "Light," and the polarities of "confusion" versus being "aligned." This would be a question either of Right Thought, or of Right View. If you consider the crystal in the heart as a seed of integral wisdom, each life-lesson that you complete releases a new ray of light from a fresh facet of that jewel. When you master the polarities associated with life's various challenges and learning opportunities, you become spiritually complete. The Crystal Mesa is an embodiment of all the polarities that you will learn and master, and a symbol of the wholeness you will attain through this process.

When we approach crystals in this manner, (that is, when we approach them with a modicum of 'Right View'), we begin to see that they are a comprehensive body of teaching and assistance embedded by the Immortals in the dark corners of this Earth. They have been waiting for eons to come forward at times of need to assist sincere seekers in all areas of life. Crystals are the "hidden treasure" that the ancient scriptures and myths spoke of, the 'buried rays of the gods' celebrated in the Vedas, the 'rainbow wisdom' in the heart of the earth which all shamans have known. It is even more evident that this is so after one takes the time to study the main elements of the Cosmic Plot as summarized in *Savitri* or in the other writings of the masters.

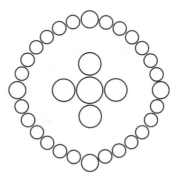

MOON LAYOUT

This layout emphasizes cyclical patterns and the movement of various elements in time, biological cycles in nature and in our own microcosm. It invites meditation and asks us to develop a feeling for connections and evolving patterns. At times we will be drawn to circular patterns because they help us to process experience in a more intuitive way. This pattern also helps users to become aware of the center, to find the inner core and thus sense who they are. With this circle, we can shift the archetype stones to different distances to find our feeling of harmony.

ATTUNEMENT

A ttunement is a bringing together of attention, thought, feeling, energy and consciousness so as to connect with a reality that is not apparent to the five senses. Through attunement, an individual human microcosm can become resonantly interactive with the universal consciousness, the Divine Reality which lies beyond physical manifestation. By connecting with something bigger than our own thoughts, feelings and energies, we transcend our self-created parameters of limitation. Thus, we become participants in the marriage of Heaven with Earth.

Crystals can serve this sacred movement toward union of the human with the divine. The *mesa* provides a way of working with crystals to realize an integral wholeness of being, both individually and collectively. The following exercises will enable you to develop your capacity for attunement with crystals, and this skill will be fundamentally important when you begin working with your *mesa*. But instead of thinking of what follows as an "exercise," let's revert to the word "play" and approach it with a childlike attitude of simply experiencing joy.

THE THIRD ATTUNEMENT: ATTUNEMENT OF ATTENTION

My attention wanders. It is dissipated into random thoughts, polarized by aversion to what I find unpleasant, and fascinated by the attractiveness of what I desire. My attention typically lacks focus. It is unstable because I have not developed its capacity for concentration.

(Holding a crystal and gazing at it with a silent mind and open heart)

In crystal, I see the perfect focus of energy. There is a harmoniously balanced flow of energy as the six sides of a quartz crystal converge at a single point of unity. This harmonious inner balance does not vary or wander, for crystal carries no internal tendencies toward interruption and dissipation. Crystal shows a perfect state of contemplative absorption. It has no personal volition. It does not lose itself in thinking activity. It does not crave new forms of pleasure; nor does it fear pain and loss. Therefore, crystal is not pushed or pulled from its inner poise. Crystal is pure and steady.

I know that energy follows thought. Crystal expresses a divine thought of harmony, purity, balance and focus. When my thought becomes crystalline, my energy will reflect this, becoming ordered and balanced. If I become clear in my mental life, beyond the turbulence of attractions and aversions, then I shall be a perfect instrument to channel those higher forces which can transform and perfect this material creation.

(Holding the crystal to the heart)

I want to approach this crystal attunement with pure intent. No longer will I exploit crystal to reinforce the disorder of my egocentric desires. Rather, I attune to the perfect meditation that crystal is always doing in the dimensions of matter and energy. And I aspire to achieve such perfect attunement of feeling and spirit in my own being, on all levels. In this new relationship of respect, I want to ask crystal to be my teacher, friend and helper.

In this spirit, I begin to approach the experience of attunement with a feeling of openness and gratitude. I breathe in slowly and deeply and relax my body completely. I am ready to begin to work with the energy and consciousness of stone with a sense of lightness and play, knowing that I can enjoy coming home to the fullness of relationship with my wider self.

THE FOURTH ATTUNEMENT: Letting Go

I take a six-sided natural quartz crystal of between three and six inches in my right hand. Holding the crystal, I concentrate on its form, and I assimilate an impression of how its exists. I observe with special care my crystal's symmetry. I appreciate its transparent clarity, as well as any veils or rainbows it may contain. I marvel at its interior stillness. My crystal has the mastery of inner silence and can teach this state of being to me if I pay close attention.

I observe that my own mind is somewhat restless. I need to let go of the noise and the random, restless thinking activity that goes on inside my head because I want to merge with this crystal teacher and experience what it has to show me. I need to release agitation and replace it with stillness.

Now, I am going to give this mental agitation an avenue of release so that it can drain away. I am going to allow my mind's agitation to express itself as physical movement; then, rather than making noise inside my head, this energy will be channeled out of my system.

I let the thumb of my right hand come into touch with the crystal at its base, and then I move my thumb along the surface of the crystal right up to its tip. After moving the thumb up and down several times on one of the crystal's six sides, I rotate the crystal and repeat the movement on the next side. As my thumb moves up along the side of the crystal, I let my attention follow its movement back and forth. I keep my attention focused on the movement of my thumb, and I feel its contact with the crystal.

I feel, as I practice this simple exercise, that the restless energy, which would otherwise express itself as wandering thoughts in my head, is now being channeled into the movement of my thumb. The movement of my thumb up and down across the surface of the crystal is draining away the mind's agitation. My attention is focused on the feeling of contact with the stone.

It is a very simple thing, moving my thumb up and down the sides of the crystal, but it brings my attention to a focus and it makes my thoughts quiet. I let my attention follow the movement of the thumb up to the top of the crystal and then down again. I feel the physical contact of my thumb with the surface of the crystal with increased sensitivity at each movement. I am paying full attention to this sensitivity of touch. I relax and enjoy the experience. I feel open to new sensations.

I notice the changes in my mind as I do this. My mental agitation is becoming quiet. The churning of the mind is winding down, becoming still and empty. The movement of the thumb becomes slower as this stillness settles into my nervous system and as I pay more attention to what the sense of touch feels like.

What do I experience through the sense of touch as my thumb moves across the surface of the crystal? I am being drawn steadily deeper into an experience of stillness. But I am not *striving* to achieve this goal, I am only paying attention to the movement of the thumb and the feel of the crystal as I touch its surface.

This experience of interior stillness grows. My attention becomes more and more focused. Without effort, without struggle, I am beginning to enter meditation.

THE FIFTH ATTUNEMENT: RELAXATION

In crystal, I see neither the absence nor the presence of feeling. I see the perfect sublimation and sacrifice of all life-activity into the clarity of divinely patterned order. I see that the creative spark within a crystal has completely centred its life in perfect order in every molecule of its body. My crystal is a perfect meditation teacher because it knows how to silence and order its every molecule. My crystal has become an unbroken flow of light and energy. It has completely consecrated itself to the expression of an archetypal form.

My own thoughts are not anchored in pure feeling. Nor are my feelings surrendered to pure thought. My feelings are pulled by cravings, and repelled by pain. I am attracted by what I like and I feel aversion to what I dislike. Because of the pulls and pushes that I allow in my emotions, I cannot become steadily centred in stillness. My wandering, dissipated attention fails to find my centre of deepest feeling. I am vulnerable to feelings that I cannot control. I experience desire, fear, anger and frustration. I taste the pain of stress as it contracts my nerves. There is imbalance within my being.

I want to connect with my deeper feelings. I want to relate my dreams and ideals to a wider dream that is taking shape in the cosmos. I would like my life to become part of a pattern that opens me to the stars.

Crystal has so much to show me in this process. The crystal I am holding in my hand has spent untold centuries forming itself into an expression of clarity, beauty and harmony.

As I sit with my crystal in my hand, I notice that there is residual tension inside my muscles. It comes in part from unresolved emotions. It is also rooted in the patterns of my thinking, both in my conscious and unconscious mind.

I now deliberately express this tension by clenching my hands into tight fists. Holding both my hands as tightly clenched as I can, I become fully aware of what this tension feels like. I have focused my inner stress there in the palms of my two hands, and I feel it gripping my crystal tightly. It's not something I have to analyze mentally or think about. I just feel it. In fact, it seems that I am drawing tension away from other parts of my being and localizing it in the palms of my hand. I can see how stress and tension act to bring about tightening and contraction. How adversely it must be affecting me when I allow it to continue unconsciously.

I will ask my crystal to help me release tension from all parts of my being.

Inhaling slowly and deeply, I breathe in peace. Then, I send a breath of pure, unconditional love flowing from my heart into each tightly-clenched fist, both the right hand and the left. Over and over again, I breathe in peace and exhale love, directing the rosy energy of love out from my heart, and down my arms into my clenched fists. Slowly and surely, they begin to release their contraction. They begin to release the stress which has had a tight grip on my life-energy. I allow my two hands slowly to open in response to the movement of deep feeling that streams from my heart. I am not using my mental will. I am allowing heart-energy, love, to express itself as a blessing on my stress. Ever so slowly and gently I exhale this energy into my hands, and ever so slowly they let go, relax, release and open up. As my hand opens up, my tight grip on my crystal relaxes.

When my two hands are completely relaxed, I try to clench them again. I notice that I cannot summon the same tightness as before. But whatever tension I can create, I begin to release it slowly and surely as before, until once again my hands are completely relaxed. In doing this, I come into a new state of openness, receptivity, care and feeling with regard to my crystal.

THE SIXTH ATTUNEMENT: A BODY OF LIGHT

At this point, I am ready to begin visualization. I have worked with attention, thought and feeling, and I am now ready to attune my energy and consciousness to the perfect clarity of my crystal teacher.

Closing my eyes, I picture my physical body changing into a subtle mist of light. I feel the atoms of the body becoming diffused until they are like mist in the air, a luminous cloud floating in the darkness of space. This luminous body of mist floating in the vast darkness of outer space is everything I have and everything I am. I float there in silence, feeling myself to be a radiant cloud. I can sense the big spaces between the particles of my body. I experience the sensation of floating, floating in silence. As a cloud of misty light, I am completely expansive and an exquisitely attuned to all sensations, but in the vast darkness everything is utterly still.

Now I begin to experience rays of sunlight penetrating my cloud-like body. The radiance of the sun enters every part of my being and penetrates it with light. I allow the sunlight to fill me and I feel what a crystal feels when it is placed in the brightness of the sun. For a moment or two, I notice the effects of being filled with light. I let myself sense how it feels in complete detail. I am super-sensitive to everything around me when I am a cloud of radiance. When I have taken in this experience completely, and described it in detail, I know how a crystal experiences sensation. I can now understand how a crystal can become programmed so responsively.

Next, I look out at the world around me from this state of being a floating cloud. My eyes are just slightly open, enough to take in the appearances of my physical setting. I experience my environment with my extended sensitivity. I sense how my floating body of light is responding to every aspect of my environment and I assimilate the experience in all its detail. How completely and absolutely I experience everything when the form in which I exist is that of a cloud of light! Every impression is exquisite. Sometimes, it almost seems that I taste or smell the things I am seeing.

I open my eyes ever so slightly and take in an object visually. Then I close my eyes and become aware of the way in which I experience that object while I exist as an empty cloud of light. My sensitivity is greatly increased when I can experience myself and my world in this way.

Now, I am going to gaze into my crystal. My crystal is an exquisite lattice of molecules. I allow the misty, formless cloud of my subtle, luminous body to drift into the physical body of the crystal. Our particles and our spaces interpenetrate each other. The atoms and the molecules of our bodies merge one into the other. I now exist as a perfectly-ordered, crystalline pillar of light. I am completely still. My attunement to the world around me is finely sensitive. I experience the merging of my body with the body of my crystal teacher. I have become a cloud of misty light interpenetrating the orderly molecules of my crystal in complete stillness.

For so long, I have been imagining myself to be the physical form of this human body with its boundaries and limits. Now I exist in another dimension of my being. The crystal has given my luminous body the power of perfect order and control. I see that I have been imagining myself into a human form, but now I have the freedom to exist in a different way. I now know that I can be whatever I can imagine. At this time, I actualize in my luminous body the perfect order and clarity of crystalline structure. Every atom and every molecule aligns in perfect symmetry and balanced pattern.

I take a few moments of silence to experience this re-assembling of my cloud-like body into crystal perfection.

This exercise in visualization has been an experience of programming my reality. I have cleared my understanding of some limiting notions; I know now that I am free to explore experience in many dimensions, and take in many things in different ways. This human body is only one physical expression of my infinitely adaptable consciousness.

My crystal shares with me the experience of stillness and clarity, and the power of perfect order. I now know that I can express my energy and consciousness in many ways. I know now that the ability to imagine, and the power to visualize, and the help from my crystal open the doorway to many more experiences of attunement and expansion. I feel that I want to make more such journeys in the future.

The sacred circle which defines the
outer perimeter of the Crystal Mesa
Logo encloses a sacred space
within which order and balance
prevail.

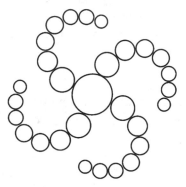

SPIRAL LAYOUT

This layout has long tentacles which resemble the arms of an aquatic 'man-of war' or the filaments of a spider web. This is a way to reach out, intuitively, to sense and explore a question or situation. It is exploratory. For example we may be trying to discover integration, or how to become pliable, flexible, more aware; we may want to explore hidden and new ways of being. If you feel stuck or bound, unable to do or understand certain things, if you seek other perspectives, this is an ideal layout. When the spiral is counter clockwise, the past is dealt with, and when clockwise it reaches out toward the future. There is no fixed order for stones, you need to use intuition.

Twin doors into the Temple of the Moon whose stones hold Primal Patterns of the ancient wisdom.

Alcoves in the Temple of the Moon where I prayed to understand the ancient tradition.

Don Sebastian, Dennis, my guide, an initiate of six years' training, and Don Sebastian's wife, Donna Maria.

The house where I stayed during my training and initiation. I was standing by the stone fence when I saw the "estrella."

Don Sebastian does an extended coca leaf reading to receive guidance
in advance of the initiation.

Don Sebastian and wife Donna Maria prepare a *despacho* to ensure the
success of the initiation.

Donna Maria returns the heartstone of my mesa after it has been blessed. This stone circle has been used for sacred ceremonies for countless generations.

Donna Maria whispers the words of power in my ear at the most sacred part of the initiation. My mesa is laid out on the red cloth before me, the stones grouped in small bags.

PALINGENESIS

In the opening chapter of *The Primal Runes* (2005), I described some of my inner experiences with the Four Sacred Elements at my retreat in the forests of the Kawartha Lakes region in Southern Ontario. There is still a palpable magic at that place. The power spots on the land continue to hold their energies, guarded by the native spirits who dwell nearby. The hardy rose bushes still flourish near outcroppings of pre-Cambrian granite. The standing megaliths, the ancient hemlock trees, and the stone circle with its lion-head altar still register the moods of dawn, noon and dusk with alternations of rain and sunshine, snow and warmth coming and going across the landscape.

After hosting a workshop in the Andean tradition here in 2004, I continued to visit Peru and experience further levels of training and initiation. A visit to the land of the Q'ero, keepers of the purest tradition of Andean indigenous spirituality, was a highlight of one recent journey, and a chance to explore the more remote regions of the ancient Inca empire. There and at a workshop held in the Royal Inca Hotel in Pisac I dived more deeply into the tradition of the *pampa mesayoq*, which is a priestly or shamanic role in the Andean tradition. Everyone who spends any time in the Andes will feel the people's intimate relationship with Mother Earth, or *Pachamama* and the importance of stone is everywhere apparent in Andean spiritual circles, for stone is considered to be the precious skeleton of Mother Earth. Certainly the initiation I took from Don Sebastion of the Q'ero was a reminder of the strong bond between my human microcosm and the body of the great goddess who is our earthly Mother. It was conducted in a stone circle under the looming mountains which embody the spirits of the *Apus.*

In this initiation and in other settings in and around Cusco, I had many occasions to become acquainted with a ritual object which is centrally important to the Andean, Mayan, Southwest Amerindian and other native traditions. I refer to the sacred *mesa,* which is a cloth bundle containing objects of spiritual significance and healing energy, and which is always carried by an Andean priest or healer whenever he or she would be called upon to perform a ceremony.

The sacred bundle is not an exclusively Mayan or Andean invention; it is fair to say that shamans and medicine men all around the globe through much of history have made and used one or another form of the 'medicine bag.' The word *mesa* is widely used in Spanish-speaking countries to refer to such a sacred bundle. As indigenous traditions become more widely known and practiced, this term is becoming more widely used to describe a collection of objects wrapped in a special cloth, a 'bundle' which is used for healing, spiritual work and ritual.

Stones predominate in many *mesas,* since they are readily available relics of nature whose uses for healing, divination and spiritual attunement have been explained in detail in quite a few books. I remember that in childhood I had a love of collecting stones wherever I found them, and in the 1980's, I wrote three books about crystals: *The Healing Gems, The Language of Crystals* and *Crystal Spirit.* These books came at the outset of a widespread interest in crystals which grew with the popularity of the New Age movement. My interest in stones, crystals and sacred bundles has grown since I began to visit various parts of the Andes and I spent many long hours wandering watercourses in the high Andes and gathering stones along the Urubamba River during my recent visits to that part of the world. Although I have studied and learned from a number of Andean teachers, and several of their advanced students, my real progress came through the inner work I did with my own *mesa.* I began to use my *mesa* more and more in meditation, and to work within a circle of twelve very large quartz crystals in a room set aside for meditation and sacred study at my home in Lindsay. An inner understanding of certain principles which are at work, or *which can be at work*, in a sacred bundle of special design began to emerge in my mind and heart. Two principles in particular stood out as this body of inner knowledge came to the fore: firstly the possibilities inherent in *crystals* (a term which includes a wide range of precious and semi-precious minerals) and secondly, the importance of *archetypes*. Other themes of significance emerged as well, such as polarity, the tree of life, the primal cosmology, the patterns of ancient mythology, the Tattwas, and the esoteric principles of *yantra* and *mantra*.

After several weeks of regular meditation with my *mesa* inside the circle of twelve large crystals, I began to feel that everything I had previously learned about sacred bundles from outside sources had been only a preliminary introduction. A much deeper awareness of *mesa* wisdom was beginning to reveal itself, a vast body of knowledge and application that had never been written about in systematic detail. There is wide understanding and application of the *mesa* in shamanic and indigenous traditions in geographic regions as widely removed as the Peruvian and Bolivian highlands, the Mayan jungles of Central America and the arid plains of the Southwestern United States. But there is a teaching that goes beyond the sacred bundle traditions that are known and practiced by indigenous peoples in the Americas (and elsewhere), and beyond what is taught in New Age workshops by a variety of teachers from South America and elsewhere. I became inwardly aware of a paradigm that underpins and antecedes the various *mesa* traditions, a body of occult understanding that is not widely known and that is hardly ever taught. This wisdom is related to its various cultural manifestations like the roots of a tree are related to the tree's trunk, or the trunk of a tree is related to its many branches. This esoteric knowledge and practice is rooted in timeless cosmology, and mystery school teachings about the primal archetypes which have mostly been confined to adepts and their pupils. The need for secrecy of the kind maintained in historic mystery schools is now by and large a thing of the past. As I meditated, elements of this cosmic paradigm began to fall into place, and the scope of what a *mesa* could be and mean and do became increasingly clear. The accumulating insights began gathering themselves into a coherent pattern that could be set down in words, and from January to May of 2005, the need to write this down in book form began to grow.

The summer solstice is almost here as I write these words, and a deepening of the inspired flow has occurred. I have awakened when it is still dark, and well before sunrise I am standing on the edge of an open field, gazing toward the ascending light. My crystal *mesa* is in a pouch hanging from my neck, centred over my solar plexus. In my left hand is a large sphere of Selenite, and in my right hand is a golden Lemurian Dow crystal. I am wearing my poncho against the morning chill. I begin to softly chant the mantra OM, and to feel its profound vibrations blending in my aura with the blessings of the rising sun. Then, at the moment of sunrise, the Spirit-Presence comes. The light of the rising Sun, just at the moment of dawn, imparts a special blessing, a living and palpable spiritual influence. But I experience it with more power and depth when I wear my crystal *mesa* like this, and when I am holding a crystal ball and a crystal point. I sense why the temple priests used to wear jewel-studded breastplates in ancient times. Breastplate or *mesa*, the effect would be the same; the precious stones convey their message of light and wholeness into the human energy-field, and into the very cells of the body. And this sacred sunrise has a special intensity for such a ritual of blessing. The day is so pure, fresh and full of possibilities at this point in time. There is no human confusion, no false "spin," only the harmony of nature and the growing light in the East. I continue to chant OM, blending the sun's rays with the energies of the *mesa* crystals, becoming one with their presence in my meditation. The spirit-light of Dawn conveys a promise of infinite possibilities. This is Isis recreating the body of a fallen god in matter. This is a glimpse of eternity touching the human face of a new day.

At a certain point, when you begin writing about esoteric matters, it becomes necessary to root ideas in history, to ground them in physical reality. The spiritual traditions of Tibet and India have an immense wealth of light and knowledge that can amplify the understanding and application of *mesa*. Just as Lord Shiva and his consort Parvati presided over the evolution of spirituality in the Himalayas, so Lord Meru and his consort Aramu have established their seat of power in the Andes where they guide a small circle of initiates who belong to a little known Mystery School. This Mystery School has an inner and an outer component. The knowledge of how to construct and use a cosmically-resonant *mesa* is well understood within this inner school. But it is a knowledge that has not yet been promulgated on the outer level, and is largely absent from the teachings that are passed on the various lineages of shamanic healers.

My understanding of *mesa* came gradually, not through a single teacher or in workshops with various teachers, although all these contacts were initially helpful. Visits to sacred power spots and temples in Peru were also important for awakening my inner desire to contemplate *mesa* and explore its possibilities At holy spots in Machu Piccu, Pisac and Ollyantaytombo I had the opportunity to reconnect with sacred energies and architecture founded on ancient cosmology. I was stimulated to re-member elements of a long-lost tradition and to re-assemble fragmented facts into a unified understanding. Gathering stones at these locations, I began the process of seeding vibrations into my subtle bodies and awakening dormant memories from past lives. With the inner help of the Muse, I entered a new attunement with the world of the archetypes and began to receive fresh inspiration. Then in the early Spring of 2005, the writing began.

The timeless patterns of prehistory are still alive and well in some remote parts of the world, and the highlands of Peru are one such place. One feels the landscape to be somehow filled with life and consciousness that is different from what can be found in other locales. The Sacred Valley near Cusco is most notably so, but all the ancient Andean ruins carry this energy to some degree. This experience, which can be clearly felt even today, has much to do with the relationship that people have always had with their local mountains, valleys and streams, something that continues unbroken right up to the present time. However, both in Incan and pre-Incan times, there was a body of highly evolved initiates who had developed a profound spiritual science and attained some remarkable degrees of occult mastery. This is reflected in some of the remaining art and architecture, some of the surviving mythology, and in elements of the shamanic tradition that is still very much alive in rural Peru, Bolivia and Ecuador. The inner meaning of a number of symbols still being woven into local fabrics, or worked into jewelry, can only be accessed by attunement to this source, which still coheres in the inner worlds.

It was the universal understanding of the Ancients in the Andean region and elsewhere that human life must honour and promote the marriage of Heaven and Earth. We see this in the way that ancient societies all over the world structured their landscapes, their temples and their rituals. For the elders, healing was and is considered a sacred undertaking, since internal harmony of the microcosm remains part of the plan that Heaven has for all humans and for planet Earth who is our Mother. However, beyond the question of individual wholeness and healing, the ancients saw politics, war, the economy and all aspects of life as being part of a sacred ritual by which the Heavenly energies are brought into resonance with Earth, and subsequently assimilated. The Celts, for example, always had Druids in attendance at battles, and there were long periods of history in which warfare was conducted according to established ceremonial, with the Gods presiding. We see some evidence of this in the Iliad of Homer.

Even to this day, in indigenous societies which have preserved the ancient ways, the old perspectives are maintained. We often fail to comprehend the ancient point of view. For example, the shaman is usually thought of by *us* as a healer of sick individuals, but traditional shamans have always thought of themselves as intermediaries who maintain right relation between the 'seen' and the 'unseen' sides of life. The healing of individuals is an incidental result of the shaman's work, which is to reconcile the balance between the human world and the world of spirit. They do what they do only in part for the comfort of the ailing individual; more importantly, they seek reconciliation with the gods, so that the right relation which should exist between the world of spirit and the world of man does not become imbalanced on a large scale. They are not primarily relievers of discomfort for ailing individuals, but rather servants of the gods, dedicated human instruments who work hard at maintaining cosmic order. This cosmic order may be seen as "right relationship" on an archetypal level, which is beyond the merely human and personal perspective which we develop in the modern educational systems of Europe and North America. The shaman's work may frequently involve the counseling and healing of sick people, but his traditional understanding and perspective on this activity is quite different than that of a New-Age healer from North America.

It is in this light that the tradition of the *mesa* must be seen. It makes all the difference in world when we come to its construction, its use, and a full understanding of its place in the relationship between the microcosm and the macrocosm. To be the keeper of a sacred bundle, and an instrument of a higher force is something quite different than to be a user of nature for one's own egoistic purposes, or one who serves the egocentric ends of others. The two are as different from each other as White and Black Magic.

The symbolism of the word *mesa* is helpful to remember; it is a Spanish term that means table, or altar. An altar is centrally important in a temple. Taken together, temple and altar exist to bring the divine and the human into alignment. In this context, it is useful to remember that the word 'religion' comes from the Latin *re-ligio*, and religion serves to re-unite what has been torn asunder. Both in North and South America, from very ancient times, long before Europeans arrived on the scene, and long before the word "*mesa*" was being applied, native shamans would assemble bundles of sacred objects to be used for ceremonies of healing and inner attunement. For most *mesa* users, these objects, wrapped in a special holding-cloth, form a kind of portable altar, a tool of spiritual power. In places as distant as Peru, Central America and the Southwest American States, indigenous cultures still give great importance to the *mesa* as a living, material expression of its user's spiritual capacity.

The objects which a *mesa* may contain are chosen by its creator and keeper. They reflect his or her personal, deep values, and each of them is carefully selected because of the meaning it has or the power it emanates. In certain cases, objects seem to call to the owner of a *mesa* and cry out for inclusion in his or her sacred bundle. Always, the keeper of a *mesa* should follow an inner feeling or instinct about what is appropriate to place inside his or her *mesa*. The urge to place an object inside a *mesa* may not be fully rationalized when it first arises as an inner impulse; the object's purpose, energy and use may not reveal itself until much later, after it has already found a home in the bundle. One may grow a *mesa* to large proportions and then see it split into two like a cell. There may be a *mesa* for healing and another for meditation, and still another for sacred ceremony. There may be a *mesa* reduced in size for travelling, and a more complete version which never leaves one's home. The process of working with a *mesa* has its own inner life and guidance and is not governed by fixed rules.

Beyond being an expression of merely personal notions and sentiments, however, a *mesa* also has scope to embody archetypal patterns. Sound knowledge of tradition always contributes to enhanced spiritual attunement and skilful application of means. For example, the *mesa* may be connected to the four sacred elements of Earth, Water, Fire and Air, and oriented to the four sacred directions. This is in fact quite commonly done, and such alignments give a *mesa* something greater than the energy of its owner's personal symbols and opinions.

The *mesa* can also be a teacher, reminding us that all life and all action, including thought and intent, are to be governed by the law of right relation. By its very structure and constitution, the *mesa* is a teaching about the relation that unifies spirit with matter, the part with the whole, the inner with the outer and the periphery with its centre. The 33 crystals of the archetypal Crystal Mesa described in this book each speak their note and vibrate their voice, and taken as a whole they are part of a cosmic pattern. The 'Tree of Life' is one expression of this pattern; *yantra* can be another. As a teacher, the *mesa* shows us how the fragmented body of a divine being can be re-membered and reconstituted, something that was hinted at in ancient myths such as the tale of Osiris and other dismembered gods.

An archetypal *mesa* is a catalyst to release the latent possibilities of life in a material world. It brings together the sacred geometry of the various crystal families, and patterns of placement that channel light and energy into the matrix of matter. This is a more powerful science than humanity as a whole can grasp, although a few have begun to appreciate and tap its possibilities. Just as a silicon chip can be configured to channel energy in a variety of ways for the purposes of computing, so the elements of the *mesa* can be so placed and activated so as to channel the energies and consciousness of the stars. Used in this way, the *mesa* helps to focus the unseen forces of light that are configured by crystalline geometrical structure. We can thus draw these rays into our microcosm, project them through geometric lenses and expedite the expression of consciousness in life. When we use crystalline grids or *mandalas* to structure and direct light, we are resuming a very ancient technology of consciousness and spirit well known to the Atlanteans and Lemurians.

No human individual can ever become so unique as to over-ride the fundamental patterns of relation between microcosm and macrocosm. One can, however, assemble and use a *mesa* in order to more consciously and wisely *build on the foundation of these timeless patterns.* To do this is to access the innate resonance of archetypes, crystals, patterns and colours more skillfully and creatively. We thus accomplish the great work which the Elders of all times have upheld, the work of linking microcosm to macrocosm, Heaven to Earth, and what is personal and private to the universal ground of being.

The power of the Source inheres in the patterns of all its cosmic manifestations. To know and apply these patterns is to tap great potential and to have the means of giving it expression. Thus, beyond being merely an extension of human individualism or personal idiosyncrasy, to be a tool of power, inevitably a *mesa* must partake in some measure in cosmic patterns that are supra-personal, and apply them in ways that are trans-personal. In fact, a *mesa* is of necessity a device that helps to interface the human microcosm with the larger macrocosm of universal light and consciousness. If it does not effect this linking of Heaven and Earth (the celestial radiance and its terrestrial reflection) either a *mesa* will lack power, or the power that it does have will be less than it might otherwise embody.

From time immemorial, light-workers have moulded space to make of it a sacred vessel. As with the ancient temples, and with sacred art, so with the *mesa* of power; either the patterns are worked out so that the empowerment of the cosmos is tapped, or this dimension is missing, in which case the *mesa* is only an expression of its owner's personal power. By the nature of the crystals we choose, their placement, the resonance of relationships, and with the added powers of sound and timing, a *mesa* can become a bridge to the supernatural worlds. With such a *mesa*, the laws that limit what is possible in the three dimensional time-space continuum can be transcended. By the application of cosmic resonance and traditional knowledge, the *mesa* becomes capable of creating a sacred space for the descent of higher energy and consciousness. A resonant crystal *mesa* can be a most significant link with the beyond, a channeling device for the higher Light that is ready to descend and effect its transformative magic in the world.

To develop a personal *mesa* which is also a mirror of the greater cosmos can be the most effective way of linking the time-bound consciousness of our limited, human continuum to vaster fields of knowledge, power and experience. Because the understanding of how to develop and use *mesas* according to an archetypal, or cosmological paradigm has not been widely shared, the present work may be of help to readers who want to work in this area. The principles and paradigms I am dealing with here are universal, not limited to any particular culture or period of history, Andean, Mayan or other. They are timeless and supra-personal, like the knowledge of occultism itself. These principles would be as applicable in ancient Tibet as they would be in modern Guatemala, or in downtown Cusco, because although human cultures rise and fall, the cosmic reality which is their backdrop, the scenery of the timeless paradigm itself, does not change.

Many people these days are interested in working with crystals. The rudiments of the subject can be learned in a very short time. However, the understanding of how to integrate cosmic principles into the deeply personal spiritual work of developing and using a crystal *mesa* is rarely taught. For many *mesa*-users, or would-be *mesa*-users, personal feelings work best when supplemented by knowledge of tradition, not necessarily the traditions of the Q'ero of Peru, or the Toltecs of Mexico (if there still are any!) or the Hopis of the United States, but the perennial tradition which is universal in scope. The perennial tradition is the tree of which these cultural variations are branches. You may know a branch or two of the tree, but still not be cognizant of the pattern of the tree as a whole. However, if you know the pattern of the tree as a whole, you will most assuredly be empowered by the essence that is being expressed in all its branches.

We are each writing the unfinished story of the soul's journey home to its Source. We each embody a force that has been toiling upward into the light since Earth began. In and through this life I call my own, there is a great world-plan unfolding. Wisdom comes. Vision grows within. The soul begins to sense and glimpse the Supreme Light. We begin to understand the Symbols of the Beyond. In common things, we begin to notice signals of eternity. In the mystery of the journeying years, an inner knowledge is revealed of how the One expresses as the many, how the formless expresses through form, and the Eternal in Time. But the vision is mystical; it needs the intuitive heart; it needs the power of a spiritual gaze. A rightly constructed Crystal Mesa is a living temple where spirit meets matter, and the magic of the stars is released.

A crystal *mesa* is:

A body of the Bodiless
An expression of the One in the Many
An assembly of divine energies
An assembly of spiritual thoughts crystallized into form,
A assembly of the symbols of the spirit's reality,
A summary of the stages of the spirit,
An image of the 'pattern-of-the-whole,'
A means through which matter may grow conscious of its soul,
A key to the magic that is frozen in material sleep.

Therefore, this is not a book about the Andean *mesa* tradition or any other *mesa* tradition in particular. Rather, it is a contemplation of a core paradigm that can be brought into play to create a cosmically resonant *mesa*. The many-branched tree of life integrates and transcends all its local expressions. Choice shaped by wisdom and sound knowledge of tradition are a very fine basis for going deeply into the world of the sacred *mesa*.

The central point of the Crystal Mesa Logo is both the clear quartz sphere that stands for Source in the Crystal Mesa, and the double terminated seed crystal which represents the *mesa*-keeper's soul, the divine presence in the human microcosm.

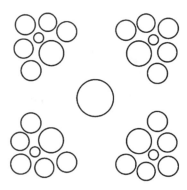

CLUSTER LAYOUT

Here we see a family situation. This layout helps us see differences between members of our family, whether it is our blood family or our circle of close connections. Families have different distances from source. There are many patterns that evolve when we start working with this pattern to sort out our feelings about family. Developing patterns of groupings by feeling and intuiting connections and distances and patterns helps you greatly to sense and see how your "family" instinct is working in your life.

THE EMBODIED WORD

The language of science is much more comfortable with "things" than with living beings or consciousness. Scientific categories of thought and scientific vocabulary becomes less and less useful when we consider the human phenomenon not merely as a mass of molecules and atoms, but as a microcosm of consciousness, intelligence, and spirit. When discussion moves into these categories, the traditional language of myth and archetype comes into play. Scientists are preferentially inclined to believe that conscious beings evolved from inert gasses and atoms. But spiritual tradition holds that physical matter devolved from spirit. According to the masters, the Divine Word was the beginning of creation. It created the various planes of reality, eventually crystallizing into physical matter as we know it. The opening words of the Gospel of John echo the Vedas and many other ancient scriptures on this point.

When the Word first echoed the mandate of the Supreme, creation began. From the One came forth two, and from the two came three; then, the three gave birth to what the *Tao Te Ching* calls the "ten thousand things," which simply means the multiplicity of creation. But its commencement was duality; the many came into existence only after the One had become dual. This twofold original force is sometimes referred to as polarity, or in the tradition of the Far East, *yin* and *yang*.

When *yin* and *yang* began the dance of creation, they gave birth to the primal pattern. The central reality of creation's primal pattern is the axis of Heaven (above) and Earth (below). *Yang's* natural home is above; *yin*'s natural home is below. The combination of these two primal dancers (*yin* and *yang*), and the two primal positions (above and below) resulted in the four primal energies.

i)   When there is yang above (in the Heaven position) and yang below (in the Earth position), we have major yang or Air.

ii) When there is yin above and yin below, we have major yin or Earth.

iii) When we have yang above and yin below, there results Fire.

iv) When yin is above and yang below, we have Water.

Each of these has also its natural home, as we have discussed. Air is North, at the top of the axis and closer to Heaven than any of the other elements except Ether. Earth is South, being heavy and dense and sinking into the depths of materiality. Fire is in the East where the sun rises and Water is in the West where the sun sets.

If we consider *yin* and *yang* from the archetypal or mythical perspective, we can speak of Mother and Father. The *yin* polarity is receptive, passive, cool, interior, soft, contracting, incoming, and tradition relates this to the feminine power in nature; the *yang* polarity is projective, active, warm, exterior, hard, expanding, outgoing, or masculine. Yang is solar, and yin is lunar, resulting in two fundamentally different processes in spiritual practice and two different paths of return to Source.

Air is the most *yang* of the four elements, and Earth is the most *yin*. Fire clings to its earthly fuel and is thus more dependent than Air; still, it strives by an ascending momentum to rise upward through the air. Thus Fire has the power of growth, evolution and aspiration and is centrally important to religious and spiritual endeavor. Water is the matrix of life in and upon the contracted, crystallized physical body of Earth.

The four great archetypal beings correspond to the four sacred elements. Earth is our Mother. In her watery womb, she gestates a divine Child who eventually is born and grows in power to become a Hero. The fiery Hero struggles to master his enemies and attain his celestial kingdom. In the end, the Hero achieves the divine or semi-divine status of a Sage, a fully realized spiritual being who is Father Heaven in human form. The Sage has evolved such wisdom, compassion and power that he can complete the work of uniting Heaven and Earth.

In addition to the stone in the centre of the *mesa*, which stands for Source, there should be four other stones in the *mesa*, immediately surrounding the centre, representing the archetypes of Mother (in the Earth position), Child (in the Water position), Hero (in the Fire position) and Sage (in the Air position). The choice of these stones should be made on the basis of personal intuition, but shaped by sound knowledge as well. You should feel when you choose a certain stone for archetypal Mother that the stone expresses the essence of the Earth-Mother. Similarly for the stones chosen to embody Child, Hero and Sage.

The inner reality of Earth Mother is that She is the creatrix of our physical body, the divine generative power who has entered the nether realms of darkness to do a great work, to manifest the Divine in matter. She has consciousness, will, power and can be experienced inwardly in consciousness if we evolve into a loving relationship with Her compassionate presence; indeed, Her inner support is indispensable for the journey of return to Source. With Her help, the seed of consciousness planted in the heart of matter at the beginning of time becomes a fully individualized being, and this takes form as the divine infant in the spiritual heart, the psychic being or archetypal Child. The Child is the blossoming soul-force, the first great achievement in the Mother's design to win Heaven for Earth. The fully developed Child archetype within the spiritual heart represents a most significant victory of consciousness over the obscurity of nescience and inconscience. The Child has achieved individualization and a separate identity, differentiated from the world-matrix. Within the Child, unfolding like a seed, will grow the latent power of the Hero. His fiery power and indomitable will eventually subsume the watery sensitivity and innocence of the Child into a more powerful expression of wholeness and build with them a surrendered instrument whose actions can complete the Mother's work.

At the end of his journey, in the completion of his struggles, the Hero experiences transfiguration and illumination. He then embodies and fully realizes all he strove to attain. The metamorphosis of the Hero into the Sage is the penultimate chapter in the master plot of humanity. It is the experience which the elders call liberation, illumination, or transfiguration.

When this transfiguration is complete, the Light of Heaven is fully established in the human microcosm. The purified mind and body of the human Hero, totally dedicated to the union of Heaven and Earth, becomes the enlightened one. The Crystal *Mesa*, and Crystal Yoga are means toward this attainment; they exist to realize the full potential that lies buried in the depth of our being, which in Vedic terms is the treasure in the cave.

Through apotheosis the human is made divine, or we can say that the inherent divinity of the microcosm is at last released from its obscure encasements and fully revealed. The Sage fulfils all the Mother's dreams. He realizes and embodies the promise that blossomed in the Child and the power that grew in the Hero. Sage and Mother then play the roles of Shiva and Shakti; together they effect the union of Heaven and Earth. (See Appendix One, The Sage)

In the *mesa* of power, the four stones which embody these archetypes must be chosen with this in mind, and treated as absolutely sacred. The work of the *mesa* is to manifest or to incarnate in this world the pattern of wholeness and perfection which exists in the higher worlds. The meaning of incarnation is that matter becomes full of light, life and harmony and is recognized to be spirit-in-form, or sacred. For the keeper of a *mesa*, this process of achieving sacred presence in physical life starts by seeing and feeling in stones, which are bones of beloved Mother Earth, the presence of the sacred.

Imperfect though they are, words can sometimes express the heart's deep bond with the Divine, which is the starting point for the work of the *mesa*. In both native and Hermetic traditions, the power of the word is essential in expressing and directing intent. The Vedas repeat this theme over and over, and it is central to the Egyptian mysteries as well, where the power of chanting was developed to a very high degree. In the Western Mysteries, and particularly the druid schools, the role of the bard was to become a master of the word, and of music, so that the power of sound could be applied to the work of spiritual attunement. A love of poetry or music can be a great asset in any field of spiritual or esoteric practice, including *mesa*. These words which follow are an example of how speech can embody sacred insights; they came to me during a car ride from Toronto to Halifax, and are an expression of devotion for the Mother:

> *She shines in the power of being,*
> *As mother, queen, womb,*

As lilt in the laughter of children,
And love that shapes their doom.
As dream finding form,
Or as light in the mist,
She does and undoes all things that exist.
From the heart to the smile, so swift and unseen,
Her breath is the spirit of all that has been;
From the soul to the tear, so subtle and sure,
Her presence is beauty in all that is pure.
She is queen of the forest, the magic in trees,
The voice of the brook, the caress of the breeze;
Her heart is life's goodness, her wisdom its Way,
Her peace is its twilight, her power its day.
She planted the rose in the heart of the child,
And buried the petals that time had defiled;
She reaps what is sown, and attracts to her heart
The lives and the loves that have broken apart.
She is all that embraces, and all that draws home,
The sleep at the end of the paths that we roam;
In the power of Being, the Mother of all
Is the unfolding soul, and the unending call.

Because the evocation of the archetypes is based on fine attunements of feeling, imagination, sensitivity and attention, inspired speech has always been considered important as a tool in their awakening. Similarly, when you experience inner contact with one or another of the archetypes, the result may be a spoken or written utterance that carries the energy of the archetype and can serve to renew contact at any point in the future. This poem, called Enchantment, expresses my own contact with the Child archetype:

In a glade of ancient hemlock wood,
There lies a hidden spring,
And those who taste its waters
Can hear the moonlight sing.
For the weaving of enchantment,
And the working of the spell,
They drink the silver waters

Where mystic powers dwell.
Who has heard the weeping loon
When twilight dims the day?
Or who has seen the swans take flight
As summer fades away?
'Tis the moon unveils their magic
To the child who finds her spring,
And her crystal chalice is a pledge
Of wonders that take wing.
She weaves an emerald ivy wreath
For those who must drink deep;
Their songs and visions lead the soul
Into a crystal sleep.
Comes then the rest of harp and voice
In the waters of the Moon,
As priestess to her bard bestows
The long-awaited boon.
Where herons haunt a hidden shore,
The moonchild seeks a nest
In timeless waves of magic light
Where dreams come home to rest.
Beneath the bending hemlock bough,
Forevermore alone,
He merges in the ancient spring
His heart has always known.

The *mesa* of power creates a sacred space within which the transformation of the human into the divine can take place. It is thus a crystal chalice, a cauldron of alchemy; when we do the work of reunification within this sacred space, we are practicing Crystal Yoga.

The enchantment of moonlight is one of the Mother's magical means for waking the imagination, which is the power that opens the Child, the Hero and the Sage to the fullness of what they can be. Those blessed by the Mother form a relation to her creative power as Muse, and their speech becomes a carrier of special energies that awaken and nurture the spirit. When the Child has grown, he becomes conscious of the future work he must do as the Hero, and more deeply appreciative of the bond with the Mother. The transition from Child to Hero is achieved in conscious dedication. While in this consciousness of soulful dedication, I once expressed it in these words:

> *I will weave a carpet of woodland fern,*
> *In gold and silver lace,*
> *And lay it low on the portal-stone*
> *At the door of your dwelling-place.*
> *When the mist has moved in lustral clouds*
> *In the aisles of the cedar-glade,*
> *I will offer you this woven skein*
> *Of the gift your beauty made.*
> *And in this gift, beneath your feet,*
> *Will rest a part of me;*
> *I am woven into the beauteous gleams*
> *That awake in all I see.*
> *Low will I rest below your door,*
> *Where your feet would touch the earth,*
> *To bear the weight of your glory down*
> *To the dust where you take birth.*

Lest the role of music and poetry and imagination in Crystal Yoga be undervalued, we should be reminded that magical power is based on imagination. Magic has been called the power to manifest intent. If you consider magic to be an occult science, then it should be called the science of imagination. Magical abilities arise from an imagination whose scope and power has been fully developed. If you have such a developed imagination (and the capacity to write poetry or compose music is evidence of it) then you have only to direct your will through your imagining and you will achieve magic. Incantation is magical speech, and the best poetry is of this sort. Such poetry has the power of the Muse, the power of the Mother, and it is indispensable for achieving the harmonies that align Earth with Heaven.

Ancient India in particular developed the tradition of inspired, or mantric speech, the mastery of word-skill which has the power to effect magical change. The Vedas, which are some of the most ancient writings in existence, show this principle at work. In these texts, which are still widely used by the Brahmins of India, we see the principles of magically empowered speech in practice. The seer-poets evoke the powers of Fire (Agni) and Wind (Vayu) repeatedly to make the Vedic sacrifice effective and attain the desired fruits of the rituals. At various points in history, the hero-seekers have achieved full attainment, but the advent of a complete and perfect Sage on Earth is a rare event. The Sage who undertakes the great labour of opening a way from Earth to Heaven is fulfilling the Mother's dream.

In the twentieth century, a very remarkable instance of this occurred. Sri Aurobindo (1872-1950) manifested the full wisdom and spiritual power of the archetypal Sage, focusing his unique spiritual capacity on deepening and widening Heaven's relationship with Earth. Equally remarkable was the career of his spiritual co-worker, Mirra Alfassa, The Mother, (1878-1973). She worked tirelessly with him from 1920 until her death to bring about the transformation of human nature and the cellular consciousness of the body. Sri Aurobindo and The Mother succeeded in bringing down of a new power called the supramental, which could help humanity to take the next step in evolution. Just as Sri Aurobindo embodied the fullness of the Sage, the Mother embodied the complete realization and the awesome power of the Divine Mother. We have made reference to Sri Aurobindo's most important piece of writing, and the longest poem in the English language, *Savitri*. It is a very important source for understanding the patterns at work in Crystal Yoga. In fact, as a revelation of Heaven's relationship to Earth, the roles of the archetypal Mother, the Child, the spiritual hero and the Sage, and the phases of their timeless interaction, it is the very best authority we have to date.

Speaking of the advent of the Sage, in Book One Canto Four of *Savitri*, Sri Aurobindo writes:

Too seldom is the shadow of what must come
Cast in an instant on the secret sense
Which feels the shock of the invisible,
And seldom in the few who answer give
The mighty process of the cosmic Will
Communicates its image to our sight,
Identifying the world's mind with ours.
Our range is fixed within the crowded arc
Of what we observe and touch and thought can guess
And rarely dawns the light of the Unknown
Waking in us the prophet and the seer.

The outward and the immediate are our field,
The dead past is our background and support;
Mind keeps the soul prisoner, we are slaves to our acts;
We cannot free our gaze to reach wisdom's sun.

In the Sage, the Divine Mother finds a perfect instrument to complete her great work. Knowing about this from his own personal experience, Sri Aurobindo's words carry the power of prophecy and revelation:

The inspiring goddess entered a mortal's breast,
Made there her study of divining thought
And sanctuary of prophetic speech
And sat upon the tripod seat of mind:
All was made wide above, all lit below.
In darkness' core she dug out wells of light,
On the undiscovered depths imposed a form,
Lent a vibrant cry to the unuttered vasts,
And through great shoreless, voiceless, starless breadths
Bore earthward fragments of revealing thought
Hewn from the silence of the Ineffable.
A voice in the heart uttered the unspoken Name,
A dream of seeking thought wandering through space
Entered the invisible and forbidden house:
The treasure was found of a supernal Day.
In the deep subconscient glowed her jewel-lamp;
Lifted, it showed the riches of the Cave
Where, by the miser traffickers of sense
Unused, guarded beneath Night's dragon paws,
In folds of velvet darkness draped they sleep
Whose priceless value could have saved the world...
The universe was not now this senseless whirl
Borne round inert on an immense machine;
It cast away is grandiose lifeless front,
A mechanism no more or work of Chance,
But a living movement of the body of God,

Savitri, Book One, Canto Three

In passages like these, throughout the roughly 25,000 lines of
Savitri, Sri Aurobindo is writing about his own personal inner experi-
ences of inner worlds where the illumining Fire, the Child Soul, the
Earth Mother and other archetypes are completely real.

The words of a perfected Sage are the most authoritative source
we have, the very best teaching we can access, for understanding the
great archetypes and the part they play in the divine plan for life on
Earth. This is why Crystal Yoga must be considered a yoga of the
masters. Some of us have already opened clear avenues of vision and
deep levels of mystical understanding, attaining glimpses and fragments of the wide picture. We each have special gifts and a specific
work to do for our own evolution and that of the Earth. All of this
has great importance for the way we use our personal *mesa*, the way
that divination or healing can work through us, making best use of
what we have evolved in our own microcosm.

This all fits into the larger picture, the cosmic pattern which only
the Sage can see, the inner destiny which defines the wider goals and
actions that *mesa* can support and empower. Only when the seeking
ego becomes a surrendered instrument of a Higher Power, following
the inner directions of divinely-inspired intuition, can the *mesa* be
made to serve its highest purposes.

An example of intuitive insight: Consider the court cards of Tarot
in light of the four archetypes we have been discussing. Who is the
Queen but the Mother? Who is the Page but the Child? Who is
the Knight but the Hero, and who is the King but the Seer? *Mesa*
and Tarot are ways of seeing, imagining, feeling and attuning to the
great mystery that underpins all true archetypes and myths. For a
most profound insight into the identity of the Mother, the Child,
the spiritual Hero, the Sage, and the work they were born to do in
us to unite Heaven and Earth, there is no better source than *Savitri*.
The selections I have included in Appendix One are well worth reading because the consciousness of the poem awakens higher levels of
awareness which help the reader's mind to reach a level where clear
seeing and magically empowered imagining can function.

THE TALE OF CREATION

Our spirit tires of being's surfaces,
Transcended is the splendour of the form;
It turns to hidden powers and deeper states.

Sri Aurobindo, *Savitri (2:2)*

O ur way of living is highly conditioned by our economic im-
peratives, social structures, educational models, culture, religious customs and beliefs, and many other ways of seeing
and relating to life that we have spun from our minds. Other people
living in other times and places have been fully human, and occasionally super-human, in very different modes of expression. Very little
of our modern mental conditioning reflects the nature of Reality. It
is mostly 'spin.' In other words, our way of thinking about and relating to life arises from our core values, and the need to expand
the economy (or to feed the acquisitive impulse) is the driving force
in the modern psyche, particularly in the West. Moreover, in the
modern, technological world, the mythologies we embrace and the
rituals we act out are *increasingly* removed from all things Primal. Our
ever-growing exploitation of Nature and our reliance on substitutes
for Nature such as artificial foods, chemicals and medicines are telling examples of this. In fact, so far are we from the original, balanced
pattern of Nature's wholeness that we are threatening to make the
planet un-inhabitable. We are at the point of destroying the planet
and ourselves because of unchecked greed.

All of this is worth understanding when we begin to think about the *mesa* and its uses. A crystal *mesa* is a connecting link to higher planes of reality. Its structure must inevitably express our understanding of the pattern of the cosmos. A *mesa's* power and capacity are necessarily a function of its correspondence to the patterning of creation. To access the full possibilities of our crystal *mesa,* we must get through the completely artificial "spin" of our modern, fractured mythos, because distortion interrupts the complete and harmonious expression of power. Revelation is a plane of consciousness which we *can* and *must* open to, and our crystal *mesa* will assist us in the ascent to this deeper, wider vision. Rightly used, the *mesa* amplifies consciousness-light; it thus deepens insight through harmonic resonance with the timeless, primal realities that structure the cosmos.

Everything that we do, say and think emerges out of our concept of Reality. When we harbour fear, we are buying into the idea that Reality is something to be feared. When we act with love, we express our faith that Reality is One, and that the seeming fragmentation of its separate parts is transcended by a pattern of deep wholeness or holiness in which our own life, and all life, participates. Thus it is that love aligns us with Truth.

What we can say about Reality always starts with a creation story. Thus before we create, we always ground our understanding in a primal foundation, a set of understandings about the nature of existence. How did creation come into being? The way we answer that question determines what we can say about creation. Our ability to discover the meaning of life hinges on how accurately our understanding mirrors the truth of things. A story of creation harmonizing with primal reality might flow very much like this:

> In the beginning, only the Great Mystery existed. It was One. There was no other to know it. It is called the Source, but in truth it cannot be named because it has no form, and is not separate from all that is. This sublime, unknowable Source exists beyond time and beyond our capacity for understanding. It simply was and is. Before any names and forms came into being, This has always been. It precedes time and space but holds them both within Itself as a tiny fragment of Its infinite life.
>
> Somehow, mysteriously, in the secret heart of the original One, a need was born, a hunger for experience. From this came cre-

ation, the 'he' of it and the 'she' of it, the light of it and the dark, the above and the below, Heaven and Earth.

Heaven and Earth between them brought forth life, which is the music of their eternal love. Although they manifest as two, they are in essence One. From this hidden oneness comes their desire to unite. Expressing their love, they beget the many, and this is the origin of the dance of creation.

Hence come all the stories that have ever been, and all the languages to tell them. Of this the poets sing. For this we laugh and weep and dance and procreate. We become lovers because of this memory we have of essential oneness, and this need in our hearts to be re-united with our Source. Even in our forgetfulness of Source and the true way of return, we have a profound need to take part in the dance of life and to fertilize the blossoming of love.

All that is to be known and felt and seen and lived between Heaven and Earth, the glory of it, the agony, the mystery, lies hidden in the heart of creation, to be brought forth and given birth in form. May the names and forms of the self-revealing dance shine clearly in our minds and hearts. And may all our thoughts, words and actions be founded on this truth.

This flow of events is not spun from my personal imagination, it is based on many creation accounts from all over the world. It is important to have a creation tale that we feel secure about, because whatever creation tale we accept generates the paradigms by which we live. Our way of seeing, being and relating to life utters (or "out-ers") the paradigm we have consciously or unconsciously embraced. In most traditional creation tales, there is an original Source. Before the beginning of time, It exists in an un-manifest state. It is infinite in consciousness and potential. In some mysterious way, this unmanifest Source gives birth to the universal creation. Our world and all the worlds are birthed by a great event original event, which modern scientists have called the "Big Bang." The un-manifest thereby becomes manifest. By the time human beings appear on the scene, there has been an evolution of intelligence and a sharpening of sensory perception. By exploring creation, we gather clues about the nature of the Source and the purpose of life.

In this evolution, we develop technologies and tools to expand the scope of our power. The electron microscope is a perfect example, because it is a tool that allows us to see the most minute particles of creation. One very ancient tool, the *mesa*, is a collection of naturally occurring objects, assembled by human understanding and configured to amplify its user's innate gifts of wisdom and power. A wisely made *mesa* will reflect the pattern of creation in its structure. Objects in themselves are not invested with meaning; it is always our way of seeing them which fits them into a story, a pattern, a use and an expression.

Traditionally, a *mesa* has a heart, an object which represents **Source**, the Absolute, the Infinite Consciousness, the Supreme. This is the starting point of the story of creation, and from its seeds unfold an ultimate destination toward which we are all headed. Our journey to this goal is the great adventure of life and consciousness on Earth; all living beings sign up to play a role in the original contract which defines the relationship between Source and Creation, Heaven and Earth.

From the One, in some mysterious way that has never been fully explained, there came to be Two. The original event of creation was thus a birth of duality from within an original unity; the mystical vision has always been a glimpse of the One in the many. Poets, seers, prophets, sages and saints all serve the Law of One in the conditions of multiplicity which form the cosmic creation. The Source and its manifestation can never be separated, but yet they are not identical.

According to many ancient traditions, from the Source comes the Word, the emanation of consciousness into creation. The Word is the power of the divine creative force to generate and modify form, and consciousness. It is fair to say that a crystal *mesa* is a representation of the action of the Word. The Word vibrates all things into harmony and oneness, thus accomplishing the plan of re-unification. The Word has sometimes been seen as the Divine Child, firstborn of the Divine Mother.

We know the seven colours of the rainbow, but we also know that infrared and ultraviolet are colours beyond our visual range. In the same way the many higher planes of consciousness have their forms, and these are ranged in an ascending hierarchy. In the first stages of creation, all is perfect, harmonious and divine. Form exists in the lofty worlds which we call the heavens, invisible to our five senses.

Our Crystal *Mesa* gives importance to four principal archetypes: The Mother, The Child, The Hero and The Sage. These archetypes arise in a transcendent domain that can be called *the Divine plane*, which in reality encompasses several levels of heavenly existence; it comprises, for example, what Sri Aurobindo calls the Supermind as well as the Overmind, which is the domain of the cosmic gods. Some have called these regions the higher heavens.

The Spirit plane is a region closer to earthly experience. The energies are very fine and pure, but it is not unusual for humans to enter or touch this plane of reality through inner attunement. Many mystics and contemplatives have experiences of the spiritual plane of being. The four sacred elements exist here in seed potential, and the Crystal *Mesa* has four stones representing Spirit Earth, Spirit, Water, Spirit Fire and Spirit Air. The Angelic realms and lower heavens are within this domain.

The Primal Plane has a marked differentiation of polarity which in its essence can be called yin and yang, but which we experience as the opposites of male and female, heavy and light, dark and radiant, high and low, and so on. The Crystal *Mesa* has Yin and Yang stones in each of the four sacred elements; in other words, Yin and Yang Earth, Yin and Yang Water, Yin and Yang Fire, and Yin and Yang Air. The inner occult domains of the higher vital and several planes of mind are included in this domain. Here the forces are heavier, less harmonious, less pure and peaceful than on the higher planes.

The Physical Plane is the domain where form can be perceived and experienced with the five senses. This is the plane where time and space and physical matter are dominant. It is the sphere of karma and evolution, struggle and loss, transformation and growth in experience and power. There are sixteen crystals in the Crystal *Mesa* representing this plane, four crystals each for Earth, Water, Fire and Air.

The crystal *mesa* expresses a flow of consciousness from the Source into the cosmic manifestation. From the Source arises the Divine and its fourfold, archetypal manifestation. From the Divine there is a further devolution to the plane of Spirit, and thence by a continued condensing of vibrations, the plane of Primal forms. Lastly, the physical world that we know materializes from these subtle forms in the invisible Ether. The *mesa* permits its user to reconnect a flow of energy from the Physical level where much of our experience is centred, back to the world of forms, further into the spiritual planes, thence to the Divine, and finally to connect with Truth, the Source. The Way of the Sage is a chapter devoted to one such approach, but there can be many approaches, and the old saying holds true: all roads lead home.

To create a crystal *mesa*, we choose crystals that embody the primal energies of the four sacred elements, and thus we reconstitute both outwardly and inwardly, through the instrumentality of name and form, our link with the pattern of original wholeness, the divine plan from which all life derives. Although the plan of creation is eternal, different cultures at different periods of history have expressed it in varying forms. Because the varying cosmologies all hinge on the fundamentals of their creation tales, we must formulate such a base if we wish to develop our crystal *mesa* into a tool for attunement to Source.

Let us, therefore, restate the tale of how creation came into existence, taking the central elements that the traditions hold in common:

The Infinite Consciousness regards its own existence in the core of its own being, in its own heart. In that instant, there comes about a division in what has ever been undivided. Within the Infinite Consciousness, in that split second, arises a notion of difference. How and why this came to be is a mystery, the ultimate mystery. But once change began, consciousness started to unfold and to take on the forms and colours of various notions. Thus came into being the distinction between knower and the knowable, the sense of separation and the experience of fragmentation. In this way, space came to be. That element later believed itself to be more dense and it manifested as Air.

After a time, from the friction of movement in Air, there emerged Fire, which sheds light. Awareness thus comes to know the difference between light and darkness. Then, this Consciousness, which had begun to experience the unfolding of its identity, entertained notions of fluidity or water; then came the notion of, earth with its characteristics of solidity and density. In this way, the water and earth elements came into existence. The traditions say that the mirage-like appearance of these four or five elements and all the worlds that arise from them came about in this split second when the Infinite Consciousness, which is the Source, considered its own intelligence in its heart-core.

This creation tale is much like the first one, yet it yields additional perspectives about the central process at work. Saying the same thing in different ways often yields insight.

Scripture, revelation and creation tales are all symbolic accounts of a process which is at work beyond the physical appearance of things. They give us clues about the possibility of return to the Source, the re-connecting (*re-ligio*, religion) of the separated part with their primal wholeness (holiness). The inner journey of return to the Source is beautifully expressed by a Tamil poem which, in translation, runs like this:

Return within
To the place where there is nothing
And take care that nothing comes in.
Penetrate to the depths of yourself,
To the place where thought no longer exists
And take care that no thought raises its head!
There, where nothing exists, is fullness!
There, where nothing is seen is the Vision of Being!
There, where nothing appears any longer
Is the sudden appearing of the Self!
This is true meditation!
There where nothing is, everything in fact is.
Penetrate this secret and you will vanish from yourself:
Then alone, in truth, YOU ARE!

The creation of a *mesa* patterned on the structures of Primal Reality can facilitate this journey inward to the direct experience of Self or Source. It all depends on the depth of knowledge and the intensity of feeling and the range of creative energies and the power of imagination that we can bring to bear in its creation and its application. This book explores how a certain kind of *mesa* can be a tool of empowerment for the journey of return to the Source.

THE AXIS MUNDI

The *axis mundi*, or staircase from Heaven to Earth, is centrally important both for indigenous spirituality, and for the cosmically resonant
mesa. The inner pilgrim travels the planes of consciousness by means
of this pillar which is also the Tree of Life. It extends from deep below
the Earth high up into the celestial light. It reaches down into the
darkness and density of material inconscience and up into the purity,
radiance and perfection of divine order. The crystal sphere at the
centre of this *mesa* represents not only Source, but the principle of
unity behind the symbol of the pillar connecting Heaven and Earth.
Mystical oneness with all that is represents the goal of our self-transcending human consciousness, and the recognition of oneness in the
pattern-of-the-whole is a most important means of ascent. We are all
at some point between the clay of earth and the light of spirit on the
ladder or stairway that leads from limitation to freedom.

Each of us has evolved in consciousness to some degree of clarity
and focus on this pathway of ascension, our progress being relative
to the mastery we have achieved over all parts of our being, and the
degree to which we have achieved identification with the truth of the
Source. For the human individual, the spinal column is the physical
expression or counterpart of the pillar of light, which is the traditional stairway or ladder of ascent into higher worlds of experience. There
are energy centres called the *chakras* all along this column, as well
as three pathways of energy known in Sanskrit as *Ida, Pingala* and
Sushumna. Some of our *chakras* are located outside the physical body,
in the auric field, but six important ones are located between the
base of the spine and the top of the head. There is growing consensus
that the seven *chakras* of tradition are only part of the picture and
that in fact the total number extends at least to twelve, and possibly
more. Some of these are below and some are above the physical body.
The Mother Power or *kundalini* rises along this channel of the spinal
column on the subtle or etheric level and brings about the union of
the individualized consciousness with the cosmic consciousness. The
crystal *mesa* has thirty-three different stones, equal in number to the
bones of the spinal column which embodies the tree of life in the
human microcosm.

If the axis of the human microcosm is the spinal column, the axis
for the planet Earth is the line from the North Pole to the South Pole.

The Earth spins on this axis, which at its top points roughly in the direction of the Polestar, Polaris. This star stays constant while the rest of the sky seems to revolve around it. Many traditions hold that this is the gateway through which souls come and go. The heavenly end of the Earth's axis points at the polestar. North thus becomes the direction which was widely understood in ancient tradition to be "up," and therefore pre-eminently "celestial." Conversely, Earth, "down" and the pull of the physical were assigned to the South. Widening our perspective beyond planet Earth into the solar system, there is also a galactic centre, and our solar system has an orientation to it. In this way, the arrangement of the cosmos also helps to suggest or determine why Heaven and the Air element lie in the northern portion of the *mesa*, and why the home of the Earth element is placed in the South.

Among the ancient Greeks, there developed some confusion as to whether Fire or Air was the truly celestial element. But again, the very arrangement of the microcosm provides the answer. The *chakras* represent stages of consciousness, with the base *chakra* being assigned to the element Earth, the sacral *chakra* to Water, the solar plexus *chakra* to Fire, the heart *chakra* to Air, and the throat *chakra* to Ether. The brow *chakra* is mind and the crown *chakra* is spirit. Air is a densification of Ether. The movement of Air creates friction which generates heat and thus begets Fire. The elements of Water and Earth represent progressive degrees of involution into the density of matter.

There are quite a few sources in the ancient East Indian tradition which recount how the sacred elements precipitated out of the Primal Source. Details may differ, but these accounts are in broad agreement as to how manifestation took place. At the beginning of its life, our galaxy existed as a formless cloud. It contained the potential for all that would later appear in creation, and it is known in the ancient Sanskrit language as *Akasha*. As this scattered cloud began to contract, it started to whirl. The 'matter' of the cloud moved as if under the pressure of some etheric wind. The spirit that is *Akasha* was churning its substance toward a condition of manifest form. The whirling motion is the essence of the sacred element Air, which is called in Sanskrit *Vayu*. The whirling particles formed a nebula, or centre, and the intensity of their whirling increased. This generated electric and magnetic energies and the friction of the particles and energies created powerful heat. This heat increased until it became luminous and Fire broke out. This condition is called *Tejas* in Sanskrit. At the climax of its motion, this nebula began to decelerate and cool down. It then coagulated into a fluid-like substance and this watery phase of material manifestation, when all flowed like lava, is known as *Apas* which we call Water. Finally, the molten substance cooled completely, solidified and formed a dense mass.

Our planet Earth is one of these dense masses of substance; or you can say that the goddess Gaia was born in physical form. At the physical level of manifestation, waves of energy manifest as particles and they move at a very slow rate of vibration, appearing to be densely packed together. This is called Earth, or *Prithivi*. These are the modalities of matter as it moves from its primordial, un-manifest condition into a finite, manifest state. This pattern of manifestation from subtle to dense, from pure to obscure and from light to dark obtains not only in matter, but also in life and even in human character. This is the hierarchic pattern of creation.

According to this paradigm, the ascending order of the elements is: Earth, Water, Fire, Air and then Ether or *Akasha*. It corroborates the placement of Air above Fire in the arrangement of the *mesa*. Fire is usually assigned to the East, because it is seen to be born there at sunrise. Fire is *yang* and governs such phenomena as light, intensity, heat, and friction. Water is the opposite of fire, being cool, passive and downward in its movement. Water, then, is placed in the West, opposite the rising Fire of the Sun in the East. The pattern of light waxing and waning is illustrated in the phases of the Moon. The time of least light, the darkness of the New Moon, is a phase of extinction and rebirth. At this time, the spark of life is reborn. It will grow through two weeks into the radiant light of the Full Moon, before waning again into darkness. The waxing light is the increase of *yang* or heavenly energy, and the darkness is a predominance of *yin* or earthly energy. Thus, the time of the New Moon is the Earth phase; the First Quarter is Fire; the Full Moon and several days on either side is dominated by the quality of Air; and the Third Quarter is Water.

This pattern is expressed in a cosmically ordered *mesa* when Earth is placed in the South, Fire in the East, Air in the North and Water in the West, with Ether or *Akasha* in the middle. Ultimately, our directional choice for the placement of Earth, Water, Fire and Air within the *mesa* will be determined by the perspective we take. If our perspective is traditional and our paradigm is cosmic, these placements suggested above will seem to have a very sound rationale. However, there are different perspectives and some *mesa* users might argue for placing Fire in the South, or in the North, with their own reasons. It is a great help in reaching a decision about placement to be aware of how the tradition has dealt with this question, and how the Ancients structured their perceptions of reality.

The still point of Infinite Consciousness at the centre of the Crystal Mesa Logo reaches out in four directions, each of which corresponds to one of the four Sacred Elements. When the mesa is laid out horizontally, Earth is positioned in the South, Fire in the East, Water in the West and Air in the North, with Ether being the Central Axis.

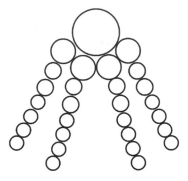

RAY LAYOUT

This layout depicts the Sun of Spirit sending out rays. The four rays may be seen as coming down the four sides of a pyramid. In fact, this layout may move you into the domain of a three-dimensional mandala layout. You may make a pyramid by using successively bigger squares of wood, or circles, placing one plane on another and gluing them together. By exploring the Rays, we sort out right relationship to Source. We acknowledge that Source is supreme in our life and we aspire to link Source to what is below, either in our own being or in our world. Themes such as "linking" or "manifesting" or "attunement" express what this layout is all about. Each ray is one path to Source, and each of us has a special affinity with one ray over the others. Remember, you can meditate on stone placements over several days, or you may place one stone per day. If you did a mesa retreat lasting several days, you could intuit a progression of energies leading to Source, and place them as an act of meditative attunement.

THE PRIMAL PATTERN

The capacity of a *mesa* to be a tool for healing and personal transformation derives from its pattern, and the awareness and capacity of its user. Knowledge of the cosmic pattern which underlies the *mesa* helps greatly in assembling a sacred bundle of effective power. *The Emerald Tablet*, which is a principle source for Hermetic and alchemic wisdom, is well known for the axiom: "As Above, So Below." This points directly to the first of nine keys to understanding the *mesa* archetype, namely the relationship of the microcosm to the macrocosm

1. MICROCOSM AND MACROCOSM

All that we see writ large in the cosmos is also present in the constitution of each and every human being, and it is for this reason that the human body-mind is referred to as a microcosm. Therefore, for example, the solar and lunar energies, the energies of the planets, the structure of crystal, and the polarities of the pillar of light are all internal to our own being. The means of ascension are part of our own makeup.

Before we take an active interest in the evolution of our consciousness, we are typically fixated on the outer world, where we seek for happiness by acquiring possessions and forming human relationships. But when we understand the relationship between the microcosm and the macrocosm, it becomes clear that we already embody all we seek, and that it is necessary to turn inward to realize our full potential. It is at this point that the use of the *mesa* may become of interest, since it is a tool of empowerment in our seeking, meditation, healing, study and attunement. The assembling of a *mesa* reflects the relationship of microcosm to macrocosm, and the more conscious we are of this principle, the more it informs and empowers our work.

2. POLARITY

Creation stories always reflect the multiplication of the One into the many by the process of polarization. *Yin* and *Yang* are the most encompassing terms for the bi-polar expression of the One which is the beginning of creation, but similar concepts of polarity such as light and dark, high and low, Heaven and Earth, matter and spirit, dense and light, masculine and feminine, reflect the same duality. Within the human microcosm, the magnetic and electric energies reflect this polarity. The nervous system is electric in its nature, which makes it possible for us to turn on a light by touching the lamp, or to direct computer information by the touch of a finger. The two sides of the brain also reflect this duality, and when they are not working in harmony, we refer to it as a 'bi-polar disorder.'

The Crystal Mesa contains the same elements of polarity. The axis or pillar of light connecting Earth to Heaven is bi-polar, Earth (the planet, not the element) being *yin* and Heaven *yang*. The elements Air and Fire are *yang* while Water and Earth are *yin*. The centre of the *mesa* is the crystal chalice, the magical cauldron where the reconciliation and transcendence of opposites can be alchemically accomplished in the core of the spiritual heart. This seven-part pattern of the *mesa* reflects the seven dimensions of the human microcosm, namely above and below, before and behind, right and left, and the centre, which is the heart. The heart stone of the *mesa* is its spiritual centre of gravity, its focus. A clear crystal sphere has both the symbolic visual perfection and the energetic range to serve for this placement. But it too will be found to be bi-polar, for the quartz crystal from which it was originally cut would have had the same areas of alternating polarity as we find in a) the human microcosm, b) the cosmos as a whole and c) the cosmically-patterned *mesa*.

3. THE SACRED ELEMENTS

The bi-polar structuring of the One becomes quadri-polar in the four sacred elements, traditionally known as Earth, Water, Fire and Air. Earth and water are *yin*, whereas Fire and Air are *yang* in nature. The four directions are traditionally co-related to the four sacred elements. There are various ways in which this is done, but Fire, for example, is often placed in the East where the sun rises to bring light to the world.

A fifth element, Ether, or *Akasha*, is also reckoned in the primal structuring of creation. It is at the centre of the sacred four and represents Spirit or the harmony of all things in balanced wholeness, integration in the journey of return to the Source. This leads us to several other key concepts. The four sacred elements are so important that we will look at this subject in greater detail in a separate chapter.

Each element is a domain of experience and mastery, opportunity and challenge. The challenges we face are in essence opportunities for growth, being the polar equivalent of our strengths. Wherever great gifts and talents are found, there also will be found corresponding degrees of challenge and difficulty. The "dark side" of the sacred elements, though not often considered, may be briefly summarized as follows:

EXAMPLES OF EARTH DARKNESS

Inept, lazy, incapable, careless, incompetent, undependable, inefficient, stingy, disloyal, gluttonous, ungenerous, disorderly, disorganized, lacking perseverance, impractical, unproductive, imprudent, unrealistic, unreliable, irresponsible, vague, unstable, unsteady, unsupporting, vacillating, naïve, compulsive, conventional, gloomy, grim, hard-headed, humourless, inflexible, intractable, intransigent, materialistic, obdurate, obsessive, obstinate, banal, overcautious, pessimistic, prim, prosaic, rigid, stiff, stodgy, timid, un-adventurous, unbending, unimaginative, uncreative, unquestioning, unspontaneous.

EXAMPLES OF WATER DARKNESS

Unaesthetic, disagreeable, lacking affection, restless, uncaring, lacking compassion, inconsiderate, undiplomatic, unemotional or excessively emotional, brooding, overly delicate, jealous, fearful, moody, escapist, fragile, frail, gushy, huffy, hypersensitive, hysterical, impressionable, indolent, introverted, lazy, maudlin, melancholy, morose, narcissistic, prissy, petulant, passive, sulky, sullen, temperamental, thin-skinned, touchy, wishy-washy, unkind, too soft.

EXAMPLES OF FIRE DARKNESS

Aggressive, brash, cocky, foolhardy, cruel, hasty, headstrong, heedless, hot-tempered, impatient, impetuous, proud, impulsive, avid, lustful, overly bold, flashy, overly confident, irresponsible, nervy, precipitous, rash, violent, restless, self-aggrandising, superficial, thoughtless, unprepared.

EXAMPLES OF AIR DARKNESS

Arrogant, autocratic, biting, blunt, cold, condescending, petty-minded, controlling, critical, cutting, indifferent, distant, dogmatic, domineering, high-handed, imperious, intolerant, judgmental, opinionated, overbearing, overly intellectual, patronizing, stand-offish, thoughtless, unaffectionate, unfeeling, unsparing, cunning, prickly, self-righteous, unjust, immoral, outspoken, overly rational.

In *The Cosmic Doctrine,* Dion Fortune writes:

> *Evil is simply that which is moving in the opposite direction to evolution. (It) is that which ... tends to revert to the Unmanifest. Evil can be viewed, if this is helpful, as the principle of inertia which binds 'the good.' Good can be seen as the principle of creative movement... (pg. 160)*

In the Andean tradition, there are two kinds of energy, light and heavy. This can be a more useful way of speaking than the polarities of "good and evil," "positive and negative." When the energy of heaviness is released, it can feed the light and empower us to higher achievement; thus it is something to work with and transform rather than to judge and condemn.

4. THE CENTRE AND THE PERIPHERY

A *mesa* has a centre and a periphery. As mentioned above, the periphery usually reflects the fourfold structure of the sacred elements and the directions of North, South, East and West. The *mesa* cloth has four sides and four corners. Elements in the bundle which embody Earth energy may be placed in one of the corners, which in turn is oriented to one of the directions. The act of doing this is an act of bringing order to a symbolic microcosm. For just as a human is a microcosm of the macrocosm, the *mesa* is a symbolic temple and altar of the human being himself.

But they all come together in the centre, which usually is the placement of greatest importance. The centre represents the One which is the Source of the many, and it is equidistant from each of the sides and corners of the *mesa* cloth. Usually, there is an object in the bundle known as the 'heart of the *mesa*' which occupies the place at the centre and co-relates in some way to the principle of spirit. The centre embodies the static aspect of creation, while the stones placed in the four quadrants express its dynamic aspects. The centre represents the inner, or the inmost reality, while the four directions represent the dynamic outer play of its potentials. In the four sacred elements, energy moves with great power and complexity, but in the centre, there is a cessation of motion. When energy and movement are stilled, mind also becomes calm and this opens doors to total awareness. Infinite consciousness is the beginning and the end of the game. The centre is the place of the one Supreme Being who is inseparable from His energy (also called his *Shakti*) and He is always Her nucleus. Energy expresses unity through diversity, undergoing many transformations while remaining ever the same, and identical to infinite consciousness. From this comes the great spiritual insight of ancient India: "All this is THAT."

Energy moves in an orderly cycle, alternating between periods of motion and rest. When in motion, energy changes and gets disordered. Then, when it enters a period of rest it is harmonized, re-ordered and made whole. This cycle of creation, dispersal, destruction, re-organization and re-creation goes on endlessly. The centre represents the 'witness consciousness,' a place of stillness from which we can see and regulate the fluctuations of mind that open us to the pulls and pushes of desire. When we move to the centre, we attain the power to stop these fluctuations, and we gradually develop the power of one-pointedness. Mastering the energies of the periphery, we attain miraculous powers, but like all else, these too are regulated by the laws proper to their own plane. *Mesa* is a tool for the eternal quest, a means of self-development, a methodology for achieving wholeness and mastery. *Mesa* gives us a picture of how the play of the universal energies works, and it can also be a teacher, demonstrating a way to move and live within these cycles of change more consciously and creatively.

Pattern and meaning are interrelated in *mesa*, and its very design speaks. The arrangement of the stones from centre to periphery forms a cross, not unlike that of the Templars. When the *mesa* is opened up, this cross is arranged horizontally, and for correct energy work it should be correctly oriented to the four sacred directions. The cruciform pattern of the assembled *mesa* corresponds to the traditional Andean symbol of the *chakana*, where the centre, an empty circle, representing formless infinity, and the four arms reach outward to the four sacred directions. Each of these in turn is matched with one of the four sacred elements. However, the Crystal *Mesa* described here is not derived from any particular South American tradition; rather, it could be considered antecedent to them all. It is archetypal in its relation to the widely differing shamanic traditions of *mesa* use and assemblage.

The roots of this tradition extend far back beyond the time of the Incas to the pre-Incas with roots even beyond that in ancient Lemuria. The revival of Lemurian, nature-oriented spirituality is a centrally important fact of our time, and much of the renewal-energy radiates out of Cusco in Peru, the capital of the Inca Empire. This empire was arranged like a mandala of power, with the Koricancha at its centre, and with the Inca Emperor presiding over the whole. The concept of a strong centre which is the focus of all outlying parts, and a spiritual axis of power uniting Heaven to Earth, with a semi divine being presiding, is ancient and universal. The Incas turned most of the Andes into a single political entity, uniting the various parts of their mountain empire into a whole, a geomantic mandala centred on the Temple of the Sun in Cusco. Their vision, carried over from earlier peoples, but never so grandly expressed on the political plane, still radiates power. The Inca phase of this unifying vision, based on the ancient tradition that Earth should mirror Heaven, was one of the last and greatest that history ever produced. Thus, Cusco is of all cities the one most associated with the ritual art of the sacred *mesa*.

The tradition of arranging precious stones around a centre is very ancient. In ancient India, the *Naoratna*, (*nararatna*) or nine-gem jewel is mentioned in a number of treatises on gems. For example, in the *Nararatnapariksha*, it is described in this way:

Centre	The Sun	Ruby
East	Venus	Diamond
Southeast	Moon	Pearl
South	Mars	Coral
Southwest	Rahu	Jacinth
West	Saturn	Sapphire
Northeast	Jupiter	Topaz
North	Ketu	Cat's Eye
Northwest	Mercury	Emerald

In the Western tradition, the emerald is usually assigned to Venus, and the diamond is associated with the Sun. The *naoratna* was a powerful talisman combining the favourable energies of all the celestial bodies in crystal form, and it was believed to be a most auspicious treasure for favourably affecting its owner's destiny. The *mesa* is based on similar principles, but its range of energies is expanded by including more than three times the number of different precious and semi precious stones.

Along with microcosm and macrocosm, centre and circumference, we must recognize the importance of inner and outer as categories of experience in working with a *mesa*. A *mesa* is an outer, physical expression of an inner understanding; it is a collection of physical objects that mirrors reality and empowers its user's inner capacity to change creation.

5. THE PILLAR OF LIGHT

The centre of the *mesa* is the connecting point where the sacred elements converge and where the many become harmonized into the One. It is a power spot where the energies of Heaven and Earth coalesce. When Earth rises into the light of Heaven, the movement is experienced as one of ascension. When Heaven manifests on

Earth in material form, it is often though of as a descent. In the New Testament, for example, this experience is seen at Pentecost when tongues of fire appeared above the heads of the twelve apostles and the Holy Spirit descended into them. The axis of ascent and descent is the channel where the celestial and terrestrial dialogue takes place, and where the relationship matures into the fullness of completion. At the upper end of the pillar of light we have the One, the Source, the Absolute, and typically some object or symbol which expresses this in material form. At the bottom end of the pillar of light we have matter, Earth, the microcosm which receives the heavenly influence and is transformed into its image. The spinal column expresses this principle in the human microcosm, with the crown chakra at the top end becoming active and open as a result of celestial attunement, and the base chakra at the bottom end serving to ground consciousness in the processes of Earth.

Light is the primary manifestation of consciousness as energy. The complete understanding of what light is has eluded science for quite some time, because light has characteristics both of a particle and of a wave. However, for our purposes the main thing to be understood is that consciousness becomes manifest as energy, and light is its principle mode of expression. Matter is an expression of energy in involution, or you could say in extreme *yin*. Yet even in matter we find that consciousness, energy, and the energies of all the sacred elements are present. This is why a *mesa*, which is a collection of material objects, can be a dynamic, three-dimensional *yantra* of transformational power.

Yantra is a Sanskrit word deriving from the root *yam*, which means to support or hold and the syllable *tra* or *trana* which means "liberation from bondage." A *yantra* is thus a 'preserver of essence' and a tool of liberation. A *yantra* holds the essence of the energy of the divine. It is a symbol, a precise, crystallized expression that corresponds to the structure of the inner life of creation. *Yantra* expresses the inner world of focus and quality, in contrast to the random order of the outer world which is extensive and quantitative. *Yantras* are painted as geometric patterns on flat surfaces such as the pages of books or the walls of temples, or occasionally on a floor or altar. The Tibetans construct elaborate *yantras* of sand which are then destroyed to express the reality of the principle of impermanence. All of the principles that govern the structure of *mesas,* such as macrocosm and microcosm, polarity, the sacred four, the pillar of light, the centre and circumference, apply to *yantra* as well. In fact, a *mesa* of power is a three-dimensional *yantra*.

A *mesa* is an assembly of symbolic objects kept in a bundle, but occasionally assembled in a certain order when the *mesa* cloth is opened up and unbundled. By using symbols, the human mind creates a situation where the particular can express the universal. Through symbols, it is possible to creatively manifest a mystery beyond the mind's grasp. The Divine is the ultimate mystery, and a cosmically ordered *mesa* can serve as a tool to facilitate in the user a withdrawal of consciousness from its outer focus so that it may be directed to an exploration of the inner world. By means of a *mesa,* altered states of consciousness can be accessed and higher levels of the central pillar of light can be achieved.

6. THE TREE OF LIFE

The stones of Earth, Water, Fire and Air total 28. The stones for the four archetypes total four, and the heartstone (source) at the centre brings the total to 33. The human spinal column also consists of 33 units, in this case, bones. Stone and crystal are bones of Mother Earth and the spinal column is the central skeletal structure of the human microcosm. The number 33 has many esoteric and arcane levels of meaning. Numerologically, the number refers to a master teacher who serves mankind in love and harmony. Such a being is considered an elder brother of humanity and incarnates for a life of service.

The human spinal column protects the spinal cord from which nerves radiate out in many directions like the branches of a tree. The human spine is the prototype for the World Tree, which is an image occurring in most of the ancient traditions. For example, in the *Bhagavad Gita* we read:

> *They say the imperishable Asvattha is with root above and branches below, of which the sacred hymns are the leaves. Who knows this, is knower of Knowledge. Upwards and downwards stretch its branches, expanded by the three Potencies; the sense-objects are its sprouts. Downwards, too, its roots are stretched,*

constraining to action in the world of men. Here neither its form is comprehended, nor its end, nor beginning, nor its support.

Elsewhere in the Hindu tradition, the World tree's leaves are referred to as "the mantras of the Vedas." These are symbolic of the supra-physical elements that maintain the universe – however they may also correspond to the pulsations of the nerve ends.

The Kalpa Tree is described by Hindu poets as a glowing mass of precious stones. Pearls and beautiful emeralds hung from its boughs. The young leaves were constituted of coral, while the mature leaves were zircon and the ripe fruit consisted of rubies. The roots of the tree were made of sapphire. The base of the tree's trunk was diamond, and its upper regions were topaz and cat's eye. In the *Rig Veda*, Brahma the creator is described in the form of a vast tree that encompasses the entire world. The gods are depicted as branches of this tree. The Buddhist scriptures described this tree as gleaming with every kind of precious stone, its smallest leaves being formed as gems more beautiful than the colours of a peacock's tail.

The Egyptians also had a tree allegory. In their sacred writings they describe a jewel-bearing tree which is located at the far East end of the world. The god Horus climbs up this tree to produce the phenomenon of sunrise. Babylonian legends tell of trees covered by precious stones. In the Gilgamesh epic, we read of a cedar tree growing in an Elamite sanctuary at Irnina. The text reads:

It produces samtu-stones as fruit;
Its boughs hang with them, glorious to behold;
The crown of it produces lapis-lazuli;
Its fruit is costly to gaze on.

Elsewhere in the same text, Gilgamesh discovers another tree that bears precious stones. The cuneiform tablet records:

It bore precious stones for fruits;
Its branches were glorious to the sight;
The twigs were crystals;
It bore fruit costly to the sight.

Ward, Seal Cylinders of Western Asia, 1910, pg. 232

In Akkadian tradition this tree was known as the Mesu tree, described in the following manner: "The flesh of the gods, the ornament of the king of the universe, that pure tree, whose roots reached as deep down as the bottom of the underworld, whose top reached as high as the sky of Anum."

The Chinese describe seven miraculous trees that flourished in the Kuen-Lun mountains. The greatest of these was of jade and it had fruit that made one immortal. The great western mystic Jacob Boehme spoke of the tree of the soul which grows up from the heart. It bears the fruit of immortality and destroys the world tree of illusion. The jewels upon its branches represent various spiritual fruits of attainment, and it bears blossoms of precious stones. This tree bestows the delight that never ceases.

The various precious and semi-precious crystals of the *mesa* relate to their centre like branches of a great tree. The four elements each form one branch, and each of these four branches has seven leaves, or seven fruits depending on how one pictures it. To contemplate the *mesa* as a Tree of Life is to open doorways of perception. When we contemplate the patterning of the crystals in the *mesa* and intuit the energies of the precious and semi-precious stones, we cultivate an archetypal way of seeing. This, in turn, makes the various powers and potencies which Mother Earth has concentrated in her crystalline bones (the precious stones) available to the keeper of the *mesa*. Only when we reclaim the eyes that can see and the heart that can feel will we be able to function as the Mother's Child, Hero, or Sage.

As a teacher, the *mesa* is ideally suited to facilitating our growth in awareness and perception. To see deeply, we need to acquire a new vision; to gaze into the heart of things, we must open the eyes of the Spirit. When we see in this way, what has been invisible becomes visible, and we can discern patterns of the hidden side of creation. Symbolic forms, the geometry of place, the varied patterns of *mandalas* and the primal structures of crystals do not "mean" in a way that our educational background equips us to recognize. *Mesa* does not speak a loud, limited, literal, rational content which the intellect can define verbally and delimit logically. Rather it opens up multi-layered levels of resonance which only become intellectual when we try to express what we have felt or perceived in words. In this way, deceptively simple patterns of stones within a *mesa* can speak far more than might at first glance seem possible. What we take in depends on the degree of insight we have cultivated, how good we are at sensing energies, linking symbols to larger patterns and intuiting mythic cycles of transformation. Symbolic arrangements of crystals on a *mesa* cloth invite us to perceive and to be aware in new ways. They challenge us to attune our powers of seeing and feeling so that we can go beyond surface appearances. It is in this way that *mesa* teaches, and only to those who are ready to listen.

7. THE GARDEN OF DELIGHT

In ancient cosmology, the Tree of Life is often found growing at the centre of an archetypal garden where beauty, harmony and peace prevail. The image of such a garden is, of course, a way of expressing "sacred space" symbolically. Whether this sacred space is called the Garden of Delight, the Garden of Eden, the Garden of Paradise, the Elysian Fields, or some other name, the image reminds us of a once-and-future golden age, a region in or beyond time and space where all things are in balance.

The Sumerians, Greeks, Chinese, Native Americans and Celts all had tales of a lost paradise where Heaven and Earth were in close proximity to each other and animals could talk with men. In this sacred space, the vegetation, rocks, people and buildings all glowed with inner light and everything was jewel-like. The description of paradise found in the Ramayana is typical: "The land is watered by lakes with golden lotuses. There are rivers by the thousands full of leaves the colour of sapphire and lapis lazuli.... The country all around is covered by jewels and precious stones with cheerful beds of blue lotus, golden-petalled. Instead of sand, pearls, gems and gold form the banks of rivers...."

There is usually, at the centre of such pristine gardens a wonderful tree of magical properties. It is tall and magnificent to behold, linking Heaven and Earth and unifying all levels of being from the material to the celestial. Often, there is a fountain in this central location, near the base of the tree, from which four streams or sacred rivers flow. The centre of this delightful garden is its most sacred area, a region of absolute reality and pristine purity, where corruption has never reared its head and where all things exist in their original perfection.

The modern view is that Paradise is not a physical location on

Earth, but rather a domain located in consciousness, a dimension accessible only after a human being has expanded his or her capacity of perception. Aldous Huxley experienced the preternatural light and luminous colours of these visionary worlds while under the influence of mescaline, but he acknowledges that mystics, shamans and visionaries of all ages have had similar experiences in contemplation. Paradise is a vision of Earth before the fall, Earth as it may yet be in the future after humanity attaining re-union with Heaven.

The archetypal *mesa* can be an access-portal, a window of profoundly mystical seeing. Through the eyes of altered awareness, we feel and sense Earth, and the world around us, as it would be if it were harmonically attuned to the celestial spheres. This pristine Earth has the jewel-like perfection that existed at the dawn of creation. The landscape of our soul's vision is often described by traditional writers in terms of the crystalline jewels because gems have the most perfect beauty and order that the mineral kingdom has been able to evolve. This has always been sensed by artistic and poetically-minded people because they seem to be more open to intuitive insight and the prompting of the Muse. Crystals *are* pristine nature. As living expressions of order and harmony they testify that something perfect can and does exist physically on Earth. In this, they are teachers and models of spiritual attainment and they have often acted as catalysts for healing and revelation for those who are receptive.

There are countless visionary descriptions in the world's literature of the Garden of Delight. These poetical and prophetic evocations depict a psycho-physical domain of beauty and pristine perfection. As long as the modern mind is committed to one kind of dreaming, a one-track, linear kind of thought called "rationalism," we will be culturally locked out of this Garden of Delight which the poets and bards of old celebrated. But in mythic consciousness, which the *mesa* helps us access, we can escape the limited parameters of rational thought and experience creation as divine dream. When we experience our individual human microcosm and the wider universal macrocosm as being full of soul, we connect with the patterns of paradise that are embedded in the deepest levels of our own being. Then, it is possible to relate to Earth and the human body as true temples, as sacred space.

As far back as the seventh century AD, a poet in Ireland wrote of the Islands of the Earthly Paradise:

There is an island far away,
Around which the sea-horses glisten,
Flowing on their white course against its shining shore;
Four pillars support it.
Pillars of white bronze are under it,
Shining through aeons of beauty,
A lovely land through the ages of the world,
On which many flowers rain down.
There is a huge tree there with blossom,
On which the birds call at the hours;
It is their custom that they all call together in concert every hour.
Colours of every hue gleam throughout the soft familiar fields;
Ranged round the music, they are ever joyful in the plain south of
Argadnel.
Weeping and treachery are unknown in the pleasant familiar land;
There is no fierce harsh sound there,
But sweet music striking the ear.
Without sorrow, without grief, without death,
Without any sickness, without weakness,
That is the character of Emhain;
Such a marvel is rare.
Loveliness of a wondrous land, whose aspects are beautiful,
Whose view is fair, excellent, without a trace of mist.
Then if one sees Airgthech,
On which dragon-stones and crystals rain down,
The sea makes the wave wash against the land,
With crystal tresses from its main.

This way of seeing and feeling is something that we too can bring
forward when we approach the *mesa* as a Garden of Delight. Seen in
this way, the *mesa* is a physical counterpart of the sacred geography
of our inner landscape, a gate through which we can enter the place
where the tree of life connects Earth and Heaven. When the crystal
stones of the *mesa* are laid out in order, they mirror an inner region
of the soul, a place of beauty, order and harmony, a heart-garden of
archetypal perfection.

How might this be done? Picture the seven Earth crystals of your
mesa as being trees. Picture your Jade stone at the centre; picture

it as a tree entirely composed of Jade, with trunk, branches, leaves and fruit of this substance. Then picture a circle of trees around this central Jade tree, six of them in total. One of these trees is composed entirely of Tiger's Eye, another of Petrified Wood, and then Pyrite, Fire Agate, Malachite and lastly Red Jasper. You can walk among these trees in your imagination, walk under leaves of these substances, touch the bark of the trees and feel what the energies are. Your intuition can sense the poetic beauty of the place, and this feeds your imagination.

Or, visualize your *mesa's* Earth-crystals as fruits plucked from the trees of this sacred grove. Imagine that these fruits are edible and that you place them like candy lozenges in your mouth one by one. Imagine placing the Jade stone in your mouth and assimilating its taste, its energy and its qualities. What do these energies feel like? What difference do they make in the way you feel? How do these energies affect your thoughts? If you were to speak under the influence of these energies, how would your words flow? By using your intuitive and imaginative faculties to relate to your *mesa* in this way, you can access an inner 'garden' of beauty and magic.

8. CRYSTAL

Crystal is the manifestation of light in three-dimensional matter. In crystal, we see a high order of molecular structure and order, which is indicative of the structuring power of light as it achieves perfect physical expression. It is crystal which transposes a two dimensional *yantra* into a three-dimensional *mesa*. It is crystal which holds energy and transmits it, making the *mesa* a place of power. It is crystal which registers and amplifies intent. Crystal manifests the successful working of heavenly energies in the physical matrix of our three-dimensional world, and is thus a promise of the successful completion of the spiritual alchemy in which our souls are engaged.

Light is primarily a spiritual manifestation of the Divine Reality. It is a power of creativity and illumination. The material light which we see emanating from the sun is a subsequent representation or conversion of this metaphysical light into matter for the purposes of a material manifestation. A crystal is a "signature" of light in matter. Each crystal will express certain of the properties from the infinity of Divine energy. The archetypal qualities which light can express are known as the *Tattwas*.

There are seven basic geometric structures that give shape to the light-substance of crystals, and give form to their possible uses and functions. These are:

1) Isometric
2) Tetragonal
3) Hexagonal
4) Trigonal
5) Orthorhombic
6) Monoclinic
7) Triclinic

Within each family, specific attunements of stone result from the colour of the stone, its variation from standard or perfect geometry, geographic origin, size, quality, clarity, the place where it is being used, the time, and the consciousness of the user. Many other factors also contribute to the unique signature of any specific stone and determine its appropriate use. Thus, beyond the cosmic patterning which we can study with the mind, or grasp intellectually, the intuition and the guidance of the spiritual heart are indispensable when we choose and assemble crystals for use in our *mesa*. A crystal is not only a victory of light in matter, but more importantly an expression of love. Love is the force that reveals the one in the many, and only the power of love and light together can bring about the perfect molecular structure that is crystal. The subject of crystal is very important, and we will re-visit it in a later chapter which is devoted entirely to this theme.

9. TATTWAS

The term *tattwa* comes from ancient India, and refers to the five elements, as well as the subdivisions into which these elements proliferate. For example Earth is the element which is a force for structuring, densification, solidification, inertia, and heaviness. However within the overall field of Earth energy, there can be several different kinds of manifestation. There can be basically Earthy energy which is manifesting in a Watery way, or in a Fiery way, or in an Airy way, or in a highly Earthy way, or even in a spiritual (Etheric) way. The

Western Mystery Schools have absorbed Eastern thinking about the elements and formulated a synthesis with their own symbols and applications.

Through the *tattwas* se see a clear expression of the many forms which light, or solar *prana*, can take on earth. For the purposes of an archetypal *mesa*, the *tattwas* provide the following categories of energy:

Earthly Domain	Watery Domain	Fiery Domain	Airy Domain
Earthy Earth	Earthy Water	Earthy Fire	Earthy Air
Watery Earth	Watery Water	Watery Fire	Watery Air
Fiery Earth	Fiery Water	Fiery Fire	Fiery Air
Airy Earth	Airy Water	Airy Fire	Airy Air
Etheric *Earth	Etheric Water	Etheric Fire	Etheric Air
Yin Earth	Yin Water	Yin Fire	Yin Air
Yang Earth	Yang Water	Yang Fire	Yang Air

* The term "Spirit Earth" will substitute for Etheric Earth, etc. in subsequent discussion.

This gives us a total of 28 manifestations of light in matter as expressed through the four sacred elements and ether. Each of these 28 is embodied in a different kind of crystal. Therefore, the energies of the *tattwas* can be expressed by including these crystals in the *mesa*, and a *mesa* built on these principles reflects a high degree of cosmically-derived order and completeness.

SUMMARY

Beyond these seven subjects, the patterning and working of a *mesa* must take into account the geometry of sacred space, the laws of geomancy, the nature and power of intent, the factor of time and some basics of astrology, the application of intent and energy through the power of sound, and the power of heart, or focused feeling.

However, it is clear from our consideration of microcosm and macrocosm, polarity, the sacred elements, centre and periphery, the pillar of light, crystal, and the *tattwas* that the pattern and the constituents of *mesa* are provided by the design of the cosmos itself. This is what empowers it to be a tool for bringing the parts of creation (the dismembered parts of a god's body) into an assembly of right relation with the Source. In ancient tradition, the sacredly planned and constructed temple had the same function. It combined all of its constituents into a harmonious whole, to express what a human is intended to be in his or her ultimate wholeness. Mankind is meant to be what R. A. Schwaller de Lubicz (*Sacred Science*) calls *anthropocosmos*, cosmic man. Every element in the crystal *mesa* concretely embodies some aspect of this complete and perfect creation which is our destined future, and taken as a whole, the elements of the *mesa* form a temple to facilitate the accomplishment of the great work of transformation.

Whereas the elements we have discussed here are the outer symbols of an inner pattern, the capacity to know the "pattern of the whole" and work with its energies through symbolic objects depends in large measure on the wisdom and spiritual maturity of the practitioner. Subjects like geomancy or astrology can be studied, but the quality of light in the heart of the student, the purity of intent in his or her will, and the capacity for steady growth in wisdom and love are very much a matter of personal choice, karma, and higher help. A later chapter entitled *A Living Relationship* will touch on the quality of the *mesa*-user's own consciousness and its importance in *mesa*-work. Thus, in the end each *mesa* must be a very unique and personal assembly of the patterns, symbols, and traditional teachings which the universe affords as tools for the inner journey of attunement to Spirit.

The vertical and horizontal arms
of the Crystal Mesa Logo meet
at a point which is the Centre, or
Source; the Infinite Consciousness
seated in the Eternal Now.

ARCHETYPE AND MYTH

In traditional cosmology, matter is simply a scaled down representation of infinite life, the life of Heaven, which exists beyond the range of our five senses on the celestial planes. The original Reality is not molecular or atomic, or even energetic, rather it is divine, blissful consciousness, full of the power of Being. Infinite consciousness is the Divine Source. In ancient India it was referred to as Sat-Chit-Ananda, existence-consciousness-bliss. It has multiplied itself into this universe of particles, energies and planes of consciousness in a fractal way such that each part reflects the pattern of the whole. If we want to understand the ladder of being on its higher ranges, we must work with a set of perceptions and a language of reference that can go beyond the scientific limits, useful as these are when dealing with matter through the lens of the five senses. Here the archetypes and the primal plot-lines of myth come into play.

The process of widening that takes place when human consciousness encompasses that which transcends it is sometimes called empowerment or initiation. As instruments of awakening and enrichment, archetypes have played an important role in this process from the earliest times. In contemplation and divination, as well as in myths, rituals, philosophy and cosmology from the dawn of recorded history, archetypes have carried us forward in our quest for Truth.

For Carl Jung, archetypes were realities that exist pre-consciously and which form the "structural dominants of the psyche." This means that they are present and at work within us even when we are not aware of them, magnetizing and energizing our thinking processes and behaviour, speaking their presence through our unconscious urges, intimations, instincts, intuitions and actions. Jung wrote:

> We understand only such thinking as is a mere equation and from which nothing comes out but what we have put in. That is the manner of working of the intellect. But beyond that there is a thinking in primordial images – in symbols that are older than historical man; which have been ingrained in him from earliest times, and eternally living, outlasting all generations, still make up the groundwork of the human psyche. It is possible to live the fullest life only when we are in harmony with these symbols; wisdom is a return to them. It is a question neither of belief nor knowledge, but of the agreement of our thinking with the primordial images of the unconscious.
>
> Modern Man in Search of a Soul, pgs. 129 - 30

An archetype such as that of the hero may be traced through history, expressed by different symbols in different cultures, but always retaining the same emotional-dynamic content, and always touching the human psyche with the same dynamic energy. Different archetypes have different effects on our consciousness, and we can see from these effects that each archetype embodies a different kind of spirit or potential. The existence and action of archetypes does not depend on human belief or recognition, but when we begin to work with archetypes either unconsciously or with awareness, our lives are enriched.

A crystal *mesa* has, as we have explained, a centrepiece or heartstone (usually a small, clear quartz crystal sphere), surrounded by four other stones which represent four archetypes:

- in Earth (South), we have Lemurian Jade representing The Mother;
- in Water (West), we have Rhodochrosite representing the archetype of The Child;
- in Fire (East), we have rutilated Citrine for The Hero;
- and in Air (North) we have Lapis Lazuli, corresponding to the Sage.

The stones chosen actually embody the energies of their associated archetypes. When we begin to work with these stones and their archetypes in the context of their relation to the total *mesa*, they not only touch and inform the mind, but more significantly, they empower it. The *mesa* archetypes, when rightly understood and accessed, arouse, energize and illumine our awareness on many levels, opening a possibility of new depths of insight and capacity. As a result, there is a deepening and widening of a *mesa*-user's inner understanding. Sometimes, we become aware of new information, and with extended practice, this knowledge ripens into wisdom.

Archetypal images and their symbols communicate to us in accordance with the kind of attitude we adopt in approaching them. When we see, feel and relate to our *mesa's* sacred space and its symbolic contents in the right way, we will invariably have an experience of inner change on some level. A profound unfolding of our inmost potential takes place in us as the full meaning of archetypal realities is contemplated and assimilated.   In order for an archetype, or image or symbol to act as a catalyst of awakening, it must be loved. With deep inner calm, one contemplates the form. Then, the heart energies are brought into play, and the sweetness of the symbol is felt. This is not an exercise of mental will, or self-effort, and it is not hampered by expectations. The fire of the heart's affection radiates into the image and brings it to life. The crystal *mesa* and its constellation of precious and semi precious gems works in such a way as to facilitate an inner alchemy of self-transformation when we relate to it in this way.

THE FOUR GREAT ARCHETYPES

The Earth has always been known to the majority of humans as a Great Mother. The name by which we recognize and honour this fact, whether it is Gaia, Pachamama, or some other epithet, is secondary in importance. What is indispensable is that we recognize how Mother Earth gives her material body, her substance and her existence to serve the cosmic plan, to incarnate the light and life of the Divine here below. *Mesa* has meaning through its participation in this centrally important divine plan that is working itself out in the material creation. The Mother cherishes the dream that the Supreme Being may incarnate in earthly form and achieve full expression of the very highest possibilities for the evolution of this planet to its full potential (see Appendix One, The Mother). That dream of the Mother resonates in the spiritual hearts of all humans; we carry it within us as the archetype of an aspiring divine child.

This archetypal divine child is sometimes called the 'psychic being' – a term that Sri Aurobindo used to refer to an evolving aspect of the soul, the form evolved by the soul as it acquires an individual identity, gathering and distilling earthly experience into an ever-growing awareness of Truth. The soul puts out a personality which develops as it assimilates the lessons of life, and in the course of time, this child-soul matures into a hero. For un-evolved human souls, the seed of the divine child is still dormant, but when spiritual progress has become the dominant theme in a human being's life, the child-soul, or psychic being, comes to the fore. It can be seen, experienced, known, heard and at some point it is recognized by the seeker as being centrally important in the journey of life. Sri Aurobindo and other masters have taught that the soul, or psychic being must come to the fore before any significant attainment is possible in the journey to Source.

As we evolve spiritually, this inner child of the spiritual heart grows up and becomes a luminous being of tremendous spiritual potential. The birth of the hero archetype from the divine child is accomplished by the power of Fire, which in ancient India was called Agni. In many of the Vedic writings, which are humanity's oldest recorded scriptures, Agni is referred to as the hero, the opener of the way, the one who accomplishes the quest and empowers the sacrifice (the self-offering of the human to the divine). Humanity as we know it is the very imperfect outer manifestation of the archetypal divine child whose home is the cave of the inmost heart. The aspiring human cultivates the many heroic qualities of Agni and, by exercising them with growing wisdom in the adventure of life, he or she eventually attains the fullness of realization, thus becoming the seer, the saint, the prophet or the master. The archetype of the Sage encompasses all these and still other forms of attainment, being a paragon of wisdom, compassion, spiritual power and ineffable equanimity.

There is an evolution which is taking place in the inner core of all earthly forms and beings. The pattern of this unfolding potential is reflected in the arrangement of the crystals of the *mesa*. Most *mesas* consist of stones, which are believed by all indigenous peoples to be the bones of Mother Earth. But beyond this, many traditions understand gemlike stones and clear crystals to be seeds of god-substance or higher light that can augment their human keeper's potential and capability.

Mesa embodies and teaches the stages of evolution by which we grow through various stages of human attainment into our divinely appointed spiritual destiny. Rightly understood, *mesa* can be a tool for accomplishing the emergence in its user of a conscious, focused will as well as a deepened capacity for observation and intuitive attunement. When used correctly, the archetypal *mesa* can be a tool to expedite the growth and individualization of the soul-element or psychic being in the spiritual heart. And finally, *mesa* can help the fully evolved spiritual warrior to accomplish his or her heroic quest and to achieve a state of attainment which the ancient Greek philosophers called *apotheosis*.

The archetype of the Great Earth Mother found in Lemurian Jade is writ large in the *mesa's* seven Earth stones. According to the mythic paradigm, the Child-seed gestates and grows in the watery matrix (represented by the Water-element stones) until, at the time of birth it emerges as a separate human individual. Thus the incarnation of the god-presence begins a new quest under the appearance of a uniquely formed human life. In the *mesa* of power, the Fire stones express the dynamic qualities of the archetypal Hero, and the Air crystals represent the fullness of the archetypal Sage. Like the higher and lower ranges of a keyboard, the Hero and Sage capacities will come fully into play only when the soul has mastered its musical instrument, its microcosm.

The destiny of the inner child, the divine seed, is to become a victor in the adventure of consciousness which is life. To be differentiated from the watery matrix of the womb and to develop a separate personality is both a challenge and a sacred opportunity for this luminous soul-child as it awakens to the full possibilities of life in a human body. For each of us, birth is a difficult passage from the primal waters of the protective womb into the cold glare of the outer world. This abrupt transition brings the experience of division and isolation for the first time into our infancy's innocent bliss. But this experience of separation is the price we must all pay in order to grow and unfold divine capabilities in a human microcosm.

When the child experiences life outside the womb, there gradually develops an awareness of right and wrong, and the inner soul tries to bring about an awakening of aspiration to encourage progress in awareness. A child's eagerness to explore the physical world is evidence of this creative potential for growth. But the child's preferred way of learning is by play, not by classroom drills and exams. In this, the wisdom of the soul peeps through, perpetually unnoticed by the institutional hierarchy of our educational system. The modern forms of institutionalized classroom schooling only pave over the intuitive wisdom of our innocence and have the result of burying the freshness of childhood under the dull conformity of adult mental conditioning.

As it grows, each human child must develop his or her own independent will, and learn to choose what is good voluntarily, free of any external pressure. This initial separation from the biological mother, followed by experiences of developing self-will and occasional disobedience (or sin) is the price that we must all pay in order to mature. So it is that a child cultivates inner power sufficient to win increased freedom by exercising his or her capacity of conscious choice. This leads to the karma of experience, knowledge of the reality of spiritual darkness, awareness of the contrasting light of joy, as well as exaltation and suffering in all their permutations.

Thus it is that the inevitable stages of the journey of life arise one after another with unavoidable certainty. But when the divine spark of the soul begins to stir, the purpose of life becomes clearer and the need for inner development is strongly felt. In some, the quest matures to its fullest and much is achieved in the course of a single life, but in many the urge for transcendence is swallowed by the dissipating tendencies of karma and scattered by the pulls of binding desire.

The awakening mind gradually acquires the capacity and the means to communicate with the spiritual heart. The intuitive mind of the awakened child who has matured as an adult into a conscious spiritual seeker is then able to develop a capacity for attunement to realms of experience that lie beyond the scope of the five senses. Each of us will sense our inner soul-presence at some time or another, in this life or in some future incarnation, and it always comes in its own uniquely convincing way. For some, the inner soul whispers to the heart a song of loving intimacy with the Divine Mother. For others, it is experienced as a summons, an imperative need for self-transcendence, or as a summons to vanquish humanity's suffering – which is how the call was perceived by the Buddha.

If this longing for light flourishes, eventually the inner child can inspire in a spiritual seeker a course of development that is in some measure heroic. Artists, politicians, scientists, writers, saints, soldiers and explorers have all in their own ways achieved heroic stature. The immature hero often expresses himself or herself as a rebel, an agitator, a cynic or an anarchist. However, when awareness evolves to greater clarity, it becomes evident that the demons and the hostile forces must first be conquered within ourselves, and only when we have achieved self mastery are we fit to lead others. The would-be hero comes to understand that it is necessary to slay his or her own devils, excise his or her own ghosts, and bring light to the dark corners of the personal microcosm, whether in the mind, vital or subconscious parts of the being. In the slaying of inner demons, the power of the spirit is clearly seen to be greater than the power of the ego or the human mind, and the hero progresses slowly and surely into a higher kind of power which is that of the archetypal Sage.

The famous conqueror Napoleon is reported to have said: "There are only two powers in the world, the spirit and the sword. In the long run, the sword will always be conquered by the spirit." (*Napoleon*, Emil Ludwig, pg. 155) A true hero must know when it is necessary to *use* the sword, but not be so foolish as to *live and die by the sword*. The power of the spirit is the power of divine love, which the ancient Greeks called *eros*. When *eros* becomes the driving force behind our worldly activities, and the awakened centre of our microcosm, all can be completed successfully. This supremely spiritual power manifests as the archetypal child's sweet dreams, the hero-warrior's struggles and conquests, and the sage's cosmic wisdom. But in all these stages of attainment the Mother, progenetrix of archetypes, is the real doer; by the power of her energy and the ultimate wisdom of her cosmic plan we live and evolve. Crystal *mesa* is form and substance of her vision, immanent manifestation of her power. Flowing from its crystalline centre, the archetypal *mesa* expresses her transformative action in the four domains of Earth, Water, Fire and Air. Each of these is a playground of the gods, a field of experience on the way home to the eternal Source, and a sacred space for completing the alchemical work of self-transcendence.

Mesa teaching, whether it follows the pattern explained in this book or is based on some other localized tradition, exists to facilitate the Mother's work of harmonizing and transmuting the human microcosm. The mysteries and powers of the cosmically resonant *mesa* can only be adequately valued or wisely applied at a certain stage of maturity in the quest. They are a revelation of the Muse to the Sage, a warrior-will for the Hero, and a gift from the Mother to the Child for his full awakening.

The desire to own and use a *mesa* will arise when the soul senses the need of some divine help to go forward in its progress. The discovery of the *mesa* may be just the answer to surmount a blockage or to strengthen the body and spirit for a coming time of challenge and testing, and it may often be discovered at the most opportune moment. We may learn about the significance of *mesa* by picking up just the right book, seemingly by chance, or perhaps by meeting a teacher, or experiencing a healing session with a *mesa*-user. Initially, the awareness of what a *mesa* is, and how it can be important, may surface as a vague impulse to gather crystals and work with them. Through this interest in crystals, the soul eventually becomes conscious at the mental level of the precious gifts which Mother Earth can provide her beloved child as sustenance for the journey of life.

From whatever source it may come, when knowledge of the meaning and use of a *mesa* eventually does develop, the seeker has within reach a marvelous tool, a progressive method, a field of study and a set of allies for anchoring higher light in the conditions of life. The inner Hero has a mythic magical gift to conquer enemies and to complete a triumphal journey homeward to Source, and the archetypal inner Sage has a teaching device to bring ever-deeper and wider revelations to the fore.

As the soul matures, the four great archetypes (Mother, Child, Hero and Sage) come fully to life and begin to exert their invisible influence. The resonant *mesa*, skillfully used, becomes a home and temple to embody and express the divine action of these great beings. They are at first sleeping godheads in the microcosm of our own body-mind. But later, through the use of crystals-in-pattern, they convey their powers to the aspiring initiate to energize the spiritual quest. Then, the journey of the soul from Mother to Child, from Child to Hero and from Hero to Sage acquires a relentless momentum, and the human life is carried from height to height in self-transcending attainment. *Mesa* is then understood in its true depth and power, as a reservoir of endless wisdom, a living temple whose creative possibilities are limited only by the scope of the seeker's own will and imagination.

The original powers associated with *mesa* magic were called the Titans by the Greeks, beings that were supplanted by the Olympian gods at a later point in history. These great primal beings have different names and forms in various ancient cultures. For example, in the earliest mythic records of India, the Vedas, we read that Indra slew his father and dragged him away from his mother, Aditi, by the feet. The original mother of the gods, Aditi, represents infinite consciousness. Indra's heroic deed enabled Surya, the Sun god, light of infinite consciousness, to rise up into the heavens and dispel darkness and falsehood. Indra is clearly a hero-god.

In Egyptian lore, Atum is the source. From him came Shu, the Air, Tefnut, the Fire, Geb, the Earth and Nut the celestial waters. The union of Geb, the Earth God, and Nut, the Sky Goddess, produced five offspring: Osiris, Arueris (the elder Horus), Seth, Isis and Nephthys who, along with the four elemental gods were called the Ennead, the Nine Gods and Goddesses. Osiris was slain by Seth. But Horus, the son of Isis, successfully battled Seth, and helped to restore the orderly reign of Isis and Osiris.

In Greek mythology, the Titans were children born from a union of Gaia, the Earth Mother and Ouranos, the Sky Father. They sided with their mother against the harshness of Ouranos, and under the leadership of Cronos they attacked and castrated him with a sickle. Then, when Ouranos died, Cronos assumed his power. He married his sister Rhea, another Earth Mother, just as the Egyptian Great Mother, Isis, had married Osiris. From the union of Cronos and Rhea was born Zeus who became the leader of the Olympian pantheon of classical history. In the mythologies of ancient India, Mesopotamia, Egypt and Greece, we see a repeated pattern of a hero-god slaying a tyrant (often a father) in order to initiate a new era of light.

The Ennead of the Egyptians, the gods of Vedic India and the Titans of the Greeks are representative of humanity's most ancient myth and magic. These elder gods reigned supreme when the institutions of tribe and clan were still dominant. The triumph of the gods over the Titans signals a period of history when the written word was gaining ground, a time when empires were outgrowing humanity's tribal roots, and the age-old customs of matriarchy were disintegrating under the impact of patriarchal sky-gods.

The Earth-energies associated with *mesa* were centrally important to humanity at the dawn of recorded history, as they still are to tribal peoples throughout the world. Thus, the archetypes of crystal *mesa* can be understood more clearly by glimpsing them at work in the very earliest mythologies where the Earth Mother is supremely important and patriarchal hierarchies are not yet dominant. The imprint of the past is still present in our collective unconscious and in our DNA. It has power which can be awakened and used when rightly understood.

EGYPTIAN ARCHETYPES

Isis was the name of the great goddess in Egypt, where she was worshipped from pre-dynastic times until well into the Christian era. As Anne Baring and Jules Cashford point out in *The Myth of The Goddess*, she has many aspects:

> *She was, variously, the milk-giving cow goddess; goddess of the serpents of the primeval waters; the star goddess Sirius, who brought about the inundation of the Nile; the fertile pig goddess; the bird goddess; goddess of the underworld, whose breath gave life to the dead; goddess of the Tree of Life, offering the food and water of immortality; goddess of the words of power, the tender, caring mother of Horus, her son; and goddess of the throne upon whose lap the king sat as her infant child in the image of all humanity. (pg. 225)*

All of this and more is encompassed in the Mother archetype, Lemurian Jade, in the crystal *mesa*.

It takes closer scrutiny to see Osiris as a primeval child archetype. He and Isis were brother and sister, and they loved each other even in their mother's womb before birth. But later, when Osiris had been killed and dismembered by Seth, it was Isis who traveled far and wide to find and re-assemble the parts of his body, thereby becoming his mother and the means of his rebirth. It is thus that Osiris can be considered the child of the Earth-Mother, the child of Isis. Some versions of this story record that Isis buried the pieces of Osiris's body in the Earth, a mythic action that accords well with the widespread ancient belief that the most precious and divine gems of the Earth are physical relics of the body of a god.

But there are other striking reasons for associating Osiris with the archetype of the child. This god was understood by the ancient Egyptians to come alive with the rising of the Nile, and to die with its falling, being therefore in one sense a Water god. 'Thou are the Nile ... gods and men live from thy outflow,' says one ancient Egyptian inscription. A very distinctively childlike attribute of Osiris is that he often seems to be helpless and passive, needing to be rescued by Isis more than once, and being constantly nurtured by her. Horus fights Osiris's battles with Seth; he himself relies on the ministrations of Isis. This is part of his watery, childlike nature, in contrast to Horus who is heroic Fire and courageous will in action. Consistent with the traditional powers of the element Water, the divine Osiris imparts to his devotees the gift of revival or resurrection, while Horus gives them power for victory.

Osiris and Horus represent two different kinds of pathways. The path of Osiris is cyclical, gradual, moving through the slow rounds of reincarnation, whereas the path of Horus is the quest of the fiery warrior, the archetypal Hero who transcends all obstacles, including ego, to move beyond matter and resurrection into eternal life in the Divine. These are examples of the constrasting solar and lunar paths we mentioned earlier, and similar examples can be found in the more extensive traditions of ancient India. In all these ancient paths, the principle of sacrifice was centrally important. In *Dreams of Isis*, Normandi Ellis explains it this way:

> *The ancient hieroglyph for adoration is a gesture of opening that signified both the receipt of divine grace and the offering of the self. When a man or woman stands before God with arms opened wide, the heart is vulnerable to penetration. Knowing that an almighty God wields swords of light that may wound and stab us, we yet offer ourselves fully for the sacrifice. We allow God to slay us, to kill that which is "other" in us, then to enter and inhabit our form in order for God to know the Divine through us, to resurrect and reconstruct us as changed creatures, as bodies more fully filled with the Light of God. (pg. 22)*

The theme of slaying and resurrecting is of course central to the myth of Osiris, who is a sacrificial victim. In the myth of Horus, the Hero-archetype is the slayer and the forces of obstruction and chaos

(Set) are his target. As humans, we have access to many sources of transformational energy, including the Earth Mother's crystals and the primal archetypes of our *mesa*, but all growth requires that we first sacrifice, or heroically slay, the idea that we are a fixed, definable identity. We do this in order to experience our essential self, which we come to know not as a "thing," but as lived process. With this realization firmly in place, our births and becomings are endless, as the elders of the Vedas and the priests of Egypt proclaimed so long ago.

Osiris is also intimately related to the lunar mystery of rebirth that is revealed in the skies when, at the time of the New Moon, the Moon's light that has been hidden for three days appears again in the resurrected sickle Moon. Plutarch explained that the years of the life of Osiris were 28 in total (in other words, a lunar month), and that the dismemberment of his body into fourteen parts refers allegorically to the days of the waning moon. Each lunar month, the dismembered light of the Moon is reassembled by Isis during three days of darkness at the time of the New Moon, and Osiris is figuratively reborn in the skies above. Isis is thus the mother of Osiris's rebirth, and he is her son-lover.

The 28 stones of the crystal *mesa*, plus the four archetypal stones for Mother, Child, Hero and Sage constitute, from the Egyptian perspective, a symbolic body of Osiris. The crystal *mesa* heart-stone can, according to this mythic perspective, be seen to stand for his spine, the Egyptian *Djed* pillar, a column, which unites Heaven and Earth. This pillar was a part of the ancient ceremonies honouring Osiris, and it was raised at the culmination of his rites to celebrate the beginning of the New Year. The lifting of this column, which is also a symbolic Tree of Life, symbolizes the victory of life over the forces of death and decay. As a symbolic backbone of Osiris, the *Djed* pillar is appropriately present at the heart of the *mesa*, connecting the eternal life of Heaven above to the cyclic alternations of life and death on Earth below. The power of resurrection that flows from Isis to Osiris (as the ancient Egyptians might express it) is thus inherent in the very structure of the crystal *mesa*.

Osiris's body is the body of a god, having been reconstituted by the divine power of the Mother, as we see in this New Kingdom hymn, where Isis is speaking to her sister Nephthys:

'Ah, Sister!' says Isis to Nephthys,
'This is our brother,

Come let us lift up his head,
Come, let us (rejoin) his bones,
Come, let us reassemble his limbs,
Come, let us put an end to all his woe,
That, as far as we can help, he will weary no more.
May the moisture begin to mount for this spirit!
May the canals be filled through you!
May the names of the rivers be created through you!
Osiris, live!
Osiris, let the great Listless One arise!
I am Isis.'

As Baring and Cashford write:

The bond between Isis and Osiris is one of the creative forces of life,
for together they are the universal soul of growth. If he is the flood-
ing of the Nile, then she is the earth that the Nile covers, and from
this union, as Plutarch said, the Egyptians make Horus to be born.

The Myth of the Goddess, pg. 236

Horus is a supremely heroic child of Isis, a fiery light generated from the watery seed of Osiris. He does battle with Seth, and defeats him, thus expressing the victorious clash of light with darkness and disorder. Horus is often referred to in the ancient Egyptian papyri as a being of light and fire, a warrior who is victorious.

On the other hand, in ancient Egyptian mythology, it is Thoth who embodies the archetype of the Sage. He is very much a lunar being whose insight is called on at various points of the Isis-Osiris tale. Thoth is the scribe, the guardian of the mysteries, the spokes-man of the gods, the holder of magical power and arcane knowl-edge, the teacher of both men and deities, the seasoned counselor. By the Greeks, he was called Hermes, and his teachings constitute the corpus of Hermetic wisdom. Iamblichus noted that the earli-est philosophers and mystics ascribed their own writings to Hermes (Thoth) as though he had written them in person. The cult of Thoth was widespread throughout ancient Egypt, but it became centred in Alexandria after the great library was established there by the pha-raohs of the Ptolemy dynasty. As the archetypal Sage, it is Thoth who keeps a balance between light and dark so that the Great Mother's work may unfold in an orderly way through the cycles of time.

There is a Hermetic nostrum that states: "The Above comes from Below, and the Below from Above – the work of the miracle of the One." The Below came from Above when Heaven impregnated Earth's womb with celestial energies, an event frequently mentioned in myths from all around the world. These heavenly energies crystallized into the precious and semi-precious gems, (quartz being the equivalent of solidified water, according to the ancients). On the day when the Sky fell, the Egyptians wrote, "Heaven was turned into the underworld." The two mountains of Heaven and Earth were fused together, one inside the other. The Earth Mother continuously gestates new life in her dark womb, time passes and the gems ripen their latent god-powers in the Underworld.

With the descent of Osiris into the bowels of the Earth, the Underworld became, according to the sages of Egypt, a home to Heaven. Understanding this, it becomes easier to make sense of the Egyptian idea that the Sky is to be found underneath the ground. For example, in the Coffin Texts, the deceased king declares:

> I have crossed over the paths of Rostau, the underworld,
> whether on water or on land, these are the paths of Osiris;
> they are in the limit of the Sky (the underworld). As for him
> who knows this spell for going down into them, he himself is a
> god, in the suite of Thoth; he will go down to any sky to which
> he wishes to go down.
>
> Coffin Texts, Spell 146
> R.O. Faulker, The Ancient Egyptian Book of the Dead, 1985.

In other worlds, one may explore the various worlds of experience by entering through a gateway from the underworld, the resting place of the body of Osiris. *Mesa* is, among other things, a gateway constituted from the most precious particles of the underworld, from relics of the body of a god. It is, additionally, an altar (the word *mesa* means that in Spanish), a temple, a microcosm, and a cosmic mirror containing all the *tattwic* energies. Alan Alford comments on this vision of the ancients as follows:

> The sacred marriage rituals of the ancients tell the same story – of
> life beginning on Earth following the impregnation of Earth by a
> falling Heaven. Hence the birth of the Titans to Gaea. Hence the

birth of Horus to Isis. Hence the eleusis of the divine child to Holy Brimo… In order to fully appreciate the ancient way of thinking, one must look upon the landscape of the Earth and observe everything that is green, trees, bushes, plants, even blades of grass. Then imagine that all of these things had formerly been growing in Heaven. Then imagine all of these things falling to Earth – not in their fully grown form, obviously, but rather as seeds. Imagine, then, that these seeds entered the Womb of the Earth, and then imagine them being watered by the Great Flood which came down from Heaven. Finally, imagine these seeds sprouting forth into the world above, transforming the surface of the Earth into a verdant paradise. This, I am convinced, was how the ancients came to regard their world. After life came death; but after death came rebirth and new life. Heaven was reincarnated on Earth, and hence all life was saved. And Earth owed everything to Heaven, the source of the seeds of life.

When The Gods Came Down, pg–. 91

THE GREEK AND MESOPOTAMIAN ARCHETYPES

The most ancient stratum of Greek mythology is reflected in the story of Gaia and Uranus (Ouranos). She was the goddess of Earth, and he the Sky god. He showered down his fertile waters and impregnated her body, leading to the birth of the twelve Titans, the three Cyclopes and the three hundred-armed giants. These offspring were displeasing to Uranus and had to remain hidden inside the body of Mother Earth. The youngest of the Titans, Cronos, attacked and castrated his father, becoming the new king and consort.

In this myth, it is explicitly stated that Uranus (the name means, literally, 'Mountain of Heaven') came down and impregnated the womb of Earth with celestial seed. The result was children born in an underworld, or planetary womb. The name of the giant Gyges, for example, means "Earth-born," but in fact all the Titans and giants are Earth-born. It is an intriguing hint about the pedigree of the crystalline gems which constitute the sacred *mesa*.

Another Earth-born god, Eros, escaped from an egg which had been laid in the "womb of darkness." He mounted up into the air on golden wings, setting hearts aflame with his fiery darts. His power was to become ultimately the most important in the accomplishment of the Mother's supreme vision for planet Earth.

What are these Earth-gods born of celestial influence? Traditionally, the precious and semi-precious minerals and crystals were believed to be the most celestial parts of Mother Earth's body. This tradition is well known in both ancient and modern India, but it was also common in the various civilizations that rose and fell on the shores of the Mediterranean, and in Mesopotamia. Jewels were considered heaven-seeds, relics of the body of Heaven that had fallen to Earth, subsumed into the womb of the Earth-Mother. It is not, therefore, a big leap for the ancients to have considered precious crystals to be Earth-gods in physical form, and to have made them the preserve of kings, priests and temples. Only kings and priests could wear the most precious gems, and the rules concerning their use were codified by longstanding precedent. The famous breastplate of the Jewish temple priests, likely borrowed from earlier precedents among the Canaanites and Phoenicians, is but one example of this. Being the relic of a god, a precious stone had to be placed in sacred ownership, and in ancient times kings were considered 'sons of Heaven,' the term frequently appearing in the list of kingly titles.

In the mythology of Mesopotamia we find parallels to this theme, as Alan Alford writes in *When the Gods Came Down* (pg. 49)

Azag, the evil Titan-like demon, (who) repaired to his 'mountain' in Heaven, which was then destroyed by Ninurta. Immediately, a huge heap of stones was released, and swept over the Earth, creating a 'great wall' upon the land. A floodwave of might waters came too – originating from 'ice, long accumulating in the mountain on the other side.' Thus was the Earth fecundated, and turned into a garden of paradise. The theme is clear. All of these legends were describing the Earth as being like a giant Womb – or perhaps we should say a Womb-for-giants. The seed fell into the Womb not from the clouds, but from the heights of Heaven, with a force which caused the seed to penetrate and enter the Womb. In Hebrew legend, the seed was the Sons-of-God. In Greek legend, the seed was Uranus – God himself. In Mesopotamian legend, the seed was the water or stones from Heaven. The seed then engendered life within the Womb.

The legends describe how a heavenly brick was placed inside the womb of Mother Earth, a brick which became the foundation of life. This brick was called a 'lapis lazuli brick,' and Ninharsag was the goddess of Earth into whose womb it was placed. In fact one of her epithets was derived from this heavenly brick, and she was sometimes referred to as 'lapis lazuli brick.' The lapis lazuli 'brick' which came from Heaven to Earth was to lie in the dark terrestrial womb for seven days. As Alford writes:

> *The penultimate line of the text (which) states that the 'vexed ones' would rejoice in the 'House of the One in Travail.' The vexed ones were, of course the Anunnaki-gods, whose workload was to be borne by the creation of man – hence their rejoicing here, and their earlier kissing of Ninharsag's feet. The key point, however, is that these Anunnaki-gods lived in the underworld – i.e. inside the Earth. Therefore, the "House of the One in Travail' must also have been the inside of the Earth. And the One who was in travail – Mami, or Ninharsag – was thus the Earth herself – the Mother-Womb. (pg. 47)*

A Sumerian poet describes the union of Heaven and Earth in detail:

> *Smooth, big Earth made herself resplendent,*
> *beautified her body joyously.*
> *Wide Earth bedecked her body with*
> *precious metal and lapis lazuli,*
> *Adorned herself with diorite, chalcedony,*
> *and shiny carnelian.*
> *Heaven arrayed himself in a wig of verdure,*
> *stood up in princeship.*
> *Holy Earth, the virgin, beautified herself for Holy Heaven.*
> *N.S. Kramer, History Begins at Sumer, pp. 303-4*

Clearly, the precious and semi-precious minerals within the womb of Earth are a heavenly infusion, a seeding of gods. Mankind is one fruit of this celestial impregnation, a child of the marriage of Heaven and Earth. According to Mesopotamian myths, and many other mythic traditions including those of the Inca, in whose lands the importance of the *mesa* is long established, humanity originated below the surface of the Earth! The evolution and growth of crystalline gems in the darkness of the netherworld is one manifestation of the Earth-Mother's work, as she labours in her womb to accomplish the development of earthly gods.

Mesa wisdom concerns the use of the Earth's precious crystalline relics to awaken in the human microcosm the latent divine beings and forces. The ancient myths of Mesopotamia had this awakening of the human to the fullness of his heroic potential as their central theme, well illustrated by the tale of Gilgamesh.

When Gilgamesh comes to a great subterranean sea beyond which lies the land of the gods, he is told by Siduri, who guards the access to the underworld, that normally it is only Shamash-Utu, the Sun God, who can cross the celestial waters. Siduri advises Gilgamesh to seek out the boatman Urshanabi, who alone might be able to help him. Unfortunately, Gilgamesh had damaged a precious device needed for the journey, something which the ancient clay tablets refer to as "the Stone Things." Urshanabi explained it thus: "the Stone Things bear me along, that I might not have to touch the waters of death." In other words, the "stone things" or "stone images" (it is translated differently by J. Gardner and A. Heidel) were a means of travelling the cosmic ocean and approaching the domain of the gods. What could these stones be, that had power to carry a seeker beyond the celestial waters, and could they work in any way similar to the stones of a *mesa*?

The Babylonian deity Marduk was a hero-god who battled and destroyed the goddess Tiamat. He then buried a large part of her body in the Earth. He built a heavenly realm in the Apsu (the underworld), designed to recreate a physical image of the 'mountain of heaven.' Thereafter, three hundred of the gods were lifted up to the celestial heavens, to become known as the *Igigi*-gods, and another three hundred remained within the domains of Earth, to be known as the Anunnaki gods. These gods of the Earth were physical; they had material bodies. Marduk constructed a temple called *E-sag-ila*, in which all of the gods, both earthly and celestial, could meet. This temple was described by the Greek writer Herodotus who visited it in the 5th century BC. The underground portion of the temple was an alchemical power-spot, a place to harness the Earthly elements and release the Heavenly elements of body mind and spirit so that a hero, or a divinely destined human, could ascend to the sky and live eternally in a body fit for life in a celestial abode.

To reach the heavenly realm was also a preoccupation of the Egyptians, even more so than the Sumerians and Babylonians. Their texts make reference to *Neter-Khert*, the "Mountain-Land of God." Both in Mesopotamia and Egypt, it was customary to refer to Heaven and Earth as 'Mountains,' and in both cultures there was a belief that the two domains were mirror images of one another, cosmic twins. Whether we consider Seth dismembering Osiris, or Marduk destroying Tiamat, or Cronos slaying Ouranos, or Indra slaying his father, the essential pattern remains the same. *A heavenly being is first destroyed, and then planted into the body of Earth. Because the divine body has been seeded into the earthly womb of the Mother, rebirth becomes a possibility for human beings.* The womb of the Earth Mother is the place of rebirth, as we read in this Sumerian Temple Hymn:

> *Mother Nintu, the lady of form-giving,*
> *(Is) working in a dark place, the heart-womb,*
> *To give birth to kings, to tie on the rightful tiara,*
> *To give birth to lords, to place the crown on their heads.*
> *(It) is in her hands.*
> T. Jacobsen, *The Treasures of Darkness, p. 107*

A "king," of course, is a widely used metaphor in ancient literature, and it means one who has achieved mastery of this terrestrial plane of consciousness, equivalent to a Sage.

In the underworld, the Earth Mother generates a higher and more perfect kind of life from the seed of the gods that has come down from Heaven. Here, she works her magic in darkness, giving birth to the divine child, to human heroes, would-be kings, as well as prophets, priests and leaders of the people. Here the bond uniting Isis and her child Horus is woven, the spell joining Inanna to Dumuzi. Here arises the transformative magic of all Earth Mothers who have given birth to divine or semi-divine beings whose tales are recounted in the myths and legends of ancient times.

A Mesopotamian temple and an Egyptian pyramid were gateways not only to the heavenly realms above, but equally important to the *Apsu*, the underworld, the womb of the Earth Mother. In the halls of the kingdom under the Earth, according to Mesopotamian tradition, gods and goddesses lived in magnificent palaces composed of precious jewels, the foremost of which was considered to be lapis lazuli. The Sumerian Sun god himself, brilliant Utu (Shamash), had a beard of lapis lazuli. When he was not traversing the skies from East to West, he was journeying through the underworld to the place where he would be resurrected at dawn. Similarly, in other traditions such as those of Egypt and India, it was only by passing through the subterranean domain of regeneration in death that a human being could find the gateway to eternal celestial life.

The Sumerian ziggurat was designed to suggest a seven-story mountain, and was considered to be a symbolic image of the seven planetary heavens, a meeting place of Heaven, Earth, and the Underworld. Such an edifice would normally be located at the centre of a Sumerian city, which was itself laid out and designed to be a microcosm of cosmological pattern. Deep within the inner sanctum of the ziggurat, in the holy of holies, would be a sacred object that embodied or expressed the essence of the sacred reality. We have no record of what the most sacred relic of such a temple might be, but we do know that in the holy of holies at Ur extensive use was made of lapis lazuli, the very stone that embodies the Sage archetype in the Crystal Mesa.

Even to this day, precious gems and gold are installed in the sacred pagodas and *chedis* of Southeast Asia and Tibet, as well as sacred reliquaries of saints and holy men. Many of these, unfortunately, have been opened and looted. But new ones are constantly being built, and endowed with treasures of precious and semi-precious stones. I have had the privilege of attending full moon ceremonies in Thailand where hundreds of people would circumambulate a chedi with lighted candles. From the perspective of Crystal Yoga, they were also interacting with the energy and consciousness of the precious and semi-precious stones within its walls, the hidden treasure of myth and fable.

Like all holy architecture, modelled on the pattern of the cosmos, and endowed with precious gems, *mesa* expresses the sacred cosmos in miniature. It is an assembly, a sacred pattern of living energies composed of precious and semi-precious gems and crystals. Symbolically, the clear quartz sphere which is the centre of a crystal *mesa* stands for the timeless 'cosmic mountain'; it is the holy of holies, the inmost sacred relic of the temple. It is *Djed* to the Egyptians, *Aditi* to the Vedic seers. It can represent a column of light that reaches high above into the skies, and deep below into the subterranean depths, but equally it comprises an alchemical sacred space for uniting Earth and Heaven in holy marriage.

From the brief account given so far, you can see that a crystal *mesa* epitomizes the entire sacred cosmology which is reflected in the mythology and religion of the ancient world.

TWO STREAMS OF TRADITION

Whereas the most ancient *mesa* teachings evolved in tribal settings, the Hermetic magical tradition, which we begin to hear about in late Egyptian and Hellenic history, evolved within the boundaries of what historians have called 'civilization.' These two streams, the prehistoric and the Hermetic, are the primary sources of the Western Mystery Tradition.

Although the sacred bundle or *mesa* is best known in the indigenous cultures of North and South America, it has counterparts elsewhere. As John Matthews writes in The Celtic Shaman:

> *Our earliest records tell of shamans carrying a bag or pouch*
> *containing various objects of special personal significance.*
> *Stones, twigs, shells, fossils or bones, for example, are imbued*
> *with magical energy, or become symbolic reference points. In*
> *Celtic tradition the crane bag has enormous significance in this*
> *respect... the crane bag contains the shaman's tool-kit, with*
> *which she or he works as diviner, healer and walker between*
> *the worlds. (pgs. 112-113)*

The cosmic patterning and wisdom that a *mesa* can embody are universal, for the energies associated with crystals are not restricted to any family of gods or any particular culture, whether Egyptian, Greek, Celtic or Andean. What we can say, however, is that the mind of primordial man saw and felt living powers and presences in nature from which the earliest magic and mythology evolved. By the time that the Assyrian, Hittite and Olympian gods had achieved ascendancy in the Mediterranean and Mesopotamian regions, humanity's tribal consciousness, and the capacity for instinctive attunement to unseen presences, was already on the wane. Increasingly, in urban settings in particular, human interaction with the gods came to be mediated by powerful colleges of priests, and religious rituals came to be completely dominated by temple hierarchies. The Iliad and Odyssey of Homer record a period of history when the gods had already departed from Earth to live as distant, mountaintop archetypes.

The energies associated with a crystal *mesa* relate to primordial, chthonic powers of Mother Earth, which the ancients believed to be celestial relics seeded into the terrestrial matrix from the skies above. Although the archetypal beings were receding from humanity's direct experience by the time of the Sumerians and Hittites, we can surmise that the contact with Earth-spirits endured much longer in the forests of Northern Europe. For example, in Celtic Scotland and Ireland, and in the tribal cultures of North and South America there is still strong evidence of this connection. I have had personal experience of these traditions in remote areas of the Andes, in Peru and in Malaysia. Similarly there are many written accounts from Central America, and the North American Southwest, as well as rural Mexico that testify to the ongoing life of ancient archetypes. The popular books of Carlos Castaneda reflect this ongoing tradition. It is in such regions that the knowledge and use of the sacred *mesa* has been kept alive.

The ancient tree of Earth-wisdom had almost died out when colonialism was at its height, but then new shoots began to sprout. Now, the Andean region and the American Southwest are places where ancient spiritual currents of power and knowledge are being restored. Many seekers are drawn to Cusco and to Sedona for the renewal of this connection, some consciously and others not quite fully aware of what they are seeking. One meets many such people when traveling.

The native tradition, which originated before the dawn of written history, is re-emerging in the guise of modern wicca and neo-paganism, whereas the Hermetic tradition, which we first hear of in classical antiquity, managed to maintain a tenuous continuity through the Dark Ages, with flashes of renewal in the Renaissance and the Nineteenth Century. Hermeticism is still very much alive and growing at the present time in a number of well known groups such as the Rosicrucians and Masons. There are also quite a few less well known magical circles such as the OTO and the Order of the Golden Dawn who work with magical energy and the primal archetypes.

Mesa derives from native tradition and ancestral wisdom, embodying an instinctive respect for Earth, the elemental forces of nature, the Great Mother, oral tradition, and the devotion of many an unrecorded, solitary shamanic practitioner. Hermetic tradition, on the other hand, is more amply documented in writing, has roots in Greek philosophy and Ptolemaic Egyptian magic, is inseparably associated with alchemy and cabala, and has tended to spawn circles or lodges of practitioners who follow secretive and exclusive fixed systems. Franz Bardon and Israel Regardie were two of the best known Hermetic mages of the twentieth century, and study of their writing sheds much light on the fundamental principles of magic, which in turn helps us to understand the full potential of the *mesa*. They both gave importance to the ancient Egyptian traditions of mythology, cosmology and sacred ritual.

A crystal *mesa* is a microcosmic model of Heaven and Earth. It is a sacred bundle, a portable power spot, an alchemical cauldron where the visible and invisible worlds can meet. In the archetypal and mythic patterns underlying a true crystal *mesa* we may discover the essence of temples, pyramids and ziggurats, the unifying pattern of myths from many lands, including Greece, Egypt, India and Mesopotamia, not to mention the Celts, Incas, Maya and lesser known tribal groups of the North American Southwest. All of these wisdom traditions foster and sustain the life of the spirit through sacred rituals with a timeless symbolism. The navel of creation, the Tree of Life, the sacred *Djed* column of Osiris, the pillar of light that joins this world to the Heavens above, these and many other keys to the primal power are symbolically present in the Crystal Mesa.

In the epic of the hero Gilgamesh, a climax is reached when the protagonist arrives at a garden made of precious jewels. In the description of this garden, the ancient clay tablets record that the carnelian stones bore vines, and the lapis lazuli bore lush fruit and foliage. Unfortunately, the record of what happened next has been destroyed. Yet it is clear that the place of heavenly attainment is a garden of jewels. *Mesa* is this garden. Its precious and semi-precious stones embody our yet unrealized potential.

The journey into full and deep knowledge of its working is an adventure as full of magic and wonder as those of the heroes of old.

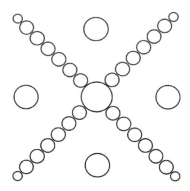

TRANSVERSE CROSS LAYOUT

This layout evolves from the Abbreviated Moon Layout. First, you work with either your archetype stones or your Spirit Element stones, and place each of the four at the correct distance from the Source Stone. This is done by moving each stone in turn closer and father from the Source Stone, back and forth repetitively until the stone just feels "right" at a certain distance. There will be a distance that seems to feel right in terms of where you are with that stone and distance from Source. The Transverse Cross layout allows you to create linkages between contiguous elements. For example, if you want to facilitate the co-operative action of Fire and Earth, you would look at all the 28 stones of the main body of the *mesa* and feel which stone might do this job. Try moving it between Spirit Earth and Spirit Fire, back and forth, until you sense the correct distance of placement. Then look at your remaining stones and see if there is another one that should be put to work in a similar fashion. You may end up with three or a maximum of four stones that can bridge and interconnect the two chosen elements. Their distances and placement will be a matter of intuitive discernment as described. The stones you place between the Spirit Element stones will balance their action within your own microcosm if the placement flows from that intent. The stones you place between the Spirit Element stones will balance their action within your own microcosm if the placement flows from that intent.

THE POWER OF PLACE

The understanding of the power of place is an extremely important component of the ancient wisdom-tradition. This tradition prevailed in large parts of China, India, the Near East and Central and South America for at least several thousand years before the Christian era. However, some esoteric teachings trace a continuity which goes back to the times of Atlantis (prior to 10,000 BC) and even beyond to ancient Lemuria and the land of Mu. Hints of this are everywhere. For example, the timelines given by Manetho for the dynasties of the Egyptian Pharaohs suggest a degree of antiquity far beyond what conventional academics can understand or accept. And Plato's account of Atlantis is something many professional historians find disturbing to their academic paradigm.

The masters of old believed that each component of the cosmos had a special position, which corresponded to its function within the pattern-of-the-whole. A planet or a person could not serve its purpose in the total scheme of things if it was displaced from its correct location. This way of thinking contributed to the rigid stratification of social classes such as the caste system of India, and from our modern point of view this result was undesirably restrictive. The relationship of Earth and Heaven was at the centre of this ancient cosmology, and cosmic harmony was the ideal toward which society and individuals were expected to aspire. For much of our past history, the good of the collective came ahead of the good of the individual, and people thought of themselves not as citizens of the world so much as members of a clan, tribe, kingdom or race.

The sages of the distant past believed that the movement of the stars and planets in the firmament provides humanity with a teaching about the nature of time and place. The understanding of what Heaven has to say to Earth was summarized in the science of astrology. When an object in the skies or on Earth is out of place, disharmony results, and disharmony can lead to disaster. What we refer to as objects in space, of course, they saw as divine or semi-divine beings, not "things," but living powers capable of affecting the destiny of Earth and its inhabitants. The ancients were very concerned with maintaining harmony on Earth, and they developed a profound understanding of esoteric ways and means to accomplish this. The prehistoric stone structures of Great Britain such as Avesbury and Stonehenge are relics of this desire that the ancients had to make the landscape reflect a more perfect harmony which, when they looked up, they saw writ large in the skies. The *mesa* is another primal technology (along with the stone circles, talismans pyramids, etc.) of right relation to Source, being used from Lemurian times right up to the present in the Americas. These and other streams of arcane wisdom such as geomancy, numerology and divination were developed to understand and adapt the human microcosm to the celestial energies and thus create conditions in which consciousness could evolve, and social stability, could be assured. The ultimate goal was complete integration and alignment of all aspects of Earth with the power and presence of the Divine. However, only the Sages and spiritual teachers had the complete picture in focus, and only they had the capacity to effect this plan for society as a whole.

In the ancient wisdom tradition, the Sun was understood to embody and manifest the light of spirit for this solar system. The Moon, on the other hand, governed and influenced the journey of the soul in time and space, a journey through matter and darkness and a return to the oneness with the original Source. The phases of the Moon were archetypal markers of the soul's journey through time's domains of light and darkness. From the Moon our earliest ancestors derived measure and law, cyclic pattern and the creative impulse of the Muse. The details of this are explored in great depth in my book, *The Primal Runes* (2005). There are four important phases in the waxing and waning of the Moon's light that extend through a lunar month of approximately 28 days. The New Moon is a time of darkness when the spark of light and life is buried deep in the womb of latent possibility (Earth). The First Quarter is the time when the

Moon's face first begins to have more light than darkness, a time of progress, energy and illumination (Fire). In terms of direction, this corresponds to the rising sun in the East. The Full Moon (Air) expresses the ascendancy of light, consciousness, power and fortune. The Moon is at the maximum yang of its power, and this highest position is considered to be the apogee, or height, and thus expressed by the element Air. The Third Quarter is a waning moon where darkness comes to dominate light and the power of expression recedes into the mystery of the watery womb (Water). Water seeks the lowest place and comes to rest on the bosom of Earth.

Through cycles of light and dark, the soul grows and evolves until its spark of spirit can shine forth powerfully and achieve a divine or semi-divine expression. Eventually, by completing the journey of return to Source, the questing human soul becomes capable of a transmutation in consciousness, an *apotheosis* as the Greeks would call it, resulting in a godlike state of attainment. One who evolves to this height of awareness may have miraculous or prophetic gifts and may live on in human memory as a sage, king or folk hero. In ancient times, and even now the path to spiritual attainment or soul mastery can involve a series of initiations. The mystery schools where the masters taught were universities of higher consciousness for this process.

The science of placement flows from the dispensations of the lunar law. The lunar law pictures to us the phases of cyclic change that darkness and light do as they weave the destiny of all sublunar beings on planet Earth. The meaning of the Moon's phases was well understood by the teachers of old, because each of the 28 days in the lunar month had its own mythology and associations. The power of the various crystals in a cosmically ordered *mesa* can be seen through the lens of their placement according to this pattern. This ordering is very important if we wish the various components of the *mesa* of power to express their full capacity so that the *mesa* as a whole is a living power and magical presence. In face, when we place the stones of our *mesa* in this configuration, they can be assembled into a permanent crystal *mesa* talisman. There are several forms this can take, but the circular arrangement of crystals expresses the lunar law, and teaches the soul lessons that relate to karma and reincarnation.

In the 28 components of this *mesa*, (or 29 if we include the Heart Stone, and 33 if we add the 4 archetype stones) we have a pattern based on the stages of the Lunar Month. The Moon in its phases of waxing and waning reveals the archetypal language of light. There are four weeks, each of seven days in a lunar month. Sun day is spirit day; Monday is Moon day (a Yin energy); Tuesday is Mars day, or Yang day; Wednesday is Woden's day, representing the kingdom of Air, abode of the gods. Thursday is Thor's day, representing the fiery will of struggle raising Middle Earth upward in aspiration. Friday is Freya's day, named for the northern goddess of the feminine qualities, or Water; and lastly Saturn is the god of Saturday. Saturn governs the processes of contraction, crystallization, and the constricting laws and binding disciplines of earthly life. Water and Earth weeks are times of lunar darkness, while Fire and Air weeks are times when the light is greater than the darkness. The four quadrants of the *mesa* reflect this pattern which cyclically repeats itself in time. Fate is woven into moon-spun pattern of time which governs all living beings on earth, but the *mesa* of power is a tool for attaining mastery of these processes. By working with nature's archetypes, using the powers of ritual pattern, crystal structure and focused intent, one who masters the use of the *mesa* can transcend the pulls of darkness and heaviness on Earth and bring the heavenly energies into play here-below.

At the heart of creation is light, the energetic expression of consciousness. Light is the medium through which consciousness interacts with its various forms and levels of manifestation, and crystals can be considered as solidified light. According to one system, there are seven rays. The archetypal pattern of seven reveals the underlying structure of the language of light and suggests the form in which it manifests on this physical Earth. However, this is not the only perspective; a different system is based on twelve rays, each with its own powers and capacities of energy and consciousness. In this system there is a relationship between the twelve strands of DNA which is our future legacy, and the twelve rays of light. Again, some people work with a chakra-system in which there are seven main chakras, and others work with twelve. I would suggest that the twelve-fold system will come more and more into play, since it expresses fuller potential. Regardless of which system one prefers to use, the *mesa* is a tool for mastery of the potential of these rays. They encompass the whole of what Heaven has to say to Earth, and one who has incorporated them with conscious mastery into his or her microcosm is well on the way to becoming a Sage.

It is through attunement that we can learn the language of light. When we practice attunement, we still the mind as well as the nerves and their pulsing energy. We focus attention through our capacity for feeling-sensitivity; or, we can say, we focus the sensitivity of feeling through the lens of unwavering attention. The intuitive level of the mind, thus focused, can register the subtle impressions radiated by crystals. Crystals are the material architecture of light. Crystals write the geometric alphabet of light physically, in matter. We know that when the body and mind are completely relaxed, our DNA expands, and in this physically extended condition, it can assimilate and work with light in a more receptive way. Diana Cooper summarizes a good swath of current thinking on the twelve rays, chakras and DNA in chapters 13 through 16 of her new book, *Discover Atlantis* (2005), and it is well worth reading.

What is this feeling-sensitivity that we need to master attunement? Simply the capacity to listen, to pay attention, and to open up to crystal energy and consciousness as if we were sharing a moment of intimacy with a very dear friend. In this opening, we place no limits on the way the crystal may communicate with us, whether it is in pictures, feelings, mental understandings, or energy sensations. We are open in all the ways we can be to become aware of some new and deeper pattern in the great mystery of life. My life and the crystal's life meet in unconditional merging – that is perfect attunement. Chapter 6 goes into the subject of crystal attunement more deeply with several practice exercises that lead to direct experience. By using my capacity for attention, feeling, sensitivity and care, I give my crystal a chance to share its light. In so doing, I help the crystal to serve the evolution of consciousness on Earth; I allow it to contribute to the unfoldment of spirit and thus fulfil its purpose in the original contract that governs our existence. My right use of crystals fulfils not only their *raison d'être*, but my own. This brings us both joy as we become more deeply aligned with our full potential.

From one perspective, the 29 components of a Crystal Mesa can be seen as the alphabet of the language of light. What can we say and express and effect if we learn to use this language? The answer to this important question is as follows: the *mesa* of power gives us the means to expedite and intensify nature's own ultimate destiny. It gives us a powerful tool for bringing the divine and earthly domains into perfect accord, both in the microcosm of our interior geography and in the macrocosm of our earthly, interplanetary and galactic horizons. Let us read on and discover how, working with the energies of an archetypal *mesa*, we can progressively realize this attainment.

THE PLACEMENT OF EARTH STONES

Let's review the basics. Earth stones are placed in the South, Fire stones in the East, Air stones in the North and Water Stones in the West. The centre of the *mesa* represents Spirit, or the *axis mundi*, which is also the 'tree of life' that unites Heaven and Earth at the navel of the world. A *mesa* is a symbol-microcosm that holds a pattern of the five sacred elements in all their phases of energy and consciousness. We note that the total number of these crystal energies is 28, the number of the lunar month.

The crystal representing Spirit Earth (Green Jade) will be placed in the Southernmost position, which is the place of the New Moon. If we picture the arrangement of the *mesa* crystals being circular, they are centred on a clear crystal sphere that stands for Spirit or Source. The crystal for Spirit Fire, or Ruby, will be placed in the Easternmost position, which is the position of the First Quarter Moon. The crystal for Spirit Air, Apophyllite, or Celestite will be placed at the top of the circle in the place of the Full Moon, and the crystal for Spirit Water (Selenite) will be placed in the Westernmost position, which is the place of the Third Quarter Moon.

In *The Crystal Mesa,* we look at this circle of stones as the potential of infinite consciousness writ large in time and space, something we could also postulate of the embodied soul and its human microcosmic body. In *The Crystal Mesa,* when we consider the question of correct placement of stones, we look from the centre outward. Imagine yourself at the middle point of the circle, in the place of the clear crystal orb that stands for Ether, (Akasha, Spirit or Source,). Look South toward the place of the New Moon and visualize there a placement of a Green Jade stone, which is Spirit Earth. Next, place Pure Yang Earth (Tiger's Eye) to its right, and Pure Yin Earth (Petrified Wood) to its left. These are the core Earth energy stones, but they are incomplete without four more.

Then, the Greater Yang Earth stone (Pyrite, or Airy Earth) is placed to the right of Tiger's Eye, and the Lesser Yang Earth stone (Fire Agate, or Fiery Earth) is placed to the right of that. Then, the stone for Greater Yin Earth, or Jasper (also called Earthy Earth) is placed to the left of the Chrysoprase, and Malachite (Watery Earth), which can also be called Lesser Yin Earth, is placed to the left of Jasper.

Thus, in the Earth quadrant of our circle, from left to right, the stones are:

1) Malachite (Watery Earth)
2) Jasper (Earthy Earth)
3) Petrified Wood (Yin Earth)
4) Green Jade (Spirit Earth, centre of the Earth Stones)
5) Tiger's Eye (Yang Earth)
6) Pyrite (Airy Earth)
7) Fire Agate (Fiery Earth)

This completes the placement of the Earth Stones. The pattern of these stones follows the design of creation, which moves from the unity of Spirit into the polarity of *Yin* and *Yang* and thence to the expression of this polarity in the energies of the Four Sacred Elements. Spirit moves on its right to express itself first as Pure Yang, thence to Greater Yang, thence to Lesser Yang, and on its left it moves to Pure Yin, then to Greater Yin and lastly to Lesser Yin. We see a mixing of darkness with light taking place in this movement from centre (spirit) to periphery (matter).

The power and truth of correct placement in the *mesa* always flows from the perspective of spirit, that is, we look with the eyes of truth or spirit outward from the still point beyond manifestation to the periphery. What is seen as a circle in space becomes in temporal expression a recurring cycle. This cycle unfolds in and as Time. The Moon is the mother of time because humanity first learned the measure of time from her cyclic phases. Time flows from the New Moon to the First Quarter, thence to the Full Moon and finally to the Third Quarter.

Let us consider in greater detail how Spirit creates Time. The Sun of Spirit radiates its light to its polar companion, the Moon, and She conveys His light, which is His wisdom, love, and blessingful compassion, into the heart of night. This light is much more than a merely physical phenomenon. Like a human being, this light is a blend of astral influence, mental energy, and spiritual consciousness. One example of the spectrum of life-nourishing subtle elements in light is the pattern of clinical depression that occurs in the populace at large during the winter months in northern latitudes. This condition of low energy and emotional disorder is caused by a lack of sunlight, suggesting that the Sun's light has implications for our lives that go far beyond the physical.

Night time has always suggested a state of metaphysical obscurity, the limiting and concealing influence of physical matter and the limitation of human capacity when faced with the powers of darkness. As the 'Mother of Time,' the Moon shines the light of spirit into the dimness of our earthly night so that we see beauty and hope in the skies high above, when the solar light of day has disappeared. Across Her face in a waxing and waning rhythm of light and dark, the polarities of creation dance. The great Moon Mother transduces or decelerates the intensity of this light to a level that can be handled by our minds, nervous systems and bodies in the conditions of physical heaviness that characterize this material planet. She suffuses time and space with the Spirit's programme for the evolution of life. Wrapped in the endless cycles of the Moon Goddess's influence, evolving life on planet Earth struggles to regain its conscious oneness with the divine Source.

From the timelessness of its non-dual reality, the Sun of Spirit speaks its truth to the Moon Goddess. She manifests the design of Spirit through endless cycles of change, weaving the destinies of living beings, and inspiring them to dream and to create. The human souls navigate this path of continuous change, gathering experience, knowledge and wisdom so that they may complete their long journey back to the eternal home.

We have seen how the stones relating to the Earth element are organized in their quadrant of the *mesa*. Let us complete the picture by setting down the placement of stones in the families of Fire, Air and Water. The *mesa* embodies the energy patterns of these remaining sacred elements as follows:

THE PLACEMENT OF THE FIRE STONES

From left to right, in the Eastern side of the *mesa*, the stones are:

1) Lesser Yin Fire (Watery Fire): Gold Labradorite

2) Greater Yin Fire (Earthy Fire): Obsidian

3) Pure Yin Fire: Rose Quartz

4) Spirit Fire: Ruby

5) Pure Yang Fire: Sunstone

6) Greater Yang Fire (Airy Fire): Citrine

7) Lesser Yang Fire (Fiery Fire): Red Garnet

THE PLACEMENT OF THE AIR STONES

From left to right in the Northern side of the *mesa*, the stones are:

1) Lesser Yin Air (Watery Air): Azurite

2) Greater Yin Air (Earthy Air): Sodalite

3) Pure Yin Air: Bluelace Agate

4) Spirit Air: Celestite (or Apophyllite)

5) Pure Yang Air: Kyanite

6) Greater Yang Air (Airy Air): Fluorite

7) Lesser Yang Air (Fiery Air): Amethyst

THE PLACEMENT OF THE WATER STONES

From left to right in the Western side of the *mesa*, the stones are:

1) Lesser Yin Water (Watery Water): Moonstone (or Larimar)

2) Greater Yin Water (Earthy Water): Chrysocolla

3) Pure Yin Water: Gem Silica (or Pink Chalcedony)

4) Spirit Water: Selenite

5) Pure Yang Water: Blue Chalcedony

6) Greater Yang Water (Airy Water): Aquamarine (or Amazonite)

7) Lesser Yang Water (Fiery Water): Labradorite

When Confucius was retained by the emperor of China to serve the Middle Kingdom as a senior administrator, he spent much of his time "rectifying the tradition." It was not clear to me what this expression meant when I first read it, but I now feel that I have a better understanding of the term "rectifying the tradition" from the perspective of my learning experiences with crystal *mesa*. When each cosmic energy is positioned in its correct place in the cosmic scheme, and when the human mind attains the knowledge of placement through a profound study of the "pattern of the whole," then rectification can be accomplished. Clarity, order, balance and harmony flow from knowledge of how each part fits into the unfolding divine plan and in what each part's appropriate placement consists. Confucius felt that this was his life work, and Chinese culture has been stamped by this influence for millennia.

A simple example of this principle at work in everyday life is the experience you get when you clean your room. When dirt and dust are swept from under the bed, and everything is polished up and placed in its right spot, and all your drawers are tidied, and your clothing and bedding get laundered, you and your room both feel different. The simple act of rectifying the order of your bedroom (by eliminating unwanted accumulations such as dust and dirt and positioning each object within the room in its rightful place) changes your consciousness for the better. Purification means the elimination of defilements, whereas rectification means correct placement according to the laws of geomancy or Feng Shui. We often accomplish both at the same time when we are moved to deal with disorder, either on the outer level or in the inner world. Feng Shui works in this way. It is the Chinese science of correct placement, which creates balanced energy in any environment where it is practiced. It has much to teach us regarding the patterns of crystal in a crystal *mesa*.

When we use a *mesa* to order and balance our interior energies by correct, conscious placement of each crystal in the pattern of cosmic wholeness, we are applying these same laws. The crystals which we keep in the *mesa* are symbolic stand-ins for our own constellation of energies. Just as when we clean or room there is a re-ordering of our own interior landscape, so the ritual of placing stones in a cosmic *mesa*-pattern brings about interior change within the *mesa's* owner. Some indefinable harmony is re-established in the microcosm of our being when we consciously place each crystal in its correct position. This is a ritual action, and it rectifies the energy and consciousness of the one who performs it in the right spirit and with the correct understanding.

The soul can only accomplish its work of reconnecting to Source by aligning the physical body, vital energy, mind and heart with the divine light and power. Yet the tools which the soul has at its disposal are few, for the art of interior alignment and rectification is little understood in the West. The *mesa* is an ideal means to accomplish an ordering of all parts of our being around their spiritual centre. The more we work with the *mesa* crystals, bond with them, energize them with intent, enlist their co-operation and grow in understanding of the processes at work, the more the soul is supported in its aspiration for integral divine alignment.

The power of place is evoked and expressed through correct and conscious placement of the stones (or crystals) within a *mesa*. The *mesa* is a representation in miniature of the complete constellation of energies and powers in our human microcosm; it symbolizes the temple that we physically incarnate when our souls take on physical form in this material world. Working with our crystal *mesa*, we are reminded that the body is the temple of the soul. Placing the stones with conscious intent, we "rectify" the various parts of our being with which the soul has chosen to work. The process of rectification involves directed intent, which implies a fully conscious application of cosmic patterns. This process is very important if we aspire to harmonize the human and the divine. The *mesa* is a perfect tool for developing and applying intent, and with practice we will discover a growing skill in placement and an increasing mastery of various energies and states of consciousness arising out of our interaction.

PARADIGM PLACEMENT

The Aztec Calendar and the Mayan Calendar can be used with the crystal *mesa* for the purpose of teaching and empowerment placements. These calendars are paradigms of the cosmos. They picture the Cosmic Light working out its plan by a radiant patterning of life. We know that galactic light pulses coded information into our solar system, and that there is a Galactic Centre around which we orbit. The radiant energy of the Sun, Moon, Stars and the Galactic Centre are the primary sources of information and vitality that infuse our life-code DNA. The ancient calendars of South and Central America were based on this relationship that our Sun and solar system have with their galactic centre. Time is only a small part of what these calendars picture; it is the quality of energy and consciousness and its changing pattern that is really being shown. A fairly detailed study of them and their cosmology would be required for using these calendars as part of our *mesa* crystal placement, and it could be the subject of an entire book. One of the beautiful things about the study of Crystal Mesa is that it opens doorways of understanding and insight in many directions, because much of the knowledge is Atlantean and Lemurian, dispersed to various parts of the Earth when the twelve tribes of Atlantis vacated their homeland at the time of its destruction. When we have insights about how to use *mesa* in different ways, we are simply re-constituting a very ancient body of knowledge what was once whole.

When you place the 28 stones of the crystal *mesa* in a circle around the edge of any of these ancient calendars (with the *mesa* heart-stone at the centre) you enhance the teaching aspect of the crystal *mesa's* potential. The 28 crystals each make a statement in light and geometry. When each crystal and its archetypal statement is placed within the 'pattern-of-the-whole' (which is expressed in exquisite detail by these circular calendars of Central America) you have a *living* paradigm, a 3D yantra, a functioning simulacrum of the light-body of the Cosmic Being. The crystal *mesa* is a way of working with light, its patterning power and its capacity to communicate life-enhancing information to our DNA. The crystal *mesa* relates to our embodied existence in a way that parallels the relationship of light to life. When used correctly, the crystal *mesa* can be a means of accessing galactic information and applying it to alignment or attunement, which helps us harmonize all aspects of our life, energy and consciousness with the divine plan. The reason why the galactic centre emits intelligent wave-information into its outlying star systems is to co-ordinate them. They are thus imprinted with the pattern-of-the-whole and empowered to align themselves accordingly. When alignment with the pattern-of-the-whole has been perceived and realized by our planetary intelligence, particularly by a substantial number of humans, a step forward in evolution can be achieved. In this way, the galaxy weaves itself a body of light fully capable of conscious, enlightened existence.

THE SEVENTH ATTUNEMENT

If your crystal *mesa* is kept in a cloth bag, it should be easy to place this bag over your chest for meditation. If the bag has the right kind of attachment strings, it can even be hung from your neck while you sit for meditation, or you can relax back into the reclining posture. Feel the weight of the crystal *mesa* on your chest. Connect with this feeling of being physically in contact with the *mesa* and its energies as you inhale slowly and deeply. From the feeling of physical contact, the sensation of being in contact with the *mesa* energies comes more easily. As you inhale, feel that you are taking all the energies of the stones into the cells of your body. As you exhale, sense your entire body glowing with these celestial energies. Continue in this way for a time. Next, visualize all the energies of the *mesa* crystals suffusing your aura as you inhale, out to a distance of several feet around your physical body. Each time you exhale, relax and feel that you are filled with the colours and energies of the crystals. Then, relax into a deeply peaceful state and begin to work with this affirmation: *I take in all the crystal energies, to re-create my DNA, to activate my full divine potential, for the highest good.* Actually, you can also repeat this affirmation while inhaling, and if you practice this way, the final peaceful relaxation can be a silent meditation.

A cosmically aligned *mesa* has a fourfold function. It *transmits* information (Air) which can be accessed by attunement. It is *electro magnetically radiant* (Fire), which is to say it emits energy. It attracts and holds patterning, which gives it a *gravitational function* (Earth), capable of grounding or anchoring light and life. Finally, it is *psychoactive, and receptive* (Water), enabling it to be a holding-pattern or matrix of evolutionary life. The *mesa* is an example of ancient technology. It uses crystals and conscious patterning to generate a world of coherence and unity, a "resonant matrix" that mirrors the cosmic intent. Using the process of harmonic resonance, there can be instantaneous transmission of information from the galactic centre, or from any of the suns or stars into the body of Earth, or of the human microcosm. There are many kinds and qualities of energy, and each has its own form-building capacity; the various families of crystals illustrate this perfectly. The *mesa* is a resonator of information, and what it has to communicate is accessed by attunement. The essence of the process is resonance. The most important result is the expansion of consciousness, not the accumulation of intellectual content in the verbal mind. For this reason, over and over again we must remind ourselves that feeling and sensing things is extremely important. With the *mesa*, we co-create a resonant field; we sense the resonance of incoming information, or the quality of energy and we attune to it, thus imprinting it into the watery matrix of our physical body, which is more than 80% water. Our conscious direction of these energies also modifies our finely tuned DNA filaments, as recent experiments have shown. DNA material in petrie dishes was examined before and after being meditated on, and the results were striking.

It is a mistake to conceptualize and verbalize experience before we have resonated with it and anchored it. Mental noise is an interference pattern and it can easily break the transmission. Mental agitation dampens the resonance of the *chakras* we use for attunement, particularly the heart and solar plexus centres, but also the brow, crown and sacral centres as well as others.

There is much more that could be said about the power of place and the art of placement in the archetypal crystal *mesa*. But the important thing is to actually work with our sacred bundle until it begins to connect us to our own inner teacher, the master who abides within the lotus of the spiritual heart. Then, our inner teacher can work consciously with the outer teacher or *mesa* to bring forward all the guidance we need, step by step, at every stage of our further unfolding development.

THE EIGHTH ATTUNEMENT

Overview: Here, we begin to use affirmations in conjunction with the *mesa*, and to work on the chakras.

Lying on a rug or bed, place the *mesa* over the region of your heart or solar plexus. Allow some time, and become aware of your mind, energy and heart integrating with the crystal energies. Then, one by one, ever so slowly and consciously, place the *mesa* on focus five different energy centers, with repetitions of affirmation thus:

- On the brow chakra: I am one with the Sage. I surrender to divine grace. I embody divine wisdom. I am fullness and completion.

- On the solar plexus chakra: I am one with Agni, the Divine Fire. I live the will of the Supreme. All that I have and all that I am burns brightly for transformation.

- On the heart chakra: I am the Divine Child. I am joy in the spiritual heart. I am all openness to light and love.

- On the navel chakra: I am one with the Mother. I am all love. I give birth to the divine in matter.
- In the region of the crown chakra and above: I am the Infinite Being. I am Existence-Consciousness-Bliss.

Each affirmation may be repeated, very slowly, until the feeling sinks in that shift of energy, or some adjustment of consciousness has occurred.

THE NINTH ATTUNEMENT

Take your *mesa* crystals out of their bag and place them in groups of Earth, Water, Fire and Air to your right on a table, or on a rug. Lay a special piece of cloth in front of you. It can be specially selected for the purpose of laying the stones, or simply a piece of cotton or silk that you find suitable for this practice.

Begin by taking your Lemurian Jade in your hands and merging with its energy. When you feel deeply bonded with this piece and all it stands for, place it on the cloth. Then, take your Spirit Earth stone, Green Jade, and hold it. Meditate in the same way, and place it beside or on your Lemurian Jade.

Visualize the room you are in as a temple chamber, and see these two stones as being placed in the center of this temple space. You may want to imagine them being much larger than they are in actuality, or you may want to picture the cloth they are on as a square altar at the center of this room.

Next, meditate with your Yang Earth stone (Tiger's Eye) in the same way, and place it to the right of the Lemurian Jade and Green Jade. As you do this, visualize the colour, texture and energy of this stone filling the region of the ceiling of the temple room you are in, which is to say, it comes to occupy the region above you. The whole ceiling is composed of Tiger's Eye, and it is a complete energy field of Yang radiance.

Then, meditate with your Yin Earth stone (Petrified Wood) in the same way and place it to the left of the Lemurian Jade. Visualize this stone, its colour and energy becoming the floor of the room you are in.

At this point, you are meditating in a space where the Yang energies are above you and the Yin energies are below. See your spine as a column, or hollow tube, running up into the celestial energies, and down into the Yin Earth energies. Let these energies flow back and forth through your spine, and meditate until you feel aligned.

Next, take your Earthy Earth stone, either Red Jasper or Green Jasper, and try to feel its energies. Feel its quality and power entering your energy-field. Then, place it on the South side of the Lemurian Jade. See one wall of your temple room (in the South) as being entirely made of this stone. Meditate on the energy of this stone as filling the entire southern portion of this room, and being most strongly established in the solid wall you have visualized.

Then, take your Watery Earth stone, Malachite, and hold it in your hands, taking in its energy and noting how you feel about it. See the Western wall of your temple room being completely formed of this material, and place the stone to the West of the Lemurian Jade.

Continue in this way with Fire Agate in the East and Pyrite in the North.

When you have thus placed all the Earth stones in this configuration, and attuned to them, you have completed the work of rectifying your Earth energies by means of the Crystal Mesa. You may want to continue on with the other three groupings of crystals, or you may feel you have done enough work for now, and leave further attunements to another time.

Close the attunement by breathing in slowly and deeply, visualizing your physical body's Earth energies completely harmonized and balanced. Then, replace the stones in your *mesa* bag and conclude the session.

The Crystal Mesa Logo
expresses, among other
things, the time-space manifestation of Lunar Law.

A LIVING RELATIONSHIP

We have seen that a crystal *mesa* has many levels of meaning, and a wide variety of applications. Among other things, a *mesa* is an altar, which means it is a meeting place where the light and power of Heaven can manifest to affect the conditions of life on Earth. An altar is usually found at the centre of an area designated as 'sacred space' – a temple, cavern, circle of standing stones, or shrine, for example. But a *mesa* is a *portable* altar. It exists in a special relationship to the one who is its keeper, caretaker or servant.

Here, an important principle must be made very clear. The keeper or maker of the *mesa* is as much its servant as the *mesa* is the servant of the keeper. All natural existence is intrinsically sacred. This sacredness does not arise out of its capacity to meet the needs of human individuals, it is a given fact, implicit in the original contract by which creation came into being. Therefore work with a *mesa* begins with right understanding and grows in right relation. The *mesa*'s true significance and power is much diminished if the human who works with it imagines a) that the *mesa* can be a personal possession; b) that the *mesa* exists to serve his or her wishes and desires; c) that the scope of the relation between human and *mesa* is a purely personal affair; d) that the 'owner' can do as he or she wishes with the *mesa*. All of these, and other similarly distorted opinions interfere seriously with the correct functioning of the *mesa*, which must always be founded in right relation to what is sacred. A relationship founded on sacred principles must transcend the wishes and desires of our human mind and ego. Alignment with (and ultimately surrender to) the Divine

Will is implicit in every activity where the original contract between Heaven and Earth is honoured. Crystal Yoga is a process for establishing this alignment and for growing its full manifestation in all parts of our microcosm.

In what, then, does 'right relationship' with the *mesa* consist? To answer this question, I would like to share a story told by Martin Prechtel in his book *Long Life, Honey In The Heart*. He had the privilege of being adopted into a Mayan community and being trained as a shaman, a process which took many years. He was actually chosen and groomed for the job by his teacher, something that he had not anticipated when, as a restless young American, he began hitchhiking through Central America.

In the Mayan community where Martin Prechtel settled down, certain sacred bundles were kept by the most advanced spiritual teachers, and it was not until an apprentice had undergone years of training and testing that he might be allowed to glimpse the contents of such bundles.

One day, some fierce looking men with machine guns came to the village and insisted on being allowed to see the most sacred bundle and to examine its contents. The keeper of the bundle complied, and after disrespectfully examining this sacred *mesa*, the ruffians went away joking. The author writes:

> *We'd been violated by what didn't love us, or comprehend the delicateness of what it took to get to the common spiritual ground where what was human could feast with the divine. The beauty had been scared off like deer in front of sport hunters. The immenseness had been diminished and trivialized. How could Chiv (the keeper) have sold us out like that? ... I'd been Chiv's student for three years now. I'd been initiated as a shaman... These men had no respect or knowledge for what they wanted to see, and yet Chiv had allowed them to peer into the most significant Holy Bundle the village had. I and the other Bundle students weren't even allowed to see inside those multiple mystical wrappings until we had undergone the requisite four years of focused training that it took to mature us enough to understand what every shred and crumb of the bundle meant. (pgs. 69-70)*

Feeling irate and betrayed, Martin approached Chiv and protested, asking how he could have opened the Bundle to these strangers while denying it to those in training. Chiv's reply was very enlightening and goes to the heart of what a *mesa* means. He said:

> *This bundle is older than any of us, and was here on the earth before any humans were created. This bundle's holiness was not created by people physically, and, for the same reason, there are no people who can destroy it by taking it apart. When people take the holy apart, they take themselves apart. Don't you think the bundle must have its own protections? The power in that bundle makes us whole but we don't make that power. …People from the outside want to take apart our bundles to see what's in them. You can take one apart in a second, but you see nothing. The only way to "see" what's in the bundle is to learn slowly how to put it together and how to take care of it, like an egg, for instance. If you want to see why the mother bird thinks her eggs are so precious, like our village loves its bundles, then you could break the egg. All you would see is mucus and yolk. But if you initiates sit, hatch, maintain, and care for the egg without breaking it, you will see in the end what an egg is all about. (pgs. 73-4)*

Then, Chiv explained something very important to Martin:

> *By looking in the bundles those people saw 'nothing,' and, seeing nothing, they took nothing away with them. … since what is in the bundle cannot be seen without going the route of learning, they saw nothing. You have to go the route, boys. This means that by going the four years you learn to see 'nothing' in a substantial way. What is in the bundle is in the seeing. We are not so primitive as to think that the bundle is the power, it is simply a home for the power to be seen. The bundle is a throne, and it takes four years for our poor human eyes to see the spirit sitting there. All of our bundles contain ordinary things that, when seen in ritual context, become the extraordinary things they really are …we have to go the full route of learning to see what's really in there. Everybody else who takes the shortcut will not see. (pgs. 73-4)*

The tale speaks volumes about what we might call 'right relation' with regard to our own crystal *mesa*. Let us consider for a few moments what this true story can teach us. According to Martin's teacher, Chiv, one could only develop the eyes to see what a sacred bundle really was by going the correct route of learning. This required an investment of four years. What a sacred bundle really is cannot be known, much less applied, if one has not cultivated the eyes to see by taking the time to walk the road toward initiation. The reality of the bundle is the power behind it, not the objects contained in the wrappings. These objects are in the nature of a throne for that inner, hidden power. We have made the point that a rightly constituted *mesa* is a miniature temple, and an altar – a sacred space which can be used to bring the divine power and presence into manifestation on this terrestrial plane where we live in physical bodies. The bundle serves to bring forth a sacred power that human eyes cannot normally see, and human sensibilities cannot normally feel. What Chiv called "the full route of learning" is the only way that sacred bundles, or *mesas*, can be known for what they really are. Right understanding and right relation go together, and would be at the heart of the initiate's training.

I myself have experienced this process in time spent with the Q'ero in remote regions of the Peruvian Andes. These people are keepers of the most pure living tradition of the ancient Andean shamanic teachings. Don Sebastian spent quite some time reading cocoa leaves to assess what the next step would be in my training, and then after long consultations and various teachings, he initiated me into the responsibilities of Pampa Mesayoq, which is one level of the ancient Andean priesthood. My friend Dennis, who guided me to Don Sebastian, had been in training in this fashion for six years. It is the ancient way, not only of the Maya and the Q'ero, but of all peoples still connected to Mother Earth, to guide those who have the shamanic call along a line of instruction that leads to direct personal experience. With experience, of course, comes progressive mastery and attainment.

Martin Prechtel is a good writer, and he uses a very beautiful expression in his writing: "the common spiritual ground where what was human could feast with the divine." This is worth thinking about. His whole apprenticeship (and the shamanic traditions of many centuries) focused on building up this sacred space of right relationship.

Martin is thinking about process here, what he calls "the delicateness of what it took to get to the common spiritual ground where what was human could feast with the divine." His words carry the weight of wisdom, and should be pondered by everyone interested in making and using a crystal *mesa*.

Working with a *mesa* is a lifelong learning choice. We begin to interact with a *mesa* in order to discover "the delicateness of what it takes" – one could not find better words than these – "the delicateness of what it takes" to bring our *mesas* and ourselves fully to life. These words of Prechtel's suggest that the right attitude is one of humility, openness, and receptivity. This receptivity implies that the *mesa* keeper must cultivate the disposition of a perpetual student, a childlike, heart-centred way of feeling and being which dispels arrogance or presumption. There is a special purity of intent and integrity of outlook which is at the core of right relationship in the field of spiritual practice. The unfettered imagination of a child has this delicacy which is so very important. Working with a *mesa* is more like playing in a sand-pile than like work. It invites us to build with imaginative feeling, with relaxed joy, with effortless concentration, with creative focus, with childlike openness. And, one might add, without preconceptions, or expectations.

For this reason, the Child Archetype must become for each of us a living reality; it is not a stage we can leap over. All progress depends on it. One can be a child of the heart only if one lives in right relationship to the Mother, the divine nurturing presence that births and enriches our dreams and aspirations.

A *mesa* is a field of experience, a magical world of possibilities, a gateway that brings us into attunement with Primal Realities. To open the *mesa* is to invoke the experience of sacred space, the equivalent of stepping into the precincts of a shrine where the living presence is palpable. This is so not because the objects we have included in our *mesa* are sacred, although they are, but because we have entered into such a relation with our *mesa* and its contents that we have cultivated and developed the eyes to see, the heart to feel and the capacity to participate in the dynamics of sacred unfoldment. Building this relation is the true work of *mesa*, it is the way in which we grow and unfold in our relationship with its potential to change our lives. In that sense, the *mesa* becomes a symbolic point of reference for the inner teacher, the preceptor or guru, the master who has the key to the power and the vision. The so-called owner or keeper of the *mesa* is an apprentice to this process, fully committed to "the delicateness of what it takes." He or she treats the *mesa* as a living temple, the home of gods and visionary power, power that heals and teaches. As one relates, so one learns and grows. It is undoubtedly just as master Chiv said.

When we go more deeply into the question of right relationship which is central to the *mesa* tradition, the essentials of the Buddhist eightfold path come to mind as a very helpful set of criteria. They are, in brief:

1) Right Views, or Understanding

2) Right Thought (and Resolve)

3) Right Speech

4) Right Action (or Conduct)

5) Right Livelihood

6) Right Effort

7) Right Mindfulness

8) Right Concentration (and Meditation)

In the Buddhist context, these terms each have specific meanings related to the Buddha's teaching. But if we use them as a springboard for thinking outside the Buddhist frame of reference, these categories of thought open up a world of understanding relevant to the use of the *mesa*. In its pure and original meaning, of course the term Buddha simply means one who has an enlightened consciousness; all paths to this attainment are going to involve the use of "buddhi," or the illumined mind. Let us consider what these precepts mean from that perspective. Rightly understood, they constitute a wisdom teaching concerning the right use of the *mesa*.

1) RIGHT VIEWS, OR UNDERSTANDING

Ignorance can be thought of as wrong views, or wrong understanding regarding one's relationship with the objects of the world, or one's relationship with oneself. The Buddha taught that all worldly things, people, experiences are imperfect, impermanent and incapable of yielding durable happiness. This is undoubtedly true.

Another Buddhist precept from the heart sutra (Mahayana Buddhism) is also deeply grounded in truth: *Form is emptiness; emptiness also is form. Emptiness is no other than form; form is no other than emptiness. In the same way, feeling, perception, formation, and consciousness are emptiness.*

Our five senses give us an impression of reality that is not completely accurate. For example, we know from the modern science of physics that so-called solid matter is mostly empty space. We know also that even the atoms of which matter is constituted are as likely to be energy waves as to be particles, and that the seemingly solid substances which we can touch are actually in a constant state of flux at the sub-molecular level. According to quantum physics, the notion that anything really solid exists, or that any form is fixed is only a convention of the senses, a distortion that comes because we see and perceive in a limited way. Everything seemingly solid is actually composed of energy-in-flux.

When we are conscious in a different way, a way that does not rely on the five senses, we experience creation in a much more open-ended manner. The way that we see ourselves and our world generates our way of relating and perceiving. From these comes the quality of experience we can have, and thus the degree of fulfilment and power we can hope to achieve in life. Clearly, these matters have importance for our interaction with a crystal *mesa*.

A big step towards 'right view' has been taken by modern quantum physics. It provides us with a model for understanding the emptiness within form and the flux within solidity. A crystal, from the perspective of 'right understanding,' needs to be understood as an energy-body rather than an object. An energy field can more easily be seen to be an expression of consciousness, as contrasted with a lifeless scientific object. When we see and relate to the crystals of our *mesa* in this way, sensing that they are both energy and consciousness, in some way alive and interactive, it makes a world of difference. This is an example of how a change of perspective, an adjustment of view, or a deepening of understanding can open up a whole new possibility for right relationship with our *mesa*. From such insights we derive a more clear, confident and effective practice. When we see the stones within a *mesa* as living, conscious beings, changing and changeable forms of mineral life, expressions of energy and consciousness, we activate latent powers of a magical nature, and then crystals become tools for effecting change.

An example of "wrong view" would be the attitude that physical things are lifeless and unconscious. From that comes the idea that nature's creations only acquire value or meaning when they are tooled and used by humans. Implicitly or explicitly this is being drilled into most children and adolescents who attend schools in Europe, North America and many other parts of the world.

To overcome this false paradigm, which is a relic of John Locke and Newtonian physics, it may be necessary to re-program your own subconscious mind. One way to begin is by deliberately attempting to speak to nature and her creations. We might start with plants, because they are obviously living. Then, we might begin to speak to stones, in particular the crystalline minerals of our personal, sacred *mesa*. In this way, we could begin to feel the possibility of relating rightly to these creations of nature as manifestations of consciousness, which they are. By speaking to them, we acknowledge that they ARE conscious, that they have life, and that therefore they are worthy of respect.

Only if we adopt this view and cultivate this understanding will we be able to receive teaching from the forces and beings connected to our *mesa*, align with its powers, and call them to us as allies of our aspiration. It is a fact of experience that we cannot work effectively with energies, consciousness or even people whose worth we disrespect or whose capacity we denigrate.

The idea that humans have supremacy over nature (based largely on the ideas found in Genesis) needs to be replaced with a different view, which might be called "biospherical egalitarianism." Many of us were trained to see ourselves as beings separated from nature, inhabiting her as our outer environment. After years of relentless drilling in this kind of thought, we come to accept it as our outlook on life. Then, invariably, we experience the anguish and limitation of an inner dissociation of sensibility which this viewpoint causes. We are separated from our own heart's ability to feel oneness with all living things. We miss this way of being, we become alienated from a very important part of ourselves, and we begin to sense that our feelings have atrophied. At this point, sometimes we start trying to get back in tune with nature, or with the deeper side of ourselves.

Perhaps individually or collectively we could create a new view, a relational, total-field world-view based on an intuited oneness with the inner life and consciousness of all things. A book by Bill Deval and George Sessions called *Deep Ecology – Living As If Nature Mattered* (1985) teaches its readers how to cultivate a state of perception in which the individual is conscious of a more encompassing "Self" that includes nature. This ecological self, or transpersonal self, would generate not so much a new system of ethics or morals (these being mental and religion-shadowed) as an entirely new way of experiencing the world. This possibility is not a mere psychological theory. It is a foreshadowing of a new way of being – or rather an ancient way of being which our modern thinking has eclipsed. Yet, as we learn when we work with a *mesa*, this holistic way of being is ready to re-awaken. *Mesa* can be our doorway, our handle and our key to the process of reconnecting with the cosmos and assuming our archetypal role in it. Only thus can we re-activate our microcosm, for its meaning can only be understood in the context of 'original contract.'

Your *mesa*, which reflects the principle "as above, so below," is a teacher of right relationship to the planet and all its manifestations, beginning with the stones and crystals which we assemble into a sacred bundle.

Consider a few more examples of "right understanding" related to *mesa* practice:

1) The world is "as you dream it." In other words, what you imagine generates what you get. Not only is our worldview fundamental to everything we do, the results we can achieve are limited (in most but not all cases) to what we believe possible.

   Remember, you effortlessly attract the energies that support your version of life. Every moment that you believe in yourself creates momentum through which you will continuously blossom light and brilliant alternatives of living. This process involves growing into the *recognition* of yourself as an equal to your stellar family. *Mesa* is an assembly or constellation of our 'stellar family.'

2) Traditional societies open themselves to multi-levelled interactions with nature whereas modern industrial and post-industrial cultures have the effect of segregating people from nature. We in the West are not even aware of how we see nature in limiting ways; the cultural matrix of our own invention has become a

surrogate environment for us, especially in cities, and especially with the advent of radios, television and computers linked to the internet. Our scientific monoculture inhibits other varieties of worldview and diminishes our capacity for right relation to Source and to nature. This suggests the need for an apprenticeship in right relation, possibly through travel, and in particular travel to regions where the old traditions are still alive.

A LITTLE STORY

By way of illustrating this second point, I want to share a personal experience. I lived in Chiangmai, Thailand for five and a half years from 1989 to 1995 and had a job teaching university there. When I arrived, I was soon impressed by how different the work habits of the Thai people are, especially construction workers, whom I had occasion to see because I would pass them by on the roads or at building sites. While working on the job, they were unfailingly cheerful, playful, light-hearted, relaxed and happy. This was an extreme contrast to my experience of factory workers or construction workers on the job in North America.

When I had been in the country longer, I learned that the Thai people can and do preface almost any verb which denotes conscious activity with the word *"len,"* which means "to play." Thus, they would speak about "play teach," or "play study" or "play growing rice" etc., and when I enquired whether one could "play work" *(len gnarn),* the answer was a definite "yes." For them, as a result, the connotation of work was very positive, suffused with a sense of fun and enjoyment. We in the West, on the other hand, usually associate work with drudgery, grim endurance and unpleasantness; for some, it's almost a "four-letter word." This, for me, was an excellent example of a cultural conditioning which made a tremendous and positive difference in the attitude and disposition of an entire populous, over sixty million people, in a centrally important area of life – their relationship to labour.

Thailand was never colonized. When I travelled and spent time in Peru, on the other hand, where the Spaniards had virtually made slaves of the indigenous people, I found a great sobriety, reserve, and impassive quality in their demeanour. This came through not so much in their relation to the land or each other, which is full of spirit and feeling, but rather in their social disposition, especially with foreigners.

Another distinct difference between the Thai people and Westerners, whom they call "farang," has to do with conversation. I learned that for Thai people, conversation was usually not about coming to a clear understanding of some subject; rather it was a kind of verbal massage whose purpose was to make participants feel good. Being intellectually earnest, or believing literally in what was said, was thus inappropriate. "Intelligent conversation" as we know it is not considered socially polite, and if attempted could lead to considerable perplexity and misunderstanding.

3) When we change our viewpoint, we can change our state of consciousness. When consciousness changes, our interaction with energy is modified automatically, and many things become possible which were not previously possible. Seeing the world differently makes the world behave differently (for the perceiver). Conversely, learning a new way to relate to the world usually effects a change of consciousness.

4) Our worldview is deeply imbedded in us not only psychologically and subconsciously. It is present even physically in our cells and musculature as a tendency to hold our body in a certain kind of posture, or a degree of tension. A language embodies a worldview; learning new languages re-programmes the brain synapses. Our very nervous system and DNA reflect the nature of our mental conditioning. Because attitudes and opinions engrave patterns into our neurological pathways, we *embody*, for better or worse, the 'way of seeing' that we buy into. This acceptance of a world-view or cultural perspective may be conscious or unconscious. The goldfish, for example, is oblivious of the existence of something called water. Our *way of relating* expresses the worldview which, consciously or unconsciously, we have adopted. New pathways of perception can be forged, and if they are used more often than the old ones, they can come to predominate. It takes some effort to initiate and then forge these new ways of seeing and relating, but unless we do so, we remain within the limited ranges of our conditioning. And you cannot keep new wine in old skins. The *mesa* works very well for re-programming our perceptual life and widening our consciousness.

5) Conversely, the limitations of what and how much can be known are built right into our genetic inheritance. Patterns imposed by culture and personal history shape the kind of nervous system we have, which in turn filters the kinds of experiences that are possible for us. The information which our planet can reveal, and the power which our *mesa* can manifest, are intimately related to the way our brains, minds, nervous systems and affective capacities work. For many people, the best that can be managed is to become aware of processed information *about* the world, rather than experiencing directly the multi-dimensional wonder that IS the world. Such people are incapable of doing or feeling magic; they were likely more balanced when they were kids watching Walt Disney on TV. It is in this sense that a university education can be both intellectually broadening and in many other ways perceptually debilitating.

6) There is a non-verbal language or communication system built into the very structure of the world. Symbols and sounds can express parts of this language. So can colours, crystals and patterns in nature. In dreaming, divination, meditation or through certain mind-altering substances like peyote and ayahuasca, we sometimes access this archetypal language. The world is constantly saying far more to us than our various filters permit us to process or comprehend. *Mesa* is a tool of primal technology. It can help us to release our cultural conditioning, clear away the filters that constrict our perception, and take a giant step towards full consciousness.

7) The healing wisdom of the Earth works through those who allow it. Our worldview is as much in need of healing as our bodies. *Mesa* is not a tool for imposing notions on Earth, or the landscape, or the minds of others, nor is it an instrument for manipulating the powers of Earth to our personal advantage. A *mesa* is rather an expression of an ancient way of being, relating and understanding, and thus a means for opening the mind to the wisdom and healing power of the primal Mother. We need to attend to the Earth symbolically through the selected crystals of our own personal *mesa* to receive its healing and be empowered by the qualities of nature and Mother Earth. If we fail to develop right understanding, nothing radically transformative can be expected.

Think for a while about other examples of right understanding and see if you can put your insights into words.

2) RIGHT THOUGHT

Right Thought springs from the heart as deep feeling. This experience of deep feeling is not the same as emotional reactivity, it is a point of connection with the spiritual heart, an echo of the inner life of the soul. Right thought is not logical analysis. It is suffused with the light of intuition. It comes from clear understanding and is founded on inner experience. It is an expression not of opinion, but of sure knowing. It aligns Earth and Heaven, or at the very least never strikes a note of dissonance. Right thought sees the unity behind multiplicity and deeply appreciates the value of silence. It does not clamour to be heard. It knows when time favours expression and also when it is right to maintain stillness. It knows the limits of its so-called knowledge and the limits of language. It senses a non-dual state of being, and from this perspective the things which are expressible by words seem to be pale distortions of reality. Therefore, right thought is not ornamented with the arrogance of superficial intellectual brilliance.

Right thought harmonizes well with simplicity and restraint. It is committed not only to the consideration of life and its meaning by the intellect, but more significantly to the actual living of wisdom. Because right thinking senses and feels the rhythms of the cosmic dance, it does not express itself through truisms or platitudes. Right thought knows that thinking is inherently imperfect, and thus it cultivates lines of concentration that lead to a wordless merging, a self-emptying transcendence. Right thought is not fascinated by novelty or curious for variety. It loves Truth. It is the handmaiden of Truth. At the same time, it does not see Truth from only one perspective; it does not become fixated in one window of the mind. Rather it enjoys different views, taking the perspective of the soul and remaining open to the magic of imagination. When vision is confined to a single, linear horizon, you can completely miss a secret wonder that is revealed by the process, or by the form of the activity in which you engage. The working of imaginative vision never boxes itself into a linear perspective. It has access to mysteries that the single-minded may miss. It is multi-valent, resonant, feeling-centred, inwardly guided and wide open to the fullness of life's possibilities.

A *mesa* which is assembled to harmonize with the cosmic paradigm can be a teacher of right thought. Right thought can easily recognize that crystals are solidified dreams of nature, manifestations of a divine plan, embodiments of a pure energy which can empower our aspiration and expedite our transformation physically, emotionally, intellectually and spiritually. Right thinking can contemplate and learn from the 32 *mesa* crystals assembled into the four houses of Earth, Water, Fire and Air, and centred on the transparent fullness of Infinity. Right thought is supremely creative. It can resonate what IS into words and is thus not bound to the human conventions of the past. Right thought is thus oracular and prophetic. Poets often touch this plane of mind; they can sometimes see or sense infinity in a grain of sand, and glimpse unearthly light in the eyes of an infant. From this inner understanding, the magic in crystals can be appreciated. This unconditioned seeing, feeling and expressing of the reality that underlies appearances is both a gift and an attainment but at all stages the *mesa* of power can support and guide its unfoldment.

The world is never something outside us; we constantly construct it with our intentionality. The landscape of our inner world is also constructed by our own lines of thought and intent. The soul, the artist in us, creates our vision of how things are, and when we are evolving in consciousness it articulates its wisdom through symbols, mystical intuitions and poetic or creative instincts. To listen to crystals, we must attend with the ears of the heart and soul, and when we do this we have moved to a frontier where the isolated individual can become a conduit of divine intention. The way we think and the way we listen determines what we may discover. If your way of thinking is dysfunctional, diminished or negative, you will never awaken to anything wonderful in your inner or outer world. When you allow your thinking to become impoverished and prosaic, the fullness of life and its rich possibilities are sadly diminished.

The soul has its own distinctive language that is communicated most often in non-verbal intimations of a very subtle nature. A symbolically ordered *mesa* is a lens of perception, an assembly of mineral allies, a bridge by which consciousness and energy can move into expression, either to register in the mind as thought or to be directed outward as potential for healing, attunement or other purposes. The *mesa* speaks to its user in such a way that he or she becomes more aware of spirit, soul, or the intuitive heart. This re-enforcement by the *mesa* of right thinking, this linking of awareness and thought to the hitching-post of essence or Source deep within us, is perhaps the greatest of all its powers. When practiced with clear intent, the eighth attunement is an excellent way of cultivating this quality of mind.

3) RIGHT SPEECH

Right speech is speech which builds oneness, heals division and fosters right relationship. Examples of right speech might include expressions of gratitude, of admiration, praise, pure joy, adoration, self-dedication, openness to Truth, receptivity, humility, and so on. In fact, any verbal expression of positive intent which tends to build loving relation could be called right speech. It might seem strange to think that we could practice right relationship to a stone, or a bundle of stones. On the other hand, if you look at this question with an open mind, why not? Isn't the strangeness only a matter of cultural conditioning? Is it not more strange to think that we are so separated from stones, or trees, or stars that we cannot speak to them? If this complete separation is true, then surely they cannot speak to us, and the relationship is so limited that little can be expected to come from it. However, most people through the course of history have believed otherwise; they lived their life in the conviction that all life is interconnected in a single web of divine weaving.

When I spent time living in the Sacred Valley near Cusco, Peru, I met people who could explain the stories associated with local stones, cliffs, mountains and springs. On several occasions a shaman would tell the tale of a prominent feature in the local landscape. This tradition survived the Spanish holocaust and has been kept alive from pre-Inca times. The landscape, reciprocally, can actually be felt to be more alive and conscious in this region. I have personally felt this many times, which is why I travel there frequently. It is magically awake because it has been treated with respect and honour both in sacred ceremony and in speech. This can also be felt in parts of England, even though the ancient traditions have been lost. The feeling is still there because it was so strongly cultivated in ancient times, and it is still the mindset of rural people in the British Isles to love their local landscape.

I have participated in Andean *despacho* ceremonies in which gifts are offered to Mother Earth, and I have performed them myself, having been initiated into the priesthood of the land in the Andean spiritual tradition. Right speech in relation to Earth and its many manifestations, including mountains, streams, and individual stones, is an important part not only of the Andean indigenous tradition, but of the ancient wisdom tradition in all parts of the world.

The practice of speaking to and about stones is very ancient. It is something that has been done by people of every level of social standing from the beginning of recorded history up to and even beyond the time of the invention of printing. This relationship with the sacred energy of the landscape, and speech expressing it, was not reserved only for priests or shamans in traditional societies, it was the common heritage of all people. For traditional societies, every significant stone, hill or spring had its own identity and story. This intimacy with the land suffered greatly under the dogmatism of Christianity. But it is only in modern times when urban culture has completely overshadowed rural culture and people's association with the land that the Earth-based mythology has been neglected. In traditional folklore, and in indigenous societies all around the world, place names and their associated stories are still celebrated and recounted as a reminder of the enduring relationship between Mother Earth and her human children.

A litany is a series of names which express the various meanings of something held to be sacred. The only litanies still in use in our culture are religious prayers, such as those in praise of the Virgin Mary. However, litany is a style of speech with a very ancient pedigree because it is ideally suited for ceremonial right speech. A good example of this is a traditional Scottish Gaelic folk prayer to the Moon:

> *Greeting to you, gem of the night!*
> *Beauty of the skies, gem of the night!*
> *Mother of the stars, gem of the night!*
> *Foster-child of the sun, gem of the night!*
> *Majesty of the stars, gem of the night!*

It is clear that a person who can look up at the Moon and say these words has a relationship of a positive kind, and openness to any energy, consciousness or influence which the Moon may exert. In a similar way, the owners of *mesas*, in particular shamanic practitioners, have nourished and fed the stones in their sacred bundles through the power of speech from time immemorial. Speech which praises, honours, or appreciates sends out good energy. This has been verified in experiments with water. Water which has been blessed, prayed over or addressed lovingly produces ice crystals of a very harmonious design, whereas water exposed to raucous music, pollutants or curses produces greatly distorted ice crystals. This experiment can easily be duplicated with a snow machine of the type used at ski resorts, placing water of two kinds, blessed and cursed, into the machine and examining the form of the snow crystals which are produced. Quite apart from noticeable effects on crystal structure (and the minerals in a *mesa* are crystalline), the act of speaking words of blessing programs the mind of the speaker, perhaps both consciously and subconsciously to right relationship, and in this condition energy and consciousness always flow more freely.

What this means, in practice, is that we do well to build a personal relationship with each and every stone in our sacred bundle, using speech as a tool for transmitting positive energy. Such speech blesses and empowers both the *mesa* and the speaker. Each stone in a *mesa* is part of a miniaturized sacred landscape. Each has its tradition, its individual form and capacity, and its appropriate uses in healing, ritual and meditation. To speak this truth lovingly is to activate the magical potential both of crystal and speaker and to unite them in purposeful and unified intent.

I was recently given a beautiful piece of green jade. Previously, I have not had any particular feeling for jade, but when I saw this stone I immediately fell in love with it. This feeling of bonding and appreciation is the ideal way of seeing each and every stone which is included in a *mesa*, and this stone will certainly have a place in my *mesa*. I find it quite easy to hold this oval treasure and speak from my heart with words similar to the Celtic litany to the Moon quoted above:

Greetings to you, green lovely one!
Beauty of the Earth, gem of green life!
Apple of nurture, crystal of wholeness!
Child of Earth's fertility, giver of healing!
So round, so perfect and complete,

Nobly enduring, patient in stillness!
Hail to you, green lovely one!
Lend me your magic now,
And share your beauty with my heart.
Ever young are you, and beautiful.
In every time and place I hold you dear,
Clasp you as a treasure of love,
Set you in a place of honour.
Green and lovely are you,
Pale jade of my dreams,
Jade of my heart's admiration,
Green lovely one!
Treasure in the assembly of mesa gems,
Magical, magical, magical earth crystal!
Jadestone of my heart's admiration.

Such speech, if it comes from the heart, feeds both the spirit of the stone and the spirit of the speaker. If set to music, this energy of right speech and right relation is multiplied, because music enhances the resonance of invocation, incantation, prophecy, or oracular speech. In fact the degree which poetry captures the spirit of incantation is the exact barometer of its magical power.

THE TENTH ATTUNEMENT

Imagine yourself holding a jade stone in your hands, and you can evoke even now the energy which makes magic possible. Imagine that you have a beautiful jade of any shade you find especially attractive, a stone about the size of a pigeon's egg. Picture its colour and shape as you hold it in your hand. Or if you actually have a jade in your *mesa*, use that. Then, with genuine feeling, say these words which I have used to express my own feeling for jade; say them over and over. The feeling will grow as you do this. If you can feel, you can project feeling. And if you can project feeling into an imaginary stone in your hands, you can project it into a real one. If you can find stones which you consider beautiful, you will not have too much difficulty to express your feelings in speech. If you can create words of praise and admiration for each of the 33 stones in your *mesa,* you will have made a very good beginning in the school of right relation and the growth process of empowerment. (Empowerment in this context means the capacity to manifest divine love.)

Actually, your ruby, which is the Passion Stone, can help you put your heart into this practice of speaking to your stones. Use it to find your voice of passion when you speak incantation.

One of the most beautiful ancient sources for this kind of sacred speech is the *Hymns of Orpheus.* Many of these were found on small sheets of hammered gold buried with Orphic initiates in Crete and South Italy, others were written down and used in sacred rituals in ancient Greece. From the ancient Orphic poetry of the Greeks comes this piece in praise of the Moon:

Goddess of silver light,
Horns of the divine bull,
Searcher in the dark of night,
We honour you.
The stars honour you,
They wait upon your orbit
As you move like a torch
Across the skies of night.
You emanate rays of blue,
But your body is amber,
Beauteous in the black vast.
All-seeing eye,
Bejewelled with stars,
Bless your watchful devotees,
Preserve them from strife.
Guide us with intuitive light,
Lamp of beauty,
Companion of the night,
Goddess of the turning wheel of Fate.
Queen of the Stars,
Artemis! Brilliant one!
Radiant lamplight veiled by darkness,

Shine down your blessed rays on us
And take with joy
Our words of praise.

Right speech is beautiful, pleasant, harmonious and musical. It soothes, elevates and harmonizes. The power of right speech can be used to suffuse the crystals of a *mesa* with active, balanced, healing energy. Some people might call this 'programming' crystals, but the connotations of the word programming are problematic in many ways. This word does not imply respect, co-operation or any bond of sacred relationship. It is not a loving or a poetic word, and it does not resonate with the living spirit of Mother Earth and her crystalline children. The worker with crystal energies in a *mesa* configuration has undertaken to create *a symbolic microcosm of living energies* that function as a kind of *conscious spiritual battery*. Right speech in this context is a language of loving, respectful relationship, evocative of the inner power and descriptive of the inner beauty which the miniature *mesa*-cosmos embodies.

According to the ancient understanding, the precious and semi-precious gems were Earthly embodiments of the Heavenly energies. Selenite, for example, was considered part of the physical body of the Moon and therefore not only beautiful but sacred. Sunstone was a bit of the Sun's own body crystallized into material form. A *mesa*, therefore, is a constellation of heavenly energies. It is conscious, innately divine, or at least celestial, and therefore spiritually precious. It was for this reason that most gems found their way into temples or royal palaces and that kings usually controlled their mining.

Think of Sunstone, or hold a piece of it if you have one, and speak aloud this ancient Orphic Hymn to the Sun:

Golden eye,
All-seeing, titanic;
You light the skies above.
We honour you.
Life-bestowing in every instant,
Your radiant chrism gladdens our hearts.
You are the Lord of the Seasons.
With your right hand, you bestow dawn,

And with your left hand you bequeath dusk.
Ancient One!
Fine and strong,
Blazing in the skies above,
Nemesis of evil, teacher of the good,
Sound for us your lyre of gold,
Lighten our world
With beams of your harmony.
Eye of brightness wending the celestial ways,
Your warmth is our life,
Your rising and setting is our delight.
Master of the World,
Lover of the brooks and streams,
Lord of Justice,
Supreme Judge,
Eye of Truth,
Sustainer of our faith,
You radiate the light of life.
Your fiery steeds
You guide by the power of your will.
Oh glorious Sun, we honour you.

Hold a Sunstone in the palm of your hand and as you look into the depths of its golden warmth, feel that it is a crystallized portion of the body of a god, which indeed it is. Then, feel your way toward saying these ancient words of praise with deepest feeling. Repeat the words over and over. Slowly, slowly the key of magical empowerment turns in the lock of consciousness and the treasure chest of the great mystery yields its riches. When you integrate with Sunstone crystal in this way, you sing your own inner sun into life. A fragment of Sunstone from the macrocosm resonates in sympathetic accord with your inner sun which has been eclipsed by materialistic mental conditioning. By the power of right attunement, it can help you find a way to release the captive beams of your inner sun and bring light into the regions that have been darkened.

In your body, gods are awakening and becoming conscious.

Divine possibilities are finding their way into expression. Presences that never before sounded their existence are beginning to resonate. The crystal of your cosmic *mesa* attune you to the light of liberation.

John O'Donohue expresses this very beautifully in his book, *Anam Cara* (pgs 94-5)

> *We so easily forget that our clay has a memory that preceded our minds, a life of its own before it took its present form. Regardless of how modern we seem, we still remain ancient, sisters and brothers of the one clay. In each of us a different part of the mystery becomes luminous. To truly be and become yourself, you need the ancient radiance of others... This tension between clay and mind is the source of all creativity. It is the tension in us between the ancient and the new, the known and the unknown. Only the imagination is native to this rhythm. It alone can navigate in the sublime interim where the lineaments of these differing inner forces touch. The imagination is committed to the justice of wholeness. It will not choose one side in an inner conflict and repress or banish the other; it will endeavour to initiate a profound conversation between them in order that something original can be born. The imagination loves symbols because it recognizes that inner divinity can only find expression in symbolic form. The symbol never gives itself completely to the light. It invites thought precisely because it resides at the threshold of darkness. Through the imagination, the soul creates and constructs your depth experience. Imagination is the most reverent mirror of the inner world.*

4)   RIGHT ACTION (OR CONDUCT)

It is an oft repeated experience that when we love what we do, we do it gracefully and beautifully. Since it is the heart and soul which bring the light of love into action, we must cultivate an attunement to that inner source, of living waters and endless possibilities. The *mesa*, rightly understood, can be a lens of perception, a school of right relationship, a living proof that "love is in the Earth." If you can find a way of working with your *mesa* that flows from a loving heart, then you will be able to make something full of beauty.

It is very clear that right action flows from right consciousness, or we can say right attunement. A single-minded, literal approach to life, while often sincere and committed, can miss the beauty of the journey. By contrast, imagination is open to a multitude of possibilities and takes the winding road rather than the straight line. Imagination moves in the spirit of creative joy because it is in love with beauty. To act with the creative joy of a lover is always to act rightly.

When work is approached only from the perspective of the mental will, it loses its expressive and imaginative dimensions and can quickly become an endurance test, a struggle against the feeling of being caught. When our image of life, or work is incomplete, the actions that flow from it create limitation, because the way we see determines how we can be. Our paradigm of reality is the lens through which we perceive life and the world around us, as well as life's possibilities and our hope of happiness in relation to it.

Also, our perception shapes the way things behave in relation to us, following the nostrum: "as you give, so you shall receive." We are responsible for creating our own paradigm and applying it to the actions that fill our lives. When the image through which we see life is open-ended, life can be rich with possibilities, but when our paradigm or lens-of-perception is limited, the inner life of things disappears and life becomes a dull monotone of sameness.

5) RIGHT LIVELIHOOD

The idea of livelihood is related to our sense of supply. Right relation with Mother Earth is full of the sense of Her bounty and abundance. This expresses itself in one's relationship not only to the community of minerals, trees and animals, but also to the community of one's human peers. When we act with overflowing fullness of trust, affection, confidence and assurance, good things come our way.

It is very interesting to compare and contrast the mythologies of hunter-gatherers with those of agriculturalists and urban-dwellers. In the former, where the relation with the Earth Mother was strong, the individual always attempted his or her quest in order to share the fruits with his tribe, clan or people. It was not a selfish pursuit of personal gain. This paradigm reflects a time when respect was accorded to nature, which was regarded as being full of life and spirit.

Later in history, the stories people told had radically changed, and the hero was a person who set out to achieve private triumph and private gain. It might have been to find a treasure, to marry a princess, or to become king of the realm, but it was always a victory for the separate self, over and against the outer world. This is the perspective of ego; you could say it's thoroughly bourgeois. In a subtle but pervasive way, most myths and stories we have inherited purvey this fractured and distorted perspective. Most heroes in these stories are egoists. The hero struggles *for his own victory, on his own behalf*, and against nature, his human enemies, or other hostile forces.

When action in the world is based on this paradigm, of separate self at the centre, struggling for separate victory, love and respect for nature dissipates; oneness with the family, tribe or society is not considered to be of importance. Such a paradigm embodies a kind of spiritual myopia. It ignores the original contract into which we are all born and within which we play out our small roles.

The action that flows from a corrupted paradigm is tinged by greed and selfishness; it is action intended to make us personally rich, powerful, famous or invulnerable. In this context we are rarely motivated to strive for the wider good of our human or natural family. People who do so are awarded prizes and written up in the newspapers because such thinking is considered exceptional. The prevailing mindset extols greed and creative accounting as virtues because they fuel the dynamism of the market place and churn out "wealth" more vigorously. There is obviously an elite of shareholders who benefit by such a paradigm, but the cost to society as a whole is great. The price we all pay includes the rape of the environment, the stressing of physical health and family unity, and the dimming down of our understanding that all life is interrelated. The idea that happiness comes from a healthy economy seems to have taken hold of the modern mind. It is, of course, a corruption of the ancient wisdom of wholeness.

When we work within the laws of nature, in harmony with Mother Earth, in right relation to all that exists, there is no limitation of abundance. Gaia is unlimited when we harmonize with her laws. There is no limitation, no disease and no hunger in the essence of Gaia. The notion of limitation is a false belief. When we buy into it, we create economies based on the myth of insufficient supply. This myth helps its perpetrators to get rich. Quite a few technologies have been developed which could operate on free energy or which could use water as fuel, only to be bought up and hidden away by the powers that be. The end of this limiting belief is entrenchment of hunger, disease and destitution. This seed thought of limitation was set in place by hierarchies concerned with preserving and extending their own political power. They concoct this idea of want and scarcity because it generates fear, which is a handle that they can use to exploit the planet and her inhabitants. Indigenous peoples living in harmony with nature always understood the abundance of supply that our Earth Mother embodies.

Right livelihood always arises from the beliefs we accept; it flows from the perspective we take on life. The corrupted myth of insufficient supply must be replaced by the original truth of infinite supply, and an exploitative relation with nature and humanity must give way to one of reciprocal service and mutual harmony. These are part of our souls' original contract with Source. When we honour this code of right relation, right livelihood becomes our natural way of harmonizing all that is.

The crystal *mesa* is an image of the unlimited wealth of Gaia, it is an assembly of precious substances set in a pattern of cosmic order and resonant harmony. Thus, it is a teacher of infinite supply and graceful livelihood. When we see the crystal *mesa*, we are silently impressed with the fact that Nature was and is complete and perfect. She is our teacher, the source of our bodies and the sustainer of our life-energy. We disrespect and exploit her at our own peril, because the first casualty is the quality of our own consciousness. Right livelihood based on right relation to Earth flows naturally, not with righteous didacticism, from the vision of completeness that the crystal *mesa* embodies.

6) RIGHT EFFORT

Right effort is not desire-motivated. It does not hunger for the fruits of its labour. Right effort is motivated by an impulse of giving rather than a need to possess. It breathes the spirit of service, not domination.

Right effort is not the struggle of an egoistic hero to triumph over his enemies and slay them. Victory can never be a merely personal agenda of private empowerment. Right effort must flow from right relation to the divine in creation, in all creation, even down to the water and bones of Mother Earth.

A *mesa* is an accord of the human and mineral kingdoms, a creation of order and alignment for the purpose of harmonizing Earth and Heaven. By the vibratory resonance of attunement, and through the power of symbolic placement, the *mesa* can mirror the self-ordering aspiration of the human microcosm. Beyond that, it can be a magical tool to effect in the material world what is envisioned in the ideal world.

Right effort is self-consciously ritualistic. It expresses the inner understanding that all action is symbolic of the consciousness and perspective of the actor. Grasping expresses the ignorance of ego, whereas giving expresses the freedom of the spirit.

Right effort can only come when personal will is aligned to the transpersonal light of the soul. In this alignment, the five sacred elements are wonderful teachers. The very form of the *mesa* is an expression of alignment of all parts of creation with the unity of their centre. The Earth-crystals represent the full range of energies of the cosmos. Water crystals symbolize the affairs of the affective and astral domain. The Fiery crystals stand for creativity, imagination and aspiration, while Air is the kingdom of the mind and the realm of intellect. Ether or *Akasha* is Spirit. It is placed at the centre of the four sacred elements and unites them to the pillar of life. A crystal *mesa* is a palette of many energies for the creative soul to express and realize its dream. The Earth element allows us to express beauty; Water is feeling and love; Fire is light and dynamism; Air is peace and wisdom; Ether is spirit and infinity. Taken together, the assembly of crystals in a *mesa* summarizes all we can be. Used rightly, they turn dreams into reality.

7) RIGHT MINDFULNESS

Right Mindfulness is steadily sustained. It is nothing less than awareness of the power of Truth, the magnetic influence of the Source, the Centre, the guiding Mandate of Heaven, whose influence radiates out to hold all things in alignment and balance.

Right Mindfulness can only be present when the heart and mind are sincere. Heart is the home of the soul, which is the representative of spirit. If mind does not listen to heart, there cannot be right mindfulness. If our education and training emphasize intellectual dissociation from the inner, intuitive light of spiritual guidance, right mindfulness is lost.

When we have right mindfulness, we constantly remember who we are and why we are here. We discover and accomplish our soul's work. Love can magnetize the memory to such a degree that steady remembrance becomes possible. Thus love is an indispensable component of our relationship to our *mesa*.

When we work with the Crystal *Mesa*, its energy and form are imprinted on the mind's eye and the inner understanding becomes aligned to its cosmic energies and pattern. This makes mindfulness of the cosmic order in which our individuality is embedded much easier. Because every molecule of a crystal is arranged in perfect order, a crystal can steadily hold an imprint of human energy and intent. It is the interior disorder of our human microcosm which makes continuous mindfulness difficult for us in a way that it is not difficult for a crystal. However, placing intent and energy into crystals where they can be sustained is a step in the right direction if we are serious about developing mindfulness. The stones in our sacred *mesa* become our allies in this work when we invite them to support our ideals and aspirations.

8) RIGHT CONCENTRATION (AND MEDITATION)

A *mesa* is an excellent mentor for helping us to enter a state of meditation. To gaze on the opened and correctly organized *mesa*, with each crystal in its place, is to assimilate a teaching of order and harmony. 'Right Concentration' steadies the mind and places it beyond the pulls and pushes of agitation. It releases the brain from restless thinking activity and opens the gateways of perception so that the meditator can assimilate the knowledge and wisdom of kingdoms beyond the pale of human mental conditioning.

Right concentration and meditation both have to do with placement. The mind likes do indulge its fancies by wandering in various worlds of thought. It has a preferential interest in certain subjects, but the underlying theme of such thinking is usually "me" and "mine" – in other words, it is ego-centric. Pause for a moment and reflect how many of your thoughts are related to the "me" idea.

Right concentration, and its spiritual deepening into meditation, leads the mind to freedom from ego. When mind feels the presence of Spirit, it can grow away from its false identification with ego. Each part of our being has its proper placement in meditation. Proper placement supports that way of orienting and relating which helps us to grow in openness and alignment with the consciousness and energy of Source. Soul, or Spirit is the inner light of our existence, the solar centre of our microcosm. When the mind opens and aligns itself to the influence of this light, we have right concentration, and this can deepen into right meditation. The experience of alignment with the inner light is both a letting go and an opening up.

We place the mind in right relationship with Source by letting go of distractions and opening up to a spiritual presence which can be felt or intuited in the awakened heart. The vital energy is placed in right relation to Source when its polarities come into a phase of balance and the breathing slows down so that the nervous system can settle into an ever-deepening stillness. The body's placement is a vigilant, relaxed quiescence. When all parts of the being are rightly placed in right relation to their Source, just like the crystals in the *mesa*, we have the possibility of going very deep or very high in contemplation. This experience of being infused by the power and presence of the Divine, if repeated at every convenient opportunity, gently moves us forward toward spiritual realization.

The horizontal arms of the Crystal Mesa Logo represent the narrow band of our waking consciousness, while the ascending and descending arms represent the deepening and widening awareness of expanding consciousness as it unfolds in the process of yoga.

THE ROOTS OF WISDOM

Isis roams the riverbank,
Dreaming her Beloved's body
Whole.

The crystals in a crystal *mesa* are symbolic stand-ins for our own constellation of stellar and microcosmic energies. When we work with them, we effect a re-ordering of our own interior landscape. The light of Spirit, the muse of beauty and the liberating joy of freedom are re-established. The soul rejoices when this work of rectification has been accomplished. It is a work of re-membering in knowledge, and it is fundamental to the working of the *mesa*.

The power that brings together what has been separated is Eros. In his book, *The Passionate Life, Stages of Loving*, Sam Keen makes the following comment about Eros:

> *Greek philosophers considered eros the prime mover, the motivating principle in all things human and non-human. It was the impulse that made all things yearn and strive for fulfillment. The acorn was erotically moved by its destiny to become an oak, just as human beings were motivated by eros to become reasonable and to form a political order as just and harmonious as that of nature. Eros was inseparable from the potentiality or promise (the potency or power) that slept in the substance of all things. Thus, in the original vision that gave birth to the word, erotic potency*

*was not confined to sexual power but included the moving force
that propelled every life-form from a state of mere potentiality to
actuality. When we limit "erotic" to its sexual meaning, we betray
our alienation from the rest of nature. We confess that we are not
motivated by anything like the mysterious force that moves birds to
migrate or dandelions to spring. (pg. 5)*

He goes on to comment that,

*Love, sexuality, and power can only be healed by returning to the
original meaning of eros… Our erotic potential is fulfilled only
when we become cosmopolitan lovers, only when potentia (power)
and eros (desire) reunite our bodies to the polis (the body politic)
and the cosmos (the natural environment). (Ibid)*

To this can be added a further perspective, namely that *mesa* is an
instrument of the work of *eros* (in its original meaning). When Isis
goes searching for the dismembered parts of the body of Osiris, she
is doing the work of *eros*. And when she retrieves and re-assembles
the body of the god into wholeness, she is accomplishing the work
of *mesa*.

Eros has three faces: desire, longing and aspiration. Desire is the
heaviest of these three, being an urge to posses, or sometimes a need
to be possessed. It is a form of love that is limited and limiting. Often
it gives rise to emotional attachment, greed, obsession, compulsion
and disregard for moral principles, but still desire is an advance over
the constrictions of inertia.

The anatomy of desire is woven into the very fabric of the human microcosm. Energy moves through its natural cycles both in the
heavens and in our chakras, and as it does this energy energizes and
activates latent desires that are stored in the microcosm. The planet
Earth is exposed to the electromagnetic currents that are the life-
blood of Eros, and our subtle bodies and subtle nerves also channel
these same currents in reduced form.

In total, the microcosmic and macrocosmic energies form the
constellation of *mesa* forces available to the *mesa*-keeper. On the level
that desire works, it is not uncommon for these energies to manifest in disordered form as restlessness, agitation, excitation, anxiety,

selfishness and greed. Religious teachings advise us to cultivate the opposites of these, such as peace, clarity, faith, generosity and compassion. However, what we need are *practical methods of cultivating and applying these principles and energies*, since knowledge of higher qualities cannot by itself make us either happy or wise. *Mesa* gives us this knowledge. The body of wisdom associated with *mesa* accepts that *eros* is the prime motivating force of the universe. It does not ask us to renounce *eros*. Rather it gives us an approach to *eros*, and a tool for developing its full potential for the highest good.

Desire does not arise because of moral deficiency in the individual. Desires are inherent in the elements, and they reside in the *chakras*. Desires can, in fact, be classified according to the elements from which they arise, and the *chakras* in which they abide. The *chakras* are the playgrounds of Earth, Water, Fire and Air, as well as Ether. Earth gives us a desire to be secure, to be grounded, to have physical comfort and protection. Water makes us attached to family, relationships, procreation, and romantic fantasy. Fire awakens in us a desire or longing for longevity, name and fame, power, wealth and authority. Air promotes instincts of sharing, affection, service and kindness. Ether or *Akasha* gives rise to knowledge and wisdom. Therefore, to transcend desire, we must master the elements and this is only possible when we work with them more consciously and skillfully. *Mesa* is a tool for doing this. It bridges matter and mind, body and spirit, the individual and the universal. It shows us how we can use the physical matrix into which we are born for the attainment of freedom and power. This would not be possible if consciousness were not inherent in matter itself, and distilled in potency in crystals.

If desire is the most problematic domain of *eros*, longing represents an advance in freedom and awareness. It is still binding, but in a more subtle way. It can be thought of as 'refined desire. By satisfying the longings of the heart, one is closer to the discovery of the connection between the individual and the universal. An interest in *mesa* work can arise at this stage, because one is sufficiently open and plastic to come into attunement with the forces that have created the structure of our psyche. Longing is love that has awakened in the heart a wish for intimacy, sharing, sweetness. It is human love at its highest, being capable of sacrifice, compassion and self-giving. Still, it is conditional and in part seeks its own satisfaction, thus maintaining an energy of separation. Aspiration is the highest form of *eros*, being an urge to achieve total oneness, to surrender to the Beloved, to merge in the identity of the Beloved.

Human life is a growth of *eros* from its most limited to its most liberating expression. Eros is the force that seeks the crystal energies of Yin and Yang, Earth, Water, Fire and Air, and brings them together in a pattern of wholeness within the *mesa*. When one feels the urge to accomplish this work of assembling a living crystal temple, a god-body in stone, then the spirit of the goddess has already been at work and her power is available to bless and complete the venture. It matters not if we name this goddess Isis, Ma, Aphrodite, Quan Yin, or if we only feel her resonance in the core of the heart; the important thing is that the action of the goddess has awakened the urge to reconstitute the body of a god. The power of the Mother, which is the seed-power of light and life in the inner world, is the only force on Earth that can bring the work of the *mesa* to completion.

As Muse, the Mother gives the *mesa*-worker a creative vision. For some, the first awakening is a sense of life's suffering, a sense of dislocation or incompleteness. One feels exiled from the intimacy and deep unity of primal being, an outsider beyond the pale of grace. Already Eros is whispering that the fragments of life need to be relocated, re-ordered, re-configured, re-assembled. Already, Isis of the deep heart has begun to seek the dismembered limbs of her beloved, the wholeness of his self-form. Only when her work is complete can life cohere and the original wholeness of our primordial being be remembered.

The hunger to achieve and express a creative vision is especially intense in the modern world. An increasing majority of human beings have no creative vision at all, having surrendered the capacity of imagination to the false images of technology, whether on the computer screen, the movie screen, or the television screen. The primal and archetypal voices have been drowned by the glossy play of surface appearances, corrupted mythologies, and the debasing values of global corporate greed. Yet there is a hunger we all cherish for something more, something deeper. We have an urge to learn a new way of being and living, an urge to awaken the sleeping gods that lie within us so that we may dance the meaning of our life more passionately and beautifully. *Mesa* provides both a creative vision and a means of creative interaction with the world.

A cosmically patterned *mesa* expresses the deeply spiritual side of our human nature and the magic of unmanifested dreams that still call us to further adventures of the soul. *Mesa* enables us to participate more fully in the joy and adventure of exploring life because it gives a true creative vision. This vision empowers, opens, centres, stills and strengthens the one who internalizes it. In this way, a well made and fully empowered *mesa* takes its keeper toward the realization of all the possibilities that reside in the deep cave of the spiritual heart. It expresses an eternal potential, the potential of the divine in the human, and it works constantly to actualize this. Your *mesa* will not rest until it materializes your dream. It is the power of Eros at work, the longing of Isis for Osiris, the deep, passionate urge we all have for wholeness and completeness in concrete form in this very life. *Mesa* mirrors to you the stability and sureness of belonging that Nature enjoys. It reminds you that you need to achieve this creative expression of your inner dream if you are to claim peace of heart.

THE ELEVENTH ATTUNEMENT

Take your *mesa* heartstone, symbol of the source, and hold it to your heart. Meditate with it, and feel its meaning and its power to actualize this meaning. Then, place it at the centre of your *mesa* cloth. Visualize a pillar of light flowing from the center of the sphere up into infinity, and down to the center of the Earth. Visualize it glowing with pure, radiant light.

Next, one by one, take and hold each of the crystal archetype stones, beginning with Lemurian Jade, the Mother, and moving on through Selenite (the Child) rutilated Citrine (the Hero) and Lapis Lazuli (the Sage). Hold each of them to your heart and meditate on the identity of each, one by one. Feel that each one embodies the potential of its archetype and is a home for the archetypal energy and consciousness. Place each one in turn in its place within the *mesa*.

Next, focus on the stones of Earth one by one. Begin with Jade, and move on to Tiger's Eye, petrified Wood, Pyrite, Fire Agate, Malachite and Jasper. Meditate with each one held close to the heart. Merge with its meaning and energy. Feel that each is a part of your own being. Feel that each is a god-energy. Feel that each one is coming to life in itself and inside your own being. Then, place each one in its correct position on the *mesa* cloth. Feel as you place each stone that you are placing that part of your being in right relationship to

Source. Repeat the true name of the stone three times as you place it. For example, Spirit Earth, or Jade is the quality of the Heart Path. So you might repeat: Here is my heart path, connected to Source. Then, for Yang Earth, Tiger's Eye, you might affirm: Here is Physical Mastery, connected to Source. Follow through along these lines with the words that come naturally to you. Be sure to do it with care and feeling, it is not an intellectual exercise but a matter of integral attunement.

Work through the stones for Water, Fire and Air in similar fashion. When the entire *mesa* has been laid out, meditate on it as a perfect expression of your wholeness and divinity.

The central point of the Crystal
Mesa Logo represents the ladder
of consciousness, the pillar of light,
the world-tree, the axis of creation,
the omphalos, and numerous
other traditional expressions of the
sacred Centre from which
all things arise.

EARTH:
THE TEMPLE OF GROUNDING

THE SACRED ELEMENTS

The five elements – Earth, Water, Fire, Air, and Ether (sometimes also called *akasha* or space) are considered to be the essence of all things and processes. The names of the elements are symbolic. For example, Earth suggests a process that brings about solidity, density and crystallization. Water fosters cohesion, fluidity and flow. Fire governs activation, illumination, transformation and intense action, which in Sanskrit is called *tapas*. Air is motion, communication, connecting and expansiveness. Ether is the portal of entry into the subtle worlds, the celestial domain, inter-dimensional experience. It is equivalent to the matrix of Spirit. Each element is a dynamic process, and each is correlated to its own characteristic human emotions, temperaments, colours, directions, tastes, physical types, disorders, mental tendencies and personality traits.

The sacred elements give birth to our five senses, our sense experience, our emotional reactions to experience, and the five kinds of wisdom that arise from mature insight into experience. In the Eastern traditions, there are five primary vital energies, or pranas, that constitute life, and these too arise from the elements. It helps to think of a sacred element as a process rather than a thing, a sacred power rather than an object. When we refer to the names and forms of "things," like crystals, we are speaking symbolically about living processes. Also, the elements are full of life, consciousness and power, they are by no means inert or unconscious. In fact, they are best seen as divine, archetypal powers of creation whose living influences and capacities can help us evolve to wholeness, happiness and fulfillment.

The elements are spiritual essences that get their power from four qualities or powers. The *dry* and *moist* qualities represent form versus flexibility. The *cool* and *warm* qualities represent union versus separation. Traditionally, Earth is considered to be *cool* and *dry*. Water is *moist* and *cool*. Air is *warm* and *moist* (it harmonizes fire and water). Fire is *dry* and *warm*. In each case, the second of the two listed qualities dominates in the element. But each of the powers and each of the elements is a complex set of dynamics that cannot be reduced to a simple definition. They manifest in the subtle worlds and in the physical world in a variety of forms.

Experientially, one might describe the "feel" of the elements like this:

Air, light and free to move.

Fire, warm and expanding.

Water, cool and contracting.

Earth, heavy like lead weight and stationary.

As the story of creation illustrates, all phenomena derive from, and relate to Source. The reality of Source is beyond finite comprehension. It is infinite existence, consciousness, bliss. But in our three dimdensional experience, it manifests as the primordial energy of existence. And this original energy manifests itself in five primal fields, each with its specific types of process. There is nothing in creation that does not arise from the permutations and interactions of these five sacred processes (which we speak of symbolically as elements).

Our very way of being, knowing and relating to the world around us takes place through the medium of the four sacred elements. The way we relate to the physical world around us involves the Earth element, and operates in the domain of perceiving. The five senses gather information which we take at face value. However, perceiving is frequently a matter of projecting our personal perspective outward rather than acquiring new data or deep insight. When we relate to the world through feeling, we are drawing on the Water element. As long as human consciousness is at the reactive level of ego, feelings tend to fall into the two categories of: "I like it" and "I don't like it";

until we attain greater light and awareness, it is easy to project our own disorders and lose objectivity.

Thinking is a third way of viewing the world, and it involves the element Air. A mental ego is usually present in people who identify with thinking activity, and thoughts frequently revolve around "me" and "mine." To this degree, they are distorted. Lastly, Fire is the element we draw on when we use our willpower and creativity. Fire can also foster an intuitive way of knowing which has more immediacy than the logical intellect.

Each of these four modes of seeing and relating to the world corresponds to a specific kind of fear. Fear is one of the great distorting factors, because when we relate to the world outside us through that attitude, it usually attracts negative experience. Earth element often generates anxieties about money, health and survival. Water-element feelings are often tinged by insecurity, loneliness, loss and sentimental attachment, and the fear of loss is behind much of this. Airy intellect can bring in doubt, suspicion, criticism and judgmental thinking. This is based on fear of not knowing, which is a subtle kind of intellectual insecurity. "Knowledge is power"; therefore if I do not know it all, I am vulnerable. Fire can generate a fear of weakness, insufficiency, or a fear that one is wrong. The more these four elements are in balance, the greater the likelihood that Ether is present, and that an opening to Spirit has taken place, and this is the best assurance of inner harmony.

All of this could remain in the abstract world of theory or philosophy, but the *mesa* is a tool for bringing its user into a creative and productive experience of living with the elements. The *mesa* enables us to use the elements positively to better the quality of our lives and to grow in wisdom and power. The elements must be encountered experientially, so explanations and systems of five serve only as a point of clarity to direct interaction. The human body itself reflects this cosmic pattern of five. The central torso has two arms, two legs and a head. Our hands and feet each end with five appendages, fingers and toes. The head is a centre of cognition through which all five senses operate, the eyes, ears, organs of smell and taste, and the brain which registers all these as well as the sense of touch which connects with the nervous system throughout the body at large.

Thus, the body we have been gifted with is a microcosm, a field-of-five, a temple with a centre (Spirit or Ether) and four important shrines located in each of the directions. The *mesa* is a symbolic tool which reflects these realities. It is an altar of sacred substances patterned in a way which can express the cosmos in miniature. Only when it is organized to reflect the structure of creation does the *mesa* function as a synergetic tool, a key to experience and interaction with the wider fivefold cosmos. There can doubtless be *mesas* based on personal notions, dispositions, attitudes, feelings and sentiments which lack this traditional grounding, but they will not be able to function in the same way that a cosmically ordered crystal *mesa* can function. The sacred elements are woven into the very fabric of our being. The soul receives its Fire (will, creativity) in the world of Fire, its mental capacities from the domain of Air, its emotional fabric from the world of Water and its physical body from the kingdom of Earth. Ether is the domain of connectedness to Spirit and it has a special relationship to the heart. The "Ether of the Heart" is a place of interior consciousness where we intuit our relationship to Source and to Spirit.

In a later chapter, we refer to Fire as the "Temple of Aspiration." From Fire comes physical warmth, the energy of digestion and energy to regulate the metabolism. Mammals have evolved a much greater bond with Fire than, for example, reptiles. On the emotional level, a hot temper of an ardent emotional nature would derive from Fire, while on the mental plane, enthusiasm, creativity and initiative are Fiery expressions. On the plane of spirit, aspiration and heroic courage derive from Fire.

From the Kingdom of Air come the airy powers. Air actually is a medium which conveys the power of Fire and facilitates its expression. It is a medium of co-ordination and communication. By means of the Breath-Spirit, or *pneuma* the Fiery soul can unite with the primeval mud of Water-Earth and sow the seeds of life. Air is moist and warm whereas Fire is warm and dry. The moist aspect of Air imparts to it the power of flexibility while its warmth empowers it with a capacity to effect differentiation. Thus, Air represents a power for active change of form. People with considerable Airy endowment are good at intellectual analysis, flexible in discernment, and full of creative ideas. Air separates things, creates divisions and distinctions, puts limits to the unlimited, and brings discrete elements together in a greater degree of unity. Ultimately, through the power of Air, the individuated soul attains oneness with the world soul, The Fool of Tarot, at the end of his adventures, comes home to The World

The energy of Water is primarily cool, which gives it an ability to bind things together, but secondarily Water is moist, from which comes its power to dissolve structure and form. The Water element mixes and holds together while being changeable in shape. It permits the growth and development of form, but is itself characterized by passive change of form. This is how the astral world appears, a fluid flow of forms – in contrast to the physical world, which has enough of the Earth element to give fixity and stability. The dissolving power of Water derives from its cooling, uniting quality. It can thus attach to solid matter of all sorts. However its moist (conforming, flexible) quality causes the result to have no fixed form. In Water all things lose their rigid structure and form and identity. A passive loss of form is typical of Water's action, and this is why we say that it has a purifying quality. Water embodies a spiritual principle of flexible union permitting both dissolution and transformation. On the emotional level, Water is connecting and relating (cool) as well as conforming and empathetic (moist). It thus gives us an ability to relate, to feel emotion, to have an inner flow of intuitive attunement which, when rightly blended with Fire, becomes a 'sixth sense.'

Earth is passive and form-imposing. It is an inflexible synthesis of stable, inert energies. The Earth energy tends to crystallize things. Earth is cool and dry. Its dryness causes things to fix into their form and structure, giving shape and solidity and pattern. Psychologically, the Earthy energy contributes to characters who are stubborn, purposeful, dependable, practical, rigid, unreceptive, inflexible, strict, concrete and grounded. Earth's' cool power unites things. It mixes, joins, synthesizes and relates things of different kinds as it contracts. It is inward-directed, *yin* in nature, concentrated and quiet. It makes for formations that are stable, steadfast and enduring. The psychology of an Earthy nature would be indecisive, undiscriminating, nurturing, careless, sympathetic, co-operative and loving.

These four sacred energies plus Ether are the raw materials from which all physical forms arise. Each element is a deep field of study in itself. Increasingly, it is the power of attunement and direct experience through which we access the qualities of the sacred elements and make use of them in our evolutionary progress.

The sacred elements are all present in every *mesa* without exception. There is no reason why we cannot combine personal feeling and sensitivity with traditional wisdom and patterning in our own *mesa* of power, and have the most complete expression of all possibilities. It has been said that imagination is the key to the experience of God, and the *mesa* gives ample scope for all forms of creativity. What is indispensable is that we proceed with clear intent and integrity, because a *mesa* should never be a tool or symbol of ignorance. The empowerment of ignorance is both dangerous and foolish, leading as it invariably does to suffering. When we refuse to learn from light, suffering becomes the teacher.

The elemental energies are within us, but we use their corresponding forms in the sacred bundle, and when we open the *mesa* and place each object in its field, we lay the foundation for sacred ritual, or magic. The energies are related to their forms, they are embodied in their forms just as a statue embodies the vision of the artist who carved it. When we trace the sacred elements into the spiritual realms, we find that they manifest not as physical forms, or "things," but as subtle energies, and then as fields of consciousness. From such the inner worlds or planes of being are constituted.

In the Tibetan tradition, the subtle, spiritual manifestation of the elements is sometimes referred to as the "five pure lights." When the elements are experienced in their refined form, they are radiant, luminous, pure and conscious, not different in essence from the cosmic gods. Each sacred element is, in essence, a divine manifestation that plays out and expresses itself in many planes of existence down to the most dense physical matter which we experience as Earth, Water, Fire and Air. This is why crystals and gems have traditionally been considered points of contact with the gods, or embodiments of the capacities and powers of the gods. For example, Sunstone vibrates some of the reality of the Solar Deity, and Moonstone resonates with the Lunar aspect of Divinity. Quantum physics has arrived at the same conclusion that everything is in essence insubstantial luminosity equally well described as waves of energy or particles of matter. The ancients used symbolic, mythical language to say many of the same things as cutting-edge modern physicists, and there is a coming together of these two paradigms which is most promising.

The *mesa* opens up for us a way of relating to the sacred. When we assemble symbolic expressions of the five sacred elements in the *mesa*, we are acknowledging that these elements are the underlying powers of existence. We affirm that everything that arises from them is also sacred. The world and all in it is essentially sacred. This human body of ours is sacred. The cosmos is structured as a space for the expression of the sacred. It is therefore, like the human microcosm itself, a temple, a house of the Divine. This temple of a human body-mind with which we have all been gifted provides us a sacred space within which the dance of consciousness unfolds. This dance too is sacred, for it gives expression to the Absolute in form. The divine is manifested with special glory in the dance of life. When we humans learn to dance life with full consciousness, the *mesa* will have achieved its purpose; it exists as nothing less than a technology or empowerment of our aspiration for fullness of life and consciousness.

Do you relate to your body as a temple? Do you feel that it is intrinsically sacred? Is your thought, feeling and behaviour motivated by a sense of your essential divinity? Do you feel that relationship is, for you, a sacred recognition? Without self-love, a sense of the sacred in our own being, it is not possible to see the objects of the *mesa* for what they really are. Or if we only occasionally glimpse that the *mesa* is special in some abstract way, we may not believe with sufficient power that we bring the *mesa*'s full potential into manifestation. Crystal *mesa* mirrors the sacred pattern of creation, the harmony of unfolding divine intent in the cosmos. If one treats one's *mesa* as a teacher, one opens inner doors for learning. If one treats one's teacher as a deity, one fosters receptivity to divine energies. But if we see the world around us, our bodies, or our *mesas* as collections of lifeless objects, from that can only come more of what is lifeless. When we see the natural world and all in it as being full of life, spirit and consciousness, then our world speaks to us. It is full of presence and power, aligned to the purposes of the soul. Similarly, a *mesa* which is honoured as a sacred temple will be charged with oracular power. Because destiny invariably unfolds from intent, and because intent is underpinned by right understanding and clear choice, we must at the very outset treat our crystal *mesa* as something most sacred. We should feel that it is equal in holiness to the temple of our physical body itself.

The interaction we have with our *mesa* must arise from our sense of what is deepest and most holy within us. In other words, it must arise from the depths of the soul, pass through the portal of the spiritual heart, and involve the body, the senses, the thinking mind and every other part and power of our being. We either choose to practice *mesa* work with totality of feeling and commitment, or we settle for being imperfect and diminished. Crystal Yoga is an integral yoga, it calls us to be total and whole.

If our sense of the sacred is not sufficient to arouse a sense of total dedication in us, we need to discover a key for greater inner opening. What is the key? Nothing other than imagination. *Mesa* is also a great help for finding or retrieving this key. Chapter 19, The Imaginarium, explores this in greater detail.

It is very likely that the key of imagination is something we had as children. Thus, when I used the analogy of *mesa* work to playing in a sand pile earlier in this book, it was not a random metaphor. Children have not yet acquired the limiting mental conditioning that defines and circumscribes the boundaries of what is possible. They see, feel and experience many subtle things that they cannot put into words. But later children learn to use words and their verbal education becomes a tool through which educators wean them away from the precious capacity of imagination.

For many of us in the West, before *mesa* can be brought fully to life as a personal experience, the faculty of imagination must be retrieved and enhanced. You will find that working with your *mesa* in the ways we describe will accomplish this. But "play" would be a better word than "work" for what we have in mind. The word play suggests joy, spontaneity, relaxation, creativity and freshness rather than the classroom mentality that made us so dull. Think of the hours you may have spent enjoying your sand pile as a child; or if you cannot remember that, observe a child at play and try to remember what that feeling is. Reconnect with that part of yourself which can live in a world of your imaginative weaving. Be in that space of consciousness when you pick up your *mesa*, and be aware that the spirit of a child is a touchstone for what is sacred within your being and truly creative in your past experience. From this dimension of our inwardness comes the disposition that can grow in fruitful interaction with the ancient traditions of *mesa*.

Do not give up until you have reconstituted your imaginative faculty and your capacity to feel and experience the sacred. Spend time in nature, especially at places you find beautiful. The atmosphere of such places speaks to your higher mind and your soul. Let a simple prayer arise in your heart when you feel yourself opening to natural beauty. Remember a melody or the words of a hymn that feels right for the occasion, and sing it to yourself. Look up into the nighttime sky at the stars and wonder about the vastness of creation. Take in the immensity and majesty of the universe; then consider the atoms of your own body to be composed of myriad such universes. Are you not sacred? Let the answer arise as a feeling rather than a verbal expression. Let go of the verbalizing mind and feel. This is attunement.

In this way, and in other ways that will occur to you, the process of preparation can unfold. When you begin to create and use your *mesa*, it will reflect the wholeness of your being back to you. It will amplify your sense of sacred presence and power. It will teach you more about yourself, your life and your soul's work if you have opened these doorways of feeling, imagination and faith. And there is nothing new in it, for it is only a retrieval of what we all had as children, before the conditioning of adulthood closed in around us. If you can remember the soul element in your childhood, you will recognize that magic is still real and very much alive in the heart of your heart where you are still an eternal child.

Wisdom grows when the blinders of our conditioning have been loosened and the pure instincts of our heart and soul are released once more into the wide spaces of their native freedom. Imagination is the ability to sense beyond what the mind can verbalize, past what human instruction can convey, and for those who believe that the *mesa* can be a tool for progress in life, imagination is truly the starting point, the gateway to Wisdom.

THE EARTH ELEMENT

Our physical bodies are largely constituted of the "Earth" energy, the energy that solidifies, provides density, crystallization and physical manifestation in matter. Water is also present in the material body, comprising between 70 and 90 percent of its volume. Fire and Air are also part of our microcosm, although in lesser proportions, as well as being present on the etheric, astral, and other planes of our integral reality.

In the sacred traditions which give importance to the *mesa*, the body is considered to be a temple of the life-force, and of the Spirit. Minerals which embody various aspects of Earth-energy work differently (in their healing and attunement uses) from those that would be characterized as Fire, Water, or Air crystals. We use the term "grounding" to encompass the full range of action of the constellation of stones that cover the spectrum of Earth energies within the Crystal Mesa. By "grounding," in this context, I mean working to incarnate Spirit in matter. The *mesa* is a tool of soul-work, and the soul comes to Earth and takes a physical body in order to manifest Spirit in matter.

From this perspective, if we consider Spirit as the artist, then matter is the canvas on which the new creation is expressed. Beyond this, matter is itself crystallized energy, which ultimately is nothing but divine consciousness in essence. Therefore, matter is not something undivine, or anti-divine as some Manichean thinkers have claimed, but it is the part of the divine which expresses itself as a solidified, physical manifestation and in many forms. Matter clothes Spirit in form; this is how it manifests the invisible. By the time the infinite consciousness has devolved to the level of matter, the One has become fully elaborated into the many, and the principle of unity is expressing itself through multiplicity. To forget the oneness that underlies the variety and to miss the divine presence and plan in the luxuriance of the creation is to live in what the Eastern spiritual tradition calls "ignorance."

In Tibetan Buddhism, in the Heart Sutra, the central theme is: "Form is emptiness, emptiness is form." It is unfortunate that the English language does not have a better word than "emptiness" to express the concept involved. It is a very poor translation for the original Pali or Tibetan term. In Sanskrit, the word *"Sunyata"* means much, more than the English word "emptiness." It is closer to the original meaning to think of it as "the un-manifest," that which is beyond the perception of our senses – even the most subtle senses. It is much closer to meaning "the unmanifest" than it is to suggesting non-existence or a complete void. In the scheme of creation, the Earth element has to do with providing physical form. When we work with *mesas,* it helps to see matter as THAT, the One, the Divine, manifesting as the many – or THAT, the Absolute manifesting in name and form (*nama-rupa*). Quantum physics provides a rich perspective which is totally in harmony with the ancient Eastern understanding of the physical world. Matter is simply crystallized, solidified energy. When we look closely at matter on the atomic and subatomic level, there is little or nothing solid about it. What we perceive as solid with our limited senses is in actuality much more in the nature of a holograph, with energy and space predominating. It is because of this that matter can be modified by energy, which in turn can be directed by consciousness.

Let us review the qualities of Earth as we move to a deeper understanding of the sacred process of grounding. Earth is COOL and DRY. The COOL aspect of Earth unites things. Earth energy thus tends to bring about mixing, joining, synthesis and relating. It unites things of different kinds. The Earth energy is inward-directed. It is characterized by concentration rather than dissipation and by quietude rather than activity. It is an energy that is stable, steadfast and enduring. Psychologically, this shows up in human character as being loving, sometimes indecisive or undiscriminating, nurturing, occasionally careless, sympathetic, co-operative and creative. The DRY power of Earth causes things to *fix* their form and structure. Thus, Earth energy is formative and determining. It gives shape, structure and solidity. It brings about the interior order which we find in crystals, which are a highly evolved expression of Earth energy in physical form. Psychologically, this DRY quality can show itself as a tendency to be stubborn, purposeful, dependable, practical, authoritarian, rigid, unreceptive, inflexible, commanding, strict, domineering, concrete, and hard. Earth, then, is *"passive form-imposing,"* like a mould into which wax is poured. Earth structures things. It is crystallizing in its relation to energy, which it causes to be dense and inert.

The human microcosm is an instrument for the grounding, or manifesting, of the Divine in the physical cosmos. It is best to think of the Earth Element as a sacred process of manifesting and grounding rather than a "thing." Traditionally, this has often been expressed by the concept of the marriage of Heaven and Earth. However, the human mind has constructed belief systems based on limitation, and this delays the divine manifestation. Therefore, the mind, the vital and even the physical must be aligned to the truth which the soul knows and which the spiritual heart can feel when it opens up and lets go of its past conditioning.

THE TWELFTH ATTUNEMENT

For the purpose of aligning the body, vitality and mind with the light of the spirit, it can greatly help to affirm and re-affirm the core truths which, from the soul's point of view, express its reason for taking on a physical incarnation. In the following affirmations, the "I" is the soul, not the ego or the personality or the small self.

AFFIRMATIONS

1)   The fullness of Truth is here now.

2)   I am a centre of Its expression.

3)   I manifests Its infinite Wisdom in my every thought, word and action.

4)   I am guided moment by moment to become a fuller expression of this Divine Truth.

5)   From the infinite supply of the Eternal Source, I draw all things necessary for my soul's work, both physical and spiritual.

6)   I acknowledge and recognize the sustained action of a Supreme Providence in every aspect of my outer and inner life.

7)   In all things, great and humble, I see the Beauty, Truth and Goodness of the Divine.

8)   Aligned with the Divine Will, my life is a courageous self-giving to the ultimate Victory of light, love and peace on Earth.

9)   In the essence of my being, I am the Light of Truth, which will one day manifest in its completeness on Earth.

10) My physical existence is a microcosm, a temple, a crystal-resonance of the Supreme, Creative Word.

Read through these statements and settle on the one which you feel is most appropriate, or which you most need to re-affirm. Then, relax completely, and say it quietly to yourself with all the feeling and care of which you are capable. You can repeat the affirmation several times.

Then, pause, and hold your Source Stone next to your heart. Connect with this crystal with the intent of seeing and feeling as clearly as possible which stone or stones in your *mesa* will support you in this affirmation. When you feel the right stone or stones, pick them up and hold them with the Source stone.

Continue to repeat the affirmation while holding these stones until you feel some shift in your energy or consciousness. Be careful not to "will" or expect a specific result. Be aware of the energy of the crystals and bring that feeling into the affirmation as you repeat the words slowly, clearly and silently to yourself over and over. You may want to visualize a light glowing in your heart each time you repeat the words, or you may inhale the energy of the crystals each time you breathe in.

A deep understanding of these truths puts the "sacred" into the process which is Earth. It is the nature of affirmations that, being often repeated with full attention, they become part of the core understanding from which we think, speak and act. It is in this way that focused attention and feeling can modify our consciousness and life-energy, ultimately effecting even a transformation of the cells.

THE ARCHETYPE OF THE MOTHER

The primary archetype for Earth is the Mother. Mother is the great mystery of the formative matrix, or womb, of life on this planet. She gives birth, She sustains and nurtures life and its evolving forms, and through death She takes back forms into Herself where they rest until they are reborn. Thus, She effects the unfoldment of the Divine Plan. The term "Mother Earth" is ancient and widely used as a verbal expression that recognizes these facts.

When the Earth energy of our human microcosm is in balance, we live in right relationship to the archetypal Mother aspect of the Divine, and to the Mother archetype in our own inner being. Many good things flow from this, such as abundant supply, health, happiness, creativity and confidence. The Mother is concerned with incarnation. Within her field of influence, Spirit becomes flesh. She governs the processes by which Spirit takes form and expresses as matter, thus "grounding" the light of Heaven in expressive Earthly manifestation.

There are, broadly speaking, two different kinds of spiritual paths. There are those like the Vedantic and the Buddhist paths which attempt to transcend or escape ignorance and suffering by going beyond the need for incarnation into another world (such as the Heavenly world), or by merging with the Void. There are other paths, tantric in nature, which aspire to effect the marriage of Heaven and Earth, which entails a progressive perfecting of Earth so that it can manifest the Divine. Any *incarnational* path (which Crystal Yoga certainly is) must of necessity give central importance to the Mother aspect of the Divine. Conversely, history has shown most escapist paths to be patriarchal in nature.

The element of Earth, and the grounding process, give us an opportunity to deepen our knowledge of our ancient evolutionary lineage, our roots, thereby connecting us to the keys of manifestation. When you understand Earth, you learn that the uncovering of Her secrets helps you unravel a number of riddles that you carry inside your own being. Just as artifacts of great importance can be hidden deep underground, so ancient understandings can be located deep within the layers of energy that make up your human microcosm. The inner explorer becomes a spiritual archaeologist, uncovering the experience and potential of the past in the landscape of unconscious memories. Earth shows us a pathway to the hidden roots of our subconscious self, and reveals to us how we can access a long-buried body of knowledge about our origins and destiny.

If we are deficient or imbalanced in Earth, we may be spacey, flighty or agitated. We may find it hard to complete what we begin and experience dissatisfaction with what we accomplish. We constantly search for what will ground us and make us secure. If our identification is with the physical, we seek to ground ourselves in substantial, external conditions; if we identify as an energetic being, we try to ground in our feelings; when we identify with awareness, we try to ground in the nature of mind; and lastly, if our identification is spirit, we identify with consciousness. However, if there is too much Earth in our nature, we become dull, inert and heavy. We are too solid, unable to move. Our thinking and our meditation becomes heavy, lacking in life-energy or creativity. Therefore, the balancing of Earth is extremely important for the process of grounding, as for transcending the various fields of experience with which we identify on our inner journey to Source.

A complete and balanced human being is a blend of both *yin* and *yang* energies, both masculine and feminine qualities. The harmonizing of life is a work in progress in the womb of the Divine Mother on Earth. It helps to understand that the Divine Mother has little to do with our notions of the female sex. The Mother is She who has the power of creation, and who exercises this power in nurturing and sustaining life on this planet so that eventually She may accomplish the incarnation of the Divine on Earth. This event is symbolized in the Christian mythos by the story of Christmas, but other religions have also had sacred births that prefigure the entry of the Divine into the human. In fact, it is fair to say that long before the beginning of recorded history, the Mother gave birth to the archetypes so that they could work out the complexity of her plan and that She far transcends them. They are part of Her creation and they work as Her instruments to effect the celestial descent on Earth. Insofar as they have forms and names, it may be that they too are evolutionary. She is not only an Earth Mother and the Mother of Earth, but She is the Cosmic Mother, the Mother of Souls. Sri Aurobindo expresses this very beautifully in *Savitri*:

> *Ever disguised she awaits the seeking spirit;*
> *Watcher on the supreme unreachable peaks,*
> *Guide of the traveler of the unseen paths,*
> *She guards the austere approach to the Alone.*
> *At the beginning of each far-spread plane*
> *Pervading with her power the cosmic suns*
> *She reigns, inspirer of its multiple works*
> *And thinker of the symbol of its scene.*
> *Above them all she stands supporting all,*
> *The sole omnipotent Goddess ever-veiled*
> *Of whom the world is the inscrutable mask;*
> *The ages are the footfalls of her tread,*
> *Their happenings the figure of her thoughts,*
> *And all creation is her endless act.*
>
> Savitri, pg. 295

The Mother of the Sri Aurobindo Ashram was an incarnation of the Divine Mother, and had a full realization of the Divine Consciousness. She once compared our inner structure to that of a house:

> *When one goes down into the depths of one's being to find the*
> *psychic being right at the bottom of one's consciousness, there*
> *is this image of descending into a deep well, going down deeper*
> *and deeper, descending, and it is as though one were truly*

*sinking into a well… As one goes on the discovery of one's
inner being, of all the different parts of one's being, one very
often has the feeling that one is entering deep into a hall or
room, and according to the colour, the atmosphere, the things it
contains, one has a very clear perception of the part of the being one is visiting. And then, one can go from one room to another, open doors and go into deeper and deeper rooms, each of
which has its own character. And often, these inner visits can
be made until this house is very familiar to him. According to
the time, the periods, it is internally different, and sometimes
it may be in a state of very great disorder, very great confusion,
where everything is mixed up; sometimes there are even broken things; it is quite a chaos. At other times these things are
organized, put in their place; it is as though one had arranged
the household, cleaned up, put things in order, and it is always
the same house. This house is the image, a kind of objective image, of your inner being. And in accordance with what you see
there or do there, you have a symbolic representation of your
psychological work. (Collected Works, Vol. 7: 271)*

The Buddha also had this image of a house in mind when he
attained enlightenment. He told Mara, the personification of ignorance, that he had penetrated the mystery of the house and the pattern of its construction. He declared that the patterning of the house
would no more contain or limit his consciousness.

A *mesa* is not only a table, or altar, it is also a temple, a house of
the Spirit. We can use the *mesa* to rectify and balance our relationship
not only to Earth, but also to the other sacred elements of our microcosm. The crystals in our *mesa* make it possible to do a symbolic,
magical work of re-ordering the elements of our inner house so that
it no longer limits the evolution of our consciousness.

THE ARCHETYPAL MOTHER – LEMURIAN JADE

The colours of Lemurian Jade range from black and gold to gray and
gold with some dark greenish hues. The gold colour comes from the
pyrite and calcopyrite that is mixed with the jade. Black represents
the inconscience of physical matter, and gold is the divine light of
the Mother which has descended into the depths to accomplish her

transformative work. This stone polarizes with Lapis Lazuli, where the blue-gold hue represents accomplished transformation, the attainment of the Sage. Lemurian Jade confers wisdom of the ancestral path, attunement to the Earth Mother, deep healing, stillness, introspection, silence, and reverence. Commenting on Lemurian Jade, JaneAnn Dow says:

It is within the dark density of this stone that one can find the nurturing of the Mother, embracing the often hidden aspects of our personality. Not only does this new stone initiate the 'new dream,' offering all of us an opportunity to set out how we see the new reality unfolding on our planet, but the minerals included also help to heal the residual old dream patterns. We carry soul memories from the first dream that we now often question to the point of not willing to take responsibility for our own creation... Meditate, pray or work with the stone in whatever shape appeals to you and watch how your perception of our planet begins to change. Be creative with this stone, imagine what kind of world needs to arise now. Take these thoughts into your dreams and be mindful of what you receive. Invite the Goddess into your life, to soften the harshness projected onto you daily thoughts. Softness does not mean weakness! In martial arts, the highest compliment one can offer another is to say they have no corners. The softness and nurturing of this stone will attest to the idea that living without corners can be empowering and strengthen your spiritual quest. Ask for guidance from Quan Yin or any of the other female goddess personalities, Isis, Mary, Mothers of our Universe.

THE SACRED EARTH STONES

SPIRIT EARTH: GREEN JADE (JADEITE OR NEPHRITE)

There is a *kundalini* factor to Jade that works well with the various *chakras*. The different shades of Jade attune to different functions and systems within the body with a healing and balancing activity. A necklace of different shades of Jade would have this effect. It enhances intelligence and perception as well as communication. Jade is nurturing and stabilizing, helping to integrate the mind and heart so they work together in harmony. It brings on meaningful dreams and releases emotional agitation. Watchwords: healing, longevity, wisdom, protection, prosperity, purity, serenity, fertility, good fortune, clarity, courage, meditation, awakening of hidden knowledge, balancing, kidneys. Key Theme: Heart Path.

YANG EARTH: TIGER'S EYE (GOLDEN)

This stone helps to lighten, brighten and warm the Earth element in our body-mind, having a high vibrational, sunny energy which is also grounded. It brings together Spirit and Earth. It helps us to ground the radiance and light from above. Tiger's Eye works best with the sacral, solar plexus and brow *chakras* where it has a balancing affect. It will absorb imbalanced energies and normalize the hormonal activity. This stone helps in the achievement of goals with integrity in action. It helps in resolving dilemmas and conflicts, especially mental ones. Watchwords: wealth, protection, courage, confidence, scattered thinking, blocked creativity, *yin-yang* balance, grounding, balance, past lives, focus, strength, conviction, psychism, headache relief. Key Theme: Physical Mastery.

YIN EARTH: PETRIFIED WOOD

In addition to having many of the qualities of chalcedony and agate, petrified wood helps with attunement to past lives in meditation. It brings inner strength, grounding, and an ability to get beyond petty annoyances. It is also good for healing dysfunctional parts of the physical body where paralysis or atrophy have set in. It helps align the skeleton and improve hearing. Petrified wood helps one to learn the lessons behind suffering and to grow beyond the need for crisis in order to learn life's purpose. Watchwords: longevity, past lives, physical protection, skin and muscles, stress, energy renewal. Key Theme: Patience.

AIRY EARTH: PYRITE

Pyrite is excellent for shielding against negative energy including pollutants; simply carrying one is enough to call in this talismanic effect. Its vibrations remind the physical body of its inherent balance and perfection, helping it to align with universal forces that will promote and actualize this wholeness. It holds and communicates the instinct for physical, mental and emotional wholeness. Additionally, it stimulates insight into the realities that underlie superficial appearances, and being related to air it promotes mental clarity and intellectual acuity. Watchwords: bone structure, protection, DNA and RNA repair, lungs, mind development, integral wholeness. Key Theme: Abundance.

FIERY EARTH: FIRE AGATE

Fire Agate expresses the spiritual flame that burns at the heart of matter. It dispels fear and creates a shield of protection, deflecting all manner of attacks from outside. It dissolves blockages in the meridians and alleviates blockages in the circulatory and nervous systems. Desires which are not in harmony with our higher aspirations are dissolved by its action. It thus fosters and supports the best level of wholeness and attainment of which we are capable, giving energy for discernment and creative expression. It has an inspirational energy that acts like a catalyst on the higher mind. Watchwords: strengthening, giving courage, healing and balancing, confidence-building, grounding, vitality, immune system, digestion, protection from radiation. Key theme: Transformation.

WATERY EARTH: MALACHITE

This stone is absorbing in nature, which is a *yin* quality. When Azurite absorbs water, it changes from blue to green and is then known as Malachite. Malachite is a powerful healer, being capable of drawing out debris from the *chakras*. It blends well with other minerals in the healing process. Malachite can work with all the *chakras*, being capable of absorbing disordered Fire, Air or Water energies for later disposal. It grounds spiritual energies into the physical expression and absorbs pollutants and negative energies, picking them up from the atmosphere and from the body. Watchwords: tranquility, vitalizing, balancing, patience, self-control, protection, inner power, clears electromagnetic smog, activates the *chakras,* opens the heart to love, intensifies transformative processes an breaks up outworn patterns. Key Theme: Emotional Mastery.

EARTHY EARTH: JASPER (ALTERNATE: GREEN JASPER)

This stone is rich in nurturing energy, a reflection of Mother Earth's own presence and power in relation to all her children. It is a stone of protection often used in sacred ceremonies of ancient North and South America. It helps keep energy high in times of illness or fasting. It aligns the energies of the *chakras* and facilitates astral travel. The positive and negative polarities of our auric fields are balanced by Jasper, and the physical, emotional and mental bodies are integrated. It has a gentle cleansing effect, helping to eliminate negative energies and knit together the physical and etheric bodies.

It is also a very good stone for grounding and stabilizing energies so that they harmonize with those of Earth. Watchwords: healing, protecting, health-supporting, mental powers, balance, grounding, stability and balance, astral travel, past life attunement, liver and bladder. Key Theme: Nurturing.

If you have these seven stones in the Earth domain of your *mesa*, you will have a collection of valuable energies which can be applied in a variety of ways and in a wide range of circumstances. Whether your own specimens are polished or rough, large or small, you will have in your Earth family stones a constellation of *grounding* energies that help the soul in its quest to incarnate spirit in the physical world.

The horizontal arms of the Crystal
Mesa Logo reveal the narrow band
of our waking awareness, with vast
domains of the Superconscious
above, and profound depths of the
subconscious below.

WATER:
THE TEMPLE OF PURITY

The predominating quality of Water is its coolness, which makes it connecting and relating; it has a capacity to bind things together. It is secondarily moist, which makes it conforming and empathetic. It is the moist quality of Water that allows it to dissolve structures and thus bring about the loss of form. The dissolving power within the element Water arises because its cool, uniting energy allows it to attach to solid matter of all sorts, while its moist energy, which is confirming and flexible causes the result to have no fixed form. For example, Water will combine with Earth to create mud, and the primal mud is where life is born. The action of Water is to make things lose their rigid structure and identity, the coolness effecting a passive loss of form, or dissolution.

Water takes on form passively. For example, a pot gives form to the water it holds, and the water passively takes the form from its container. At the same time, Water permits the growth and development of form because it nurtures. The essence of Water, then, is to mix and cling together while being changeable in shape. Water embodies the spiritual principle of flexible union, which permits both dissolution of form and transformation.

The psychological qualities of Water include: relating, emotion, feeling, inner flow, intuitive awareness, spiritual attunement, and relationship.

THE CHILD ARCHETYPE

The archetype most expressive of the sacred element Water is the Child. In childhood, the intellect is not developed, and the feelings are uncomplicated. There is thus an innate purity of being and spontaneity of expression. The ego has not burgeoned, and quite often the heart is open. All this points to the quality of purity, which is one of the outstanding powers that Water has, the power to purify. Childhood is the time for fantasy, dreaming, play, spontaneity and discovery. Energy flows at this time – fluidity being one of the important characteristics of Water. The flexibility of childhood makes it a time of maximum learning, and water nurtures growth.

The archetypal Child is in a phase of growth after separating from the Mother (Earth), but before entering the quest of the Hero (Fire). Childhood is a time of effortless attunement to Nature, the spirits of Nature, the angels, and the archetypes. This attunement is not intellectual, but purely a matter of feeling-affinity. Within the Child archetype, we find several aspects including the Wounded or Orphaned or Abandoned Child, the Magical or Innocent Child, the Child of Nature, the Hidden Child and the Divine Child. Finding the Inner Child has become a popular branch of New Age psychology. When we confront the Child archetype within, we have a potential for a fresh beginning in life, because this part of our being is intimately connected to the creative energy of the heart, its flow or its blockage. Where innocence needs to be re-established, or wounding needs to be healed, the sacred energy of Water and the archetype of the Inner Child have much to offer. From the heart-space of our inner child, we are empowered to explore life's possibilities with freshness, beyond the restrictions of our conditioning, without the editing of our mind. The inspirations that come in this attunement are often intimations from the soul which can help us find a path to wholeness and balance. Unless we can again become vulnerable and open, life's promise will remain at best only partly fulfilled.

The Child within us embodies an intersection or crossroads, a place where transformation can occur. When we identify with this part of our inner being, we can reconfigure and re-pattern our self-expression. The Child centers us in a place of revelation, discovery and new emergence of fresh possibilities. Whether it brings us to an intersection of mind and imagination, or mind and emotion, or mind and body, we can be enriched by exploring this crossroads domain of expanded potential. For transforming the patterns that we have inherited, or re-working the habits we have acquired, there is no more beautiful and enriching place to be than centred in the Inner Child. The Inner Child sits at the crossroads where two or more different realms intersect. This is the place of intervention, the place where grace is most active, the domain where the potential of re-configuration is released. It is through this part of our being that Spirit takes shape and outers itself into expressive form. Renewal and rejuvenation are most favoured in this part of our being, especially the re-creation of the emotions. If we can feel that we are only four years old and relate to life with that innocence, then our thoughts begin to explore new domains and the old grooves no longer contain our life-potential. We can break into new domains of imagination and from there we can see and feel a wider way of being.

To find this part of your inner being, imagine you are a child again. Feel in your heart that you are fresh, free, clean and clear. Smile. When you smile, you bring heart-energy to the fore, and it is heart-energy that brings the Inner Child fully to life. If you can locate your heart's sweetest smile and radiate it through your mind and body, you will be able to attune to the Inner Child. If you can give birth to a sacred child in the cave of your heart, you can re-write the destiny before you and come closer to fulfilling your dreams.

THE ARCHETYPAL CHILD: RHODOCHROSITE

The energy of love is very evident in Rhodochrosite. It is a dreamy, balancing, meditative love energy that one may melt into. At the same time, Rhodochrosite has a definite connection with Earth Mother, and a balancing, purifying action on the base, sacral and heart *chakras*. It cleanses and renews and balances energy at all these levels, with a special emphasis on opening to love, the child-mother love of innocence and openness. The mind is aligned to the higher self so that spiritual attunement is made easier. Watchwords: affection, peace, love, dreams, happiness, romance, forgiveness, physical energy, immunity, intuitive attunement, Earth healing.

THE SACRED WATER STONES

SPIRIT WATER: SELENITE

Selenite connects us with Spirit. It builds a transition from our physical body and auric fields to the highest frequencies of light that we can assimilate. The human microcosm and Selenite work together to ground pure white light into physical manifestation. It brings clarity of mind and an opening of the crown *chakra*, enhancing telepathy and receptivity to higher spiritual energies. Thus, the capacity for feeling-attunement to light, the ability to dissolve disharmonious emotions, and the opening and activation of the crown *chakra* are ideally suited to Selenite. Watchwords: clarity, spiritual attunement, deepening of meditation, healing, soothing, balancing of the nerves, attunement, opening to light. Key Theme: Light Activation. (Alternate choice: Iolite)

YANG WATER: BLUE CHALCEDONY

Blue Chalcedony helps one to be more open-minded so that new information can be integrated into one's life. When the mind is adaptable, it is able to listen more carefully to signals from all directions, and communication is improved. The memory is stimulated and all kinds of learning are made easier by Blue Chalcedony. A positive outlook on life is promoted by this stone, and a more realistic perspective on one's personal issues. Watchwords: perspective, verbal dexterity, enhanced communication, positive outlook, improved self-assessment, enhanced immune system, anti-inflammatory, healing for the lungs. Key Theme: Gaining Perspective.

YIN WATER: PINK CHALCEDONY

Pink Chalcedony is gentle and compassionate, bringing out the affectionate and open qualities of the childlike heart. Like Blue Chalcedony, it supports openness to newness, but it does so from the heart rather than the mind. Creativity is enhanced with this stone, and inner harmony is promoted. When the heart is relaxed and open, greater trust can come to the fore. This stone supports the immune system too, as well as the heart and the lymph system. Watchwords: gentleness, openness, trust, relaxation, kindness. Key Theme: Graceful Love.

AIRY WATER: AQUAMARINE

Aquamarine clarifies the mind and promotes the capacity for reasoning and orderly thought. Thus, if knowledge and wisdom are desired, it would be excellent. As with all Water stones, it purifies, but it is good for providing order, structure and balance to the mind as well working harmoniously with issues of emotional sensitivity. It counteracts darkness and pollutants, while harmonizing its surroundings. It works well with the throat chakra, where it has a stimulating, cleansing and activating effect. It shields the aura and aligns the *chakras*. Watchwords: purification, calming, stabilizing, creativity, meditation, tolerance, communication, clarity, promotes insight and clears confusion, sharpens intuition and promotes clairvoyance, inspiration, serenity, cleansing, release of judgementalism. Key Theme: Honesty.

FIERY WATER: LABRADORITE

The energy of Labradorite helps keep the auric energies in balance. It also unifies the subtle bodies and links them to the physical and etheric bodies. Intuitive thought is expressed more easily by its influence. One writer refers to it as the "matriarch of the subconscious mind," because it inwardly teaches those who use it, giving insight, mental clarity, serenity and a peaceful mind. Along with Astrophyllite, it brings energies from the stars and planets into the *chakras,* and links with the Moon in particular, which gives it the watery vibration. This stone acts to deepen understanding, thus helping to support the aspirations that enter into meditation and spiritual attunement. It supports the work of inner transformation, and the unique and original path the soul must tread to that end. It is a stone of mystical, contemplative and psychic experience, helping the mind and heart to assimilate the energies of illumination and embrace the uncertainties of transformation. Watchwords: spirituality, originality, courage to be an individual, finding the soul's work and expression, creativity, meditation, galactic attunement, contact with higher beings and inner teachers. Key Theme: Magic.

WATERY WATER: MOONSTONE

The energy of Moonstone is introspective and reflective, lunar and feminine with a strong water affinity. It helps with the beginnings and endings of life cycles, relating more to the emotions than to the mind, a stone for feelings rather than intellectualizing. It connects well with lunar energy, and in meditation could help with attunement to the Divine Mother. Things stored in the unconscious parts of the being are made more conscious. Psychic abilities and clairvoyance are enhanced. It is calming, balancing of male-female energies, and it tones down aggressive tendencies. Watchwords: nurturing, divination, psychic awareness, protection, happiness, longevity, balance, flexibility, relaxation, reproductive organs. Key Theme: Attunement.

EARTHY WATER: CHRYSOCOLLA

This stone brings together the energies of Earth and Water. It revitalizes and calms the base chakra as well as the sacral and solar plexus. It can help ease emotional disorders, renew strength and balance, and facilitate communication because it works well with the throat *chakra* as well. There is great inner strength and energy in this stone which, if tapped, can be a remedy for lethargy. It draws off negative energies of all kinds, and imparts steadiness. All the *chakras* are energized, pacified and opened by this mineral, which makes attunement to the divine easier. Gem Silica is very similar in its substance and action. Watchwords: peace, wisdom, discretion, confidence, provides motivation where it is lacking, facilitates communication, helps to inspire creative expression, soothing, balances metabolism, supports good digestion, eases arthritis. Key Theme: Physical Temple.

The perfect balance of the Centre
with the Periphery, the parts with
the Whole, and the inner with the
outer is illustrated in the Crystal
Mesa Logo.

FIRE:
THE TEMPLE OF ASPIRATION

I n Fire, the warm quality predominates. This quality acts to separate things, working to bring about a re-arrangement of structure. The Fiery energy causes things of the same kind to join and things of different kinds to go apart. It differentiates, discriminates, dissociates, finds oppositeness and creates opposition. Fire expands and moves in an outwardly directed way, hence its luminosity and its radiance.

In Fire, heat predominates and the dry quality is present in a secondary way. Dryness is formative, determining, shape-giving. It gives solidity. (In Earth, where dryness predominates, we can see this at work.) It causes things to fix their form and structure. Psychologically, the dry quality is stubborn, purposeful, dependable, practical, possibly rigid, unreceptive and inflexible. It can also be authoritarian, commanding, strict, domineering, concrete and grounded.

Fire is the primary element that acts as an agent of change. Being warm and dry, it actively creates distinctions and imposes form (as a blacksmith does with his forge). Among the other elements, Fire is an agent of action. It is *energy* whereas the other elements are manifest as 'states of matter.' The Divine is often experienced in mystical contemplation as a great light, a spark of which embraces the evolutionary soul. It is this soul-spark, or soul-flame of hidden divinity which gives a human life its precious potential. The Divine Light of the soul is analogous to the essence of the stars, and in many ancient cultures it was believed that after death the souls of the just would ascend to live among the stars. Earth also has its central fire deep underground

244 Crystal Yoga One: The Crystal Mesa

at the centre of its being. The Fire that is below the Earth and the Fire of the stars above resonate this message to the kingdom of Middle Earth and its human inhabitants: aspire to be all that you can. Fear not change. Go forward bravely.

Psychologically, Fire sharpens the power of discrimination and thus enables decision-making and decisive action. The dry power of Fire makes decisions, once taken, inflexible. Fire fuels the willpower. The Fiery will clearly conceives its purpose and cannot be swayed from the path of action. Fire's decisive discernment is self-determined (in contrast to the receptive quality of Water). Those who are empowered by Fire are not swayed by external influences or circumstances. Often, Fire irrupts into life like a bolt from the blue, a flash of brilliance that shows the way forward, a stroke of creative genius that opens up understanding of how best to proceed. Fire strives to actively impose a pre-determined form on things, thus fulfilling the expressive potential of the creative impulse. The faculties activated by Fire include the human psychological factors of will, inspiration and creativity. Fire energizes action and illumines understanding, being a power either for great good or for destruction.

In the Vedas, the most ancient scriptures of India, composed thousands of years BC, Fire stands as a symbol of the soul. The *Rig Veda*, which is the oldest of the Vedas, begins with the image of the Fire sacrifice as a metaphor for the underlying process of all existence. In essence, it is saying that all our actions and thoughts are offerings to our soul. They generate experience, which helps the human being to grow and evolve in consciousness. For the ancients, life was seen as a pilgrimage of return to the Source, a sojourn of the soul in a world of ignorance and challenge. Fire manifests the spiritual consciousness that enters into creation as the soul and evolves a divine destiny from within. It is the seed and source of all we are and all that we can become. Agni, the god of Fire in ancient India, is a power for change that nothing can limit or overcome. All the forces of Nature are mothers of this luminous child who is poised between our earthly life of limitation and the infinite, eternal vistas of the beyond. Agni builds up and then inhabits the various life-forms as he journeys onward and upward to infinity. He imparts not only warmth, but also light, colour and energy. These are his outer attributes. Inwardly, Agni magnifies consciousness, enhances perception and promotes discernment, thus helping humans to attain the full expression of the inner light.

In Vedic thought, Agni is the ruling spirit or deity of Earth. Similarly wind, or Vayu, is the deity of the atmosphere, and the Sun, or Surya is the deity of heaven. Thus the Gayatri Mantra begins: "Aum, Bhur, Bhuvah, Svah," invoking the three planes of manifest existence as we know it. In these three spheres of our experience the creative light of sacred Fire brings about the transformation of existence. We see the manifestations of earthly Fire in volcanoes as they push up from the centre of the Earth to erupt in great displays of heat and light. Minerals express the potential of Fire in a very pure form in gemstones and in precious metals like gold. Agni is also present in all crystals that have the purity to conduct cosmic, spiritual and physical healing forces. It helps to remember that minerals are elementary life forms that are evolving, growing, developing and changing, and that the force within them for change is Agni, the sacred Fire.

Agni is in essence a sacred divine power, a forceful heat and a Fiery will. As a radiant force of knowledge, Agni descends from the Heavenly plane to build up the worlds; he is seated at the heart of matter, a secret deity, one who initiates dynamic action and progression. Agni confers power in action, strength in the inner being, beauty of form, magnificence of presentation, glory and greatness. Once entirely birthed from the constraints of limitation, he is revealed as the solar godhead of love and light. On the earthly plane, Agni assails, penetrates, envelops, devours, re-constitutes all things physical. His flaming force is filled with the light of divine knowledge; his is the seer-will that can effect alchemical transformation. He is a seer, a priest, a hero and an accomplisher. His accomplishment is to purify and raise up the soul struggling in Nature, to bring light where there has been darkness, power where there is debility, and progress where there is stagnation.

Sri Aurobindo writes:

No sacrifice is possible without Agni. He is at once the flame on the altar and the priest of the oblation. When man, awakened from his night, wills to offer his inner and outer activities to the gods of a truer and higher existence and so to arise out of mortality into the far-off immortality, his goal and his desire, it is this flame of upward aspiring Force and Will that he must kindle; into this fire he must cast the sacrifice. For it is this that offers to the gods and brings down in return all spiri-

tual riches, – the divine waters, the light, the strength, the rain of heaven. This calls, this carries the gods to the house of the sacrifice. Agni is the priest man puts in front as his spiritual representative (purohita), a Will, a Force greater, higher, more infallible than his own, doing for him the works of the sacrifice, purifying the materials of the oblation, offering them to the gods whom it has summoned to the divine ritual, determining the right order and season of its works, conducting the progress, the march of the sacrificial development... this flame is a light which, when it is perfectly kindled and in proportion as it mounts higher and higher, enlarges itself into the vast light of the Truth. Flaming upward to heaven to meet the divine Dawn, it rises through the vital or nervous mid-world and through our mental skies and enters at last the Paradise of Light, its own supreme home above where joyous for ever in the eternal Truth that is the foundation of the sempiternal Bliss the shining Immortals sit in their celestial sessions and drink the wine of the infinite beatitude... In the end we overpass all crookedness of falsehood and error, emerge from the low and broken and devious ground to the straight path and the high and open levels. Will and Knowledge become one; every impulse of the perfected soul becomes conscious of the essential truth of its own self-being, every act fulfils it consciently, joyously, victoriously. (The Immortal Fire, pgs. 4,5)

When we read the Vedas, we find that Agni is referred to in many ways. He is the priest of the sacrifice, the God-will, filled with delight, the young sage, the master of our gated dwelling place, the lord in the creature, the divine child, the invincible warrior. He is also the leader on the journey toward immortality, one who advances the pilgrim human seekers. Agni is the immortal within the mortal microcosm, the toiler whom the gods have established in mankind. He is unobstructed in knowledge, infinite in being, a vast and flaming sun of truth who consents to be buried in the obscurity of matter and ignorance; from this obscure beginning, he works his way upward into release and wide freedom. Agni brings divine perception, light, inspired vision, and inner joy, filling the imagination of his bards and poets with a flaming ecstasy. It is his force, his power of knowledge and his shining brilliance which are most often celebrated in the Vedas. He is the child both of Father Heaven and of Mother Earth, and the accomplisher of the great work of their reunion. As the hero-warrior, he dwells in the solar light and flame; as the wise sage he dwells in the heaven of purified mind, and as the psychic child, he dwells in the rivers and waters of our earthbound terrain. As the hero, he brings to humanity the triumphant will to persevere and attain victory in the struggle of life; by his flaming light, he destroys the hostile forces who attempt to prevent out ascent toward the Divine Source.

Our souls are sparks of Agni, for his is the light of life that fills our senses, breath, mind and consciousness. We are manifestations of a spiritual and universal Fire that generates strength, colour, warmth, energy, motion and aspiration. The inner brilliance of this climbing Fire grows as it attains mastery through our repeated cycles of Earthly experience. Because the energy of Fire is concentrated in crystalline formations of matter such as crystals, they have a place of special importance in the *mesa* of power. This is an interaction between humans and the mineral world which stretches back to lost Atlantis and even beyond to the times of Lemuria.

What we see as light is in essence this spiritual power called Agni, but on the physical plane it manifests as the sacred element of Fire. Fire is the physical manifestation of the Divine Force which we call Agni, or the archetypal hero; it works out the process of dynamic transformation on the most obscure levels of matter and inconscience. Fire does not accomplish its work of building life into a temple for Spirit without congress with the other sacred elements. Water is connected to Fire and can be its carrier. Salt water is closest in composition to our own blood whose red, warm and life-carrying properties are fiery in nature. The great oceans of Mother Earth absorb the solar Fire from sunlight, becoming the original matrix, or watery womb, for the gestation of life. The sap of plants carries their life, energy and heat. Plant Fire is watery in nature, while mineral Fire is more Earthy in nature. But Agni is more awake in plants than in rocks because plants demonstrate greater dynamism and movement of life-energy. In flowers, plants manifest Fire in the form of colour, fragrance and expansive form. Plants are easily dried and burned, thus releasing the expression of their inherent Fire energy.

Fire, having awakened in plants, achieves further expression in the animal kingdom. Animals have a central zone in their physical bodies where the digestive Fire is at work. It provides nutrients and energy to the whole body, and is found in the deep interior of the animal's physical structure, just as Fire is found at the core of the body of Mother Earth. The solar plexus chakra in humans governs the digestive Fire and related organs. Respiration, which oxygenates the body, is also a Fire activity. Mobility, speed and dynamism are Fire qualities, which animals demonstrate to a greater degree than plants.

With the appearance of human beings, we see a new type of Fire which takes the form of intelligence. This gift of Fire permits us to see beyond the outer forms of things and to become aware of their invisible energy and consciousness. By means of directed intelligence, we can increase the presence of light, wisdom, harmony, peace and divinity that is present in our world. The animal Fire still burns strong inside human nature, but a higher reality can be forged by the inner Fires of rightly directed will. *Tapasya, (or tapas)* is the Sanskrit word for fiery intensity of applied spiritual effort. It is *Tapasya* which brings about spiritual regeneration and causes consciousness to evolve beyond the animal and even beyond the human into a phase of godly or divine manifestation. This fuller expression of Agni was always present in creation, just as the oak tree is present in the acorn, but it is only revealed when the creative potential of matter is organized to a higher level of order such as we see in crystals. Humans are meant to demonstrate the intelligence of Fire, the fullness of its inner potential and its radiant powers. When the soul spark comes to the fore as a radiant flame of will, human nature becomes ready for the process of divinisation. The soul-Fire is the divine possibility within the human microcosm, a spark of the Source and surrendered to its plan to unite Heaven and Earth in the fullness of time. When we nurture this Fire in the heart, it eventually outshines all forms of limitation and reconnects the limited human individuality with the infinite consciousness.

As the inner Fire grows, the higher powers of consciousness are revealed and we move through various inner worlds or realms of consciousness from the most earthly and dense to the highest, formless heavens. The ascending Fire brings about an ever-widening capacity for action as it completes its journey of return to the Source. Where Fire is acting in a pure expression, we find the gifts of creativity, prophecy, intuitive insight, inspired intelligence and universal love.

Fire fills words with consciousness and moves thought from the plodding logic of prose to the inspirational meters of poetry.

The creators of the Vedas, the bards of the Druids, the prophets and oracles of all times and cultures have preferred this inspired speech for the expression of their wisdom. The inspired dynamism of Fire is present in all truly inspired music and speech, and the rhythms of inspired speech are best suited to convey the power of Fire. The following is an example:

In the beginning of time, a secret Fire was kindled
To burn at the heart of the world,
An imperishable flame at the core of creation,
Spark of the Primal Light that shone
Before the Sun and Moon were born.
In every flame of every firelight ever kindled,
Not less in the golden Sun above,
That light abides.
Gaze on Fire and it will sing to you its secret spell.
Out from the flames rise fragments of knowledge,
For Fire releases the mounting will and the soaring aspiration.
Fire engulfs all things created,
Consumes them in the holocaust of its light.
In Fire, a spark of the Divine
Begins to sense its presence and its power.
Fire brings the radiance of purity to the heart of life.
Fire melts all things into its great beauty.
To contemplate Fire,
To merge in Fire,
To touch the very heart of Fire,
Is to find within the deep soul of inward knowing
The power that can dare to BE,
Accepting without fear, without question
What truly IS.
Fire consumes what is inessential, and leaves what is pure.
In the crucible of the silent mind,
In the ether of the spiritual heart,
The alchemy of Fire transmutes all things into Divine Gold.
Therefore, we contemplate this Fire

Which gives light to our understanding,
Power to our will,
And magic to our words.

Sri Aurobindo describes the work of Agni in Canto XII of *Savitri:*

Out of the depths where life and thought are tombed,
Lonely mounts up to heaven the deathless Flame.
In a veiled nature's hallowed secrecies
It burns for ever on the altar Mind,
Its priests the souls of dedicated gods,
Humanity its house of sacrifice.
Once kindled, never can its flamings cease.
A fire along the mystic paths of earth,
It rises through the mortal's hemisphere,
Till borne by runners of the Day and Dusk
It enters the occult eternal Light
And clambers whitening to the invisible Throne.
Its worlds are steps of an ascending Force:
A dream of giant contours, titan lines,
Homes of unfallen and illumined Might,
Heavens of unchanging Good pure and unborn
Heights of the grandeur of Truth's ageless ray,
As in a symbol sky they start to view
And call our souls into a vaster air.
On their summits they bear up the sleepless Flame;
Dreaming of a mysterious Beyond,
Transcendent of the paths of Fate and Time,
They point above themselves with index peaks
Through a pale-sapphire ether of god-mind
Towards some gold Infinite's apocalypse.

Savitri, pgs. 279-80

Alchemy is a craft of transmutation in which the power of Fire purifies and exalts the base substances of human nature, including the inertia of the Earth element, into something radiant. Fire and its deep power of transmutation is indispensable to the *mesa*; working with the crystals which embody different aspects of Fire expands our awareness of this process. Because Fire is conscious and a divine power, it can teach us the forms of practice most consonant with our own nature. Indeed, a sacred *mesa* serves best when it helps us attune to higher guidance in contrast to being a tool for the attainment of limiting desires.

THE HERO ARCHETYPE

The predominant archetype of the sacred element Fire is the Hero. Possibly the best book ever written on the Hero-Archetype is Joseph Campbell's *The Hero With A Thousand Faces*. On page 19 of the Meridian 1970 edition, he writes:

> *The hero, therefore, is the man or woman who has been able to battle past his personal and local historical limitations to the generally valid, normally human forms. Such a one's visions, ideas, and inspirations come pristine from the primary springs of human life and thought. Hence they are eloquent, not of the present, disintegrating society and psyche, but of the unquenched source through which society is reborn. The hero has died as a modern man; but as eternal man – perfected, unspecific, universal man – he has been reborn... to return then to us, transfigured, and teach the lesson he has learned of life renewed.*

In this classic work, Campbell traces the hero's quest through several stages: departure from the security of home and hearth, initiation into a quest, attainment of a goal, and ultimately a return home with blessings for all. He makes many references to mythology and history, giving examples of the hero as warrior, as lover, as world redeemer and as saint. We might add that the great creative breakthroughs of thinkers, scientists and artists place them in a heroic world of attainment as well. The hero archetype has a special relation to the concentrated intensity and persevering will of the element Fire, something often represented in iconography by the saint's halo, or the world-redeemer's radiant heart.

Fire is lesser *yang* because in contrast to Air (greater *yang*), which expands everywhere with no limits, Fire must cling to its Earthy fuel in order to manifest. Fire relates to Earth as a bringer of catalytic change. Fire consumes, irradiates, transmutes and re-creates material forms and substances. Fire fuels the alchemical crucible of sublimation and purification. At the same time, Fire infuses life energy into water and sublimates it.

The hero has this same relationship with the earthly plane as Fire does to its fuel. The hero must struggle against the density, heaviness, resistance and ignorance of earthbound reality to achieve victory for the light. This fiery labour can only be accomplished in the conditions of connection and struggle, just as a flame must grapple its fuel. Both Fire and the hero must grapple with the raw materials of Earth and wrestle them into something better. The victory of light over darkness has been a central theme of myths and legends from our earliest recorded history, and it continues to be so in our own time. The hero is the light-bearer, the sun-warrior, the brilliant victor who liberates the life-potential that has been obscured by earthy darkness. The work of Fire is to achieve a victory of the Divine Beloved in the transmutation of matter.

THE HERO STONE – RUTILATED CITRINE, OR RUTILATED SMOKEY QUARTZ

Rutile directs intention, energy and will. Strongly directed and focused will is the essence of the hero or warrior. When rutile alignments occur in Citrine, the golden fiery energy is excellent for the mind and solar plexus *chakra*, promoting courageous thought and energetic action. When rutile strands occur in clearly aligned paths in Smokey Quartz, the lower and more obscure dimensions of consciousness and energy can be cleared and opened to light. The heroic action always involves *tapas*, which is concentrated, focused direction of will and energy. Rutile expresses this potential no matter what matrix it occupies, but the heroic action is most clearly emphasized in Citrine and Smokey Quartz.

THE SACRED FIRE STONES

SPIRIT FIRE: RUBY

Ruby gathers and amplifies energy and motivation, stimulating concentration and awakening the higher qualities of the heart such as wisdom, compassion and idealism. It is good for shielding from psychic attacks and for dispelling darkness and depression. It integrates will with love and releases blockages of energy from the subtle bodies. It also can help access spiritual levels of attunement in dreams and meditation or the transmission of information from spirit guides. Ruby stimulates and balances the heart chakra in particular, and is an excellent shield against psychic attack. It supports inspiring dreams and powerful visualization, being good for meditation of a heart-centred kind. Watchwords: wealth, protection, joy, will, confidence, amplifying, vitalizing, love, release of anger, leadership, courage, spiritual devotion, circulation, heart. Key Theme: Passion.

YANG FIRE: SUNSTONE

Sunstone brings vitality, joy and abundance as well as protection from hostile forces. It clears and brightens all the energy centres, working to alleviate stress and dispel fear. It is traditionally considered a stone of good luck and improved fortune. It has a special connection to light, especially solar light, being connected to the sun's cleansing, inspiring and revitalizing powers. It helps to cut energy lines to other people which tend to drain away the life force, and it makes it easier to say "no" when we have to. Negative feelings and attitudes are eased by Sunstone, and it is excellent for clearing away issues related to the solar plexus *chakra*. Watchwords: protection, physical energy, health, rejuvenation, vitality, regulates the nervous system, relieves depression. Key Theme: Solar Alignment.

YIN FIRE: ROSE QUARTZ

This pink, crystalline form of quartz has a calming, cooling energy that can work on all the *chakras* to push out and eliminate negative patterns. The colour of Rose Quartz energy is gold-white, and it has a special affinity for the heart and crown *chakras*. The vibrations of Rose Quartz are soft and silky, clearing fluids in the body's cells, and releasing impurities. Rose Quartz has a gentle action that is benign and feminine in nature. It helps the heart centre to open and dissolves stress and tension. This releasing action is then radiated from the heart to other energy centres. Rose quartz can act as a rejuvenator both of the physical body and of the emotions. Its tender, loving quality can help to deal with problems related to the emotions, sexuality, and relationship. It can be used for spiritual attunement to the energy of love. Watchwords: happiness, peace, love, fertility, compassion, forgiveness, self-esteem, nurturing, stress. Key Theme: Compassion, esp. Self-Love.

AIRY FIRE: CITRINE

Citrine clears, brightens, lightens, cheers, and builds up the light force in the subtle bodies. It is a cleanser and regenerator *par excellence* being the mediator of a gold ray of light which links the navel and the crown *chakras*. It does not hold negative energy, but dissipates it, which is a very rare quality. It helps to attract wealth and to balance yin-yang energy. It is good for focusing the mind, and also for the solar plexus and navel *chakras* in particular, clarifying issues of intellect and emotion and cleansing any negativity. It works also with the crown chakra to perfect the intellect and stimulate the awakening of intuition, thus being very useful in solving problems and promoting awareness. Citrine helps to awaken the higher mind. It helps to attract abundance and to maintain it. Self esteem and self confidence are supported while motivation and joyous endeavour are encouraged by the energy of this light and cheerful energy-battery. Watchwords: protection, creative energy, cheerfulness, abundance, energizing and recharging, nerve tonic, digestive aid, detoxifying. Key Theme: Clarity.

FIERY FIRE: GARNET (ALMANDINE)

Garnet promotes health, transmuting negative into positive energy in all the *chakras.* It links the base and crown *chakras,* having access both to spiritual and physical planes of energy. As a regulator of energy and a balancer of the body's auric fields, it is unsurpassed. This makes it a regenerative stone of a high order of effectiveness. Both emotional and intellectual processes are enhanced by its action, which accounts for its use in rosaries in ancient Tibet. It opens the higher mind and stimulates compassion simultaneously. Its energy discourages chaos, disruption or disorder, helping to bring stability and harmony to all levels of the microcosm, while purifying and cleansing whatever is negative. Watchwords: protection, healing, creativity, love, intensity, courage, strength, purity, compassion, heart and blood, anger issues. Key Theme: Sacred Body.

WATERY FIRE: GOLD LABRADORITE (CLEAR)

As a Feldspar mineral, clear gold Labradorite helps in detaching from old patterns and encourages new and original departures in one's personal quest. It promotes the development of self-awareness and self-esteem. It also works well to help uncover and make sense of inner messages one has received. As with blue flash Labradorite, there is an inter-stellar connection and an enhancement of communication with galactic energies, but clear gold Labradorite has a much stronger lunar connection. Insight is clarified, and detached awareness of intuitive information is facilitated. In fact all kinds of Labradorite bridge the connection between the intellectual and the intuitive mind. Watchwords: attunement, spiritual work, discernment, creative expression, universal awareness. Key Theme: Union.

EARTH FIRE: OBSIDIAN

Obsidian works best with the sacral, solar plexus and throat *chakras*. Being volcanic glass, it has a Fiery energy that helps promote internal change, specifically letting go of what no longer is useful. It exposes flaws and reveals truth in a powerful way, impelling growth by changing negative conditions. It vitalizes the soul's purpose in life and helps dissolve obstacles to that choice. We are able to take the right course of action and see the issues that confront us more clearly though the light of this dark fire-stone. It shields against negativity and disperses disharmonious thoughts. Gold sheen Obsidian in particular seems to have an energy that pierces the outer appearances of situations and allows us to discern the heart of an issue, being in addition a valuable stone for scrying. Watchwords: strongly protective, grounding, emotional catharsis, soaks up environmental pollution, divination (especially gold sheen), peace, objectivity- especially revealing reasons for stress, and supporting its release, over-sensitivity. Key Theme: Protection.

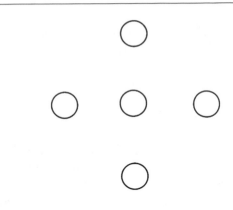

ABBREVIATED MOON LAYOUT

We can also create a version of this layout involving only the Source stone and the stones for Spirit Earth, Spirit Water, Spirit Fire and Spirit Air. To use this layout, move each of the four stones in and out until you receive an intuitive feeling about what distance it seems to come to rest from the center. This distance reflects our current state of balance or imbalance with regard to the four elements. The greater the distance from Source, the less light is working in that element, and the greater the potential for disharmony. After intuitively moving each stone in and out, you will feel your way toward a placement that represents for every stone its relation to Source (expressed as distance) When you see and reflect on what the pattern of placement means, after each stone's difference has been determined, you may gain insight into what your inner balance is, or in what area you need to pay attention. If we feel a disharmony with any of the elements, we can work with the stone or stones involved, moving and adjusting them in relation to center, either closer or farther away, to a comfortable distance, in the awareness that we are changing the relevant energies inside ourselves. This works best if we have developed a good bonding with the stones involved. The ideal is to have the stones a relatively similar distance and closer rather than farther. But it is important to feel where each stone actually is and place each one accurately according to this intuitive feeling.

AIR: THE TEMPLE OF WISDOM

*A*ir is moist, which gives it the quality of flexibility, and it is secondarily warm, giving it a power for differentiation. Therefore, Air represents active change of form. On the level of human psychology, this manifests as an ability for analysis, flexible discrimination, and for a comprehensive fund of ideas ordered by a clear intellect.

Air can bring about the fusion of Fire with Water. It has warmth in common with Fire, and moistness in common with Water, so it forms a bridge between them. This union of opposites is centrally important to the alchemical process.

Air conveys the power of Fire, and facilitates Fire energy. Air is a conduit that transmits powers and influences, a vehicle of co-ordination and communication. Air is the active spirit (*pneuma*) which operates on the passive structure of Earth and on the fluid flux of Water. Spirit, the breath, is the means by which the fiery soul can unite with the primal mud (Water-Earth).

Air operates like intellect; it separates things, creates divisions, and brings about distinctions. Air puts limits to the unlimited. It also unites things on a higher spiritual synthesis, helping the many to become one.

THE ARCHETYPE OF THE SAGE

The archetype which stands out in the domain of Air is the Sage. The perfection of Air is omniscience, and the Sage is one who has attained a degree of wisdom bordering on omniscience.

By virtue of being conscious, we humans can be attuned to all beings and know the relation of the whole to the part, the inherence of the part in the whole, and the truth of their identity. "I am THAT" is another way to express the spiritual realization of the Adept or Sage. This profound wisdom is the transcendence of struggle, which is invariably present in the archetypal hero's quest. Completion comes with spiritual realization, and the Sage is the archetype of one who has attained ultimate wisdom, a state of permanent identification with the Infinite Consciousness. The archetypal Sage has realized that 'all is consciousness.' He has seen that infinite consciousness is the matrix within which all forms arise and to which they return. He knows consciousness to be the ultimate field that pervades the entire creation.

Like Air, the mind and heart of the Sage dwell in lofty heights of freedom and purity. Having ascended above the pulls and pushes of the life force and the struggle of light with dark, the Sage can abide in the non-dual awareness of inner liberation. He may choose to live in the world and serve the Beloved in the world, but he is no longer of the world. He has become the philosopher's stone of alchemy a perfect instrument for furthering the divine plan on Earth. The Sage may be a prophet, a spiritual master, an avatar or a bodhisattva. Or he may live a life of obscurity and humility, unrecognized. His work is an inner one, but the outer appearance of his earthly life can be a teaching and an impetus for the spiritual progress of all whose paths he may cross.

The great masters have embodied various aspects of the archetypal Sage, qualities such as compassion, purity, detachment, wisdom, sublime peace, and inner power. Sometimes, the Sage may be a miracle worker, but the real miracle he constantly works is the capacity to raise the consciousness of humanity. He embodies attainment; for him, the struggle of the hero is over. His struggle is only to transmit what he has and is into the consciousness of aspiring humanity. Whether he lives in the world or in contemplative seclusion, the life of the Sage is an expression of the transcendental freedom of the Divine Beloved.

In Chapter 20, The Way of the Sage, certain aspects of this archetype are explored in greater depth, and their relevance to *mesa* practice is considered. If you have a master on the inner plane, he or she may be your archetypal Sage. You can relate to this being when the Sage archetype comes up in *mesa* work.

LAPIS LAZULI – THE SAGE STONE

This stone has been a connector with spiritual wisdom for countless millennia. It activates and energizes the third eye and throat *chakras,* clearing them of debris and preparing them for spiritual attunement. It helps in meditation because it facilitates the expansion of awareness. The intuitive and psychic capacities are facilitated, and there is greater mental clarity. Lapis Lazuli carries consciousness upward toward the Source, preparing for this ascent by an action of mental and emotional purification and clarification. As a protective stone, it helps build up our connection with inner spiritual guides. Additionally, it integrates the physical, mental, vital and spiritual levels of the being so that they function in harmony.

Lapis Lazuli helps us not only to uncover and see truth, but also to express it through a harmonising of the throat *chakra.* The higher mind is activated and creativity enhanced. Watchwords: healing, psychic work, protection, enlightenment, balance, focus, creativity, Spirit guide connector, thyroid cleansing. Key Theme: Wisdom.

THE SACRED AIR STONES

SPIRIT AIR: CELESTITE

The celestial realms have their own elevated energy, and we can intuit this with Celestite. Like Selenite, it is rather soft. But it does elevate consciousness by deepening mental peace and refining the vibrations of thought from lower to higher frequencies. In this sense, it enhances spiritual aspiration. For spiritual work of all kinds, including clairvoyance, dream recall, astral travel and distant healing it is excellent. The quiet openness of deep contemplation, free of noise and mental conditioning is the great gift of Celestite. It works well with the third eye and the throat *chakra,* having an ability to heal the aura and uncover hidden truths. It cools, calms and sedates, helping the mind and body to relax into meditation. Balance, alignment and interior harmony are qualities which Celestite will promote. It opens the third eye to universal energies and brings mental clarity and a smooth flow of communication, thus it would facilitate channelling. Watchwords: mental stillness, spiritual experience, clearing, inner peace, strength, communication, lucidity, dream recall, healing, transmutation of energy, intuition. Key Theme: Listening.

YANG AIR: KYANITE

This crystal aligns the energies of the etheric body with the consciousness of the causal body, activating higher *chakras* and facilitating spiritual experience. It brings light into the mental plane of experience. Like Citrine, it never needs clearing, it will not accumulate negative energy. It aligns all *chakras* without needing conscious intent. Its calming effect helps deepen meditation and it is especially valuable with the brow chakra where it works to attune the higher mind to the very highest spiritual vibrations. For all kinds of spiritual work, it is excellent. It aligns the *chakras* and subtle bodies, clears the meridians and balances *chi*; it awakens compassion, grounds spiritual energy and facilitates dream recall. For eliminating subconscious or semi-conscious fears and blockages, it is excellent, because it has a sword-like cutting quality that pierces these obstacles to understanding and awakening. For entering or deepening meditation, it is an ideal choice. Watchwords: creativity, communication, serenity, contemplation, alignment with spiritual light. Key Theme: Clearing.

YIN AIR: BLUE LACE AGATE

This stone is excellent for spiritual attunement to high worlds of energy and consciousness, bringing a sense of movement, lightness, and harmony. A feeling of softness, gentleness, coolness and soothing sweetness characterise this stone. Its inspirational influence makes it excellent for meditation. It clears energy blockages from the nerves and blood vessels, and helps to eliminate physical growths. Also, any suppression of free self-expression, which is a throat *chakra* issue, gets attention from Blue Lace Agate; we are able to speak our truth more confidently by tapping its energy. Watchwords: peace, happiness, calm, lightness, soaring, patience, spiritual attunement. Key Theme: Balance.

AIRY AIR: FLUORITE

This crystal acts to dissipate chaotic energy. It brings order to the mental, emotional, physical and spiritual parts of the being. It favours detached intellectual analysis, being an excellent tool for concentration and study. It is purifying, cleansing, and it has a wide scope of action through its different colours. As a tool for insight meditation, it would be excellent. Beyond this, Fluorite is useful for protection, particularly on the psychic plane. It balances and cleanses the entire aura, and it works very well against electromagnetic energies such as we find in computers. Anything that is in need of cleansing, purifying, dispersing or re-ordering within the body can be attended to with Fluorite. The mind can attune to spiritual realities more quickly under its influence and the physical and emotional parts of the being are also aligned with this higher opening, since Fluorite grounds high vibrations in all the bodies. Watchwords: intellect, a help for study and learning, promotes creativity, enhances intuition, focuses concentration, deepens meditation, grounding, stabalizing, balancing, healing, bones and teeth, emotional disorder, mental work. Key Theme: Mental Order.

FIERY AIR: AMETHYST

Amethyst connects to the violet flame of spiritual transcendence. It purifies and transmutes lower energies, clears the aura, and promotes peace and stability. As a protection stone, it guards against psychic attack. It is excellent for meditation, and it is excellent for healing and cleansing. It helps bring matter and Spirit together in harmonious balance because it has the capacity to open human consciousness to a higher realm of reality. In meditation, it brings the mind to tranquillity and deep interiorization of attention; at the same time it helps with visualization and intuitive dreaming. Negative emotions such as rage, grief, anxiety and fear are melted by its purifying energy. Watchwords: healing, peace, meditation, purification, inspiration, balancing, centering, elevates consciousness toward spiritual awareness. Key Theme: Aspiration.

WATERY AIR: AZURITE

Azurite stimulates the higher spiritual seeker within one's being, working well with the third eye and inner vision. It helps promote insight and psychic attunement as well as the ability to process information which is intuitively received. Creativity is enhanced, and minor irritations and mental agitation are smoothed away. Besides the third eye, which is its true home, Azurite works very well with the sacral *chakra* (Water) and the heart *chakra* (feeling) where it helps to awaken compassion and empathy. It aligns all the *chakras* and builds connectivity between the physical and etheric bodies. Watchwords: dreams, healing, meditation, inspiration, cleansing, inner peace, self-development and self-transformation. Key Theme: Freedom.

EARTHY AIR: SODALITE

Sodalite helps to open the third eye. It is the most dense and grounding of the blue stones and works well with the mind to bring reflective calm and an opening to meditation. It embraces the full spectrum of mental capacities including intuition, logic, spiritual perception and practical organization. Intellectual understanding, the clearing of old mental patterns, and transcendence of astral illusion are all promoted by Sodalite. It especially helps us to bridge the worlds of spiritual and practical experience so that we have an integral harmony. It can be used to block electromagnetic pollution. Watchwords: tranquillity, meditation, wisdom, objectivity, communication, harmony, balance, grounding, creativity, breaking bad habits. Key Theme: Understanding

EARTHY AIR (ALTERNATE): CHRYSOPRASE

This stone helps to balance *yin* and *yang* energies. It helps to activate and open the heart centre, so that it can bring the love energy into physical expression. Chrysoprase supports deeper states of meditation, especially heart-energy meditation. It heals a broken heart and favours the development of adaptability and a capacity to be accepting and non-judgmental. It promotes personal insight and stimulates the awkening of creativity while helping its owner to overcome compulsive or impulsive thoughts and actions. It is good for helping to restore security and trust when these have been shaken, as well as stimulating forgiveness and compassion. Watchwords: friendship, protection, healing, eloquence, personal insight, calming, helps relaxation, opening – especially of the heart, fertility, clarity, balancing, joy, memory improvement. Key Theme: Courage.

2

THE IMAGINARIUM

An innate knowledge of the Gods is coexistent with our own very essence.

Iamblichus, De Mysterii

When we imagine, let us understand that we are building up an image which can help us express ourselves more completely. Let us remember that the way in which we see ourselves and our world, our self-definition, is a synthesis of perception and experience which we constantly create and sustain. We live in our imagination, however static or full of life and creativity this inner world may be. We constantly create the world of our experience through our imagination, our weaving of a story from random events.

Crystal Yoga, Chapter 21

*M*esa is a map for journeying to the Otherworld. The more we use our intuitive guidance, enhanced with the energies of the *mesa*, and follow the hints that come to us from within, the more our meditations will reveal the true nature of this hidden, inner terrain. Like explorers, we venture into a little-known landscape where we seek to experience first-hand realities which are deemed to be mere fantasy or myth by those who have never lifted and peered beyond the veil. *Mesa* slowly reveals the workings of the central intelligence of this universe. The primordial powers, long supplanted by the gods of history, are still there in the energies of a resonant *mesa*, still there as dimmed lights in the very cells of our bodies and still present in the rocks and earth beneath our feet, as in the stars above.

Mesa is a key to the wholeness of creation's pattern, a doorway or point of entry for the journeying between dimensions, a lens through which to see and feel the completeness of creation, a revealer of the soul's way beyond the labyrinth of karma. When we know how to use a crystal *mesa* in meditation, ritual, and healing, we slowly attain access to deeper levels of consciousness and we witness within ourselves the emergence of a vast and complete understanding of creation. Our ancestral roots are embedded in the same energies that generated the gems of the Earth; the primordial wisdom of the foretime lives still in the constellation of energies that comprise a crystal *mesa.*

But to use a *mesa* effectively is much more difficult than to merely read about the subject, or to assemble one, although selecting the right stones can take months of searching. The techniques of the shaman and mystic require continuously renewed practice, unstinting effort supported by deep study and sustained by intense dedication. Although the work of a *mesa*-keeper may seem romantic when viewed from the outside, there is in fact tremendous self discipline required to sustain a practice of daily meditation, mastery of the mind, refinement of perception and release of any limitations that could limit the work. This growth of experience may include, ultimately, the transcendence of ego. But by walking this path with determination, we reclaim our patrimony of boundless wisdom. We recover our ancient symbols, and the ability to interpret dreams and insights and to follow these to their source. We open our mind and heart to an influx of revelation which is at once new and timeless, and thus we mature in the understanding of the hereditary wisdom of a very ancient tradition. We become living embodiments of the timeless archetypes, forerunners along the path of humanity's eventual *apotheosis*. Earth, its stones and especially its precious crystalline gems hold secrets concerning who we really are, and what constitutes the fullness of our cosmic being; *mesa* offers us a key to unlock the story of our star-heritage so that it may be told anew in our own time.

Everything we have mentioned is predicated on our capacity to enter into the *imaginarium*, which is the domain of magical creativity. The meditations described in this book are based on traditional pathways that open up into other worlds, or planes of being. The more frequently you walk the path, the more clear and strong your experience becomes. You may, if it helps, record the inner journeys which you intend to practice on tape, leaving extended pauses to visualize and bring to life the experiences described. Have your *mesa* constantly with you, and use it as directed. When you visualize a progression of events during an inner journey, remember to look through your own eyes at the scenes before you. Instead of seeing yourself in the setting, be there and see only the setting, not yourself. Be alive in your imagination within the setting which you bring into focus in your mind's eye, or on the screen of your consciousness. When you have finished your meditation, make notes of your experience. Do this while the impressions are fresh so that you will not lose them. Repeat each exercise a number of times and see how your experience evolves.

The *mesa* you work with will help you to energize and maximize your inner experience during these sessions. You will develop an ever-clearer perception of the primal powers that live beneath the surface appearances of things, and in particular the powers that manifest through the elements of your *mesa*. This knowledge will allow you to serve the Great Plan with humility and wisdom.

The intention with which you begin your practice, and each individual session, is extremely important. It always helps to state your intent and goal succinctly in words, as this defines the parameters of your experience, and in a sense strengthens and protects you. Each exercise should be repeated until you are familiar with it. But remember that you alone possess the key to bring your practices fully to life. Find your own way of working with your *mesa* tools, a way that feels right for you. You are walking a pathway which is a journey home to the truth of your own inner being. This must always be remembered.

The way you use your imagination is nothing short of your chosen style for self-creation and self-definition. Imagination and its use does not imply the construction of something unreal. To imagine, for the purposes of *mesa* studies, means to construct an image through which we express focused intent.

We are all blessed with several levels of imagination. Using our interpretive imagination, we take the sensory input of the outer world and the intellectual input of the mind, and we weave our own structures of perception and belief. Sometimes, we may use another and higher level of the imaginative faculty to bring these new creations into the world. Every aspect of our culture, from cars to gardens, buildings and paintings was originated using this power of creative imagination. Most of us have some experience of these two kinds of imagination.

However, the kind of imagination that has most to do with the *mesa* serves us on a still deeper level. This level of imagination has been called the *qualitative* imagination or the *incarnational* imagination. We use it to extend awareness into areas beyond the known boundaries of space and time. We use this form of imagination to access higher dimensional images, subtle patterns or archetypes that we then download and express in the specifics of our human reality in time/space. For those who are not visionary, these energies may be experienced more as qualities than as forms. The soul uses the faculty of imagination to apprehend creative qualities or forms or energies inwardly, and then we have the opportunity to draw them to ourselves and give them expression. If we do this, we become more than just physical beings, for we can use these higher images and energies to transcend the cultural and mental conditioning which has defined and limited us. The *mesa* is a resource or tool for developing and applying this faculty of *qualitative imagination*. When we apply and draw on these qualities of the inner plane, first creatively imagining them with our minds and feelings, and then expressing them in our lives and relationships, we widen our consciousness.

Your *imaginarium* is a world of unlimited possibility. If you can see and feel an inner possibility, you can actualize it. This is the fundamental principle of magic. If you can establish personal contact with the energies and forces assembled within your *mesa*, the potential of your inner work will be enhanced. The Earth energies may be visualized in the dragon form, or in any other archetypal symbols to which you find yourself naturally attuned. But for your growth in inner experience to succeed, you will have to bring to life the world of the *imaginarium*, the living, visionary, inner landscape of empowering forms. At present, this outer world in which our physical bodies take birth may be a ruined, barren landscape where hundreds of sacred sites lie abandoned, or even desecrated. For many of us, this outer distopia takes the form of an industrial wasteland, or an urban jungle, or a treeless suburban housing project, or a strip mall. But certain sacred sites *within* you are still active, and you must build on their power, for they can send ripples of energy to every other domain of your inner geography. Once you have re-awakened the principle inner temples of your own microcosm you can, as George Russell wrote in *The Candle of Vision*, "stand in a place that is holy ground and ... breathe the intoxicating exhalations as did the sibyls of old." (*The Candle of Vision*)

When you want to work with the archetypal form or power of the Earth Mother, face South; when you work with the archetypal crystal *mesa* described in this book, you can access Her presence and energy most directly in this orientation. When you are working with the archetype of the Hero, face East where the Fire of the Sun arises each day at Dawn. In sessions where you are attuned to the archetypal inner Child, be present with your heart fully open in a Westward direction. And when you invoke the Sage, face North. You will understand which sections of your *mesa* correspond to these archetypal beings, and you can open and orient it accordingly. In general, your inner journeys will follow a sacred track to a holy place within your very own inner landscape where you will encounter an archetypal presence. In this place, having made this connection, the essence of the meditative experience will begin to unfold.

It helps if you keep your *mesa* cloth clean, and possibly scented with a pure fragrance from essential oils. If you read about the various natural fragrances, you may feel drawn to certain ones by an intuitive affinity. Or, you may learn that certain combinations are magically potent, having the power to charge and sustain energy fields of intent. The fragrance of your *mesa* cloth will be a reminder to your consciousness, every time you open it, of your consecration to the sacred work. This same principle is present when the smell of incense in a church helps us to remember and recollect ourselves in spiritual focus. The mnemonic power of fragrance is a wonderful catalyst for activating magical capacity.

THE THIRTEENTH ATTUNEMENT

Take five or ten minutes to relax. Breathe slowly and deeply, and relax each part of the body in turn. Suitable background music would be helpful for this visualization. You might like the pure sounds of crystal bowls, or Tibetan bowls, or chanting, or you might have other preferred music.

Begin by visualizing a set of stone steps leading downward into a stone grotto. The steps are fifteen in number. Step down onto each one in turn, consciously and slowly, breathing deeply at each step. When you have reached the bottom of the steps, you are facing the grotto-entrance to a cave-like tunnel.

You begin to walk down this tunnel, and after ten steps, you come to a torch which is attached to the stone walls on your right hand side. You continue another ten steps, and come to a torch similarly attached to the cave wall on your left side. Then, after ten more steps, you come to a circular staircase leading upward into a room filled with light.

You climb these steps slowly. There are fifteen in total. You mount the first step slowly and surely. Then the second. Then the third, and so on until you are standing in a room filled with light. The ceiling is a glowing white crystalline substance, opalescent and radiant; the floor is dark and crystalline. A circular opening in the dome of the ceiling allows a shaft of light to descend onto a large quartz sphere, perfect and clear, which is in the center of this hall, resting on a square altar, which is at the center of a square stone platform three steps high.

The room you are in has four sides, but each of these sides has a large, square portal opening into four further rooms. One of these smaller temple rooms is in the North, one is in the South, one in the East and one in the West. Thus, the layout of the temple as a whole is in the form of an Andean Cross, or *chakana*.

In each of the four corners of this room stands one of the archetypes. To the right of the Southern portal stands the Mother. To the right of the Western portal stands the Divine Child. To the right of the Eastern portal stands the Fiery Hero. And at the Northern opening, on the right, stands the Sage. You gaze on each one in turn, slowly establishing a deep heart connection of love with each.

The Mother comes forward and takes your right hand. She takes you toward the square altar in the middle of this large chamber in which you are standing. You step up three steps with her, and you find yourself gazing into the center of the radiant, perfect quartz sphere. It is about a foot in diameter and perfect in every way. The light of this quartz sphere is beautifully radian. It draws your gaze into itself. You hear the Mother's voice:

Here, all that can be is alike in not having originated;
Here is the wonderment of pristine cognition, beyond duality;
Here is the dynamic range and reach of utter openness and
utter lucency;
Here is the unchanging continuum, the Ground of Being;
Here is the Primordial Enchantment, the consummate clearness;
Here, the mistaken presentations of your dreaming are no more.
Gaze deeply into this light.

As you gaze into the sphere of light, you enter deeper and deeper into its peace, stillness and blissful emptiness.

Allow this part of the visualization to deepen, and you may hold the clear quartz sphere from your *mesa* as you meditate in this way. Take as long as you like, and when you have finished, become aware once more of the Mother holding your hand.

When you are finished your silent meditation, the Mother takes you down the three steps, toward the Sage. He holds your right hand as she backs away, and he speaks to you:

That which we call our 'reality' turns out to be only our intended meanings. They present themselves like a dream from nowhere, and out of nothing. And this alleged reality is no more than a dream. It is we who have given it meaning and order. You have gazed into the infinite nowhere and nothing from which the elements of your dreaming arise. You have gazed into infinite consciousness, the Source from which the 'reality' you dream takes form, and to which it returns. Now, come with me into the temple of Air.

You pass between two pillars, one of dark blue Sodalite, and one of medium green Chrysoprase into a square chamber. In the center on a tripod is a large sphere of clear Apophyllite (or light blue Celestite, your choice). The ceiling is made of indigo-coloured Kyanite, and the floor of light Bluelace Agate. The Northern wall is of golden Fluorite; the Eastern wall is of clear, gold Citrine, and the Western wall is of dark blue Azurite.

The Sage guides you to the sphere of clear Aphophyllite, and you put your two hands out to encompass it on both sides. First, you gaze through the clear crystal of Apophyllite at the wall of Golden

Fluorite, ahead of you to the North, and assimilate the energies of Golden Fluorite and Apophyllite together. Then you gaze through the clear crystal of Apophyllite at the wall of golden coloured Citrine, taking in their two energies together, the energy of Citrine passing through the clear crystal into your hands and eyes. Then, you gaze at the Western wall and take in the energy of Azurite. Lastly, you choose one of the pillars, and gaze at it through the sphere, either Sodalite or Chrysoprase depending on which one you feel drawn to, taking in its energies and the Apophyllite together.

Remember while you practice this exercise that you can shift awareness into your subtle body as you learned to do in an earlier attunement exercise. Remember also that you can use your breathing to consciously inhale energies, and you can then visualize these energies being distributed through your entire being.

Finally, the Sage steps up and puts his hands on the sphere. You feel you have become the sphere and that you are being held in his hands. Feel that you are a clear crystal sphere, held in the hands of the Sage. Feel that your hands are his hands, and you are the sphere he is holding. The depths of his meditation becomes yours, and you merge in the most profound stillness. Some considerable amount of time passes, and when you open your eyes again, you are standing at the top of the stairs which lead down to the tunnel, ready to depart. You nod meaningfully to each of the archetypes, who are standing in their places, and then you descend the stairs, one by one.

Slowly, step by step you retrace your way down the long corridor of stone, noting the torches to your right and left at ten step intervals. Then, you slowly climb the fifteen steps that lead up into the sunlight. The attunement is over.

You may return to this inner temple, called the Imaginarium at any time, and deepen your acquaintance with the various archetypes. You may invite any of them to take you into their chambers, or you may ask any of them to take you up the three steps to meditate on the central crystal sphere. You may ask any of them for advice, help, or guidance. You may ask any of them to meditate *with* you or *for* you or on you. You may hold any of the *mesa* stones that are suitable to co-ordinate with inner work that you may choose to do in this temple. Because this is the Imaginarium, you should allow your heart to show you various ways of meditating and working with the energies that are here. Or you can study the experience of primal Reality which the Source crystal embodies, entering into deeper and deeper states of silent meditation and ultimately merging in the non-dual consciousness.

This is your inner-plane temple corresponding to the physical temple symbolized by your *mesa* stones. This is the place where the crystal powers come alive and fully available to you on the subtle planes for the inner work you intend to do. Let your soul guide you in this work, and may your *mesa* align and teach you as you move forward. The following seed thoughts will help you to make the most of your Imaginarium:

- My personal beliefs, and the collective beliefs of others form the parameters of my life experience. But these beliefs are only agreements about reality. I am creating the world I live in all the time. I choose a wider and more beautiful world of possibilities to be and become all that I can dream possible.

- If I can be more aware of what I feel, think and say, I can structure my life with impeccable clarity. My *mesa* is a crystalline temple of perfect integrity, a living embodiment of my full potential.

- I choose to see, identify and recognize all that happens to me on all levels.

- I will speak the truth as I see it with courage and clarity.

- I have at my disposal an unimaginable power, the power of consciousness. It fills me with energy, making me alive, intelligent, responsive, sensitive, dynamic and full of awareness.

- All parts of my environment are similarly endowed with consciousness and energy of varying frequencies, and I can be in rapport with the whole of existence by this recognition of our shared matrix.

- I know that my choices determine my attainment. The degree to which I become self-realized will depend on how I recognize and evaluate the many frequencies and vibrations I encounter in life, and how I bring forward my soul's purpose in the midst of my life experiences.

- No longer will I deny, forget, deactivate or disdain the wonderful possibilities my soul has dreamed.

- I choose to be free of the mass-induced trance of powerless living. I accept responsibility to be all that my soul's divine plan has predestined.

- I acknowledge that I am my own creation I love and accept myself for who I am.

- I recognize that the love I have been seeking outside myself is alive and well in my own heart and soul. I will develop inside myself the greatest gift that I have to offer the world, my own unique love frequency.

- I will begin by loving and honouring every opportunity for spiritual growth and expansion which life brings.

- I will make full use of my imagination to recognize and explore the subtle realms within and around my microcosm.

- My thoughts create the reality I experience. My beliefs are the underlying foundation for the experiences that come my way. I have the power to structure the reality of my life according to my soul's light and intent. I will be aware of this power and use it to the fullest at all times.

- In the Imaginarium, I use my willpower, my time, my energy and my imagination to create a new possibility. In my inner Imaginarium, I generate the frequencies of thought and energy that will shape my future.

- Therefore, I join with the Mother, the Child in my heart, my own heroic will and the Sage, who is the Master of Wisdom, and I say "YES!" to all divine inspirations, both now and in the future.

These are the principles and the choices that will allow you to maximize the transformational potential of the Imaginarium. Review and affirm them from time to time as you progress in the work.

THE WAY OF THE SAGE

Nowhere is the wisdom of the archetypal Sage more comprehensively revealed than in the traditions of ancient India. In *Gods, Sages and Kings: Vedic Secrets of Ancient Civilization* (2001), David Frawley dates the time of the early Rig Vedic texts of India, the world's oldest scripture, to a period between 6,000 and 4,000 BC, and the later Rig Vedic texts to a period between 4,000 and 2,000 BC. (pg. 198) They are thus by far humanity's oldest recorded historical documents, having been passed down orally for millennia until they were at last written in Sanskrit. When we look for precedents relevant to the meaning of *mesa*, the Vedas in particular are valuable because they are a record of the spiritual wisdom of sages who lived in the region of the Indus Valley. This phase of ancient history unfolded prior to 1800 BC (a point in history when the Saraswati River Valley dried up).

The great sages of ancient India discovered a body of higher knowledge, and formulated it for humanity as a path to spiritual attainment. These primal sages meditated on the intuitions that rose up from the depth of their souls, and then cast their visions and realizations into sacred and enlightening words of power. They held these thoughts of light steadily in their awareness, and thus became enlightened, which means that they achieved the blissful fullness of the divine consciousness in all parts of their being. They invoked swift streams of divine power (the gods) to flow down from celestial heights and flood them with supreme knowledge. In these sages of elder times, the Truth-Consciousness was fully established, and the way of its attainment was revealed. Their works and words were enshrined in the Vedas. The Vedic chants are an ancient record of the human soul's hymn to the gods, and a richly detailed vision of the entire journey from darkness to illumination.

In this tradition, gems, jewels and crystalline minerals have had an important place. The Sanskrit word for wealth is "*ratna*" or jewel. Gemstones played a very important role in the history of India, having been used both for adornment and for their occult powers. An ancient Sanskrit text "Ratna-Pariksha" is the authoritative Indian source on the science of gemstones. According to this work, there are 84 "*Ratnas*" (gemstones) which are further divided into two categories of "*Maha-Ratna*" meaning major gems and "*Upa-Ratna*" meaning minor gems. Out of the 22 listed as *Maha-Ratna*, 9 are classified as "*Nav-Ratana*" literally meaning nine gems. Examples of ratnas are: *Vajra* (diamond), *Indranila* (sapphire), *Marakata* (emerald), *Karketana* (chrysoberyl), *Padmaraga* (ruby), *Rudhirakhya* (carnelian), *Vaidurya* (cat's eye), *Pulaka* (garnet), *Vimalaka,* Raja-mani, *Sphatika* (rock crystal), *Sasikanta* (moonstone), *Saugandhika* (a variety of sapphire), *Pushparaga* (topaz), *Brahmamani, Jyotirasa, Sasyaka, Mukta* (pearl) and *Pravals* (coral). Varha Mihir, the famous 1st century BC astrologer of ancient India has devoted a full chapter to gems and precious stones in his monumental work *Brihat Samhita*. He detailed the outstanding characteristics of diamonds, sapphires, emeralds, and other precious crystals, and explained how they are associated with different deities.

If the Vedas comprise humanity's oldest wisdom tradition (fragments of which are also found in sources from ancient Egypt, Greece and Mesopotamia), Sri Aurobindo is a twentieth-century sage who has unique and outstanding mastery of these texts in their spiritual fullness and depth. He is universally acknowledged to have been a fully realized spiritual master who had direct experience of the inner planes of reality. It is no co-incidence that India celebrates its national day on his birthday, and that his image appears on India's five-rupee coin, along with the words: "All life is yoga." His *The Secret of the Veda (VS)* is, in my opinion, the best book ever written on the subject of the Vedas. It is an invaluable contribution to our understanding of *mesa* because it gives a completely authoritative explanation to the archetypal symbols, meanings, mythic patterns and cosmology of a human society that flourished in ancient India from about 6,000 to 2,000 BC. It is in the Vedas that we find intact the main lines of ancient spiritual thought and practice as shaped by a great lineage of ancient sages.

The term 'Veda' means knowledge, a term which in the Eastern spiritual tradition designates not information but the direct experience of the highest spiritual realities. This supreme knowledge was expressed in hymns that "have been the reputed source not only of some of the world's richest and profoundest religions, but of some of its subtlest metaphysical philosophies" (SV 3) According to Sri Aurobindo:

> *The aspiration of the Vedic seer was the enrichment and expansion of man's being, the birth and the formation of the godheads in his life-sacrifice, the increase of the Force, Truth, Light, Joy of which they are the powers until through the enlarged and ever-opening worlds of his being the soul of man rises, sees the divine doors (devir dvarah) swing open to his call and enters into the supreme felicity of a divine existence beyond heaven and earth.*
>
> Sri Aurobindo, *Hymns to the Mystic Fire*, 1973, pgs. 53-4

When we construct and use a crystal *mesa*, we have begun practicing one form of Crystal Yoga for achieving precisely this goal. A crystal *mesa* holds clues to many ancient wisdom-traditions, of which the ancient Indian and Tibetan streams are two of the richest. Of all the mystery schools of historical cultures in various parts of the globe, these have survived up into our own time, while many others have not. In the Vedas, Upanishads and other source writings of India the central thought is that the meaning of life centres on a quest for Truth, Light, Immortality. Sri Aurobindo writes:

> *There is a Truth deeper and higher than the truth of outward existence, a Light greater and higher than the light of human understanding which comes by revelation and inspiration, an immortality towards which the soul has to rise. We have to find our way to that, to get into touch with this Truth and Immortality, **sapanta rtam amrtam**, to be born into the Truth, to grow in it, to ascend in spirit into the world of*

Truth and to live in it. To do so is to unite ourselves with the Godhead and to pass from mortality into immortality. This is the first and central teaching of the Vedic mystics. The Platonists, developing their doctrine from the early mystics, held that we live in relation to two worlds, – a world of higher truth which might be called the spiritual world and that in which we live, the world of the embodied soul which is derived from the higher but also degraded from it into an inferior truth and inferior consciousness. The Vedic mystics held this doctrine in a more concrete and pragmatic form, for they had the experience of these two worlds. There is the inferior truth here of this world mixed as it is with much falsehood and error, **anrtasya bhureh,** *and there is a world or home of Truth,* **sadanam rtasya,** *the Truth, the Right, the Vast,* **satyam rtam brhat,** *where all is Truth-conscious,* **rtacit.**

Sri Aurobindo, Hymns to the Mystic Fire, 1973, pgs. 53-4

According to Sri Aurobindo and other masters, Truth is multi-layered, moving from a multiplicity of forms and energy upward to a unified state of infinite consciousness. The pilgrim soul journeys through this inner terrain in a return journey to Source:

There are many worlds between up to the triple heavens and their lights but this is the world of the highest Light – the world of the Sun of Truth, **svar,** *or the Great Heaven. We have to find the path to this Great Heaven, the path of Truth,* **rtasya panthah,** *or as it is sometimes called the way of the gods. This is the second mystic doctrine. The third is that our life is a battle between the powers of Light and Truth, the Gods who are the Immortals and the powers of Darkness. These are spoken of under various names as Vritra and Vritras, Vala and the Panis, the Dasyus and their kings. We have to call in the aid of the Gods to destroy the opposition of these powers of Darkness who conceal the Light from us or rob us of it, who obstruct the flowing of the streams of Truth,* **rtasya dharah,** *the streams of Heaven, and obstruct in every way the soul's ascent. We have to invoke the Gods by the inner sacrifice, and by the Word call them into us, that is the*

specific power of the Mantra, – to offer to them the gifts of the
sacrifice and by that giving secure their gifts so that by this
process we may build the way of our ascent to the goal. The
elements of the outer sacrifice in the Veda are used as symbols
of the inner sacrifice and self-offering: we give what we are
*and what we have in order that the riches (**ratna**, wealth*
or gems (my insertion)) of the divine Truth and Light may
descend into our life and become the elements of our inner birth
into the Truth... The Gods, the powers of Light and Truth
are powers and names of the One, each God is himself all
*the Gods or carries them in him: there is the one Truth, **tat***
***satyam**, and one bliss to which we must rise.*

Sri Aurobindo, Hymns to the Mystic Fire, 1973, pgs. 53-4

There is a profound meaning in this passage for the work we do with a *mesa*. The central sphere of clear quartz of the Crystal Mesa represents the Sun of Truth. The other gems which form the body of the *mesa,* including the four archetype stones, are its rays. They are nodules of its spiritual light crystallized into material form, each being in essence a *deva* or god. Every one of these rays of divine power brings its capacities of light and energy to the *mesa*-keeper for the holy work of realizing the soul's oneness with Source. Under the appearance of crystalline stones, the *mesa* assembly is in reality, when correct attunement and understanding dawns, a family of gods, a congress of their sacred powers and potencies gifted to us from Mother Earth and the Sages of all times for completing the soul's journey of sacrifice and ascension. As a tool of ritual, healing and contemplation, the *mesa* is thus a living embodiment of all that the ancient tradition has to say about the journey to Source. This way of seeing and relating to the Crystal Mesa is passed down by masters who have attained the fullness of realization, and is thus called the Way of the Sage. The Sage brings together both spiritual and occult capacity to manifest the divine in matter.

Within Crystal Yoga, the "Way of the Sage" refers to the process of working with *mesa* in the Eastern tradition, most specifically Indian and Tibetan, for the attainment of the highest spiritual goals. India and Tibet have always given great importance in their cultures to the spiritually perfected man who accomplished the work of Heaven on Earth. The way of the hero has been more prominent in the west. And the way of the Mother has been prominent in tribal, shamanic societies.

In the Indian tradition, the Vedas and Upanishads are the foundation upon which all else is built. According to Sri Aurobindo, the legend of the recovery of the lost cows of the sun from the cave of the Panis is at the very heart of the Vedic tradition, and holds the key to the significance of the entire Veda – and what is true in the Veda invariably opens an effective line of practice in our relation to the *mesa*. In this legend, the cows of the Sun represent Divine Light, and the cave signifies the concealing and obscuring power of darkness, which limits and obscures consciousness. The *rishis* who composed the Vedas also referred to this metaphysical darkness as Night.

Sri Aurobindo summarizes the plot of this important myth as follows:

> *Vala dwells in a lair, a hole (**bila**) in the mountains; Indra and the Angirasa Rishis have to pursue him there and force him to give up his wealth; for he is Vala of the cows, **valasya gomatah** (I.11.5) The Panis also are represented as concealing the stolen herds in a cave of the mountain which is called their concealing prison, vavra, or the pen of the cows, vraja, or sometimes in a significant phrase, gavyam urvam, literally the 'cowey' wideness of in the other sense of go (cow, light) "The luminous widenesses," the vast wealth of the shining herds. To recover this lost wealth the sacrifice has to be performed; the Angirasas or else Brihaspati and the Angirasas have to chant the true word, the mantra; Sarama the heavenly hound (intuition) has to find out the cows in the cave of the Panis; Indra, strong with the Soma-wine, and the Angirasas, the seers, his companions, have to follow the track, enter the cave or violently break open the strong places of the hill, defeat the Panis and drive upward the delivered herds. (SV 134-5)*

It is clear that many elements of this story are reflected in the tales of Egypt, Greece and Mesopotamia, where a god is hidden under the ground, and then rescued or resurrected. The god is invariably a being of Light, often a Solar deity. In the Vedas, the gods represent universal powers generated by the Truth-Consciousness to raise up the harmony and full potential of the worlds, and to bring about humanity's progressive perfection. Each god is a custodian of an aspect of the Divine Plenty and he fulfils this function by promoting it, both in individual humans and in the cosmos. By referring to the 'herds of cows,' the Vedic symbolism suggests that Truth is Light and that this Light has many rays, many colours, powers and potentials, a range of energies and powers. Each of these has a name and is considered a god. These are represented in the crystal *mesa* by the precious and semi precious stones. For example, the stones for Spirit Water, Yin and Yang Water, Watery Water, Earthy Water, Fiery Water and Airy Water represent a storehouse of spiritual treasures that we can access in the feeling side of our nature. Similarly the Earth stones represent blessings, harmonies and enrichment on the physical plane. The Air stones bring the many lights into the mind, and the Fire stones enrich our dynamic will, creative vision and inner intensity. The emotional, physical, intellectual and vital parts of our being are all able to house the gods represented by the various crystals. The installation of these powers and capacities into our microcosm is part of the Way of the Sage, and is a Vedic approach to working with the Crystal *Mesa*.

There is a certain learning curve, and it may be a long or a short one, but in time we discover that the crystals within our *mesas*, under the appearance of being mere stones, actually function as rays of the One Eternal Light, the lost cows of Vedic legend. Through the veil of material density, when we develop the sensitivity of attunement, it becomes self-evident and abundantly clear that these crystals are potencies and powers (gods) of the One Source. Each is alive, and each can be activated into dynamic potency by the keeper of the *mesa*. Just as the rishis of ancient times called down and installed the gods in their light bodies, the keeper of a Crystal *Mesa* has the means to accomplish this same work. Such a *mesa* helps us to prepare the chakras, nadis and auric sheaths for full attunement to the light of the soul, and hastens the descent of divine forces from above.

There are many variations to the legend of the lost herds. In some of them it is Brihaspati (the archetypal sage) who recovers these lost herds of buried light, while in others it is Indra (god of the illumined mind), or Agni. Brihaspati is the godly power by whose influence seers, sages and rishis deepen, widen and perfect their illumination. Whichever kind of hero may be at work, in the Vedic accounts his supreme task is to release the hidden illuminations so that spiritual light is raised up, restored and placed beyond the concealing and binding power of Night. The result will be the manifestation of something divinely potent, capable of perfecting the world. Our archetypal Hero stone, which represents Agni, is especially significant in this work, being a power for *tapas*, a Sanskrit term which means: 'intensity of directed will and intent developed through concentrated spiritual practice.'

The principles which underlie this ancient symbolism are at the core of all mystical endeavour and experience; they are not historically dated, and have never ceased to be operative in the inner life of aspiration. Always the seekers of light have struggled, persevered, been tested, progressed and eventually triumphed in the quest to go beyond limitation and achieve oneness with the infinite consciousness. Higher help, prophetic revelations, boons and blessings have come at many points of the spiritual journey to help each hero-seeker overcome a difficulty and release an obstruction. The role of the gods and of ritual in preparing the body-mind for ascension is ancient and universal. The keeper of a *mesa* will see each of his or her crystals as a physical nodal point of the action of a divine energy. Each crystal represents a spiritual potency directly applicable to the inner work of the quest. When we open the sacred bundle, activate the stones, place them in sacred patterns, and work other rituals of attunement we re-establish in our own bodies the lost herds of the spiritual Sun of Truth.

For the Vedic seers, in their symbolic ritual poetry, cows were the thoughts of truth; for the *mesa*-keeper, stones hold the energy and consciousness of the primal thoughts of Truth. These thoughts have been systematically named and described in the section on Tattwas in Chapter 2, The Primal Pattern; for example, the seven Tattwas of Earth, for crystal *mesa* purposes, are: Earthy Earth, Watery Earth; Fiery Earth; Airy Earth; Etheric Earth (or Spirit Earth), Yin Earth and Yang Earth. These are the seven rays, or rivers that flow down from Heaven (to use Vedic language) as they become embodied in the Earth element. We have these same seven rays or rivers of light in the other elements as well.

We know that the crystalline minerals of the *mesa* have always, from the esoteric point of view of the ancient cultures, been considered nodules of planetary and stellar light fixated into material form. For the ancients, the bodies in the heavens above were gods; thus, crystals were seen occultly as holy fragments of the body of a god. We know from many historic sources that gems and gemlike crystals were considered physical fragments of planetary and stellar gods, condensations of divine light crystallized into physical form. It was quite common to create talismans with the gems representing the planetary gods. One of the more common settings has the Ruby, representing the Sun, in the centre; the Diamond (Vajra) representing Venus in the east; a Sapphire (Indranil) representing the Saturn in the west; a Cat's eye (Vaidurya) representing Ketu in the north; a Coral (Moonga) representing Mars in the south; an Emerald (Marakatam) representing Mercury in the northeast and a Jacinth (Gomed) representing Jupiter in the northwest of the Navratna Pariksha. Tibetan singing bowls, and other sacred implements, are often made of seven sacred metals including copper, tin, zinc, silver, gold, iron and mercury. The best bowls are made with meteoric iron, because it has a 'stellar' origin; this tradition has prevailed right up into recent times in the remote areas of Tibet, Bhutan and Nepal where these bowls are made in the old way.

In many cases, the name of the stone indicates the association, as for example in Sunstone, Moonstone, Selenite, Neptunite, Iolite, Heliotrope, Celestite, and Astrophyllite. Their many pure colours expressed the seven rays, or seven streams of energy, or seven rivers of power which flowed from the primal Source, or in Vedic terms, from the udders of Aditi, the Mother of the Gods, the divine Cow. The heroic act of going under the ground into the womb of Mother Earth and releasing the concealed 'herds of light' from the darkness of subterranean caves liberates many streams of celestial potential from their deep places of concealment. These then become available for the great sacrifice, the work of elevating the consciousness of spiritually awakened humanity. *Mesa* is an assembly of crystals (each crystal being a solidified light) into a unified body of power. When the lights and energies which Mother Earth has been holding in her womb are released and assembled into a unified body, they become a true *mesa*, a tool of spiritual self-transformation.

If you ever fly in and out of airports, it is very interesting to look down at the streets of a city below you and see what is going on. The people and the cars become smaller and smaller as the plane rises up into the sky. The higher you get, the more insignificant they seem, and it's not long until a city looks just like an anthill, a busy heap of small beings rushing around doing very petty things. That is how we urbanized humans must look to the sky gods. I once saw a bird that had died only a few hours previously, but already ants were swarming over its body and taking pieces of its eyes and flesh back to their nest. I have many times been to gem and mineral shows where people swarmed over the pieces of the body of Mother Earth, selecting morsels they liked best and buying them to take home. There, no doubt, they would enjoy the energy or the colour, or some other indefinable qualities of the crystals and minerals that they had purchased. Something about the energies of precious stones attracts and nourishes the consciousness of even the average shopper who has no interest in spiritual philosophy. In that respect, we are a little like ants, or like the dwarves of ancient European legend who were the seekers of the hidden wealth that lay buried deep in the bowels of the earth. They were hoarders of treasure, toilers in the tunnels of the underworld for jewels and gold.

If you pause and think about these divergent examples, you may begin to see and sense a pattern, and this is exactly what was known and described in the most ancient texts of India. In the womb of Mother Earth, there are treasures which have special energies that greatly assist us to reconstitute our bodies, energies and understanding into a pattern of wholeness and perfection. These precious and semi-precious gems feed us in some special way. It is no co-incidence that the ancient societies where gold and gems were widely used and worn progressed to high levels of culture and spiritual attainment.

Vedic symbolism and legend speak to the core realities of crystal *mesa*. Both Veda and *mesa* can involve speech, song and story. Both in Vedic tradition and in *mesa* cosmology, symbols and archetypes can only speak to us when they are connected to a living story. M*esas* and the crystals that comprise them only teach and heal when the *mesa*-keeper is aware of their grammar, their language, the stories they were made to tell and the roles that the powers of light and darkness can play in these stories. All of this is what we mean by cosmology, and it is the need for this framework of understanding which necessitated earlier chapters that dealt with the story of creation.

If you want to consider more deeply who Vala or Vritra (villains of the Vedic story) are, simply refer back to the dark side energies of the four sacred elements. These villains act as hostile forces of concealment, distortion, constriction, limitation, and even destruction. The liberating actions of the hero-gods Indra and Agni, as well as the archetypal Sage Brihaspati, are not performed once and for all time in some historical past which is now over. Indra (the illumined mind) and Agni (the divinely empowered will) continually repeat their seeking out of the lost rays (or herds of light) and their rescuing action so that the concealed wealth of Mother Earth can be used by seekers of Light and Truth. Brihaspati continuously imparts and empowers the words of power that activate and direct the powers of light toward the sacrifice of transformation. The Vedas can supply a student of *mesa* with precious insights for releasing and applying the many-rayed lights of the Earth Mother's gems in the work of self-transformation. It is worth considering some aspects of this ancient teaching.

The Vedic gods are different names and powers of the one Deity seen working in nature and expressed in symbols taken from nature. Representing as they do the different forms, powers and personalities of the one Supreme Being, their work is to restore unity out of the chaotic divisions which have prevailed in the lower worlds as a result of the hostile powers. They bring light, harmony and order where there has been darkness, fragmentation and disorder. For the Rishis who composed the Vedic hymns, each deity was at once an internal and an external power of universal nature. Thus, the Sanskrit word *"go"* meant both cow and light. The cow was the symbolic form of Aditi, the infinite consciousness, Mother of the Gods. Her earthly representative in the crystal *mesa* is Lemurian Jade. From within the crystalline matrix of earthly matter, she gestates the divine child, Agni, the future hero, and ultimately the royal Sage; these archetypal beings will emerge from the dark web of matter through her power, when her work of birth-giving reaches its term.

In the primal legends and Vedic hymns, the seven rays and the seven rivers symbolize the various powers of this creative light which the Mother gestates to fullness in the heart of matter. The Vedic hymns were meant to be chanted at public rituals, and in their verses the gods are continually referred to as 'priests of the offering'; it is by their power that the inner spiritual work is accomplished. Agni, who is outwardly called the Fire God is inwardly the illumined Will, the divine Force. Agni's action is supremely important because he takes up the inner work of the consecrated sacrifice and brings it to a successful conclusion so that it bears fruit and yields an increase of divine potential.

It is the sages who have made us aware of gods like Agni, and sages who have composed the hymns to these gods by which the ritual sacrifices were made effective. Sri Aurobindo has translated many of the Vedic Agni hymns into English, and certain passages from these can be excellent for meditation, for example:

The flame adorable by the ancient sages
Is adorable too by the new.
He brings here the Gods.
By the flame one enjoys a treasure
That verily increases day by day,
Glorious, most full of hero-power.
O Fire, you, being born, hither bear the Gods
For the sacrificer who spreads the holy seat,
You are our desirable summoning priest.
He who with the offerings
Approaches the divine force, for the Birth of the Gods,
O Purifier, on him have grace.
He is born to us as if a son, rapturous in our house
Like a glad horse of swiftness he carries save through their battle
the peoples
When I call to the beings who dwell in one abode with the Gods
The flame attains all godheads.
He forms within us the seer-wisdoms of the eternal creator
Holding in his hand many strengths, powers of the god-heads
May fire become the treasure-master of the riches
Ever fashioning all immortal things.
O Fire, you are overwhelming in your strength
You are most forceful for the forming of the gods,
As if a wealth for the forming of the gods;
Most forceful indeed is your rapture and most luminous your will.
So they serve thee, O Ageless Fire,
Those who hear thy word serve thee.

> *Hymns To The Mystic Fire, 1973, random selections.*

The two chief results of the Vedic ritual sacrifice were wealth of cows and wealth of horses, which according to the higher or inward interpretation means an abundance of light and a plenitude of vital energy. In working with a *mesa* of power, results come only when we have awakened, invoked and harnessed the powers of the crystals. The Vedic seers, had they left us any treatises on *mesa*, might have spoken of the 'gods' of the crystals rather than 'archetypes,' this latter term being one with which the modern western mind is more comfortable. But the choice of words is of secondary importance as long as we are clear about the realities at work. These are explained very clearly by Sri Aurobindo:

> *The gods I found to be described as children of Light, sons of Aditi, of Infinity; and without exception they are described as increasing man, bringing him light, pouring on him the fullness of the waters, the abundance of the heavens, increasing the truth in him, building up the divine worlds, leading him against all attacks to the great goal, the integral felicity, the perfect bliss. Their separate functions emerged by means of their activities, their epithets, the psychological sense of the legends connected with them... (SV 43)*

What was the goal of the Vedic Rishis, and of the Brahmins who still perform pujas and other similar sacrifices according to the ancient way? It is the same ultimate goal towards which we are working when we assemble the crystal *mesa*, namely to eliminate all deformations of energy and consciousness so that harmony and Truth could be established both in the human microcosm and in the wider macrocosm. The ancients would have expressed it more succinctly as an aspiration to "bring together Heaven and Earth." The Truth toward which spiritual seekers strive is described in the Veda as a progressive attainment of wholeness, happiness and eventual immortality. By working with ritual tools to establish the reign of light, purity and full awareness, both the Vedic seeker and the more modern *mesa*-user go beyond the domains of limited consciousness, transcending all forms of ignorance to eventually attain enlightenment. It is worth remembering that the Vedas are chanted by the Brahmins of India (and elsewhere)to this very day, just as they were in the distant past. Moreover, *mesas* are being assembled and used by indigenous people and a growing body of spiritual seekers from various backgrounds throughout North America, South America and even beyond. These ancient pathways to wholeness have never exhausted their power; indeed, in our own time there may be more people actively practicing them than at any other point in human history.

Foremost among the Vedic gods is Agni. He is described by Sri Aurobindo as *"the divine power that builds up the worlds, the immortal in mortals, the divine power in man, the energy of fulfillment, the divine will perfectly inspired by divine Wisdom, the active or effective power of the Truth-Consciousness, the god in humans, the immortal in mortals, the divine guest."* (SV 61-2) In Sri Aurobindo's *Collected Works*, we read:

> *Our sacrifice is a journey, a pilgrimage and a battle, – a travel towards the Gods and we also make that journey with Agni, the inner Flame, as our path-finder and leader. Our human things are raised up by the mystic Fire into the immortal being, into the Great Heaven, and the things divine come down into us. (Vol. 11, pg. 18)*

Fire is the manifestation of Divine Light, and the crystals of our *mesa* are physical nodules of this metaphysical light. They are, as Sri Aurobindo phrased it in *Savitri*:

> *The prophet hierophants of the occult Law,*
> *The flame-bright hierarchs of the divine Truth,*
> *Interpreters between man's mind and god's,*
> *They bring the immortal fire to mortal men.*
> *Iridescent, bodying the invisible,*
> *The guardians of the Eternal's bright degrees*
> *Fronted the Sun in radiant phalanxes.*
> *Afar they seemed a symbol imagery,*
> *Illumined originals of the shadowy script*
> *In which our sight transcribes the ideal Ray,*
> *Or icons figuring a mystic Truth,*
> *But, nearer, Gods and living Presences.*
> *(Book II, Canto IX, pg. 265)*

He is actually writing in this passage of the Vedic gods, or Deva archetypes (of which certain crystals are physical manifestations on Earth).

In the crystal *mesa*, Agni is represented by the hero archetype, which is Citrine (or Smokey Quartz) containing strands of Rutile. This stone has the property of focusing and directing willpower and energy. (A possible substitute for Rutilated Citrine would be rutilated Smokey Quartz in its natural form). Both Veda and *mesa* proceed on the basis of correspondence, a correspondence between symbolic forms that nature provides and the spiritual realities that these express. Fire is not only the flame that burns wood, but on a higher plane it is vitality and internal heat of intensity, and beyond that flame signifies willpower charged with purpose. At the highest level, Fire is a divine power of alchemical transformation, a god whose presence makes the supreme spiritual attainment possible. The outward ritual of a Vedic Fire Ceremony, (or a more modern application of crystalline Fire energies through *mesa*) corresponds to an inward rite in which, as Sri Aurobindo says, "there is communication and interchange between the mortal and the Immortal."(SV 62) The ancients always summoned Agni to preside over the ritual in the inner worlds: "Let him come, a god with the gods."

Nature holds Divine Force concealed in the density of her material forms and in the passionate disorder of her vital energies. In developed human beings, the mind becomes conscious of this, and when a truth-seeker undertakes spiritual practice, progressively higher and wider ranges of consciousness are experienced. These exalted states of illumined consciousness cannot be preserved unless they are guarded from the hostile powers that conceal and distort. In an early phase of the spiritual life, the Mother-Power in creation achieves the birth of a conscious being of inner light, a flame or spark of consciousness in the spiritual heart that slowly grows and eventually becomes a mounting will for spiritual attainment. This is the birth of the psychic being, the heart-child, from the oceans of the subconscious obscurity. Sri Aurobindo translates the "Second Hymn to Agni" thus:

*The young Mother bears the Boy pressed down in her secret being
And gives him not to the Father;
But his force is not diminished,
The peoples behold him established in front in the upward workings
of things.
Who is this Boy, O young Mother, whom thou bearest in thyself*

When thou art compressed into form,
But thy vastness gives him birth?
For many seasons the Child grew in the womb;
I saw him born when the Mother brought him forth.
The Secret of the Veda, 1971, pg. 367

In the crystal *mesa,* Lemurian Jade, as we have mentioned, represents the Mother Stone. It is black and dense, suggesting the power that matter has to conceal and obscure In the Sage, or Lapis Lazuli, we see specks of gold embedded in a deep blue of celestial consciousness, showing the fullness of the action of spirit. But in the dark condensation that is Lemurian Jade, we also see specks of gold held in a dense matrix of black (symbolizing inconscience). These specks of gold in the mother-matrix of Lemurian Jade foreshadow the emergence of a being of light, a divine child who will be born in the ether of the spiritualized heart at a time when conditions make the miraculous event possible.

In the Vedic hymns, Agni is called the "Child of the Waters." When he first appears in his youthful form he is white, but as his power grows, he becomes ruddy and powerful, eventually growing into the fiery hero, Agni. The Child of the Mother has many births. In *mesa* parlance, we could say that the first birth of Agni takes place when the Earth Mother conceives a Child in the watery womb. In our *mesa,* the archetypal Child takes the physical name and form of Rhodochrosite. When the work of the gods has proceeded further, the Child is reborn as a fiery Hero, represented in the *mesa* by Rutilated Citrine. Lastly, the Mother's Child and Hero (in Egyptian cosmology, Osiris and Horus) are reborn as Lapis Lazuli, which the seers of the Veda would have referred to as 'the Brihaspati-power,' the Sage, the king of wisdom who is the knower and attainer of the fullness of divine realization. It is by the power of sacrifice, the deliberate letting go and oblation of what binds us, that Agni frees a spiritual seeker to move toward the divine.

These, according to Sri Aurobindo, are the principle ideas of the Vedic Rishis:

the conception of a Truth-consciousness supramental and
divine;

the invocation of the gods as powers of the Truth to raise man
out of the falsehoods of the mortal mind;
the attainment in and by this Truth of an immortal state of
perfect good and felicity;
and the inner sacrifice and offering of what one has and is by
the mortal to the Immortal as the means of the divine consum-
mation (SV 64)

In ancient India, the Veda set forth the path of attainment followed by the early Sages, the way empowered by Agni and Brihaspati, the way of the power of the Word. When we incorporate crystals into our *mesa* and use them in conscious ritual, the *mesa* can become a means of accessing the power and wisdom of the Elders, not only those of ancient India, but all masters in the inner world who align themselves with this work.

The power of Brihaspati the Vedic Sage is hymned in Rig-Veda IV. 50. Commenting on this Rik, Sri Aurobindo writes:

In the hill of the physical being there are dug for the soul those
abounding wells of sweetness which draw out of its hard rigidity
the concealed Ananda; at the touch of the Truth the rivers of honey,
the quick pourings of the wine of Immortality trickle and stream
and break out into a flood of abundance over the whole extent of
the human consciousness... Vala is not himself dark or inconscient,
but a cause of darkness. Rather his substance is of the light, vala-
sya gomatah, valasya govapusah, but he holds the light in himself
and denies its conscious manifestation. He has to be broken into
fragments in order that the hidden lustres may be liberated. Their
escape is expressed by the emergence of the Bright Ones, the herds
of the Dawn, from the cavern below in the physical hill and their
driving upward by Brihaspati to the heights of our being where
with them and by them we climb. He calls to them with the voice
of the superconscient knowledge; they follow him with the response
of the conscious intuition. They give in their course the impul-
sion to the activities which form the material of the sacrifice and
constitute the offerings given to the gods and these also are carried
upward till they reach the same divine goal. (SV 309-11)

The clue for the ritual of sacrifice is then given:

To the Purusha (the unmanifest Divine) under the name of Brihaspati the Rishi would have us dispose in the order of a sacrifice all the materials of our being by sacrificial action in which they are given up to the All-Soul as acceptable oblations offered with adoration and surrender. By the sacrifice we shall become through the grace of this godhead full of heroic energy for the battle of life, rich in the offspring of the soul, masters of the felicities which are attained by divine enlightenment and right action. (SV 311)

The result of the ritual of sacrifice, correctly performed, will be attainment of the fullness of the Truth-Consciousness. It is a royalty of light and power creative of the highest good. In one who has the blessings of this Sagely wisdom, the growth of spiritual potential is continuously "cherished, fostered, increased by all the divine cosmic powers who work for the supreme consummation."(SV 312)

COLLECTIVE ATTUNEMENT

The individual, or group are seated and readied for meditation. This preparation can be through slow deep breathing, or the sound of Tibetan Bowls. The meditation begins with the chanting of OM.

Each person who has his or her *mesa* present may hold it over the heart center. When inhaling, feel that the totality of crystal energies are flowing into the cells of the body and all corners of the mind. When exhaling, relax into this radiant energy. After some period of such meditation, the ritual can begin.

1)   The altar is prepared in advance, and purified with incense such as sandalwood or frankincense; its four sides are oriented to the four directions. Four candles are placed on the altar, one in each of the four corners.

2)   The one performing the sacrifice will have bathed and purified both body and mind. He or she should also meditate, pray or chant to center awareness before beginning.

3)   The one performing the sacrifice meditates with the clear crystal ball representing Source. The ball should be placed so all who are

present can see it and meditate on it. The meaning of the ball and the meditation are briefly explained by the celebrant at the start. The meditation is to align and identify the totality of mind, heart, body and Soul with Source, using the crystal sphere as the symbol of THAT. With all present chanting OM three times, the sphere is placed at the centre of the altar, symbolizing the act of centering.

4) Then, the celebrant states: "We meditate on THAT Supreme Being, the Source, the Infinite Consciousness, the Absolute." Several minutes of silence are allowed at this point for the meditation. The essence of this meditation is to be one with the Supreme on all levels.

5) The priest of the sacrifice takes the Sage Stone, Lapis Lazuli. The meaning of the stone is explained as it is held for all to see. Chanting OM, Mani, Mani, Mani, OM, the celebrant invokes the presence of the Divine as Master and Guide to preside inwardly over the sacrifice at all stages and to be the priest of sacrifice and co-celebrant of the ritual on the inner planes. Each person present may visualize or feel whatever name or form of the Divine Guide comes naturally, but it should be understood that the mantra "Mani" expresses the jewel-wisdom and the jewel-light of the Sage Archetype, or the inner master. The Lapis Lazuli stone is a symbol and embodiment of this presence for the ritual. When the invocation seems complete, the stone is placed in the North. Then, the celebrant states: "We meditate on the Supreme as Master, Lord of the Sacrifice, the Sage, full of Wisdom, the inner Guide." Several minutes of silence are allowed for meditation. The celebrant should explain that the essence of the meditation is to visualize the Master as present above the head or within the heart, in any form that comes naturally, including the form of blue-gold Lapis Lazuli.

6) The priest of the sacrifice takes the Child, either Rhodochrosite or Rose Quartz, and after a brief explanation, chants OM, Padme, Padme, Padme, OM. While chanting, those present visualize the lotus of the heart (to which the mantra "Padme" refers) opening and blossoming and the Golden Child of the Divine Presence nestled there. The stone is visualized in the form of this lotus in the ether of the spiritual heart, and the chanting continues until the feeling of the Presence is real.

Then, the stone is placed on the West side of the altar. Then, the celebrant states: "We meditate on the Divine Child within the spiritual heart, the light of the soul, the Living Presence within the human temple." Several minutes of silence for meditation are allowed, the celebrant explaining that the meditation centres on the presence of the Divine Child in the heart centre in any form that comes naturally, but the lotus of the heart is envisaged in the colour pink, as in Rhodochrosite or Rosy Quartz.

7) The priest of the sacrifice takes the Hero stone, Rutilated Citrine, Smoky Quartz or Quartz, speaks briefly about Agni, or the Hero Archetype, and then chants: OM, Hum, Hum, Hum, OM. The mantra "Hum" is the seed syllable of Agni, the sacred fire, the hero-warrior who effects the sacrifice. Those present visualize the stone which is being held out visibly as an embodiment of flame, light and power in physical form. The person performing the sacrifice chants until the invocation feels complete, and then places the stone on the East side of the altar. He or she then states: "We meditate on Agni, the Fire, the Hero, the Divine Light which accomplishes all things and brings them to perfection." Allow several minutes for silent meditation. The meditation should be explained to those present: to envisage a sacred flame of gold-bronze rutile colour, inside which one's body and aura are being steadily purified and activated. The purifying and uplifting energy of the flame blazes through all parts of the being.

8) The priest of the sacrifice takes the Mother stone, Lemurian Jade, and after a brief explanation chants: OM, Ma, Ma, Ma, OM. While chanting, the celebrant feels and visualizes the living power and presence of the Mother coming into all parts of the being, and the chant should be continued until this experience becomes very real and living. Then the Mother stone is placed on the South side of the altar. The celebrant states: "We meditate on the Mother Divine, Mother of the Gods, Mother of the New Creation, in whom we have our being, to whom we offer our life-breath and our heart's love." Several minutes of silence for meditation. The meditation is a feeling-centred meditation of being placed in the very depth of the Divine Mother's loving compassion. Lemurian Jade may be part of this visualization, or not, depending on the natural inclination of each individual. One may visualize a womb or matrix of this substance in which one

is nestled like a golden child, or any other image which comes naturally.

9) Then, with two hands extended over the stones on the altar, the priest of the sacrifice chants: OM, MANI PADME HUM, MA, seven times, while visualizing a pillar of light that extends through the stones to the centre of the Earth and up from the altar to the highest heavenly realm. The visualization is explained before the chanting begins so that all present visualize the same image. The pillar is envisaged as a flow of golden light descending from Heaven into the Earth, and blessing all things on Earth.

10) Breathing in, slowly and deeply, each person present raises all the energies and consciousness up the pillar of the spine, drawing it from below the feet, from the depths of the Earth, and lifting it high into the sky as the hands are raised above the head. Then, turning the palms downward, visualize the golden light of Heaven descending through one's body-mind, through the feet, and dispersing into the body of Mother Earth. This is done with full attention, and with a feeling of loving devotion. Several minutes are devoted to this practice.

11) Each person present brings some offering. One may select a *mesa* stone which symbolizes the aspiration or request. The stone or object is placed over the third eye and filled with the aspiration or request. Then each person places it on the altar.

12) The person performing the meditation, and all present fold the hands and chant OM three times.

13) Incense is wafted over the various stones on the altar.

14) Flower petals are distributed to all present and each person places some on the stones.

15) The person celebrating the ritual may at this point conclude the ritual in an appropriate way. There may or may not be a short talk after or before the ritual is concluded. At the conclusion of the ceremony, the four candles are extinguished and the ritual is declared closed.

16) At some point later on, each person may reclaim the offering and take it away, with the understanding that it has been blessed. The offering should then be placed on one's altar at home.

A NOTE ON SACRED SOUND

The power of the Word is centrally important in the Vedic spiritual tradition. According to the most ancient sources, cosmic evolution proceeds from the unconscious, unmoving, unknowable and unmanifest to the conscious, moving, knowable and manifest. The human microcosm emerges after many millions of years of such sojourn. Our human evolution is a return journey from the experience of the exteriorised physical plane of a human microcosm back to the infinite consciousness of the Absolute. In the phase of manifestation and creativity, the divinely emanated force from the Source is centrifugal; in the journey of return, it becomes centripetal.

In the Tantric schools of Indian spiritual thought, sound, as a vibration of undifferentiated Intelligence, is the catalyst that sets into motion the unfolding of the manifest cosmos. A primal vibration or Word arouses the slumbering equilibrium of Shakti and generates rajas, the active principle which then brings about the creation of the manifold universes. The causal vibration, Shabdabrahman, is undifferentiated, soundless Sound. It is the wavelength that many mystics experience as "God," which is not the same as what Meister Eckhart called the 'Ground of Being.'

This great Cosmic Vibration splits Shakti into two fields of magnetic force, and projects it as two aspects, Nada and Bindu. As centrifugal, positive male force, Bindu is the ground from which Nada operates. Other terms for this primal duality are *Purusha* and *Prakriti, Ishwara* and *Shakti.* The centripetal, negative female force, however it is named ("Yin" in the Chinese tradition) unfolds the manifest universe. Yin and Yang, Nada and Bindu are regarded as Mother and Father aspects of the Supreme Power. The bifurcation of Shakti is a duality in unity, not a separation.

Like a lotus blossom, the universe unfolds and expands. After the first differentiation containing the seed energies of the universe, the vibrating mass of energy continues differentiating and expanding as wavelengths. By the fifth differentiation, the energy evolved on the gross plane, with the creation of fifty articulate sounds or *varnas. Varnas* denote colour, and all sounds have corresponding colour vibrations in the invisible world.

From the combinations and permutations of these root sounds, the universe of forms is created. Sounds, as physical vibrations, are able to produce predictable forms. Combinations of sounds produce complicated shapes. The Vedic chants, and in particular the seed syllables of Tantra were based on this principle. Repetition of the exact note and pitch create a predictable duplication of a given form; for this reason, a tradition of oral transmission was passed on from teacher to student through many millennia until finally the Vedas and Upanishads were written down in Sanskrit. However, the period of prehistory when this tradition began is even more ancient than that.

According to the spiritual tradition of ancient India, the fifty primeval sounds and their varying combinations underlie all the forms of the physical world; their varying oscillations generate everything that we can perceive with the five senses. This manifest world that we take in through the senses is considered to be *maya* or illusion. Because of the oscillatory nature of matter and of mind as perceiver, the world of manifest forms can only be experienced in distortion as illusion. Knowledge of the fifty basic sounds has faded with the passage of time, and is largely lost to human memory. The Sanskrit language, however, is directly derived from them, as are mantras in Sanskrit, and of all languages it is the closest approximation. Mantras are sound powers evolved from the seed syllables and revealed to the ancient sages of India. From this tradition of the masters of India, we have the following:

The first element is Earth, represented by a yellow square: This element governs beginnings and firm foundations. The Bija mantra is "LUM."

The second element is Water, symbolized by a silver crescent moon. This is the sphere of the unconscious dream world, relationships, partnerships, networking, consulting, and consorting. The Bija Mantra is "VUM."

The third element is Fire shown as a bright flame-red triangle, apex down. This element rules the domain of passion, creativity, promotions, enthusiasm. The Bija Mantra is "RUM."

The fourth element is Air, depicted as a sky-blue circle or globe. Air influences everything to do with surviving trial and test periods, emotional stability and attention to fine details – as well as creative imagination. The Bija Mantra is "YUM."

HUM *(pronounced Hoom) is a mantra of the inner fire. It calls the divine down into us and offers our soul upward to the Divine for transformation in the sacred light of awareness. Through it we can offer ourselves or our impurities into the Divine for purification and transformation. A mantra of very ancient derivation,* **HUM** *is a Vedic mantra of Agni or fire. It is the mantra used to consign offerings into the sacred fire. It also is used to call or invoke the fire and to make it flame up more brilliantly. It represents the soul hidden the body, the Divine immanent in the world. It governs the planet Earth and the material sphere in general.*

OM *is the universal mantra from which all others derive. It is used at the beginning and at the end of most all vedic and invocations.*

The horizontal line of the Crystal Mesa Logo represents the creative cauldron at the centre where the Sacred Elements blend to form the Philosopher's Stone.

USING THE MESA: PART ONE

*All this perfection which we are going to acquire is not for a
personal and selfish end, it is in order to be able to manifest
the Divine, it is to put at the service of the Divine. We do not
pursue this development with a selfish intention of personal
perfection; we pursue it because the divine Work has to be
accomplished.*

The Mother (The Great Adventure, pg. 159)

In much of Latin America, the *mesa* is referred to as a *"mesa* of power," meaning that it is a tool of action. It can, of course be an
instrument of contemplation, or a symbolic device for exploring
metaphysical reality as well, but the *mesa* has most often been understood in shamanic practice as an extension of the personal power of
the healer who has assembled it.

As the tradition goes, after being instructed by one's mentor on
the subject of how to assemble and use a *mesa*, each person has complete freedom to choose articles and artifacts of his or her own liking
for placement in the *mesa* bundle, and in practice most healers and
shamans follow their own personal instinct in this matter. Usually, as
per the tradition, the *mesa* has an object, or small assembly of objects,
which represent its "heart" or centre. Also, there may be some organizing principle in the contents of the *mesa* in terms of cosmology;
certainly in the 'Crystal Mesa' we have been describing, this is so.
The organizing principle may be the four sacred elements, the various
directions of the compass, the important spirits of the local region,

one's own familiar spirit(s), etc. It may be some mixture of the above without any logical pattern. There is no fixed and universally agreed procedure that governs the process of creating a personal *mesa* of power. There is a wide-ranging variety of traditions related to different tribes and shamanic traditions, mostly in the Americas, much of the lore being highly local or even highly personal in nature.

I have taken pains to point out in earlier chapters of this book that beyond the personal talent of the individual practitioner, there are occult laws which may be brought into play to empower a *mesa* and make it effective. Where these laws are followed, the resulting *mesa* will gain power, and where they are ignored, the deficiency will be present. A *mesa* may function very well as an extension of its owner's own personal vital energy, but this kind of *mesa* is less likely to be a widely used learning or teaching device, or to accord with ancient and universal tradition. The power of such a *mesa* is largely individual, idiosyncratic, unique. The cosmology and occult principles that could be applied to making a cosmically-resonant *mesa* were far better known in ancient Egypt, Atlantis and Lemuria than they are at present, but it has become possible to resurrect and apply the central principles of this knowledge. In *Crystal Yoga*, we are looking at the assembly and use of a *mesa* from a comprehensive perspective, drawing on laws and cosmic patterns that underpin and support all aspects of *mesa*-wisdom and *mesa*-use.

A cosmically-patterned *mesa* will have an intentional rather than a random structure. The layout of such a *mesa* will reflect the cosmology which is its background, the operative occult laws, some kind of spiritual philosophy, and almost invariably, certain principles of sympathetic magic. A *mesa* of this sort does not lose its intensely personal meaning for its owner, but it transcends what is merely personal and unique insofar as it reflects a widely understood pattern. Let us consider some of the elements of pattern or paradigm which are at work, many of which were considered in greater detail in Chapter Ten, The Primal Pattern.

A *mesa* modeled on traditional wisdom-teachings will have a centre, and at least four regions surrounding the centre, possibly more. The sacred elements, Earth, Water, Fire and Air, are the likeliest themes for the constellation of energies which surround the centre, which is often designated *Ether* or *Akasha*. The centre represents the Source, the *axis mundi*, the heart, the Tree of Life, or living interior unity of the *mesa*, and for this reason it is special. It serves like the hub of a wheel, bringing together the spokes that radiate out to the circumference. The owner of the *mesa* will follow a personal instinct, and hopefully a well-informed understanding when the centrepiece of his or her *mesa* is chosen.

For this, two processes need to be understood, processes which are constantly at play in this bi-polar world of ours. The projective principle is at work when energies flow from the centre to the periphery. On the other hand, the receptive process predominates when energy flows to the centre from the periphery. Some crystals are projective and some are receptive and often we use terms like *yang* and *yin* to designate the differences between them. Thus, when we have bundles of stones embodying Earth, Water, Fire and Air energies in the four sacred directions defined by the *mesa* cloth, each of the stones within these assemblies has its own balance of *yin* and *yang*. Yin and *yang* are everywhere, but in different proportions. The knowledge of patterned variability in these proportions is central to understanding not only what is at work in a *mesa,* but in science, cosmology and the ancient wisdom tradition itself.

A background of cosmology is always at work when we undertake to assemble a *mesa* in full consciousness. The universe, its galaxies, and our own solar system reflect this same principle of 'centre and periphery' touched on above. Earth is a sphere which rotates on its axis, and the axis of the world stands as a symbol for the centre, the core, the place of wholeness and balance which is so important to the ancient wisdom tradition. The *axis mundi*, which is also the pillar of light or the Tree of Life, permits two kinds of movement, firstly upward from Earth to Heaven, and secondly downward from Heaven to Earth. In the first kind of movement, energy and consciousness rise to their highest degree of refinement, light, order and power. In the second kind of movement, something from on high descends into the domain of physical expression. For this reason, an object shaped like a pillar could be a suitable choice for the heart of the *mesa;* alternately, a sphere can be a physical expression of completeness and perfection. In particular, a sphere of clear quartz can function very well, both energetically, and symbolically, to play the role of a heart or centre for a *mesa* of power.

In ancient times, the landscape was regarded as a reflection of the higher order that prevailed in the stars above. A city would usually be organized around a sacred building with a relic of special cosmic significance. From this centre, lines of energy radiated out like spokes from a wheel to other sacred places in the surrounding countryside, knitting the whole together in a pattern much like the archetypal *mesa* which we are discussing. I have seen this pattern at work in cities and landscapes as distant as Chiangmai, Thailand, and Cusco Peru, but it was widespread through the British Isles, mainland Europe, the ancient Middle East and elsewhere. The belief was that if the landscape could be organized like a *mesa*, and the energy centred within the city, then the king or high priest could hold the various parts of the kingdom together in unity with their centre. Such a city-state could be a power-base for a priesthood or royal family, and the fulfillment of the heavenly mandate (or royal ambition) could be accomplished more surely than if everything was left, for example, to the random forces of market economics. This way of thinking prevailed in China for several thousand years, right up into the early decades of the twentieth century. The emperor was considered the 'son of heaven,' a semi-divine being mandated to preside over his kingdom's unified centre, to maintain the kingdom in power and peace and bring the celestial blessings to all.

Since this way of thinking has been discredited by our democratic values and our egalitarian educational system, the understanding of building unity through hierarchy must be cultivated in other ways. The likeliest way to gather information about the approach of the ancients is through reading, but there is not much in writing about the subject of the *mesa*. Better still would be to meet a master and learn directly from personal instruction and experience, but how many masters have devoted themselves to the topic of *mesa* and have any of them written about it from a universal, esoteric perspective?

Sometimes, one may catch hints of the ancient wisdom in movies. For example, the very popular Harry Potter series supplies us with a main character who lives the archetypal pattern of the mythic hero, which Joseph Campbell explained so clearly and comprehensively in *The Hero With A Thousand Faces*. Young Harry Potter is a magically gifted child (aren't we all at the beginning?), but he finds himself an orphan in a very unsympathetic and materialistic family. Harry feels out of place, and he is. Luckily, he makes his way to an occult college where his magical abilities are recognized, accurately valued, and cultivated. During his summer holidays, he returns to his foster family and must try to fit into "normal" society, but when he goes back to the college of applied magic, he is much more happy and alive because he is doing what he was born to do. There, he can be who he really is, a magical child. There is an element of play, an element of systematic instruction, and a dollop of personal passion and genius in Harry Potter's magical apprenticeship. The pattern at work is just the same as we find in the life of anyone drawn to study and use a *mesa*.

Very few people understand or care about *mesas*. Nor does the ancient tradition from which *mesas* derive interest many. Teachers of the subject are few and far between, and books written about the *mesa* are hard to come by. However, if, by great good fortune one learns how to make and use a *mesa*, the gateways of perception open up into a magical world of boundless interest and experience. The opened *mesa* bundle with its sacred objects assembled in cosmic order is a college of arcane teaching and esoteric experience. To enter this world with the crystal stones, symbols and materialized energies of the hidden magical domain is possible when one 'enters the stream' and links with the power and passion of the *mesa* transmission. The possibility that many souls are secretly called to a life of magic and adventure is confirmed by the popularity of the Harry Potter movies and books, Lord of the Rings, The Narnia series and fantasy as a literary genre. Given the widespread appeal of mythic, fantasy and magic movies, one suspects that many more *mesas* would be in use if adults, writers and spiritual seekers knew what a *mesa* of power really is and how it can be assembled and applied to make life rich with creative energy and vision.

A *mesa* is a symbol-microcosm, a living energy-reservoir, a sacred space of endless possibilities. A symbol becomes a tool for sculpting reality both in the inner and outer worlds when we invest it with energy and link it with our inner consciousness and vitality. We do this linking and empowerment through the faculty of imagination, which we often see being expressed by children at play. A child on a rug playing with toy soldiers, creating miniature campaigns, struggles and battles, is investing his or her toys with inner life of archetypal heroism in the world of imagination. The child may not be able to ride a real horse or wield a sword or a gun, so it works with (plays with) toy counterparts instead. Toys are thus symbols. They stand in for realities of the outer world which is dominated by adults.

Play is "imagination-at-work." If imagination is encouraged and allowed to do its work without interruption, the capacity for magic slowly grows and develops within the child, and the child carries this over into adolescence and adulthood. Magic means the ability to manifest change by conscious intent. When intent focuses on the miniature world of a well-patterned *mesa*, the *mesa* becomes a powerful instrument of manifestation. However, one does not arrive at empowerment by leaping over the gentle inner school of fantasy, imagination and play. The soul can teach the outer parts of the being, such as the mind and vitality, through spontaneous, imaginative play and this is the best way to cultivate a capacity for self-transformation and for re-visioning and re-creating the world according to a higher pattern – or, to use a simpler expression, to awaken the gift of magic.

The typical adult mind has become literal, practical, dull and cautious. Many adolescents are in a state of psychological pain at seeing their inner magic eroded by educational institutions which they are forced to attend. The soul-qualities of their childhood ideals are ignored, devalued or ridiculed in a system of schooling which emphasizes the rational intellect, conformity, the market economy and material practicality. But in every child who has been dulled down into adulthood, there remains still a memory of magic, a spark of creative light that can be fanned into a flame. Some of the most popular movies of our time celebrate just this theme, and testify to the need we have for a re-balancing of life in favour of fantasy, play and imagination. We all aspire to be inwardly complete; we all have souls and hearts hungry for richer lives. We graduate from highschools or universities into jobs and thence into family life with its responsibilities, and it all feels like progress. But the imbalances and deficiencies of our training and social conditioning inwardly cripple us. Weaned away from our innate intuition, disempowered by the devaluation of our dreams, we lack the capacity to play, to create, or in some cases even to even imagine a better world. In the ancient tradition, the apprenticeship and tradition of the *mesa* serves as an answer to this crying inner need of our time. In a traditionally patterned *mesa*, the wholeness, power and harmony of nature *is* accessible. Such a sacred bundle invites us to enter a world of archetypal energies, living forces and beings who help us to expand our imaginative horizon until we embrace the fullness of all that we can be.

CHOOSING AND BONDING

Bonding develops through appreciation. Each stone in your *mesa* should be personally selected by you on the basis of how you feel about it. When you see a stone that you consider particularly beautiful, and you feel that it wants to be in your *mesa*, that is the stone to buy. Do not buy crystals for your *mesa* primarily because they are the "right price," according to some conceptual notion of what your budget is.

Remember that each individual crystal within your *mesa* is a friend, a mineral-being that you respect and work with. Your *mesa* will function best when you feel personally connected to every piece within it, just as a doll has a personality and an identity for the child who owns it. Each crystal should be a living entity that you feel you could talk to, and to which you are eager to listen. It should have a kind of beauty that might inspire you to write a poem or a song , that you could praise with heartfelt enthusiasm, a treasure that you like so much that you would stretch your budget for the privilege of being its caretaker, a stone you want as your companion.

Let's drop the idea of being an "owner" in relation to the *mesa* we create. Let's think instead of having the privilege of being allied with a very special society, a band of friends who have remarkable magic and mystic powers. The *mesa* that grows in our keeping is a living body, and each of its 33 parts has a power and personality all its own. In the ideal relationship, the *mesa*-keeper's heart and desire would be turned toward each and every one of the 33 *mesa* crystals with appreciation and fondness. Thus, piece by piece, usually by acquisition and purchase, always according to intent, and hopefully guided by intuition, we grow the family of our sacred *mesa* bundle.

If you are serious about your *mesa*, it will be the treasure of your life, the pearl of great price, and you will go out of your way to have the company of stones you really love. These need not be the most expensive ones. For example, large ruby and emerald crystals of great beauty, energy and presence can be had for as low as ten dollars. When you feel an inner pull or connection with a stone which is available for a price, and then you hesitate because the cost is steep, in that very moment examine the sincerity of your attitude. If money means more to you than the friendship of the individual pieces in your *mesa*, at least be aware of your scale of values. Where your heart is, there also is your treasure, and unfortunately the pocket-book is often the barometer of the degree to which we care. Your *mesa* represents your heart's treasure, your deep passion, your bond with the cosmos and beyond it the light of infinity. If it is something other than or less than this for you, be aware of the limitation you have introduced to its possibilities.

In ancient times, the masters enforced long apprenticeships on their disciples. Part of their reason for doing this was to awaken a deep sense of value in their hearts. By testing, delaying, making them work hard, the masters inculcated an attitude of total commitment and earnest sincerity. The conditions of our age and society make this almost impossible; the modern mindset and mostly the degree of inflation in the modern ego works against this ancient system. Therefore, the burden is on the individual to cultivate sincerity.

Reading books about any given topic is not in itself evidence of sincerity, for the urge to collect information may be simply a sign of intellectual curiosity, which is not an adequate basis for doing yoga or working with a *mesa*. Only the application of willpower in action can show the presence of sincere aspiration, and this is what we need for transcendence and attainment. Deeply felt prayer is a most significant form of inner action. Selfless service is a form of outer action. As for money, it represents energy and has value only when spent. The love that is in the Earth includes us, for we are its children, and the avatars of this love in the mineral kingdom are the crystals. The paper bills in your wallet are only a human notion of wealth. True wealth is the love that is in your heart. But, your passion for crystals can be a key to its awakening and a sign that it is ready to come to the fore. When you link your individual capacity for love to the love that is in the Earth, or the love of the Mother, profound possibilities come into play. Sri Aurobindo writes:

> *All wealth belongs to the Divine and those who hold it are trustees, not possessors. It is with them today, tomorrow it may be elsewhere. All depends on the way they discharge their trust while it is with them, in what spirit, with what consciousness in their use of it, to what purpose. (The Mother, Ch. IV)*

Crystals are precious parts of the body of Mother Earth. This is something to constantly remember. As such, each one is a relic of the sacred divine body of our own Goddess-Mother. A *mesa* is a reliquary of the Divine Body into which we are ascending with the support of our Earth Mother. It is because of this original contract between Earth and Heaven that crystals have power and a role to play in our great adventure of consciousness and its return to Source. When we recognize the privilege of becoming co-creators in this original plan, we will be used as active channels of the Divine influence. As the wise teachers repeat, those who do not have eyes to see and a heart to feel will be blind to the mystic reality of things, and they are not yet ready to be the caretakers in the sacred *mesa* tradition.

Building up a living relationship with your stones can be accomplished in a number of ways, but one of the best is by using the power of speech. For example, you can verbalize your admiration. Simply hold a stone in your hand, consider its beauty, and begin to speak: "I love you because...." Find as many reasons as you can why you feel that this crystal is loveable, beautiful, or significant and put each reason into words. Elizabeth Browning's poem, "Why do I love thee?" is a very good model for this kind of deeply appreciative speech, and the bonding it nurtures. Sit with your crystal and express your love with care and tenderness in the best words that come to you. Repeat the most beautiful phrases until there is such depth of feeling in your heart that tears come to your eyes. Not until you have let the salt tears of your love touch the crystal have you reached the depth of your sincerity, and if you cannot feel and express the depth of your passion, you cannot expect your crystals to give you their all in the power of the *mesa*. Write down your words and keep them as a formula to renew and intensify the feeling of relatedness that you have with your stone or stones.

INTUITIVE GUIDANCE

Once you have your *mesa*, you may find that certain stones call out to you. This happened to me in Summer and Autumn of 2005. Moonstone kept coming into my mind. Over and over again, I would think of the etheric blue glow that a fine Moonstone has. I actually acquired a very beautiful oval Moonstone like this and had it set into a silver ring during this period. Times like this, when a certain stone comes to mind often, are the best times to compose your words of relationship to the stone in question. This came home to me one day after meditation when I opened *Savitri* by Sri Aurobindo, and settled upon the words:

> *The heavens of the ideal Mind were seen*
> *In a blue lucency of dreaming Space*
> *Like strips of brilliant sky clinging to the moon.*

I looked up the word "moonstone" in a concordance for *Savitri* and found that the only use of the word in the entire poem was:

> *Caught in the song that sways the Apsara's limbs*
> *When she floats gleaming like a cloud of light,*
> *A wave of joy on heaven's moonstone floor.*
> *Behold this image cast by light and love,*
> *A stanza of the ardour of the gods..*

However the term "moon-flame" was also listed in my *Savitri* concordance, and so I looked it up too:

> *Our souls can visit in great lonely hours*
> *Still regions of imperishable Light,*
> *All-seeing eagle-peaks of silent Power*
> *And moon-flame oceans of swift fathomless Bliss*
> *And calm immensities of spirit space.*

From these references, I was helped to express my own feelings of relation:

> *Moonstone beauty,*
> *'Blue lucency of dreaming Space,'*
> *Ether of the spiritual heart,*
> *You are the light and love divine,*
> *The 'moon-flame ocean of swift, fathomless bliss,'*
> *Door to 'calm immensities of spirit space,'*
> *And sweet release, and peace of homecoming.*
> *Still radiance of the Presence,*
> *In the temple of your etheric light,*
> *My heart's devotion blossoms*

And I hear the fullness of the ocean of infinity
Sounding waves of ecstasy along the distant shore of my mind.

I wanted the master's words to be woven with my own because they capture a high meditative consciousness and express just what I was intuiting but was unable to write. If, as I mentioned earlier, "bonding develops through appreciation," then the expression of our feelings and our appreciation for each crystal within the *mesa* in words, and the repetition of this *'paean'* at appropriate times, helps greatly in developing a full and interactive relationship with the *mesa*. When you approach this aspect of the work, it may be helpful to think of the physical stone as the body of the crystal, and the living spirit within that body as the 'Deva.' Remember that the words are directed to the spirit of the stone, the living Deva, whose physical body we can perceive with the five senses as a crystal.

If poetry helps to actualize the "heart" side of one's relationship with *mesa*-crystals, study does much to deepen the intellectual side of the relation. For example, I looked up Moonstone in Melody's book, *Love Is In The Earth,* and found:

The energy of moonstone is balancing, introspective, reflective and lunar. It is capable of helping one with the changing structures of one's life on the physical, emotional, mental and spiritual levels. The energy relates to "new beginnings," allowing one to realize that these "new beginnings" are, in actuality, the fruition of each "end." It is a stone for hoping and wishing; it allows one to absorb that which is needed from the universal energies, not necessarily, however, furthering that which is wanted. It helps one to recognize the "ups and downs" and to gracefully acknowledge the changing cycles. It can assist one in sustaining and maintaining and understanding the destiny one has chosen. It works to bring the galactic evolved energies from other worlds to accessibility. It is a stone for "feeling" and understanding via intuition and emotional "thoughts" rather than via intellectual reasoning. It brings flashes of insight, banishing the possibility of neglecting ones profit from that which is experienced. It stimulates intuitive recognition and helps one to apply the intuitive knowledge in a practical sense... (*pgs. 271-2*)

We are all in a learning curve in our relationship to stones, and it IS possible to make mistakes. For example, about a year previous I had bought a lovely Moonstone ring. At least, I fully believed that the stone in the ring was a genuine Moonstone, and it was sold to me as such. In fact, it turned out to be something called "opalite," which is a resin that closely resembles high-grade Moonstone. To complete the deception, this "resin" had a little flaw inside it that looked like a crystalline fissure. The very attractive price should have alerted me.

Not long after buying this lovely "Moonstone" I had it removed from its original ring-setting and commissioned a jeweler to create a new setting for it. Only after having the stone examined by gemology experts at a gem show many months later did I learn that my "Moonstone" was fake. Not long after that, at another gem and mineral show, I found a real Moonstone that had just the qualities I so admired. Perhaps this "mistake" had value for me as a learning experience; perhaps I became more conscious of how important Moonstone (the real thing) was for me personally. One also experiences this bonding with particular intensity when a stone drops out of the ring one is wearing (which has happened several times with me). The joy and relief at finding the lost stone can be immense; or, the permanent loss of the stone, or of any other crystal, can be very disappointing. In any case, this kind of interest and care about one's crystals is a very important element when you begin to develop your *mesa*. You have to be able to feel a bond with your crystals. The care that you have for them is the living energy that you bring to your *mesa* work. It is the life-force that births the evolving *mesa* magic.

As I review these words about Moonstone, I have already been into a several month phase of attunement to Labradorite, which I much prefer to think of as 'Magic-Stone.' It seems to remind me of past life attainments in this field, and to carry my awareness into the domain of the stars. I could easily write a whole chapter on this, and writing about the effect that Labradorite has on my mind and spirit would be a good way to become more conscious of its action and claim it more fully. Alas, this will have to wait.

HATCHING DRAGONS

The energies of light often flow through the veins of Mother Earth in a form traditionally referred to in the ancient myths as the dragon.

A precious or semi-precious stone can be seen as a dragon's egg. Try holding a rounded stone from your *mesa* and thinking of it in this way. As the keeper of its energy, you may wish to incubate the crystal dragon's-egg and release the sleeping power that is inside it. The incubating is done with attention, feeling, speech, association, and most of all, with love. If you lavish these energies on your crystal dragon's egg, you can bring to life its inner spirit.

Not all dragons are alike. They have different colours and energies. Be non-specific in your expectation until the energy involved reveals itself to you. You can visualize your seven Earth Stones as a nest of Earth-Dragon eggs, if you like, and it helps if they are a size and shape that makes it possible for you to really feel that there is a life within each stone waiting to be awakened. Holding a rounded crystal in the warmth of your hand will infuse it with your energy and consciousness, which is the catalyst of the awakening process. Or, you can hold all seven at once, as if the palms of your hands formed a nest of love. Allow the love energy to flow into the eggs so that they will release their potential and come fully to life in service within the *mesa*. Again, you may wish to use words to convey the energy.

Hatching a dragon will, for many of us, involve a conceptual shift. In the normal paradigm we grow up with, we are taught to conceive of stones as "things." In reality, most of the perceptual boundaries we erect concerning "things" are little more than our own cultural conditioning, but each boundary can shift or change when we open up a new way of perceiving or relating. A boundary, seen from a fresh angle, can become a point of entry into a greater and wider condition of being and knowing. Approach the apparent fixity and hardness of your 'stone-things' in this way, remembering that the possibilities they can release will be a function of what you feel and believe possible. The potential is not, after all, only in the stones, but also in ourselves; the power we release is our own.

Using the language of light, as we have been doing, we have previously referred to crystals as 'nodules of light.' Let us be aware of the choice we have in this matter. We may continue to think of the crystals in our *mesa* as "particles," which is the normal Newtonian, old-paradigm approach – or we can try to perceive these specially selected stones as "waves." When we see a particle as a wave, we open a new world of insight, and consequently a wider domain of experience. Or, to put it another way, when the horizons of perception open, we can hatch a dragon.

You had a reason for choosing these crystals and bringing them together, didn't you? This is it.

We release dragons from crystals by deepening relationship. We human beings, in our own inner world of thought and feeling, are far more like waves than 'things,' and this wavelike aspect of our inner being is inherently relational. The capacity to relate is a primal power of being which many of us have allowed to atrophy. It is a power by means of which we can hatch, or awaken, the dormant dragon in the stones of our *mesa* and the dormant vibrancy of our imaginative range. The reason that we acquire a particular stone in the first place is most often an impulse of relation, a feeling, desire, wish for connection – a wave of perception that triggers the impulse to reach out and grasp.

There is a saying from the Caribbean Islands that runs: "Thoughts are things with a thousand wings." The way that a crystal can function flows in large measure from what we feel and imagine it to be. This *affective thinking* can be filled with imagination, feeling, creative joy, respect and intuitive attunement. The more of these energies we pack into our dealings with stones, the richer their possibilities ripen. When we see a stone as a wave rather than a particle, part of our own inner being becomes more receptive. The image of stone as 'contracted, frozen energy' is melted; the idea of a bigger possibility begins to grow inside the musing mind; our imagination comes to life. It is this released creative energy which can activate a crystal, through whatever ritual we may choose to express it. The ritual is secondary to the life-energy we infuse into it.

In her book, *Riding the Dragon* (Brisbane, 1994), Roselle Angwin gives a brief synopsis of what the dragon concept can mean:

> *The serpent/dragon has long been a symbol of primal energy, power, wisdom, healing, ... initiation and transformation. Its ability to shed its outgrown skin is important symbolically. In China the dragon has always been seen as benevolent, but in the West, largely due to Christianity and its fear of this raw energy (often associated with Eve and therefore womankind) it has become identified with evil, hence the obsession with killing dragons (also killing-off the 'old religion'). The danger with killing it is that unless something equally powerful is put in its place it leaves a deadness of spirit. A more positive way*

*of working with dragon-energy is to give it its due recognition
and respect (this prevents it from rampaging all over the place)
and then to find a way to channel dragon-power into creative
expression. If you suppress it, you will be burned by it. If you
acknowledge it and its wisdom, you may ride on its back. Any
work of art – music, poetry, painting, dance, performance
– that has the power to move us deeply uses dragon-power. As
does sex. As a fire-beast it symbolizes vision, and also guards
the treasure-hard-to-find buried deep in the unconscious. (pg.
76)*

The dragons you hatch within your *mesa* may have dimensions
of meaning touched on in the above quotation, or they may be *devas*
(nature spirits) connected with the crystal. There is no reason why a
watery or airy dragon cannot emerge from your time spent gestating
the crystal into activity. Much depends on how you work with and
relate to the energies involved, and this is a very personal thing.

When we imagine, let us understand that we are building up
an image which can help us express ourselves more completely. Let
us remember that the way in which we see ourselves and our world,
our self-definition, is a synthesis of perception and experience which
we constantly create and sustain. We live in our imagination, however static or full of life and creativity this inner world may be. We
constantly create the world of our experience through our imagination, our weaving of a story from random events. It is we who spin
a meaningful pattern and a personal perspective from the events we
live through. No one imagines his or her world of experience into being in exactly the same way as anyone else. In one sense, everything
we live is filtered into our mind through our imagining faculty.

But beyond *sustaining a coherent view of the world*, imagination also
serves a more *creative purpose*. By means of higher imagination, we humans birth new creations and bring them into expression. Everything
around us in our culture was brought into being in this way. It was
all *imagined* into being. Imagination incarnates possibilities that have
not yet crystallized into our three dimensional world. We have to
go beyond our own time-space continuum to access things that are
there in the cosmic flow, the formless soup, the universal mind, and
then bring these new energies into expression in this world. In this
way, we transcend the images that normally define and limit us. The

most useful images for reaching into this realm of 'incarnational imagination' are those that are dynamic rather than static. In other words, think "wave" rather than "particle," and imagine "dragon's egg" when you see "crystal." Cultivate the magic that can hatch *mesa*-stones into dragons.

This new-paradigm understanding where we can think both wave and particle has also to do with right and left brain perception. Creative work draws more on the right brain, while linear logic tends to be a left brain function. A shift of perception such as we describe here may help you to hatch a few dragons with your crystals, or to unleash the wings of your own thoughts so they fly to wider horizons. When you treat your *mesa* and its contents as you would a multi-faceted, respectful friendship, you develop a new, open-ended relation with a whole range of invisible energies and possibilities that would otherwise have stayed dormant.

If you go down this path even a short distance, you will find that crystals can become co-creators and friends in your journey of self-discovery.

ESTABLISHING PURE INTENT

At this point, it will be helpful to re-read the quotation which begins this chapter. The intent behind our actions is all-important, of this there can be no question. If we assemble a *mesa* which is empowered by the cosmic pattern, but exploit it for selfish ends, we have misused a most precious boon. The work which the *mesa* can help us accomplish is actually the Mother's work. Our contribution is, like that of the *mesa*, to be a co-worker, a conscious instrument for attaining and manifesting a higher order of possibilities on Earth. Any personal spin, egocentric ambition or obsessive desires we bring should be abandoned. The real doer of the *mesa* work is the higher power that comes from the Source. Our primary reason for unfolding various capacities must, if we cherish pure intent, be to serve that larger divine vision. Any other motivation or purpose is adding to karma and delaying the day of our liberation.

There is a very beautiful passage in Sri Aurobindo's poem *Savitri* where the Supreme speaks to the human instrument and expresses this divine vision:

Now will I do in thee my marvellous works.
I will fasten thy nature with my cords of strength,
Subdue to my delight thy spirit's limbs
And make thee a vivid knot of all my bliss,
And build in thee my proud and crystal home.
Thy days shall be my shafts of power and light,
Thy nights my starry mysteries of joy
And all my clouds lie tangled in thy hair
And all my springtides marry in thy mouth.
O Sun-Word, thou shalt raise the earth-soul to Light
And bring down God into the lives of men;
Earth shall be my work-chamber and my house,
My garden of life to plant a seed divine.
When all thy work in human time is done,
The mind of earth shall be a home of light,
The life of earth a tree growing towards heaven,
The body of earth a tabernacle of God...
I will possess in thee my universe,
The universe find all I am in thee.
Thou shalt bear all things that all things may change,
Thou shalt fill all with my splendour and my bliss,
Thou shalt meet all with my transmuting soul.
Assailed by my infinitudes above,
And quivering in immensities below,
Pursued by me through my mind's wall-less vast,
Oceanic with the surges of my life,
A swimmer lost between two leaping seas
By my outer pains and inner sweetnesses
Finding my joy in my opposite mysteries
Thou shalt respond to me from every nerve.

Book 11, pgs. 699-700

These are lines of truth and revelation uttered by a true sage. These words summarize the intent of the divine plan itself, which is the will of the Supreme for his chosen instruments. A *mesa*-keeper who can embrace and identify with this mandate from on high can then relate to his or her *mesa* in similar terms. These same words, spoken by the *mesa*-keeper to his or her *mesa*, summarize the work that they will undertake together. This is a work of the divine, for the divine, and in no way a play of ego.

When, in all honesty, one is incapable of the highest and purest intent, one should work to clarify the underlying motives for assembling and working with a *mesa*. Putting these motives into words often helps. Once you have clarified and written down your real intentions, evaluate their karmic implications and try to raise your intent to the loftiest and most disinterested level of which you are capable. For your own protection, and for the welfare of all associated with you, this is the best thing you can do before proceeding further in working with your *mesa*.

ACTIVATING THE CRYSTALS

From ancient times, a number of seed syllables, called *Bija Mantras* in India, have been passed down. These sounds are powerful tools for activating certain kinds of energies – or as the ancients would say, for invoking the powers of the gods. A seed syllable is an excellent way to apply the power of sound to awakening the full potential of a crystal, or of an entire *mesa*. Here is a list of such syllables *(Bija)* that may be used to good effect; an alternate set (to the right) of purely Hindu seed syllables you may also work with:

BIJA		HINDU	
EARTH	LUNG	EARTH	LAM
WATER	VANG	WATER	VAM
FIRE	RANG	FIRE	RAM
AIR	YANG	AIR	YAM
ETHER	HANG		
SUN	ANG		
MOON	MANG		

Focused concentration and clear intention are necessary when using a mantric sound for activation. The best idea would be to hold the crystal, focus attention on it, and chant the sound out loud, clearly and repeatedly until you feel that the crystal is charged with energy. Earth mantra is used with Earth crystals, Water mantra with Water crystals, and so on. Sun energy and Moon energy can be used when and as desired. The ANG sounds are pronounced like "rung," as in a rung on a ladder. The "U" in UNG is pronounced like "moon."

MAGICAL ARCHETYPES AND THE PRIMAL GARDEN

If you want to experience spiritual renewal, it is quite important to be in contact with the magical child inside your heart. Archetypes empower various ranges of our life-possibilities, and the magical child awakens the imagination to the possibility that life can become anything we firmly believe and clearly envision. Sometimes, movies can help us remember and get in touch with archetypes. For example, Harry Potter is a magical child. So is Charlie Bucket from the movie *Charlie and the Chocolate Factory*. In this movie, the magical child finds himself growing up in the bleak and impoverished urban wilderness of a city in England. Scion of destitute parents, he has few prospects, only a dream that he might find the golden ticket in a Wonka chocolate bar. Willy Wonka is an archetypal hero. He has the courage to create a whole world of possibilities inside his factory. In one scene, we see him fighting his way through jungles with his machete, and slaying a monstrous insect in order to discover new flavours for his candy creations. Willy Wonka has what Charlie needs, a creative vision of life's infinite possibilities; by the end of the movie, Charlie has been empowered, and the magical child within the hearts of the movie viewers has been given a wakeup call. If you see this movie from this perspective, the best thing to do is take the awakened energy away and keep it alive in your imagination so that you can apply it to your *mesa*, or work with your *mesa* from within your awareness of being a magical child. The magical child within each of us dreams, creates fantasies, visualizes possibilities that stir the heart.

Let us consider a specific example of how this might be applied to *mesa*. Within the movie, *Charlie and the Chocolate Factory*, there is an extraordinary scene where Willy Wonka leads the selected children and adults into a huge chamber which is a magical garden. Every part of the garden is made of candy. There are candy apples hanging like rubies from the trees, grass as green as Emerald, pumpkins like big

Carnelians, in short just the kind of Eden-garden that the ancients pictured in their heroic and mythic tales.

The exercise you can do with your *mesa* is actually a lot of fun. Imagine a garden very much like the one in Charlie and the Chocolate Factory, but made of jewels rather than candy. This should not be too difficult because you can remember the garden from the movie and tweak your imagination by calling to mind the visual images you actually saw on the wide screen. Picture this imaginative garden as residing inside your *mesa*, and go there in your imagination. In other words, your *mesa* becomes a real place you can visit in the domain of imagination, like the chocolate factory in the movie.

Imagine that the garden which you are about to visit has four areas. In one area, all the jewels are from the Earth section of your *mesa*. For example, there can be Jade-green grass and leaves. The trunks and branches of the trees can be made of Petrified Wood; the flowers can be Red Jasper and Pyrite. Certain beautiful bushes can have huge tropical leaves of Malachite, with stems and blossoms of Tiger's Eye. Picture this down to the last detail. The gems do not have to be hard and glassy, they can be soft and edible, because this is the world of imagination and creative interaction. The surfaces of the gems can be like the television in the movie, where you can put your hand right through the glass surface and reach into the interior. In your imagination, move to whatever gem-fruits or mineral-leaves attract you, and interact with them as you like. You can taste, shape, smell, touch, and interpenetrate the flesh of any part of this gem garden. Assimilate each of the gems in all the ways you can. Imagine their flavours and fragrances, and take these into yourself by tasting and inhaling. Feast on the jewel-energies of your *mesa*-garden in your imagination. Have fun. Enjoy the experience as if it were a visit to the chocolate factory in the movie.

The more creative and enjoyable you make this imaginative journey, the move vivid will be the energies that you activate both in your personal *mesa* and in your own microcosm. Remember, the magical child is the inner archetype that can resurrect your imagination from the drab sterility of its current neglect; and the inner hero can empower you to go forward and create your future life with verve and passion.

You can similarly visit the other sections of the jewel-garden which relate to the energies of Fire, Water, and Air. If you want hero power to bring your magical child fully to life, you may envisage your Hero Archetype stone as coming to life, with a human shape and a capacity to dialogue and guide you from experience to experience. In this way, you can take the stimulated imagination from the movie theatre right into your *mesa* work and apply it to the resurrection of your inner, magical child. If you do this, you will be able to build up just the right relationship to the energies of your *mesa* so as to bring fully to life its magical potential.

The great work cannot be accomplished unless we connect with our inner archetypes. Therefore, to find and identify with the Child in the heart, the inner Hero, the Sage, and the compassion of the Mother must be our constant aspiration and endeavour. The archetype stones can be very helpful in this process. They can be programmed by speaking our intent clearly to each one of them. Then, they can be placed in our hand when we meditate, or on any of the *chakras* during moments of deep relaxation. Sometimes, a stone may speak to you; this can happen as an intuitive nudge that touches the back of your mind, or it can come as an impulse to act. When you feel the urge to hold one stone in particular from within your *mesa*, do not neglect to act on it. Some stones other than the four designated archetype-stones may be very helpful in the work of linking your mind and heart to your principle archetypes. Remember also that there may be other archetypes beyond these four which arise for your recognition. The Major Arcanum of the Tarot is a good inventory of esoteric archetypes, and familiarity with these 21 inner forms is very helpful for attunement to this domain of the inner world.

MESA MEDITATION

The word "meditation" can mean many things, and no two people meditate in exactly the same way. Nevertheless, a *mesa* can support, deepen and sustain its keeper's meditation, and it is very simple to use in this way. One simply holds the *mesa* over the heart centre, or over the solar plexus while sitting in meditation. It is helpful to bring the *mesa* formally into the meditation by a simple affirmation. The one that I like to use is: "Now, we meditate." This recognizes the *mesa* as a part of one's own microcosm, and also sends a clear signal of intent and an invitation to collaboration. This can be strengthened by concentrating for a few moments on the components of the *mesa* and giving instructions or invitations for full co-operation. The love-bond is the most powerful and intimate of all, and if you feel that your own physical body and the body of the *mesa* are merging in love and becoming one glowing field of spiritual aspiration, a very good result will come.

Affirmations are like homework assignments both for your own subconscious mind, and for the energies at work in your *mesa*. If you can centre on a very few key themes that you feel are important, and impregnate the *mesa* with the same verbal expressions repeatedly, the work will go very well. For example:

> *"We constantly, consciously, become the best that can be on all planes."*
>
> *"We constantly transcend all limits."*
>
> *"We are one ever-growing body of light and love."*
>
> *"We deepen and widen our peace, light and bliss at every moment."*
>
> *"We draw energy and light in abundant measure from all sides at all times."*

These and other expressions of intent, if repeated slowly and consciously, will be like a program for the *mesa* to work on, and each time you hold the *mesa*, you can rejoin this flow toward realizing the affirmations. Again, the key to success with this method lies in: a) focusing intent; b) creating succinct and positive statements; c) repeating the same words each time; c) impregnating the *mesa* with conscious affirmations frequently.

A MESA-LABYRINTH MEDITATION

The *mesa* can be used as a labyrinth in a very simple way. Place the stones on your *mesa*-cloth organized by houses, with Earth stones in the South, Air in the North, Fire in the East and Water in the West. Place the Earthy, Watery, Fiery and Airy stones within each element in the outermost area, so that they form a circle. Then, closer to the centre, and forming a second circle within the first place the *yin* and *yang* and spirit stones for each element. Then, beyond the four Spirit stones and closest to the centre, place the four archetype stones. The heartstone is at the centre, and is the destination.

You may want to begin your inward journey to the centre by a conscious focusing of aspiration. It may, for example, be a journey of deepening love at each step, or a movement into the most profound peace and stillness. Or it may be a gathering of light, or an awakening and healing that you seek; again, you may have the intent of attunement for information or knowledge that the *mesa* (or certain of its components) can bring to you. The more clear you are about your intent, the more specific the results you can expect.

To move your consciousness through this crystal *mesa* labyrinth, you will place your fingertips one by one on each stone and pause to meditate. Begin by placing the fingertips of your right hand on the stone for Earthy Earth, and tune in to its energies. When you feel your time in this energy-field is done, move on to Watery Earth, Fiery Earth and Airy Earth, meditating however long you feel appropriate at each stone. Then, move to the next element in the outermost circle and continue around until you have completed all 16 stones in the outer circle.

At this point, place your fingertips on the first of the twelve stones in the second circle and continue around until you have completed each. When this is complete, move through the four archetype stones one by one, connecting with that archetype inside your own being until you feel you have been able to bring the consciousness of each to the fore. Finally, when you have contemplated all 32 stones surrounding the centre, move your fingertips so that they rest on the clear crystal sphere which is the heartstone. Here, take the time to enter into your deepest meditation, resting in total silence in the depth of Eternal Being.

When you exit, move outward in the same order. Your meditation at each stone may be somewhat more brief, pausing only where you feel drawn, but remaining alert for impulses and insights that may come to you inwardly.

At the end of the exit, before completing the meditation with the last stone, feel a soulful sense of gratitude and offer this energy to the *mesa* as a whole. Then, when the exit is complete, place both hands on your lap and remain silent for a few moments, gazing on the *mesa* as a whole to be aware of any other information or sensation that may come. Finally, complete the journey with a brief prayer of intent in which you may invoke protection, or send blessings to the world, or direct healing or light and love to those who are in need.

FEEDING THE MESA

After my initiation with Don Sebastian of the Qero, he explained the principles involved in feeding a *mesa*. When we feed the *mesa*, we energize its life. This can be done in a number of ways. The ancestors of the Incas living in the Qero villages often use wine as a feeding energy for the *mesa*, or chicha which is a local beer made from fermented corn. In that part of the world, it is customary to fill the mouth with a kind of local wine called *pisco*, and then spray it over the object being fed by means of the breath. This has the advantage of mixing the tiny droplets of liquor with the life-breath, and this is a potent kind of magic. Feeding a *mesa* involves both intent and a knowledge of how certain energies work.

Someone who is well known to me had the experience of purchasing two wooden statuettes in Bali, special carvings which he found unusually beautiful. He liked to rub sandalwood into them and soon found that each of the two statuettes was inhabited by a spirit. The more he thought about and cared for his statues, the stronger the spirits within them became. This example shows how sacred rituals can bring results even when the intent is not focused, simply by virtue of the powers involved; it came as quite a surprise to this person that two elemental life-forms had taken up residence in his newly acquired statues, for this was not his intent.

The life energy contained in essential oils can be very compatible with many crystals, but some care should be exercised with soft minerals in this regard so that any given essential oil will not affect their chemical structure. Selenite, Malachite and Turquoise come to mind as examples of soft minerals with which care should be exercised. I personally like to purchase pure rose water and place it in a plastic bottle so that I can mist a crystal with this purifying and nurturing energy. Crystals like water, but when the water is filled with the energy of roses, it feeds them with a very pure and high vibration.

Other sources of energy are to be found in the Sun, the Moon, and the soil of Mother Earth. The period of the Full Moon is especially powerful for impregnating the *mesa* crystals with lunar energy, and solar energy can be accumulated within the stones by placing them in the full sunlight on any cloudless day. Burying crystals in the Earth for a few days not only clears and purifies their energy, but works well to un-stress and replenish them.

Sound also clears the energy of crystals, activates them and feeds them. Crystal bowls, Tibetan bowls and tingsha cymbals are excellent for this purpose. With Tibetan and crystal bowls, you can place a soft cloth, folded, in the centre of the bowl, with your *mesa* resting on it, and when you sound the bowl, the intensity and purity of the tone will clear the energy of your crystals and activate the entire *mesa* for your use.

The stones of the *mesa* can equally well be purified and nourished with incense smoke, flower petals, or movements of a feather, which is swept over the stones with focused intent either to clear away stagnant energy, or to awaken and feed the existing powers of the stones. After moving a crystal through sacred smoke, breathe on it, and feed it with your life energy. This can be repeated several times until you feel that the crystal has been charged with *prana*.

HEALING

It is traditional in *despacho* ceremonies for the celebrant to bring his or her *mesa*. This is held with the bundle of offerings before the final burning or burying, and swept up and down over the bodies of those present for healing. Your *mesa* can be a healing tool in similar fashion. While you may not want to pass it to anyone else to hold, you should be able to sweep it back and forth above the *chakras* of a person in need of healing and effect a change for the better. If you receive a message that a certain stone within the *mesa* is needed for the healing, use it according to your inner guidance. Sometimes, it may be the stones of one element that are called for, or several stones that have no obvious connection. Physical contact with the person who needs healing may not be necessary, simply holding the stone in the aura over the right area is often all that needs to be done.

The crystals for the four sacred elements are ideal for balancing the chakras. Place the Spirit stone at the centre of the chakra, and arrange the other six stones in a circle around it. The Fire stones are most useful for the solar plexus chakra. The Air stones work well with the heart centre and any of the chakras above it. The Water stones work well with the sacral chakra. Because the base chakra is not a flat surface, you may place the pouch containing these seven stones over it without any attempt to lay them out in the circular pattern mentioned above. While doing this exercise, any of the archetype stones may also be placed where you feel they are appropriate, or if you prefer, they may be laid above the head in the region of the crown chakra. Self healing may be practiced on the chakras in this way, or on others. Slow breathing, deep relaxation, visualization and affirmation all help the process. When you begin working with your *mesa*, you will intuit your own way of helping to balance energy in those who ask for your intervention. Finding and believing in your own style of healing is a stage of growth that comes naturally when you have worked with your *mesa* and grown familiar with its meaning and power.

The Crystal Mesa Logo is a
centering pattern for the Crystal
Mesa. It brings together and
combines elements of the
Teaching and the Lunar
crystal layouts.
(See pages 48 and 82)

USING THE MESA: PART TWO

One very useful application of a crystal *mesa* has to do with retrieval. In order to understand what retrieval work is, and how the *mesa* can facilitate it, we must have some understanding of the process by which human beings become alienated from their true nature. Many diseases have their root causes in emotional and mental disharmonies, and this in turn comes from unawareness of essential being. Alienation from Self means forgetfulness of who we truly are. This condition has been recognized from earliest times by all the masters as the root cause of suffering. In the ancient spiritual tradition of India, this forgetfulness of Self is called 'ignorance'; it is often accompanied by a sense of inner emptiness, and anxiety which in turn can generate psychosomatic and physical disorders. The work of retrieval is all about finding that which we have lost or forgotten, re-discovering the true Self which is deep within, covered over by the personality and by ideas arising out of the ego. As a process of reconnecting to the qualities and energies of the Self, retrieval is an indispensable part of the journey from ignorance to enlightenment.

Only when we have found deep within the answer to the question of questions: "Who Am I?" will we fulfill our potential and attain true freedom. A number of schools and methods have evolved which teach the processes by which the knowledge of our true and essential nature can be re-claimed. The discovery or attainment of the true Self cannot be communicated by verbal instruction, because it is not a packet of information. Realization of Self is an experience, and it arises spontaneously. The experience can be had only by doing the necessary work; those who undertake to do the work are said to be "on the path"; they have dedicated themselves to following "the Way." Only a small percentage of human beings undertake the path of return to Source, and of those who do, only a few complete the journey. The qualities needed for realization of the Self are many. One teacher I studied under summarized the qualities as: "simplicity, sincerity, purity and humility." To this we could add determination, focused will, a capacity for total self-giving, patience, and infinite good will. These, and other qualities, should they be lacking, may be retrieved or developed in the inner journey of return to Source.

In order to make a deep and sincere commitment to the inner work of retrieval and realization, a student must face all his or her unconscious fears, especially the fears related to 'loss of identity.' For most beginners, the only identity they know is the outer personality, which is a construction of ego. Students are taught that surrender to the higher Self is necessary for the transcendence of ego, but ego and personality fear to let go. The unconscious mind believes that if the individual commits fully to the quest, he is going to lose himself. It is true that the false personality will be outshone by the true self, but for this to happen it is necessary to work through all fears and particularly fears related to loss of identity. As A. H. Almaas put it:

> ...it has always been difficult to do the Work because the com-
> mitment, the will, the understanding are generally not avail-
> able to us due to repressed fears and resistances, which are
> completely unconscious, which control our behavior, and which
> get stronger if we push against them. Since the false personal-
> ity is the barrier we need to pierce through to get to our true
> nature, the Work has always required that people begin to
> make changes in some actions and patterns of behavior which
> are manifestations of the false personality.
> Diamond Heart, Book One, pg. 40

In order to transcend the false personality, it helps to understand how it has arisen. The word "conditioning" is often used to summa-rize a whole host of characteristics we acquire from outside ourselves in order to accommodate to our environment. This conditioning is a complex structure of beliefs, unconscious notions, fears, defences, and patterns of action and reaction. It does no good to demolish conditioning unless there is something to take its place. The core work of the path is to connect with the light, love, peace and power of the Self and to bring this to the fore so that the false personality can gradually be released and replaced by our inner, essential being. If we define meditation as attunement to the true Self, we can see that it is indispensable to the Work.

As far back as the time of Plato and Socrates in the West, and long before this in India, the masters have referred to self-realization as a matter of remembering, not of finding or attaining anything new. For example, when a moment of grace happens and we remember how to love, we reclaim a part of our own being that feels very familiar; we are not getting something from outside us. We reclaim the Self by remembering it. Each time we retrieve a vision or feeling of essential Self, it comes to us as something we have known and been, but which we misplaced. This memory of essence exists in all of us. Retrieval is the process of remembering who we are and restoring ourselves to our true nature. This is what the myths of retrieval are all about. When Isis re-assembles the parts of Osiris, she is re-membering the divine wholeness. The work of Isis is the work of the Divine Mother, the universal doer of the Work, and the body of Osiris is our own lost wholeness of Being.

Our lost essence has may facets or aspects. When we love deeply and truly, we have experienced one aspect of our deep essence. When we reclaim the quality of humility, we have retrieved one limb of our original Being. In the past, probably during childhood and adolescence, we felt inadequate in our capacity to function in the world of ignorance outside and around us. We compensated for this by detaching from soul (or spirit) and filling up the resulting empty spaces with a constructed personality, an individuality based on ego. The deficiencies or holes in our makeup arose because, in the course of adapting to the world around us, we forgot to be who we truly are. We wanted to be accepted, to fit in, to please our parents and teachers, to win approval, to attain recognition, and so we created a social personality that would allow us to be successful in a disfunctional family or society.

This social personality is a mask, not our essential self, but when we wear it and function through it long enough, we forget that we are truly other than our learned patterns of behaviour. The constructed personality serves the requirements of the ego, but obscures the presence and power of Spirit. As we lose contact with our inner "essence," or our soul-qualities, we acquire other adaptations of outer behaviour, and we use them to substitute for these losses. Where a quality of Spirit has been lost, a quality of personality has generally been manufactured to replace it. Once we begin the path of return to Source, this manufactured personality becomes a source of great unease. The ego and the false personality taken together represent the great obstacle to enlightenment. Retrieval is the work of letting go and going beyond; we let go of the constructed personality, and we go beyond the agenda of the ego. Retrieval means releasing our acquired conditioning and reclaiming the true soul qualities of our essential Being.

The crystal *mesa* can assist us in the work of retrieval because it is an embodiment of energetic completeness and an empowered icon of harmoniously balanced focus. Each stone within the crystal *mesa* stands for a living energy or soul quality that is an indispensable component of our light body. The light body is harmonized and activated when the physical, emotional and mental alignment of our entire being comes into attunement with the light of the soul. *Mesa* and retrieval work taken together are a means to this end. The heart of the *mesa*, a clear quartz sphere, the 'heartstone,' is the key to this understanding. It symbolizes our essential Being, our true Self, our unmanifest divinity. In that clear space, we know that we are one with the Source. In that crystalline domain of clarity we are fully identified with the presence and radiance of Spirit.

The power of the Source is expressed through the four sacred elements. In Earth element, for example, there is the Archetype of the Mother, the stone for Spirit Earth, the Yin and Yang Earth stones, and then the four variations of Earth energy, namely Earthy Earth, Watery Earth, Fiery Earth and Airy Earth. These stones correspond to parts of our own inner being. If our Earthy Earth energy has been denied, repressed or blocked, there will be a deficiency in our manifestation of Spirit; in other words, our life energy will not be radiating Spirit. By working with the *mesa* as a whole, and the stone for Earthy Earth in particular, we can find our way toward retrieval, or re-activation of that part of the being, and then a linking of its energies with our inner Source. Each time we reclaim or retrieve one of our sacred energies, the heartstone can manifest it.

The key stone represents the seed crystal in the spiritual heart which enables the yoga, so it helps to link consciously with that part of our being in all our work. When we do this, we will be able to feel and embody and express the full range of our life-energy in our microcosm, and we will be able to radiate our life-force outward to manifest our soul's plan. We will be able to link the inner and outer worlds in action which comes from the depth of our own spiritual heart. The spiritual heart is to our human microcosm what the crystal sphere and the key stone are to the *mesa*, namely the abode of the spirit, the home of soul.

Another way of expressing this is through the image of the mystical rose. When we do the work of retrieval, we re-constitute the mystical rose in our spiritual heart. Each of the 32 peripheral stones of the *mesa* represents a petal of the mystical rose which abides in the spiritual heart. The crystal sphere is their centre, and it is capable of reflecting the colours and energies and capacities of the petals when they have been retrieved, or healed. In alchemy, the rose symbolizes the wisdom of divine love, and the rosarium, the rose garden, is a symbol of the Great Work of self transformation. The mystical rose was originally the symbol of Venus, goddess of love, and then it became the symbol of the Virgin Mother, Mary, in Medieval Christian Europe. Sri Aurobindo has written a beautiful poem on the meaning of the mystical rose, entitled Rose of God:

Rose of God, vermilion stain on the sapphires of heaven,
Rose of Bliss, fire-sweet, seven-tinged with the ecstasies seven!
Leap up in our heart of humanhood, O miracle, O flame,
Passion-flower of the Nameless, bud of the mystical Name.
Rose of God, great-wisdom-bloom on the summits of being,
Rose of Light, immaculate core of the ultimate seeing!
Live in the mind of our earthhood; O golden Mystery, flower,
Sun on the head of the Timeless, guest of the marvellous Hour.
Rose of God, damask force of Infinity, red icon of might,
Rose of Power with thy diamond halo piercing the night!
Ablaze in the will of the mortal, design the wonder of they plan,
Image of Immortality, outbreak of the godhead in man.
Rose of God, smitten purple with the incarnate divine Desire,
Rose of Life, crowded with petals, colour's lyre!
Transform the body of the mortal like a sweet and magical rhyme;
Bridge our earthood and heavenhood, make deathless the children of Time.

Rose of God, like a blush of rapture on Eternity's face,
Rose of Love, ruby depth of all being, fire-passion of Grace!
Arise from the heart of the yearning that sobs in Nature's abyss:
Make earth the home of the Wonderful and life beatitude's kiss.

The Mother has also spoken about the meaning of roses. For example, a multi-coloured rose signifies Love from the Divine; pink roses signify the state that can be obtained by surrendering to the Divine; red roses signify human passions changed into Love for the Divine; white roses represent integral Love for the Divine; and yellow roses represent mental Love for the Divine.

These roses actually hold the soul-energies designated. Thus, the crystal *mesa*, as it applies to the work of retrieval, can be seen as a symbolic counterpart of the mystical rose of the heart, and the retrieval of the qualities embodied by each crystal makes it active in the heartstone, which is to say in symbolic language, active in the spiritual heart of the *mesa* keeper, and therefore capable of being manifested in life.

The work of soul-retrieval is an ancient shamanic practice, and there is no single procedure that will be successful for everyone. A few suggestions may be made for retrieval work with your crystal *mesa*. If you are intuitive, you can ask a question and receive an answer, or if you have experience using a pendulum, you can focus your questions and answers quite specifically.

Try to feel which sacred element is most in need of retrieval. Then try to feel which crystal or crystals from your *mesa* you should work with. For example, if your Fire energy is weak, focus on the Fire stones. Either intuitively, or through the pendulum, find one or more stones that you feel can fill a space within you, or help you attune to energies and qualities in which you may be temporarily deficient. The stone will be a battery of this energy for you to draw on. Try to name that hole or empty space that needs filling, or affirm the quality in the stone that you can feed on. It is best to work according to your own inner feelings, but also to be aware of the qualities that the stones are generally believed to embody based on past experience of others in the field. Intuition works best when it is supplemented by a sound knowledge of tradition.

After you relax and meditate, you may want to lie on a rug or on your bed and place the stone you will use first on your physical body on the location that seems to be the centre of the deficiency. Inhale the energy of the stone into your being. Each time you breathe in, slowly and deeply, visualize yourself inhaling the colour and energy of the stone into that part of the body, and then when you exhale,, see the energy dispersing to all the cells of the body, and into your aura. When you feel you have filled your entire being with that energy from the selected crystal, relax. Working in this way, use all the stones in the *mesa* that speak to you, and replenish yourself with their energies. The pendulum can be a very helpful tool to confirm whether the work is complete, or how much progress has been made in any session of working with your *mesa* stones in this manner.

THE SOUL MANDALA

Your *mesa* becomes your soul mandala when you internalize its structure, energy, and consciousness. This is only possible if you discover in yourself an interest in your *mesa* such that you feel you want to have it with you, you feel pulled to meditate with it, to open it and gaze on it, to speak to it, to listen to it, to learn from it, and to cherish it in your heart. Short of this kind of relationship, no ritual or mechanical activity can bring out the reality of Soul Mandala from your Crystal Mesa. But the following exercise is proposed for those who feel they want this degree of connection with their *mesa* and are prepared to do what it takes to deepen and realize their fullest connection with it.

The twenty-eight stones of the *mesa's* outer ring constitute one lunar cycle. The Earth stones comprise the time and energy of the Moon's darkest phase. Spirit Earth is the day of the New Moon. Yin Earth is the day preceding this, and Yang Earth is the day following. Fiery Earth is the day following Yang Earth and Airy Earth is the day following that. Earthy Earth precedes Yin Earth, and Watery Earth precedes that. Thus, the sequence for stones in and around the New Moon is: Spirit Earth on the day itself, with Yin Earth, Earthy Earth and Watery Earth preceding, and Yang Earth, Fiery Earth and Airy Earth succeeding.

The First Quarter is Spirit Fire. The day preceding it is Yin Fire; the day before that is Earthy Fire, and the day before that is Watery Fire. The day after Spirit Fire is Yang Fire, then Fiery Fire and lastly Airy Fire. This pattern is followed with Air and Water stones.

You should lay your stones out in this pattern on your altar at the time of the New Moon, and meditate to set your intention. The intention in this case will be to merge your *mesa* with your soul's light so that the *mesa* becomes an expression of your soul-force and your soul-destiny for this lifetime. This means that you have chosen to fully appropriate and individualize the *mesa* archetype in the inner world. When you have done this, its dynamic capacity will come fully alive for you. In this way, your meditation with each stone will bring about a synthesis of its crystalline energy (and its capacity) with one facet of your soul's expression.

Read the profile for each stone that you work with day by day, but do not be bound by the information you read. Once you take in the information, feel for yourself what the crystal for that day means to you. Another way to put it is: see the crystal for that day as a projection of one aspect of your soul, and try to clarify your understanding of how that crystal will project this ray of your soul into manifestation for you in this life. A crystal may convey information, or even awaken wisdom; it may symbolize a spiritual quality, or activate that quality in your life; it may radiate healing energy, healing for you personally, or healing that you can apply to others if that is your calling. It may show you a work to be done within your own being for further progress on the path, or it may have other levels of significance.

When this is done with care and deep feeling, the *mesa* becomes a living projection of your soul-power, consecrated to the realization of your soul's mission in this life. It is important to set this intent clearly and with deep feeling at the outset of this work so that you actualize this deepest level of meaning for each crystal within your *mesa*.

On the day of the New Moon, you will begin working with the stone for Spirit Earth. You may be inwardly guided about how to incorporate this crystal into your Soul Mandala. Whatever procedure you follow, it will have an aspect of deep feeling and another aspect of clear understanding, and both should be in balance. You may use sound, spoken word, invocation, prayer, meditation and affirmation, as well as any other appropriate methods for achieving this end. The work will not proceed identically with each stone. It is in essence a creative work, not a rote routine. You must feel and discover your way with each individual crystal facet of your being in this matter. If you do not have the inspiration to do this, perhaps you are not ready to undertake the work. In this case, simply meditate on (or with) the *mesa* stones daily at a particular time and wait for inner guidance about how to proceed. When the guidance comes, of course, follow it; but the guidance that comes may not be the complete picture, it may only be a few hints about how to begin. Accept the hints and make the beginning. Be open to what else will come. This is the way that true transformation of the *mesa* into Soul-Mandala can be done, there is no shortcut.

THE REVELATION MANDALA

Place all the stones of your *mesa* in one pile and place your hands over the crystals. Spread them out and feel their energies. Look at them and feel which one you are most drawn to at that time. Place this stone in the centre of your *mesa* cloth.

Continue to do this with your crystals, choosing four more for a total of five. Each time you discern the next crystal that most calls to you, feel where you want to place it in relation to the central crystal. You may place a crystal in the Earth section of your *mesa* cloth, or in the Fire quadrant, or in Air or Water, but only one crystal in each position. Do not think this placement through with your mind, rather follow your feeling, your sense of what placement feels right at the time you do it.

When you complete the placement, you will have a pattern that is an outer representation of your own relationship to life at that time. If you have asked a question, the pattern which you lay out on the *mesa* cloth will be an answer to that question. If you have a desire for self-understanding, the pattern will speak to this need. Your intent may be focused or unfocused, and each time the result will vary according to the way you engage the process. If you have asked for healing, the pattern will address that need. If you have invoked a blessing, it will be so.

All of this is predicated on having completed the work of making your *mesa* a soul-mandala, although the soul can work with you at any time you sincerely invoke it, and even before your apprentice training is complete. However, good preparation is the foundation of excellence, and the true depth of this exercise is prepared in that earlier use of *mesa* to link with soul.

When you can do this for yourself, you can do it with others, and the *mesa* can be a tool of healing, discernment, teaching or spiritual counsel.

GEM REMEDIES

Each of the stones within a crystal *mesa* can be used to generate a liquid tincture, which holds the essence of the vibration in water. Gem and crystal tinctures can be used therapeutically to get at the core disorders which underlie the more obvious physical pathologies. Physical and psychological health problems are often compensations which the organism creates to hold and express a deeper weakness in higher bodies. Speaking generally, we can say that at the soul level, where Spirit is most present in its interface with matter, there can be a seed, or idea of a disease that inhibits full health, and may eventually manifest as a fullblown, even a fatal, pathology. These disorders may be referred to as "psycho-spiritual." They are profound and subtle disharmonies which impact the spiritual life, the psychology and often the physical health of their carrier. The ancients used to use the language of music as an analogy for health, and in this frame of reverence, these seed-disorders might be termed deep-seated disharmonies.

One may use gems and crystals to formulate a set of vibrations that form a mirror image of this deep disharmony. There is no standard formula in this work. Each formulation must be customized. Also, there may be a need for several different formulations to cover the full spectrum of the disharmonies. Gurudas has gone into this subject in great detail in his books about *Gem Elixirs and Vibrational Healing*. The essences may be sucussed and potentized as in homeopathy to direct them into the more rarefied energy fields of the human microcosm. The analysis may be in the form of a series of questions, or it may be intuitive, using a tool such as a pendulum, or it may be a combination of both these, as well as muscle testing and other modalities. Each healer will have his or her preferred method.

The result of finding effective formulations will be a harmonizing of energy with Spirit, and of both with the physical cells of the body. This enhanced flow of energy and Spirit often precipitates heightened states of awareness, and it is when energy and spirit flow most freely that true, deep, lasting healing can be effected. The gem tinctures may be taken orally, or as a mist on the skin. It helps to understand that there is no transfer of physical particles from the gems or crystals, but only a seeding of healing vibratory patterns into the subtle bodies of the patient. When the correct formulation is applied, there will be a harmonizing effect on the flow of energy at the subtle level, and this will frequently be mirrored by an enhancement of consciousness. This, then is integral healing, healing of spirit, vitality and body. The vibrations of gem remedies are pure enough to interface perfectly with the highest vibratory fields of the various subtle bodies of the human microcosm. Typical results of a good treatment would include: relaxation, expanded awareness, a feeling of release, open-mindedness, clarity of perception and judgement, and a feeling of creative energy at one's disposal. This is sometimes called an "altered state," but it is actually the natural state, the state before "the fall."

When you work with gem remedies, the suprasensible element is to the fore. If we look for parallels, the action of flower essences comes closest to the action of gem remedies. In neither is there a need to research or explain any physical medicinal value, because there is no ingestion of physical matter. There is no need to analyze the chemical properties of the gem or mineral involved, because it is in fact the dynamic, subtle energy of a gem which is the real healer. Each mineral and gem has its own "signature" or characteristic pattern of action, as the writings of Bhattacharya and Gurudas explain very clearly. For example, writing about Jade, which we call "Spirit Earth," Gurudas says:

> *Jade generates Divine Love, which is unconditional love. Articulation of psychic abilities increases, as does a discriminating, altruistic nature. There may be an inability to articulate one's feelings, especially in the family unit, when one is in need of jade. The astral, emotional, and etheric bodies are aligned to function as a single unit. This aligns the entire personality to the level of the biological personality... This other personality is very ancient, and through this vehicle one attunes to the earth. The kinship between the earth and the physical body has been in place a very long time. The biological personality is of great benefit when one has forgotten about one's earth connection.*
> *Gem Elixirs and Vibrational Healing, Vol. I pg. 117*

Just as an essential oil is a storehouse of dynamic potential which reflects the essence of all aspects of the source plant, so a gem remedy holds the vibratory essence of a crystal, with all its complexities and subtleties. There are many schools of esoteric healing which can be accessed to advantage when one studies the uses and applications of these remedies, but all of this is incomplete unless the healer can apply his or her intuitive faculty in the process of analyzing the patient and the locate the unique patterns of the disharmonies which are at work.

The use of gem remedies for healing is a holistic form of medicine, a spiritual, non-clinical art capable of reorganizing the most subtle disharmonies and releasing them into balance. When deeply held disharmonies are re-balanced, the entire human microcosm, including the physical body, is ameliorated.

It must be said that the specific genius of gem remedies is to create health within the deep patterns of the life-energy, and even within the consciousness, or spiritual expression, of the soul involved. Gem remedies are perfectly complementary with the kind of care provided by allopathic and naturopathic doctors. They work in subtle, but sometimes dramatic ways for spiritual healing and deep re-balancing of the subtle bodies, an area which few other healing modalities can access.

MESA AS TEACHER

You may feel that you are drawn to a certain crystal. You may find that it is on your mind or of special interest to you, as I described earlier in my experiences with Moonstone and Labradorite. If so, it is good to open your mind to the possibility that this crystal in particular has something to teach or show you at this time. The window for interaction may not be long, so seize the opportunity when you first become aware. How will you learn from your crystal?

The first thing to do is to prepare the crystal for sacred ceremony by purifying it with water, salt, sunshine or some other means. Then, feed it with your heart's love energy, with words, music, with sound (such as Tibetan bowls or bells or tingshas) or by anointing it with sacred oil (such as essential oil of rose). You may also breathe onto the crystal to bless and impregnate it with your life energy, as a gift of spirit. Then, either place the crystal in your hand, or on an altar and begin to meditate on it with the eyes open. Let your mind become very quiet as you gaze at the crystal.

When you have the energy and colour and form of the physical crystal well fixed in your mind, close your eyes. Picture the crystal as a holograph, a space that you can step into. Picture your own body as being extremely light and vapourous, a subtle body which you can use to move into the body of the crystal. This we have practiced in our attunement training. Then, imagine that you move in this subtle body into the interior of the crystal. You find yourself in a space resembling a room where all four walls, and the floor and ceiling are crystal, similar in structure, energy, form and colour to your own crystal.

In this space, wait for a while. Intuit how the space feels. Open your heart in a sense of reverence and sincerity and call upon the spirit of the crystal. Express your respect to the living Deva and ask to be shown anything that can be of help to you. You might have specific questions such as: how can this energy be of help to me at this time? Then, with an open mind, be alert to any impressions, feelings or information that come to you. Be open to the unexpected. Keep all possibilities open.

At the end, when you feel you have completed the process, express your thanks, exit back into your physical body and bring the session to a close.

Using your crystal *mesa* is a lifelong learning experience. As one limb of Crystal Yoga, your *mesa* training will open doors of awareness and capacities of interaction that will make every other practice you do richer. In time, you will internalize the crystal energies, or activate their counterparts within your own microcosm. Then, your memory and intuition will be sufficient to let you continue with the work by having a mental link with the reality behind the *mesa*, the configuration of energy and consciousness which sustains our embodied souls and makes possible the work of ascension. The *mesa* is a symbolic counterpart of all you are and can manifest, but remember that its sacredness is only realized by living in right relationship to its archetypal reality. Through the humble physical forms of stones and crystals, the energies and consciousness of cosmic gods can be brought to the fore in your microcosm and in your consciousness.

In the end, *mesa* will be all that you can believe and dream. Therefore, set your sights high. Aim for the stars. Allow the best that can be to shine through. In this way, not only is the full potential of your Crystal Mesa actualized, but you realize the magnificent destiny that your soul has chosen as the ultimate goal of your life.

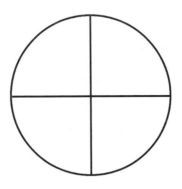

CRYSTAL MESA LOGO

The Crystal Mesa Logo has many levels of meaning, despite its visual simplicity. It shows how the Centre connects to its phyical manifestation (the outer circle) through the arms of the four elements (the inner cross). It expresses the fundamentals of time (especially the four stages of the lunar cycle), space (especially inner space and its relation to the outer world) and form (which is based on number and geometry). This very ancient symbol is found in many temples, caves and ancient manuscripts, and is also significant as an alchemical teaching device.

THE CRYSTAL ORACLE

A new creation from the old shall rise,
A Knowledge inarticulate find speech,
Beauty suppressed burst into paradise bloom,
Pleasure and pain dive into absolute bliss.
A tongueless oracle shall speak at last,
The Superconscient conscious grow on earth,
The Eternal's wonders join the dance of Time.
                                    Sri Aurobindo, Savitri, pg. 330

Use of the crystal *mesa* brings many openings and awakenings, but it does more than stimulate and release its keeper's hidden potential. When engaged with sincere intent, the *mesa* aligns this potential with the divine plan and it brings the soul closer to full mastery. In this way, the spiritual dimensions of our being fill our human form, and we grow into our destined role in the cosmic drama. Inevitably in this unfolding process, the oracular consciousness comes into play. Not only is the *mesa* an oracle, its keeper realizes the attainment of oracle.

An oracle is a person through whom deity can speak; however, the word 'oracle' can also refer to the shrine in which the deity resides, (in this case the crystal *mesa*) whence the hidden knowledge and divine purpose manifest. An answer or decision given by an oracle is sometimes also called an oracle. All of these meanings have a very ancient and rich history which has given birth to many religious and cultural expressions of this theme. In the end, when we have studied much and grown greatly, we come to recognize that the very structure of our being is innately oracular. Our cells and our DNA are encoded with this potential before we leave the womb. The Higher Self is a priest and mediator of this inner fullness. The illumined mind is a mirror of Spirit's infinite possibility and a seer of the invisible forces that orchestrate a gradual revelation of divine purpose on Earth.

The crystal *mesa* is certainly a shrine or temple assembled to manifest all these possibilities, but what it can manifest is always measured and limited by its keeper's openness. Whatever we can believe, we can actualize. Yet before we believe, we must conceive. Thus, the awakening of our mind and imagination to the infinity of possibilities is often the starting point on the road to the oracular consciousness. The experiences of those who have gone before us on the way are of inestimable value, especially the masters whose words carry the living power of their realization.

The complete attainment of the oracular consciousness is something rare and precious. In *Savitri*, Sri Aurobindo communicates his own lived experience of this height:

> *A high vast peak whence Spirit could see the worlds,*
> *Calm's wide epiphany, wisdom's mute home,*
> *A lonely station of Omniscience,*
> *A diving-board of the Eternal's power,*
> *A white floor in the house of All-Delight.*
> *Here came the thought that passes beyond Thought,*
> *Here the still Voice which our listening cannot hear,*
> *The Knowledge by which the knower is the known,*
> *The Love in which beloved and lover are one.*
> *All stood in an original plenitude,*
> *Hushed and fulfilled before they could create*
> *The glorious dream of their universal acts;*
> *Here was engendered the spiritual birth,*
> *Here closed the finite's crawl to the Infinite.*
>
> *Savitri, pgs. 297-8*

The master is describing a plane of consciousness where:

Silence listens with still heart
To the rhythmic metres of the rolling worlds,

Here,

He heard the ever unspoken Reality's voice
Awaken revelation's mystic cry,
The birthplace found of the sudden infallible Word
And lived in the rays of an intuitive Sun.

Savitri, pg. 299

One who grows into this consciousness experiences a constant flow of revelation, and should he or she express this revelation in words, those words carry the light and transformative power of revelation.

If you have undertaken a serious relationship with your crystal *mesa*, then you are in a position to explore this domain of experience and bring the oracular potential fully to the fore. What will this attainment be like? Certainly it can never exceed the measure of your faith or the extent of your mind's openness. But the mind's conception of what is possible can be widened. One way of doing this is by reflecting on the experiences of those who have full mastery. Using words of oracular dignity and depth, Sri Aurobindo continues, in this section of *Savitri*, (Book XI) to describe how the seeker becomes the seer:

There Knowledge called him to her mystic peaks
Where thought is held in a vast internal sense
And feeling swims across a sea of peace
And vision climbs beyond the reach of Time.
An equal of the first creator seers,
Accompanied by an all-revealing flight
He moved through regions of transcendent Truth
Inward, immense, innumerably one.
There distance was his own huge spirit's extent;
Delivered from the fictions of the mind
Time's triple dividing step baffled no more;
Its inevitable and continuous stream,

The long flow of its manifesting course,
Was held in spirit's single wide regard.
A universal beauty showed its face:
The invisible deep-fraught significances,
Here sheltered behind form's insensible screen,
Uncovered to him their deathless harmony
And the key to the wonder-book of common things.
In their uniting law stood up revealed
The multiple measures of the upbuilding force,
The lines of the world-Geometer's technique,
The enchantments that uphold the cosmic web
And the magic underlying simple shapes.

Savitri, pg. 299

Engraved on the doorway to the ancient Delphic oracle (in Greek, of course, not Latin) the following proclamation confronted all pilgrims who came seeking answers to life's challenges: *Vocatus atque non vocatus deus aderit:* Summoned or not, the deity is always present. This famous injunction may be coupled with another which history tells us was carved on the lintel of Plato's academy: "Know Thyself." These two statements point to centrally important themes of the oracular process. If Sri Aurobindo gives us a glimpse of the summit-experiences at the end of our soul's long journey, the *mesa* is for its keeper a most significant door-opener, a vehicle of ascent on the Way, a co-creator spiritual progress. As well as supplying answers to oracular questions and being a shrine of revelation, *mesa* can be a source of teaching and guidance to its keeper's mind and heart. The crystal *mesa* can open and awaken consciousness until eventually the seeker becomes the seer, the pilgrim grows into the attainment and the lover merges in the Beloved.

Of course, intent is centrally important at every stage of this process. If we do not knock, the door may not open. If we do not seek, we are not likely to find. If we do not inquire about the truth of our being and aspire to uncover a spiritual destiny, there is no need for deity to appear or to speak. Divine help is required only when an intense need to know oneself has arisen. At this point, there is a very good chance that the right conditions prevail either to approach an oracle, or to become one.

Spiritual Knowledge, or Gnosis, is much more than intellectual insight, nor is it merely an ability to spin philosophical or theological words. The oracular consciousness is gnostic, and one who attains it is a seer, a sage, or a spiritual master. However, prior to that attainment, the very process of using the *mesa* as an oracle lays a foundation for lofty realization.

The oracular use of the crystal *mesa* implies much more than technical, mechanical methods for seeing into the future. Although the *mesa* permits its user to interrogate the future, it always tends to move consciousness toward a fuller and more profound understanding of divination. When rightly assembled and understood, a crystal *mesa* enhances the faculties that provide access to higher planes of consciousness where the past, present and future are simultaneously present. As a spiritual master, Sri Aurobindo, describes this domain of experience in the passages quoted above, and in other sections of *Savitri.* These are real worlds of inner experience. However, accessing them requires us to release unfulfilled desires, wishes and illusions. As the light of consciousness grows, the questions one needs to ask become more and more centred on relationship to Source, less and less coloured by ego and its fascination with pleasure. We no longer try to wrestle oracular messages into the confines of our mental understanding. We are more willing to contemplate the mystery of the Word and feel its implications for our life. When one who has consulted an oracle does not understand the deity's revealed Word, this is a sign of being disconnected from the deeper Self. By misunderstanding, or through inappropriate attitude, such a seeker brings about his or her own downfall, and in such a case it is not the oracle but estrangement from right relation to Source that causes the outcome.

For this reason, the ancient oracles were approached with awe and respect, and the rituals involved were always conducted with solemnity. The oracle shrine or temple was recognized as a place where the deity descended to Earth, a power-spot connecting terrestrial affairs to the celestial powers that govern them. Being a house of the god, the oracle would frequently be endowed with precious treasures, famous works of art and noble architecture. Such was the case with Delphi, Dodona and other famous oracles of the classical world. One would feel their numinous energy as one crossed the threshold and entered the inner sanctum. The seeker would have prepared for the event by fasting, and by offering a goat or sheep in sacrifice. At each step, appropriate rituals would be enacted and an aura of sacred expectancy would come to the fore both in the questioner and in the one who gave voice to the deity. At the time when the verdict of the god was spoken, a lofty oracular speech would clothe its meaning in suitably significant phrases. From start to finish, the performance had to be conducted prayerfully and in a manner worthy of the divine.

Since oracles are very much concerned with the power of the revealing Word, it is very helpful to study passages of true revelation for deeper understanding of the oracular path. It is quite significant to recognize that this attainment is not self-chosen, but rather an election from above. The Divine communicates to the seeker:

I lay my hands upon thy soul of flame,
I lay my hands upon thy heart of love,
I yoke thee to my power of work in Time.
Because thou has obeyed my timeless will,
Because thou hast chosen to share earth's struggle and fate
And leaned in pity over earth-bound men
And turned aside to help and yearned to save,
I bind by thy heart's passion thy heart to mine
And lay my splendid yoke upon thy soul.
Now will I do in thee my marvellous works.
I will fasten thy nature with my cords of strength,
Subdue to my delight thy spirit's limbs
And make thee a vivid knot of all my bliss
And build in thee my proud and crystal home
Hearts touched by thy love shall answer to my call,
Discover the ancient music of the spheres
In the revealing accents of thy voice
And nearer draw to me because thou art:
Enamoured of thy spirit's loveliness
They shall embrace my body in thy soul,
Hear in thy life the beauty of my laugh,
Know the thrilled bliss with which I made the worlds

Savitri, pgs. 698, 701

When an oracle is at work, it is the divine which is using the human to express itself. One must therefore approach the use of *mesa* for oracle work with a soul-deep disposition for surrender and merging in the divine providence. Through a surrendered oracle, the divine accomplishes its work:

A few shall glimpse the miraculous Origin
And some shall feel in you the secret Force
And they shall turn to meet a nameless tread,
Adventurers into a mightier Day.
Ascending out of the limiting breadths of mind,
They shall discover the world's huge design
And step into the Truth, the Right, the Vast.
You shall reveal to them the hidden eternities,
The breath of infinitudes not yet revealed,
Some rapture of the bliss that made the world,
Some rush of the force of God's omnipotence,
Some beam of the omniscient Mystery.

Savitri, pg. 704

The depth of this merging which takes place between the human and the divine in the surrendered oracle is scarcely understood by the average seeker. But Sri Aurobindo makes it very clear how deep the indentification runs:

Then shall the embodied being live as one
Who is a thought, a will of the Divine,
A mask or robe of his divinity,
An instrument and partner of his Force,
A point or line drawn in the infinite,
A manifest of the imperishable.
The supermind shall be his nature's fount,
The Eternal's truth shall mould his thoughts and acts,
The Eternal's truth shall be his light and guide.
All then shall change, a magic order come
Overtopping this mechanical universe.

Savitri, pg. 706

Moreover, this transformation of the individual oracle is only a prelude to a worldwide transformation of the consciousness of humanity as a whole. It is particularly valuable to appreciate the prophetic and oracular power of the master's language when he speaks words of prophetic revelation:

A soul shall wake in the Inconscient's house;
The mind shall be God-vision's tabernacle,
The body intuition's instrument,
And life a channel for God's visible power.
All earth shall be the Spirit's manifest home,
Hidden no more by the body and the life,
Hidden no more by the mind's ignorance;
An unerring Hand shall shape event and act.
The Spirit's eyes shall look through Nature's eyes,
The Spirit's force shall occupy Nature's force.
A heavenlier passion shall upheave men's lives,
Their mind shall share in the ineffable gleam,
Their heart shall feel the ecstasy and the fire.
Earth's bodies shall be conscious of a soul;
Mortality's bondslaves shall unloose their bonds,
Mere men into spiritual beings grow
And see awake the dumb divinity.
Intuitive beams shall touch the nature's peaks,
A revelation stir the nature's depths;
The Truth shall be the leader of their lives,
Truth shall dictate their thought and speech and act,
They shall feel themselves lifted nearer to the sky,
As if a little lower than the gods.
For knowledge shall pour down in radiant streams
And even darkened mind quiver with new life
And kindle and burn with the Ideal's fire
And turn to escape from mortal ignorance.
The frontiers of the Ignorance shall recede,
More and more souls shall enter into light,
Minds lit, inspired, the occult summoner hear
And lives blaze with a sudden inner flame
And hearts grow enamoured of divine delight,
And human wills tune to the divine will...

Savitri, pgs. 707, 709-10

A crystal *mesa* oracle-worker is a fore-runner of this divine destiny.

He or she realizes and attains what all will one day realize and attain. The oracle's revealing Word is not only information, it is power for integral transformation. One comes away from a true oracle in some measure changed, more charged with light, more available to Spirit, and this is so whether one approaches the oracular function of the *mesa* seeking wisdom for oneself, or for others. It is in this way that the oracle fulfils the ancient Greek command: "Know Thyself." Through deep self-knowledge, the harmony of microcosm and macrocosm is accomplished, and thus Earth becomes a reflection of Heaven.

It was well understood in ancient times that the seriousness of the question must conform to the sacredness of the place. Often a cave would be the site of an oracle, or a natural setting of dramatic beauty. Vast sums were spent on buildings which would impress the visitor with the sacred power of the forces at work. This dimension of awe and mystery may have been lost in our own day and age when Tarot decks or sets of runes are widely available at little cost, and proper training in the ancient tradition of divination is almost impossible to find. In the oracles of Greece, Egypt and Mesopotamia, when all the right conditions were realized and there was no flaw either in attitude or in the execution of the rituals, the experience of consulting an oracle would take on a spiritually revitalizing quality. The revealed Word of the deity acted to renew and surcharge the pilgrim if he (or she) had sought out the truth in all sincerity, and with appropriate humility. As revelations of the deity's wisdom, the ancient oracles were always considered extraordinary, not ordinary. It was hardly possible in such a cultural context to reduce their role to the trivial level of a parlour game, as we often see these days.

The faith of the ancients, and our faith too, if we are to make right use of the *mesa* for oracle-working, is that the deity will be fully present when the question and the questioner meet the required standard of respectful integrity. If these conditions are not met, either the oracle will refuse to answer, or the answer will be misleading. A proper and serious question always probes, in one form or another, the issue of the individual or the collective harmony with the cosmic order. In its deepest sense, a proper question would refer to the connection, or disruption of connection, between the human and the divine. The burden of formulating a proper question, and responsibility for approaching the oracle in the right spirit had to be met by the seeker. In the ancient world, one visited an oracle at one's own peril, and usually at considerable expense. The oracular sacred space brought the soul into direct confrontation with the forces of fate and the ultimatums of destiny. When the question met the god's standard of seriousness and correctness, and when the various aspects of accompanying ritual were carried out correctly, the ancient oracles functioned brilliantly. Evidence to this effect can be found throughout classical literature, where we read that many oracles became not only famous but immensely rich. It must be added also that some were corrupt – such, it seems, is human nature.

The ancient tradition has much to teach us regarding our own portable temple, the crystal *mesa*. The *mesa*'s construction is intertwined with its keeper's intent from the very first instant that its planning begins. Where due attention has been paid to the correspondence between macrocosm and microcosm, the divine and the human, the *mesa* will be a teacher, helping its keeper to accomplish the mandate: "Know Thyself." It will constantly send out energies which reinforce the will to attain wisdom; it will steadily emanate a signal to the soul that says: "Live up to all that you truly are."

The *mesa* is, after all, a repository of knowledge that can best be tapped by an oracular approach. As a point of connection between our normal human level of mind and experience, and the suprapersonal domain of deity, the *mesa* is intrinsically sacred. When we construct and maintain a crystal *mesa* correctly, we have started living the process of right relationship to the sacred more consciously, a theme discussed at some length in Chapter 13. The *mesa* and its various parts activate aspects of our own microcosm, including the *chakras*, meridians, DNA, and the nervous system. The *mesa* is a teacher because it makes us more conscious of the subtle domains of our own being that are otherwise incomprehensible. At the same time, it presents us with a pattern of wholeness and interconnectedness based on the interrelation of the four (or five) sacred elements, and their relationship to Source. In this way, the totality of the unconscious and supraconscious is mirrored and the awareness of our psyche is made clear to us in the various interactions we experience.

The *mesa* constantly proclaims: "I give spiritual nourishment." Each seeker who chooses to develop and interact with a crystal *mesa* has the responsibility to learn his or her own uniquely personal way to tap, assimilate and share this nourishment. The *mesa* as oracle opens up one of many possibilities for self discovery and service to the divine plan. By briefly reviewing the ancient tradition, we set the stage for a contemporary approach to right relation and right use of the *mesa* in its oracular function.

CRYSTAL MESA DIVINATION

The first step is to meditate and enter a deeper level of consciousness. When you feel that your heart is open and the mind silent, either formulate the question, or look at the question you had intended to ask and see if it is the true question. Also, try to find the perfect words to express this question. Do not ask a question that can be answered by "yes" or "no." Write the question down on a slip of paper.

Take the clear quartz sphere which represents Source in your crystal *mesa*, and attune to it in your consciousness. You may want to do the meditation which takes you to your inner temple (see The Thirteenth Attunement in Appendix II) and concentrate on this crystal sphere as it appears there, while simultaneously holding your physical crystal sphere from the *mesa*. As you meditate with this sphere, come to understand it as a living extension or symbol of the Supreme. It is the central axis of your *mesa* temple, and it is continuously aligned with the Truth consciousness. You may feel or visualize this alignment and enter into it through your meditation.

One or two suggestions concerning this important meditation: You may have a crystal ball which you prefer to hold while you meditate, possibly because you have used it this way for some time, or because its size or its quality make it suitable. You may substitute this crystal sphere for the one in your *mesa*. As you hold the crystal sphere, close your eyes and take in its presence through the sense of touch. As you hold the crystal sphere, remind yourself: "This is the Great Mystery." Understand that in this meditation, you will be contemplating the Great Mystery which the crystal sphere embodies. The perfection of clear quartz, solidified light, holds within itself the entire mystery of creation. Visualize the sphere as a gently glowing region of light which you can enter. Use *the intelligence of your heart* to contemplate the Great Mystery. This intelligence is synonymous with your capacity for intuitive feeling. Moving into the perfect corridors of light in your crystal sphere, going deeper and deeper with the intelligence of your heart, contemplate the Great Mystery which is cradled in your hands. At this time, you may ask the Mother, the Child, the Hero or the Sage to meditate through you. If you do this correctly, this divine archetype will become the doer of the meditation. The possibilities are immense. You may intuit that in reality, you are Creator holding creation in the palms of your hands, and this is not untrue. The only thing separating you from God is the smallness of your thinking.

When you are in this space of alignment, you make a sacrifice of some kind mentally. It may be an offering of a prayer such as love or gratitude. Or it may be an expression of praise. Or you may visualize yourself ritually anointing the crystal sphere with water, or rose petals, or with a sacred oil, or with incense. You may also include a prayer for a successful divination.

The four archetype stones of your *mesa* will not be included in this divination, nor the Source stone, but the rest will. They should be in a bowl or cloth bag. Since your Selenite crystal is very soft, you might want to substitute Iolite for divination purposes. At this point, the divination can proceed in several ways. You may choose to draw only one crystal, or you may draw two. The first stone you draw may indicate the area within your own being where you should look for an answer or seek balance and healing, or on whose strength and capacity you should build, depending on the question. Or, the first crystal you draw may indicate the area in which to look for an answer, and the second crystal may indicate the specifics of the answer, what to do or how to think and feel, or what change to make. You should draw with the question clearly in mind, the mind quietly focused, and the eyes closed, selecting intuitively and quickly so you do not have time to recognize any stone by its size or by the sense of touch.

You might consider questions such as: In what area of my being do I most need light? What energy should I strive to increase and develop? What crystal energy has most to teach me at this time? In what area is my relation to Source most in need of improvement? Each system of divination has its specialty and strength, and the crystal *mesa* oracle is well suited to questions related to health and inner development.

You will always have two different forms of awareness for what any given crystal means. Firstly, you will have your own personal intuitive feeling. And secondly, you will have information that you know mentally by having read about the stone. You should take the stone and hold it, and even carry it with you and meditate on it until it reveals to you its answer; and in the case of two stones, follow the same procedure. Here, you revert to the heartspace of unknowing, the domain of Yin Fire which we considered in a previous chapter.

If you choose to read up on the stone you have selected, this is acceptable, but remember you are should not engage in an intellectual quest for an intellectual answer. The question has been asked, and the stone has been chosen to communicate to you its answer. The answer may not come in the form of information, but rather in the form of insight. A crystal vibration may not be expressible in words, and yet it can contain just the right answer. The gift of a true oracle is to put the inexpressible into some verbal form that does minimal distortion.

Remember what class the stone falls into, whether it is Airy Earth, or Yang Water, or Spirit Fire, for example. That information can be helpful. Contemplate the stone from this perspective, and see this element both in its own essential nature, and as it exists in your own microcosm. Remember that your question is ultimately about finding a harmony, a balance, or a re-balancing of energy and consciousness. The real question may not be as you have discerned or phrased, but the stone will be the answer to your need if you have been sincere. Be alert to the possibility of a disconnect between your ostensible question and what you need to know. What you need to know is encapsulated in the stone or stones you have selected. You can only read that meaning by placing the stones and their energy before the mirror of your soul.

Also, be aware that you will, over time, grow into your own way of crossing the threshold into the oracular consciousness and discerning the meanings of the stones. The same stone may not speak the same meaning on two consecutive occasions – or, it may.

Remember, the stone you have chosen is an invitation to contemplate a mystery, not to create a verbal success formula, although that may come too. If you want to imbibe more of this stone's energy, you may place it in a glass of water in sunlight for a day or two and sip the liquid, which will be a crystal tincture. Also, keep in mind that you may work with a wider set of stones than the 28 stones of your *mesa*. The *Crystal Lotus Handbook* provides a good description of stones in terms of the inner issues they deal with, and would be a handy manual for crystal oracle work.

When the divination has been completed, return the crystals of the *mesa* to their bundle. Personally, I have sown up four bags of flannel, black for Earth, red for Fire, white for Air and turquoise blue for Water. I keep the Selenite crystal in its own small pouch. These four smaller pouches are placed inside a single larger pouch which I obtained during my travels in Peru.

It is always advisable, as Don Sebastian made it a point to urge me, to feed my *mesa*. This can be done by using the breath, by sunlight or moonlight, by speech or music, and mostly through loving intent. In Peru, as mentioned earlier, the belief is that wine or alcohol is very nourishing to a *mesa*.

It helps to hold and bond with each stone individually, and to become aware of the stones' different characters. In time, they come alive for you, and each has its own note which it contributes to the symphony of the whole. At this point, you have a living community, which means that the energies of mutual communication will flow more freely, and the crystal *mesa* may even at times speak to you, or one stone may send you a signal, even when you have not approached it for divination. Be alert and aware of all these possibilities as you care for your *mesa* and grow in loving relationship to all it represents.

You may, as I mentioned above, have a crystal sphere that you use for meditation. If you visualize it as a stand-in for the crystal sphere at the centre of your *mesa*, the power of all your meditations will be linked into the *mesa*. You may begin any meditation by making an inner journey to your *mesa* temple (see Appendix 2, Attunement 13), and once there, you may invite any of the four archetypes to bless your meditation.

"As above, so below" is illustrated in the Crystal Mesa Logo, the horizontal line being the band of earth-centred consciousness which separates them.

EPILOGUE

The first chapter of this book was entitled "Facets of the Jewel." The meaning of the title was not explained, but at this point a more profound understanding of this phrase will be possible. Now, you have completed the reading of this book about Crystal Yoga. You have perhaps felt the pull of a mysterious presence in the centre of your being, summoning you home.

The jewel of the heart is the self-evolved form that the soul has been gestating and treasuring over many lifetimes for its ultimate realization and manifestation. It is not unlike the psychic being, and may be considered one form or expression of the psychic being; we can say that the heart-jewel is a self-form that a certain family of souls develops and works with in the unfolding of the divine plan.

At one point during an interview with the Deva for Crystal Yoga, I asked the question: What is the relationship between Sri Aurobindo, my spiritual master, and the writing I am doing on the subject of Crystal Yoga? The answer was brief, but illumining. "Sri Aurobindo was a crystal yogi." I asked my Higher Self what it meant that Sri Aurobindo was a crystal yogi. The answer was: "A yogi is one who dwells in the Divine." Sri Aurobindo was that and more. He had identified himself with the Divine. The crystal quality has to do with complete alignment. Crystal is total alignment of all parts to a single ideal. A yogi is one who has accomplished complete alignment to the Divine. Sri Aurobindo had this accomplishment and more. He was crystalline and more. There may be additional information that one could access in answer to this question, but this is what came to me when I turned inward and asked the question.

It follows from the above that that *Savitri*, the summation of Sri Aubobindo's inner vision and experience, is the spiritual biography of a crystal yogi, and hence should be considered a foundation of study for Crystal Yoga, at least the approach to Crystal Yoga (and its four core archetypes) which I have been describing in this book. Apart from the present volume and a growing collection of crystals, a copy of *Savitri* is all that one needs to make a good start. The CD "Crystal Yoga" is a helpful option as well (see description at the end of this book).

You will find many quotes from *Savitri* in Appendix One of this book, selected for their relevance to the subject of Crystal Yoga. However, the quotes are taken only from the first two or three hundred pages of the complete text and represent less than a third of what is there. If reading this present volume, *Crystal Yoga One,* opens your mind to the study of other works by Sri Aurobindo, this will certainly lead to an enhancement of your practice. To make contact with a master on the inner planes is to be blessed with the most supportive of all friends on the journey home to Source.

It is to be understood that the power of the Word is indispensable to one's progress in yoga, and a master's written or spoken words must always be a most significant component of our awakening to yogic knowledge and attainment. The master incarnates and lives the radiance of the Word to show the way forward for others; the master speaks and writes the Word to make its power accessible to the thinking mind.

Savitri does indeed constitute a most important source of supplementary reading for a serious student of Crystal Yoga. Why? *Savitri* holds the consciousness which is to be realized, and *Savitri* awakens that consciousness mantrically in the mind and heart of the reader. Spending time in the world of *Savitri* activates the crystal in the lotus of the spiritual heart, and unfolds the petals that surround this jewel to reveal and manifest the soul. In Book Seven, Canto V, *The Finding of the Soul*, Sri Aurobindo describes in detail the rock temple and the great rock doors which the seeker must penetrate to claim the inmost treasure. As the epic's main character, *Savitri*, nears her inmost goal, Sri Aurobindo gives us the following picture:

Then through a tunnel dug in the last rock
She came out where there shone a deathless sun.
A house was there all made of flame and light
And crossing a wall of doorless living fire
There suddenly she met her secret soul...
Here in this chamber of flame and light they met:
They looked upon each other, knew themselves,
The secret deity and its human part,
The calm immortal and the struggling soul.
Then with a magic transformation's speed
They rushed into each other and grew one.

                                    Savitri, pgs. 525-6 & 527

What is this soul that the seeker has found and claimed? The
master writes:

As a mother feels and shares her children's lives,
She puts forth a small portion of herself,
A being no bigger than the thumb of man
Into a hidden region of the heart
To face the pang and to forget the bliss,
To share the suffering and endure earth's wounds
And labour mid the labour of the stars.
This in us laughs and weeps, suffers the stroke,
Exults in victory, struggles for the crown;
Identified with the mind and body and life,
It takes on itself their anguish and defeat,
Bleeds with Fate's whips and hangs upon the cross,
Yet is the unwounded and immortal self
Supporting the actor in the human scene.
Through this she sends us her glory and her powers,
Pushes to wisdom's heights, through misery's gulfs;
She gives us strength to do our daily task
And sympathy that partakes of others' grief
And the little strength we have to help our race,
We who must fill the role of the universe
Acting itself out in a slight human shape
And on our shoulders carry the struggling world.

This is in us the godhead small and marred;
In this human portion of divinity
She seats the greatness of the Soul in Time
To uplift from light to light, from power to power,
Till on a heavenly peak it stands, a king.

Savitri, pgs. 525-7

This discovery of the soul is a most significant moment in the spiritual life:

In the brief stade between a death and birth
A first perfection's stage is reached at last;
Out of the wood and stone of our nature's stuff
A temple is shaped where the high gods could live.
Even if the struggling world is left outside
One man's perfection still can save the world.
There is won a new proximity to the skies,
A first betrothal of the Earth to Heaven,
A deep concordat between Truth and Life:
A camp of God is pitched in human time.

Savitri, pg. 531

Crystal Yoga is a journey of inner discovery that brings the seeker to the cave of the heart and unites body, mind and will with the divine light of the hidden deity. It is a work accomplished by the divine doer, She whose light the soul is, whose compassion constitutes the journey home, whose bliss is the consummation of being re-united with Source. The seeker is at once the child of the Mother, the flaming light of the inmost sanctuary, and the king-sage of full realization. But it was necessary for the unfolding of the divine plan for the soul to journey through lifetimes of pilgrimage before the homecoming could be effected. The *Crystal Mesa* is a physical counterpart not only of the divinely human temple which the soul has woven for itself from mind and matter, but of the sanctuary at the temple's centre, the region of shadowless light where consciousness is at last fully awakened to its oneness with Source. Working with a *mesa*, we learn to transform all aspects of our microcosm into instruments of the guiding light of the soul.

To find the cave of the heart, to journey through the darkness and beyond the barriers into the dwelling place of the soul and finally to merge in its light is to complete the first stage of the bringing together of Heaven and Earth. To live as a crystal yogi is to treasure Truth, Light, Love and Beauty above all else, and to make one's life an act of self-giving to the Transcendental Bliss. Through our exploration of the crystal *mesa*, we have built up a deep bond with the great archetypes whose presence in us makes it possible to begin and to complete the journey. The child of the heart is that aspect of our seeking humanity which can awaken the loving compassion of the Mother and place us in a more or less constant state of grace. The fiery hero in us is the doer of the work, the forward momentum of the journey, the agent of the sacrifice and accomplisher of its completion. Agni's work being complete, the royal sage emerges like a phoenix from the ashes of the old self, radiant in wisdom, full of the soul's living power and presence. The seeker can say of all of these archetypal aspects of his or her own being: I AM THAT.

I began this book by sharing several of my own experiences of THAT. I leave you with the avowal that no other aspect of life can fulfil your hungry heart in the same measure as discovery of the soul. To the question: Who Am I?, this is the answer. To the question: Why am I here?, this shows us the reason we took birth. To the question: Where am I going?, this radiant inwardness of our existence lights the path forward.

I began writing the words of this Epilogue at 3:30 in the morning, having been wakened from sleep by a spiritual dream, and then inspired by the Spirit to set down a few final words to bring the book to a close. I had thought in completing the Foreword two days ago that the labour was finished, but one never knows.

Outside, a fresh layer of snow has fallen. My bedroom window on the second floor of an 1873 Victorian home overlooks a stately avenue lined with maple trees, now bare in the chill radiance of moonlight. Millions and billions of snowflake crystals lie in drifts all around the house. They bring purity, freshness and simplicity to the landscape. The crystal in my heart responds to their beauty with quiet joy. The skies above have settled a pure white blanket over the face of the Earth, and it will be here for the next four months and more. It's cold out there, and warm in here, but the inner and the outer are no longer separate.

We are moving toward the solstice time when the Sun will stop his southern journey, and begin the long, slow return northward, and from the cold depth of winter the divine child will be born. It is a season redolent with mystery and steeped in spiritual richness. It is a time both of conclusions and new beginnings, a spiritual transition point for turning inward and remembering who we truly are.

In the wee hours of the morning as Advent darkness begins to thin around the trees in my front yard I can see the snowflake crystals that cover the frozen soil and stones of Mother Earth's physical body, and as the Moon plays lost and found among the clouds in the sky, I ask the Mother to bless all those who will make use of and awaken the spiritual possibilities inherent in Crystal Yoga.

The approaching dawn is already turning the eastern horizon grey. Soon, the sunrise edge of the sleeping world will change to rosy gold with the blessed influence of light from on high. I wish you the full realization of all the crystals in your *mesa*. Most of all, I wish you a happy homecoming to the jewel in the cave of your heart, the deep and eternal Truth of your being.

When we find *that jewel* in the centre of the lotus of life, *we have truly come home*.

Lindsay, December 3, 2005

APPENDIX ONE

SAVITRI ARCHETYPES

1 The Child
2 The Hero
3 The Work of the Hero
4 The Hero Becomes the Sage
5 The Sage and His Relation to the Mother
6 The Sage
7 Gems of the Earth
8 The Tree of Life
9 The Identity of the Mother
10 The Mother's Attainment of the Goal
11 Mesa

The following selections from Sri Aurobindo's *Savitri* constitute the
insights of a true sage into the archetypes of the Mother, Child, Hero
and Sage, and wisdom that correlates to the theme of *mesa*. It is a
limited selection from a vast pool of possible choices, drawn from
the longest poem in the English language, *Savitri*.

THE CHILD

> *A mystic passion from the wells of God*
> *Flows through the guarded spaces of the soul;*
> *A force that helps supports the suffering earth,*
> *An unseen nearness and a hidden joy.*

There are muffled throbs of laughter's undertones,
The murmur of an occult happiness,
An exultation in the depths of sleep,
A heart of bliss within a world of pain.
An Infant nursed on Nature's covert breast,
An Infant playing in the magic woods,
Fluting to rapture by the spirit's streams,
Awaits the hour when we shall turn to his call.
In this investiture of fleshly life
A soul that is a spark of God survives
And sometimes it breaks through the sordid screen
And kindles a fire that makes us half-divine.

Book Two, Canto Five, pg. 169

Into a wonderful bodiless realm he came,
The home of a passion without name or voice
A depth he felt answering to every height
A nook was found that could embrace all worlds
A point that was the conscious knot of Space
An hour eternal in the heart of Time.
The silent Soul of all the world was there:
A Being lived, a Presence and a Power,
A single Person who was himself and all
And cherished Nature's sweet and dangerous throbs
Transfigured into beats divine and pure.
One who could love without return for love,
Meeting and turning to the best the worst,
It healed the bitter cruelties of earth,
Transforming all experience to delight;
Intervening in the sorrowful paths of birth
It rocked the cradle of the cosmic Child
And stilled all weeping with its hand of joy;
It led things evil towards their secret good,
It turned racked falsehood into happy truth;
Its power was to reveal divinity.
Infinite, coeval with the mind of God,
It bore within itself a seed, a flame,
A seed from which the Eternal is new-born,
A flame that cancels death in mortal things.

Book Two, Canto Fourteen, pgs. 290-91

THE HERO

His soul lived as eternity's delegate,
His mind was like a fire assailing heaven,
His will a hunter in the trails of light.
An ocean impulse lifted every breath;
Each action left the footprints of a god,
Each moment was a beat of puissant wings.

A spirit that is a flame of God abides,
A fiery portion of the Wonderful,
Artist of his own beauty and delight,
Immortal in our mortal poverty.
This sculptor of the forms of the Infinite,
This screened unrecognised Inhabitant,
Initiate of his own veiled mysteries,
Hides in a small dumb seed his cosmic thought.

Book One, Canto Three, pg. 23

THE WORK OF THE HERO (THE WORK OF FIRE)

A flaming warrior from the eternal peaks
Empowered to force the door denied and closed
Smote from Death's visage its dumb absolute
And burst the bounds of consciousness and Time.

Book One, Canto Two, pg. 21

A brilliant passage for the infallible
Flame Is driven through gross walls of nerve and brain,
A Splendour presses or a Power breaks through,
Earth's great dull barrier is removed awhile,
The inconscient seal is lifted from our eyes
And we grow vessels of creative might.
The enthusiasm of a divine surprise
Pervades our life, a mystic stir is felt,
A joyful anguish trembles in our limbs;
A dream of beauty dances through the heart,
A thought from the eternal Mind draws near,
Intimations cast from the Invisible
Awaking from Infinity's sleep come down,
Symbols of That which never yet was made.

Book Two, Canto Two, pgs. 108-9

Our spirits break free from their environment;
The future brings its face of miracle near,
Its godhead looks at us with present eyes;
Acts deemed impossible grow natural;
We feel the hero's immortality;
The courage and the strength death cannot touch
Awake in limbs that are mortal, hearts that fail;
We move by the rapid impulse of a will
That scorns the tardy trudge of mortal time.

Book Two, Canto Eleven, pg. 262

THE HERO BECOMES THE SAGE

And when that greater Self comes sea-like down
To fill this image of our transience,
All shall be captured by delight, transformed:
In waves of undreamed ecstasy shall roll
Our mind and life and sense and laugh in a light
Other than this hard limited human day,
The body's tissues thrill apotheosised,
Its cells sustain bright metamorphosis.
This little being of Time, this shadow soul,
This living dwarf-figurehead of darkened spirit
Out of its traffic in petty dreams shall rise.
Its shape of person and its ego-face
Divested of this mortal travesty,
Like a clay troll kneaded into a god
New-made in the image of the eternal Guest,
It shall be caught to the breast of a white Force
And, flaming with the paradisal touch
In a rose-fire of sweet spiritual grace,
In the red passion of its infinite change,
Quiver, awake, and shudder with ecstasy

Book Two, Canto Five, pg. 171

A flame in a white voiceless cupola
Is seen and faces of immortal light,
The radiant limbs that know not birth and death,
The breasts that suckle the first-born of the Sun,
The wings that crowd thought's ardent silences,
The eyes that look into spiritual Space.
Our hidden centres of celestial force

Open like flowers to a heavenly atmosphere;
Mind pauses thrilled with the supernal Ray,
And even this transient body then can feel
Ideal love and flawless happiness
And laughter of the heart's sweetness and delight
Freed from the rude and tragic hold of Time,
And beauty and the rhythmic feet of the hours.
This in high realms touches immortal kind;
What here is in the bud has blossomed there.
There is the secrecy of the House of Flame,
The blaze of godlike thought and golden bliss,
The rapt idealism of heavenly sense;
There are the wonderful voices, the sun-laugh,
A gurgling eddy in rivers of God's joy,
And the mysteried vineyards of the gold moon-wine,
All the fire and sweetness of which hardly here
A brilliant shadow visits mortal life.
Book Two, Canto Twelve, pg. 279

THE SAGE AND HIS RELATION TO THE MOTHER

His thought stretches into infinitude;
All in him turns to spirit vastnesses.
His soul breaks out to join the Oversoul,
His life is oceaned by that superlife.
He has drunk from the breasts of the Mother of the worlds;
A topless Supernature fills his frame:
She adopts his spirit's everlasting ground
As the security of her changing world
And shapes the figure of her unborn mights.
Immortally she conceives herself in him,
In the creature the unveiled Creatrix works:
Her face is seen through his face, her eyes through his eyes;
Her being is his through a vast identity.
Then is revealed in man the overt Divine.
Book One, Canto Three, pg. 24

In his wide sky she built her world anew;
She gave to mind's calm pace the motor's speed,
To thinking a need to live what the soul saw,
To living an impetus to know and see.
His splendour grasped her, her puissance to him clung;

She crowned the Idea a king in purple robes,
Put her magic serpent sceptre in Thought's grip,
Made forms his inward vision's rhythmic shapes
And her acts the living body of his will.
Book Two, Canto Three, pg. 125

Amidst live symbols of her occult power
He moved and felt them as close real forms:
In that life more concrete than the lives of men
Throbbed heart-beats of the hidden reality:
Embodied was there what we but think and feel,
Self-framed what here takes outward borrowed shapes.
A comrade of Silence on her austere heights
Accepted by her mighty loneliness,
He stood with her on meditating peaks
Where life and being are a sacrament
Offered to the Reality beyond,
And saw her loose into infinity
Her hooded eagles of significance,
Messengers of Thought to the Unknowable.
Identified in soul-vision and soul-sense,
Entering into her depths as into a house,
All he became that she was or longed to be,
He thought with her thoughts and journeyed with her steps,
Lived with her breath and scanned all with her eyes
That so he might learn the secret of her soul.
Book Two, Canto Six, pg. 191

Ever disguised she awaits the seeking spirit;
Watcher on the supreme unreachable peaks,
Guide of the traveller of the unseen paths,
She guards the austere approach to the Alone.
At the beginning of each far-spread plane
Pervading with her power the cosmic suns
She reigns, inspirer of its multiple works
And thinker of the symbol of its scene.
Above them all she stands supporting all,
The sole omnipotent Goddess ever-veiled
Of whom the world is the inscrutable mask;
The ages are the footfalls of her tread,
Their happenings the figure of her thoughts,
And all creation is her endless act.

His spirit was made a vessel of her force;
Mute in the fathomless passion of his will
He outstretched to her his folded hands of prayer....
Mastered by the honey and lightning of her power,
Tossed towards the shores of her ocean-ecstasy,
Drunk with a deep golden spiritual wine,
He cast from the rent stillness of his soul
A cry of adoration and desire
And the surrender of his boundless mind
And the self-giving of his silent heart.
He fell down at her feet unconscious, prone.

Book Two, Canto Fourteen, pg. 295-6

A vast surrender was his only strength.
A Power that lives upon the heights must act,
Bring into life's closed room the Immortal's air
And fill the finite with the Infinite.
All that denies must be torn out and slain
And crushed the many longings for whose sake
We lose the One for whom our lives were made.
Now other claims had hushed in him their cry:
Only he longed to draw her presence and power
Into his heart and mind and breathing frame;
Only he yearned to call for ever down
Her healing touch of love and truth and joy
Into the darkness of the suffering world.
His soul was freed and given to her alone.

Book Three, Canto Two, pgs 315-16

THE SAGE

For him mind's limiting firmament ceased above.
In the griffin forefront of the Night and Day
A gap was rent in the all-concealing vault;
The conscious ends of being went rolling back:
The landmarks of the little person fell,
The island ego joined its continent.
Overpassed was this world of rigid limiting forms:
Life's barriers opened into the Unknown.
Abolished were conception's covenants
And, striking off subjection's rigorous clause,
Annulled the soul's treaty with Nature's nescience.

All the grey inhibitions were torn off
And broken the intellect's hard and lustrous lid;
Truth unpartitioned found immense sky-room;
An empyrean vision saw and knew;
The bounded mind became a boundless light,
The finite self mated with infinity.
His march now soared into an eagle's flight.
Out of apprenticeship to Ignorance
Wisdom upraised him to her master craft
And made him an archmason of the soul,
A builder of the Immortal's secret house,
An aspirant to supernal Timelessness:
Freedom and empire called to him from on high;
Above mind's twilight and life's star-led night
There gleamed the dawn of a spiritual day.

Book One, Canto Three, pgs. 25-6

The body's rules bound not the spirit's powers:
When life had stopped its beats, death broke not in;
He dared to live when breath and thought were still.
Thus could he step into that magic place
Which few can even glimpse with hurried glance
Lifted for a moment from mind's laboured works
And the poverty of Nature's earthly sight.
All that the Gods have learned is there self-known.
There in a hidden chamber closed and mute
Are kept the record graphs of the cosmic scribe,
And there the tables of the sacred Law,
There is the Book of Being's index page;
The text and glossary of the Vedic truth
Are there; the rhythms and metres of the stars
Significant of the movements of our fate:
The symbol powers of number and of form,
And the secret code of the history of the world
And Nature's correspondence with the soul
Are written in the mystic heart of Life.
In the glow of the spirit's room of memories
He could recover the luminous marginal notes
Dotting with light the crabbed ambiguous scroll,
Rescue the preamble and the saving clause
Of the dark Agreement by which all is ruled
That rises from material Nature's sleep

To clothe the Everlasting in new shapes.
He could re-read now and interpret new
Its strange symbol letters, scattered abstruse signs,
Resolve its oracle and its paradox,
Its riddling phrases and its blindfold terms,

Book One, Canto Five, pgs. 74-5

He saw the unshaped thought in soulless forms,
Knew Matter pregnant with spiritual sense,
Mind dare the study of the Unknowable,
Life its gestation of the Golden Child.
In the light flooding thought's blank vacancy,
Interpreting the universe by soul signs
He read from within the text of the without:
The riddle grew plain and lost its catch obscure.

Book One, Canto 5, pg. 76

His privilege regained of shadowless sight
The Thinker entered the immortals' air
And drank again his pure and mighty source.
Immutable in rhythmic calm and joy
He saw, sovereignly free in limitless light,
The unfallen planes, the thought-created worlds
Where Knowledge is the leader of the act
And Matter is of thinking substance made,
Feeling, a heaven-bird poised on dreaming wings,
Answers Truth's call as to a parent's voice,
Form luminous leaps from the all-shaping beam
And Will is a conscious chariot of the Gods,
And Life, a splendour stream of musing Force,
Carries the voices of the mystic Suns.

Book Two, Canto Eleven, pg. 265

In the kingdom of the Spirit's power and light,
As if one who arrived out of infinity's womb
He came new-born, infant and limitless
And grew in the wisdom of the timeless Child;
He was a vast that soon became a Sun.
A great luminous silence whispered to his heart;
His knowledge an inview caught unfathomable,
An outview by no brief horizons cut:
He thought and felt in all, his gaze had power.
He communed with the Incommunicable;

Beings of a wider consciousness were his friends,
Forms of a larger subtler make drew near;
The Gods conversed with him behind Life's veil.
Neighbour his being grew to Nature's crests.
The primal Energy took him in its arms;
His brain was wrapped in overwhelming light,
An all-embracing knowledge seized his heart:
Thoughts rose in him no earthly mind can hold,
Mights played that never coursed through mortal nerves:
He scanned the secrets of the Overmind,
He bore the rapture of the Oversoul.
A borderer of the empire of the Sun,
Attuned to the supernal harmonies,
He linked creation to the Eternal's sphere.
His finite parts approached their absolutes,
His actions framed the movements of the Gods,
His will took up the reins of cosmic Force.

Book Two, Canto Fifteen, pgs. 301-2

GEMS OF THE EARTH

In a splendid extravagance of the waste of God
Dropped carelessly in creation's spendthrift work,
Left in the chantiers of the bottomless world
And stolen by the robbers of the Deep,
The golden shekels of the Eternal lie,
Hoarded from touch and view and thought's desire,
Locked in blind antres of the ignorant flood,
Lest men should find them and be even as Gods.
A vision lightened on the viewless heights,
A wisdom illumined from the voiceless depths:
A deeper interpretation greatened Truth,
A grand reversal of the Night and Day;
All the world's values changed heightening life's aim;
A wiser word, a larger thought came in
Than what the slow labour of human mind can bring,
A secret sense awoke that could perceive
A Presence and a Greatness everywhere.
The universe was not now this senseless whirl
Borne round inert on an immense machine;
It cast away its grandiose lifeless front,

A mechanism no more or work of Chance,
But a living movement of the body of God.

Book One, Canto Three, pg. 42

Our earth is a fragment and a residue;
Her power is packed with the stuff of greater worlds
And steeped in their colour-lustres dimmed by her drowse;
An atavism of higher births is hers,
Her sleep is stirred by their buried memories
Recalling the lost spheres from which they fell.
Unsatisfied forces in her bosom move;
They are partners of her greater growing fate
And her return to immortality;
They consent to share her doom of birth and death;
They kindle partial gleams of the All and drive
Her blind laborious spirit to compose
A meagre image of the mighty Whole.

Book Two, Canto One, pg. 100

Each power that leaps from the Unmanifest
Leaving the largeness of the Eternal's peace
They seized and held by their precisian eye
And made a figurante in the cosmic dance.
Its free caprice they bound by rhythmic laws
And compelled to accept its posture and its line
In the wizardry of an ordered universe.
The All-containing was contained in form,
Oneness was carved into units measurable,
The limitless built into a cosmic sum:
Unending Space was beaten into a curve,
Indivisible Time into small minutes cut,
The infinitesimal massed to keep secure
The mystery of the Formless cast into form.
Invincibly their craft devised for use
The magic of sequent number and sign's spell,
Design's miraculous potency was caught
Laden with beauty and significance
And by the determining mandate of their gaze
Figure and quality equating joined
In an inextricable identity.

Book Two, Canto Eleven, pgs. 266-7

The unseen grew visible to student eyes,
Explained was the immense Inconscient's scheme,
Audacious lines were traced upon the Void;
The Infinite was reduced to square and cube.
Arranging symbol and significance,
Tracing the curve of a transcendent Power,
They framed the cabbala of the cosmic Law,
The balancing line discovered of Life's technique
And structured her magic and her mystery.
Imposing schemes of knowledge on the Vast
They clamped to syllogisms of finite thought
The free logic of an infinite Consciousness,
Grammared the hidden rhythms of Nature's dance,
Critiqued the plot of the drama of the worlds,
Made figure and number a key to all that is:

Book Two, Canto Eleven, pg. 269

Each mysteried God forced to revealing form,
Assigned his settled moves in Nature's game

Book Two, Canto Eleven, pg. 270

The symbol modes of being

Book Three, Canto One, pg. 307

THE TREE OF LIFE

In the immutable nameless Origin
Was seen emerging as from fathomless seas
The trail of the Ideas that made the world,
And, sown in the black earth of Nature's trance,
The seed of the Spirit's blind and huge desire
From which the tree of cosmos was conceived
And spread its magic arms through a dream of space.
Immense realities took on a shape:
There looked out from the shadow of the Unknown
The bodiless Namelessness that saw God born
And tries to gain from the mortal's mind and soul
A deathless body and a divine name.

Book One, Canto Three, pg. 40

Alone it points us to our journey back
Out of our long self-loss in Nature's deeps;
Planted on earth it holds in it all realms:

It is a brief compendium of the Vast.
This was the single stair to being's goal.
A summary of the stages of the spirit,
Its copy of the cosmic hierarchies
Refashioned in our secret air of self
A subtle pattern of the universe.
It is within, below, without, above.
Acting upon this visible Nature's scheme
It wakens our earth-matter's heavy doze
To think and feel and to react to joy;
It models in us our diviner parts,
Lifts mortal mind into a greater air,
Makes yearn this life of flesh to intangible aims,
Links the body's death with immortality's call:
Out of the swoon of the Inconscience
It labours towards a superconscient Light.
If earth were all and this were not in her,
Thought could not be nor life-delight's response:
Only material forms could then be her guests
Driven by an inanimate world-force.
Earth by this golden superfluity
Bore thinking man and more than man shall bear;
This higher scheme of being is our cause
And holds the key to our ascending fate;
It calls out of our dense mortality
The conscious spirit nursed in Matter's house.
The living symbol of these conscious planes,
Its influences and godheads of the unseen,
Its unthought logic of Reality's acts
Arisen from the unspoken truth in things,
Have fixed our inner life's slow-scaled degrees.
Its steps are paces of the soul's return
From the deep adventure of material birth,
A ladder of delivering ascent
And rungs that Nature climbs to deity.

Book Two, Canto One, pgs. 98-9

THE IDENTITY OF THE MOTHER

At the head she stands of birth and toil and fate,
In their slow round the cycles turn to her call;

Alone her hands can change Time's dragon base.
Hers is the mystery the Night conceals;
The spirit's alchemist energy is hers;
She is the golden bridge, the wonderful fire.
The luminous heart of the Unknown is she,
A power of silence in the depths of God;
She is the Force, the inevitable Word,
The magnet of our difficult ascent,
The Sun from which we kindle all our suns,
The Light that leans from the unrealised Vasts,
The joy that beckons from the impossible,
The Might of all that never yet came down.
All Nature dumbly calls to her alone
To heal with her feet the aching throb of life
And break the seals on the dim soul of man
And kindle her fire in the closed heart of things.

Book Three, Canto Two, pg. 314

THE WORK OF THE MOTHER

The inspiring goddess entered a mortal's breast,
Made there her study of divining thought
And sanctuary of prophetic speech
And sat upon the tripod seat of mind:
All was made wide above, all lit below.
In darkness' core she dug out wells of light,
On the undiscovered depths imposed a form,
Lent a vibrant cry to the unuttered vasts,
And through great shoreless, voiceless, starless breadths
Bore earthward fragments of revealing thought
Hewn from the silence of the Ineffable.
A Voice in the heart uttered the unspoken Name,
A dream of seeking Thought wandering through Space
Entered the invisible and forbidden house:
The treasure was found of a supernal Day.
In the deep subconscient glowed her jewel-lamp;
Lifted, it showed the riches of the Cave
Where, by the miser traffickers of sense
Unused, guarded beneath Night's dragon paws,
In folds of velvet darkness draped they sleep
Whose priceless value could have saved the world.

A darkness carrying morning in its breast
Looked for the eternal wide returning gleam,
Waiting the advent of a larger ray
And rescue of the lost herds of the Sun.

Book One, Canto Three, pgs. 41-2

The Earth-Goddess toils across the sands of Time.
A Being is in her whom she hopes to know,
A Word speaks to her heart she cannot hear,
A Fate compels whose form she cannot see.
In her unconscious orbit through the Void
Out of her mindless depths she strives to rise,
A perilous life her gain, a struggling joy;
A Thought that can conceive but hardly knows
Arises slowly in her and creates
The idea, the speech that labels more than it lights;
A trembling gladness that is less than bliss
Invades from all this beauty that must die.
Alarmed by the sorrow dragging at her feet
And conscious of the high things not yet won,
Ever she nurses in her sleepless breast
An inward urge that takes from her rest and peace.
Ignorant and weary and invincible,
She seeks through the soul's war and quivering pain
The pure perfection her marred nature needs,
A breath of Godhead on her stone and mire.
A faith she craves that can survive defeat,
The sweetness of a love that knows not death,
The radiance of a truth for ever sure.
A light grows in her, she assumes a voice,
Her state she learns to read and the act she has done,
But the one needed truth eludes her grasp,
Herself and all of which she is the sign.

Book One, Canto Four, pgs. 50-1

An immortal godhead's perishable parts
She must reconstitute from fragments lost,
Reword from a document complete elsewhere
Her doubtful title to her divine Name.
A residue her sole inheritance,
All things she carries in her shapeless dust.

Her giant energy tied to petty forms
In the slow tentative motion of her power
With only frail blunt instruments for use,
She has accepted as her nature's need
And given to man as his stupendous work
A labour to the gods impossible.

Book Two, Canto Two, pgs. 108-9

She stooped to make her home in transient shapes;
In Matter's womb she cast the Immortal's fire,

Book Two, Canto Three, pg. 130

She conquers earth, her field, then claims the heavens.
Insensible, breaking the work she has done
The stumbling ages over her labour pass,
But still no great transforming light came down
And no revealing rapture touched her fall.
Only a glimmer sometimes splits mind's sky

Book Two, Canto Four, pg. 134

This is her secret and impossible task
To catch the boundless in a net of birth,
To cast the spirit into physical form,
To lend speech and thought to the Ineffable;
She is pushed to reveal the ever Unmanifest.
Yet by her skill the impossible has been done:
She follows her sublime irrational plan,
Invents devices of her magic art
To find new bodies for the Infinite
And images of the Unimaginable;
She has lured the Eternal into the arms of Time.
Even now herself she knows not what she has done.

Book Two, Canto Six, pg. 178

On every plane, this Greatness must create.
On earth, in heaven, in hell she is the same;
Of every fate she takes her mighty part.
A guardian of the fire that lights the suns,
She triumphs in her glory and her might:
Opposed, oppressed she bears God's urge to be born:
The spirit survives upon non-being's ground,
World-force outlasts world-disillusion's shock:
Dumb, she is still the Word, inert the Power.

Here fallen, a slave of death and ignorance,
To things deathless she is driven to aspire
And moved to know even the Unknowable.

Book Two, Canto Six, pg. 179

Ever she summons as by a sorcerer's wand
Beings and shapes and scenes innumerable,
Torch-bearers of her pomps through Time and Space.
This world is her long journey through the night,
The suns and planets lamps to light her road,
Our reason is the confidante of her thoughts,
Our senses are her vibrant witnesses.
There drawing her signs from things half true, half false,
She labours to replace by realised dreams
The memory of her lost eternity.

Book Two, Canto Six, pg. 181

To create her Creator here was her heart's conceit,
To invade the cosmic scene with utter God.
Toiling to transform the still far Absolute
Into an all-fulfilling epiphany,
Into an utterance of the Ineffable,
She would bring the glory here of the Absolute's force,
Change poise into creation's rhythmic swing,
Marry with a sky of calm a sea of bliss.
A fire to call eternity into Time,
Make body's joy as vivid as the soul's,
Earth she would lift to neighbourhood with heaven,

Book Two, Canto Six, pgs. 195-6

THE MOTHER'S ATTAINMENT OF THE GOAL

A vision meets her of supernal Powers
That draw her as if mighty kinsmen lost
Approaching with estranged great luminous gaze.
Then is she moved to all that she is not
And stretches arms to what was never hers.
Outstretching arms to the unconscious Void,
Passionate she prays to invisible forms of Gods
Soliciting from dumb Fate and toiling Time
What most she needs, what most exceeds her scope,
A Mind unvisited by illusion's gleams,

A Will expressive of soul's deity,
A Strength not forced to stumble by its speed,
A Joy that drags not sorrow as its shade.
For these she yearns and feels them destined hers:
Heaven's privilege she claims as her own right.
Just is her claim the all-witnessing Gods approve,
Clear in a greater light than reason owns:
Our intuitions are its title-deeds;
Our souls accept what our blind thoughts refuse.
Earth's winged chimaeras are Truth's steeds in Heaven,
The impossible God's sign of things to be.

Book One, Canto Four, pgs. 51-2

MESA

An mystic Form that could contain the worlds,

Book One, Canto Five, pg. 81

It moves events by its bare silent will,
Acts at a distance without hands or feet

Book One, Canto Five, pg. 85

A mediatrix sith veiled and nameless gods
Whose alien will touches our human life,
Imitating the World-Magician's ways

Book One, Canto Five pg. 86

This was a forefront of God's thousandfold house,
Beginnings of the half-screened Invisible.
A magic porch of entry glimmering
Quivered in a penumbra of screened Light,
A court of the mystical traffic of the worlds,
A balcony and miraculous facade...
It lodged upon an edge of hourless Time,
Gazing out of some everlasting Now,
Its shadows gleaming with the birth of gods,
Its bodies signalling the Bodiless,
Its foreheads glowing with the Oversoul,
Its forms projected from the Unknowable,
Its eyes dreaming of the Ineffable,
Its faces staring into eternity.

Book One, Canto Five, pg. 88

This overt universe whose figures hide
The secrets merged in superconscient light,
Wrote clear the letters of its glowing code:
A map of subtle signs surpassing thought
Was hung upon a wall of inmost mind.
Illumining the world's concrete images
Into significant symbols by its gloss,
It offered to the intuitive exegete
Its reflex of the eternal Mystery.
Ascending and descending twixt life's poles
The seried kingdoms of the graded Law
Plunged from the Everlasting into Time

Book One, Canto Five, pg. 88

Images in a supernal consciousness
Embodying the Unborn who never dies,
The structured visions of the cosmic Self
Alive with the touch of being's eternity
.... form-bound spiritual thoughts
Figuring the movements of the Ineffable.
Aspects of being donned world-outline; forms
That open moving doors on things divine...
The symbols of the Spirit's reality,
The living bodies of the Bodiless

Book Two, Canto One, pg. 96

A passage for the Powers that move our days,
Occult behind this grosser Nature's walls,
A gossamer marriage-hall of Mind with Form...
Heaven's meanings steal through it as through a veil,
Its inner sight sustains this outer scene.
A finer consciousness with happier lines,
It has a tact our touch cannot attain,
A purity of sense we never feel;
Its intercession with the eternal Ray
Inspires our transient earth's brief-lived attempts
At beauty and the perfect shape of things.
In rooms of the young divinity of power
And early play of the eternal Child
The embodiments of his outwinging thoughts
Laved in a bright everlasting wonder's tints

Book Two, Canto Two, pg. 104

A tissue mixed of the soul's radiant light
And Matter's substance of sign-burdened Force, –
It drops old patterned palls of denser stuff,
Cancels the grip of earth's decending pull
And bears the soul from world to higher world,

Book Two, Canto Two, pg. 105

It brings to us the inevitable word,
The godlike act, the thoughts that never die.
A ripple of light and glory wraps the brain,
And travelling down the moment's vanishing route
The figures of eternity arrive.
As the mind's visitors or the heart's guests
They espouse our mortal brevity awhile,
Or seldom in some rare delivering glimpse
Are caught by our vision's delicate surmise.

Book Two, Canto Two, pg. 110

APPENDIX TWO

THE FOURTEEN ATTUNEMENTS

In this Appendix we bring together and list in order the thirteen attunement exercises presented at various points in the main body of this book. These forms of practice develop a foundation for further practical work with the *mesa,* which is described in the last chapters of this book on the subject of using the *mesa.*

THE FIRST ATTUNEMENT: INTERACTING WITH CRYSTAL ENERGIES

Overview: This exercise begins the process of finding your own personal way to interact with the energies of crystals.

You may have some stones that you have collected or saved over the years. This would be a good time to get them out, place them in front of you, and see which one speaks to you most. In doing this, you are starting your journey in Crystal Yoga. There may be more than one stone that you feel drawn to at any given time. Feeling your way forward in this matter is how we learn attunement. Choose the stone or stones that most interest you, and one by one tune in to the impressions or feelings you get from each. You need not be able to verbalize these impressions, it is enough to note them. Crystal Yoga is possible simply because stones do catch our attention, engage our interest and call be held and considered by us.

From the most ancient times to this very day, stones engage us to interact with the body of Mother Earth. They call to us to discover our own unique way of feeling and sensing life's deep mystery and purpose. If you can feel this call, or if you have this interest to touch, to hold, to interact and to explore the mysteries of crystals, then you are ready for the experience of attunement. There is no better time to re-affirm the experiential pull that stones and crystals have than this very moment. When you have done this, you have completed your first attunement. It is as simple as that.

THE SECOND ATTUNEMENT: CONNECTING WITH CRYSTAL AND WITH THE SACRED ELEMENTS

Overview: In this exercise, you learn to attune to crystal energies through the sacred elements. Because crystals are already embodiments of Earth energy, the other three elements (Water, Fire and Air) are used as avenues of access.

The sacred element of Air is very important for connecting, linking, and communicating. It connects consciousness to that which our mind may consider to be 'other' or outer. In *Savitri*, Sri Aurobindo reveals some fascinating aspects of Air that can help us in meditation. It emerges that 'air' can refer to a state of consciousness, as in the lines: "A thinker and toiler in the ideal's air"(22) and "A breath comes down from a supernal air" (47). Among many interesting references to this element (there are almost one hundred and fifty in *Savitri*!), we find the following:

> *Air was a vibrant link between earth and heaven; (4) His spirit breathed a superhuman air; (82) Immaculate in the Spirit's deathless air; (109) In the white-blue-moonbeam air of Paradise; (234) The Thinker entered the Immortals' air; (263) In gleaming clarities of amethyst air; (264) A silent touch from the Supernal's air; (272) Breathe her divine, illimitable air; (276) a crystal mood of air; (289)*

For this exercise, you may want to hold a crystal, or to imagine that you are holding one. It can be a point or a sphere, the larger the better. Begin by breathing in slowly and deeply. Quiet the mind and body and relax completely. Imagine that you are in a space where the air is crystalline. You are inhaling a "crystal air." Feel the crystalline qualities of clarity, purity, freshness and light entering every cell of the body as you inhale. Then, as you exhale, vibrate these energies in the cells of the body by intoning "OM."

Sri Aurobindo refers at one point in *Savitri* to "amethyst air" (see above). You may want to visualize that the air you are inhaling has the colour and energy of Amethyst, or you may picture any other crystal whose qualities you intuitively sense will be nurturing. For entering the heartspace, Rose Quartz is ideal. For vitality, cleansing and lightness, Citrine would work very well. You have many choices. Slowly and surely visualize yourself merging into this "crystal air" as you inhale and exhale. Continue this conscious breathing until the mind is perfectly still. At this point, you will experience a deep state of peace. Merge in that state of silence and peace. Rest there as long as you can remain focused. If you want to attune to any of the crystal energies through the Water element, imagine the crystal as a flowing liquid washing over and through your mind and body. If you want to attune to a crystal energy through the Fire element, visualize the crystal as a flame inside which your entire being is situated; feel the crystal flame permeating all parts of your being.

When the mind starts to become active, resume the conscious breathing and see if you can again enter the state of peace. It may help to recall phrases like "Immaculate in the Spirit's deathless air," or others. These affirmations can permeate the subconscious mind and re-program it to greater openness and more profound relaxation.

THE THIRD ATTUNEMENT: ATTUNEMENT OF ATTENTION

Overview: An approach to concentration with crystals

My attention wanders. It is dissipated into random thoughts, polarized by aversion to what I find unpleasant, and fascinated by the attractiveness of what I desire. My attention typically lacks focus. It is unstable because I have not developed its capacity for concentration.

(Holding a crystal and gazing at it with a silent mind and open heart)

In crystal, I see the perfect focus of energy. There is a harmoniously balanced flow of energy as the six sides of a quartz crystal converge at a single point of unity. This harmonious inner balance does not vary or wander, for crystal carries no internal tendencies toward interruption and dissipation. Crystal shows us a perfect state of contemplative absorption. It has no personal volition. It does not lose itself in thinking activity. It does not crave new forms of pleasure; nor does it fear pain and loss. Therefore, crystal is not pushed or pulled from its inner poise. Crystal is pure and steady.

I know that energy follows thought. Crystal expresses a divine thought of harmony, purity, balance and focus. When my thought becomes crystalline, my energy will reflect this, becoming ordered and balanced. If I become clear in my mental life, beyond the turbulence of attractions and aversions, then I shall be a perfect instrument to channel those higher forces which can transform and perfect this material creation.

(Holding the crystal to the heart)

I want to approach this crystal attunement with pure intent. No longer will I exploit crystal to reinforce the disorder of my egocentric desires. Rather, I attune to the perfect meditation that crystal is always doing in the dimensions of matter and energy. And I aspire to achieve such perfect attunement of feeling and spirit in my own being, on all levels. In this new relationship of respect, I want to ask crystal to be my teacher, friend and helper.

In this spirit, I begin to approach the experience of attunement with a feeling of openness and gratitude. I breathe in slowly and deeply and relax my body completely. I am ready to begin to work with the energy and consciousness of stone with a sense of lightness and play, knowing that I can enjoy coming home to the fullness of relationship with my wider self.

THE FOURTH ATTUNEMENT: LETTING GO, PHASE ONE RELAXATION

Overview: An approach to relaxation using crystals.

I take a six-sided natural quartz crystal of between three and six inches in my right hand. Holding the crystal, I concentrate on its form, and I assimilate an impression of how its exists. I observe with special care my crystal's symmetry. I appreciate its transparent clarity, as well as any veils or rainbows it may contain. I marvel at its interior stillness. My crystal has the mastery of inner silence and can teach this state of being to me if I pay close attention.

I observe that my own mind is somewhat restless. I need to let go of the noise and the random, restless thinking activity that goes on inside my head because I want to merge with this crystal teacher and experiences what it has to show me. I need to release agitation and replace it with stillness.

Now, I am going to give this mental agitation an avenue of release so that it can drain away. I am going to allow my mind's agitation to express itself as physical movement; then, rather than making noise inside my head, this energy will be channeled out of my system.

I let the thumb of my right hand come into touch with the crystal at its base, and then I move my thumb along the surface of the crystal right up to its tip. After moving the thumb up and down several times on one of the crystal's six sides, I rotate the crystal and repeat the movement on the next side. As my thumb moves up along the side of the crystal, I let my attention follow its movement back and forth. I keep my attention focused on the movement of my thumb, and I feel its contact with the crystal.

I feel, as I practice this simple exercise, that the restless energy, which would otherwise express itself as wandering thoughts in my head, is now being channeled into the movement of my thumb. The movement of my thumb up and down across the surface of the crystal is draining away the mind's agitation. My attention is focused on the feeling of contact with the stone.

It is very simple thing, moving my thumb up and down the sides of the crystal, but it brings my attention to a focus and it makes my thoughts quiet. I let my attention follow the movement of the thumb up to the top of the crystal and then down again. I feel the physical contact of my thumb with the surface of the crystal with increased sensitivity at each movement. I am paying full attention to this sensitivity of touch. I relax and enjoy the experience. I feel open to new sensations.

I notice the changes in my mind as I do this. My mental agitation is becoming still. The churning of the mind is winding down, becoming still and empty. The movement of the thumb becomes slower as this stillness settles into my nervous system and as I pay more attention to what the sense of touch feels like.

What do I experience through the sense of touch as my thumb moves across the surface of the crystal? I am being drawn steadily deeper into an experience of stillness. But I am not *striving* to achieve this goal, I am only paying attention to the movement of the thumb and the feel of the crystal as I touch its surface.

This experience of interior stillness grows. My attention becomes more and more focused. Without effort, without struggle, I am beginning to enter meditation.

THE FIFTH ATTUNEMENT: PHASE TWO RELAXATION

Overview: An approach to deepening the relaxed stated through the use of crystals.

In crystal, I see neither the absence nor the presence of feeling. I see the perfect sublimation and sacrifice of all life-activity into the clarity of divinely patterned order. I see that the creative spark within a crystal has perfect order in every molecule of its body. My crystal is a meditation teacher because it knows how to silence and order its every molecule. My crystal has become an unbroken flow of light and energy. It has completely consecrated itself to the expression of an archetypal form.

My own thoughts are not anchored in pure feeling. Nor are my feelings surrendered to pure thought. My feelings are pulled by cravings, and repelled by pain. I am attracted by what I like and I feel aversion to what I dislike. Because of the pulls and pushes that I allow in my emotions, I cannot become steadily centred in stillness. My wandering, dissipated attention fails to find my centre of deepest feeling. I am vulnerable to feelings that I cannot control. I experience desire, fear, anger and frustration. I taste the pain of stress as it contracts my nerves. There is imbalance within my being.

I want to connect with my deeper feelings. I want to relate my dreams and ideals to a wider dream that is taking shape in the cosmos. I would like my life to become part of a pattern that opens me to the stars.

Crystal has so much to show me in this process. The crystal I am holding in my hand has spent untold centuries forming itself into an expression of clarity, beauty and harmony. It shows me how to build perfection of form slowly and surely, with total dedication.

As I sit with my crystal in my hand, I notice that there is residual tension inside my muscles. It comes in part from unresolved emotions. It is also rooted in the patterns of my thinking, both in my conscious and unconscious mind.

I now deliberately express this tension by clenching my hands into tight fists. Holding both my hands as tightly clenched as I can, I become fully aware of what this tension feels like. I have focused my inner stress there in the palms of my two hands, and I feel it gripping my crystal tightly. It's not something I have to analyze mentally or think about. I just feel it. In fact, it seems that I am drawing tension away from other parts of my being and localizing it in the palms of my hand. I can see how stress and tension act to bring about tightening and contraction. How it adversely it must be affecting me when I allow it to continue unconsciously!

I will ask my crystal to help me release tension from all parts of my being.

Inhaling slowly and deeply, I breathe in peace. Then, I send a breath of pure, unconditional love flowing from my heart into each tightly-clenched fist, both the right hand and the left. Over and over again, I breathe in peace and exhale love, directing the rosy energy of love out from my heart, and down my arms into my clenched fists. Slowly and surely, they begin to release their contraction. They begin to release the stress which has had a tight grip on my life-energy. I allow my two hands slowly to open in response to the movement of deep feeling that streams from my heart. I am not using my mental will. I am allowing heart-energy, love, to express itself as a blessing on my stress. Ever so slowly and gently I exhale this energy into my hands, and ever so slowly they let go, relax, release and open up. As my hand opens up, my tight grip on my crystal relaxes.

When my two hands are completely relaxed, I try to clench them again. I notice that I cannot summon the same tightness as before. But whatever tension I can create, I begin to release it slowly and surely as before, until once again my hands are completely relaxed. In doing this, I come into a new state of openness, receptivity, care and feeling with regard to my crystal.

THE SIXTH ATTUNEMENT: ACCESSING THE LIGHT BODY

Overview: Training to shift into the subtle body in preparation for later visualization exercises. This practice also helps to activate and develop the imagination, which has much importance in subsequent practice.

At this point, I am ready to begin visualization. I have worked with attention, thought and feeling, and I am now ready to attune my energy and consciousness to the perfect clarity of my crystal teacher.

Closing my eyes, I picture my physical body changing into a subtle mist of light. I feel the atoms of the body becoming diffused until they are like mist in the air, a luminous cloud floating in the darkness of space. This luminous body of mist, floating in the vast darkness of outer space, is everything I have and everything I am. I float there in silence, feeling myself to be a radiant cloud. I can sense the big spaces between the particles of my body. I experience the sensation of floating, floating in silence. As a cloud of misty light, I am completely expansive and am exquisitely attuned to all sensations, but in the vast darkness everything is utterly still.

Now I begin to experience rays of sunlight penetrating my cloud-like body. The radiance of the sun enters every part of my being and penetrates it with light. I allow the sunlight to fill me and I feel what a crystal feels when it is placed in the brightness of the sun. For a moment or two, I notice the effects of being filled with light. I let myself sense how it feels in complete detail. I am super-sensitive to everything around me when I am a cloud of radiance. When I have taken in this experience completely, and described it in detail, I know how a crystal experiences sensation. I can now understand how a crystal can become programmed so responsively.

Next, I look out at the world around me from this state of being a floating cloud. My eyes are just slightly open, enough to take in the appearances of my physical setting. I experience my environment with my extended sensitivity. I sense how my floating body of light is responding to every aspect of my environment and I assimilate the experience in all its detail. How completely and absolutely I experience everything when the form in which I exist is that of a cloud of light! Every impression is exquisite. Sometimes, it almost seems that I taste or smell the things I am seeing.

I open my eyes ever so slightly and take in an object visually. Then I close my eyes and become aware of the way in which I experience that object while I exist as an empty cloud of light. My sensitivity is greatly increased when I can experience myself and my world in this way. This way of experiencing is not merely intellectual; it is a complete and integral attunement.

Now, I am going to gaze into my crystal. My crystal is an exquisite lattice of molecules. I allow the misty, formless cloud of my subtle, luminous body to drift into the physical body of the crystal. Our particles and our spaces interpenetrate each other. The atoms and the molecules of our bodies merge one into the other. I now exist as a perfectly ordered, crystalline pillar of light. I am completely still. My attunement to the world around me is finely sensitive. I experience the merging of my body with the body of my crystal teacher. I have become a cloud of misty light interpenetrating the orderly molecules of my crystal in complete stillness.

For so long, I have been imagining myself to be the physical form of this human body with its boundaries and limits. Now I exist in another dimension of my being. The crystal has given my luminous body the power of perfect order and control. I see that I have been imagining myself into a human form, but now I have the freedom to exist in a different way. I now know that I can be whatever I can imagine. At this time, I actualize in my luminous body the perfect order and clarity of crystalline structure. Every atom and every molecule aligns in perfect symmetry and balanced pattern.

I take a few moments of silence to experience this re-assembling of my cloud-like body into crystal perfection.

This exercise in visualization has been an experience of programming my reality. I have cleared my understanding of some limiting notions; I know now that I am free to explore experience in many dimensions, and experience many things in different ways. This human body is only one physical expression of my infinitely adaptable consciousness.

My crystal shares with me the experience of stillness and clarity, and the power of perfect order. I now know that I can express my energy and consciousness in many ways. I know now that the ability to imagine, and the power to visualize, and the help from my crystal open the doorway to many more experiences of attunement and expansion. I feel that I want to make more such journeys in the future.

THE SEVENTH ATTUNEMENT: Conscious Breathing

Overview: This exercise further develops the importance of breathing for attunement, and combines it with feeling to increase capacity to sense and assimilate crystal energies.

If your crystal *mesa* is kept in a cloth bag, it should be easy to place this bag over your chest for meditation. If the bag has the right kind of attachment strings, it can even be hung from your neck while you sit for meditation, or you can relax back into the reclining posture. Feel the weight of the crystal *mesa* on your chest. Connect with this feeling of being physically in contact with the *mesa* and its energies as you inhale slowly and deeply. From the feeling of physical contact, the sensation of being in contact with the *mesa* energies comes more easily. As you inhale, feel that you are taking all the energies of the stones into the cells of your body. As you exhale, sense your entire body glowing with these celestial energies. Continue in this way for a time. Next, visualize all the energies of the *mesa* crystals suffusing your aura as you inhale, out to a distance of several feet around your physical body. Each time you exhale, relax into the feeling that you are filled with the colours and energies of the crystals. Then, relax into a deeply peaceful state and begin to work with this affirmation: I take in all the crystal energies, to re-create my DNA, to activate my full divine potential, for the highest good. Actually, you can also repeat this affirmation while inhaling, and if you practice this way, the final peaceful relaxation can be a silent meditation.

THE EIGHTH ATTUNEMENT: The Power of the Word

Overview: Here, we begin to use affirmations in conjunction with the *mesa*, and to work on the chakras.

Lying on a rug or bed, place the *mesa* over the region of your heart or solar plexus. Allow some time, and become aware of your mind, energy and heart integrating with the crystal energies. Then, one by one, ever so slowly and consciously, place the *mesa* on focus five different energy centers, with repetitions of affirmation thus:

On the brow chakra: I am one with the Sage. I surrender to divine grace. I embody divine wisdom. I am fullness and completion.

On the solar plexus chakre: I am one with Agni, the Divine Fire. I live the will of the Supreme. All that I have and all that I am burns brightly for transformation.

On the heart chakra: I am the Divine Child. I am joy in the spiritual heart. I am all openness to light and love.

On the navel chakra: I am one with the Mother. I am all love. I give birth to the divine in matter.

In the region of the crown chakra: I am the Infinite Being. I am Existence-Consciousness-Bliss.

Each affirmation may be repeated, very slowly, until the feeling sinks in that shift of energy, or some adjustment of consciousness has occurred.

THE NINTH ATTUNEMENT: RITUAL

Overview: Here we begin the practice of placement. This is combined with visualization. Taken together, they create an exercise in placement which is an internal ritual. This ritual works very well to rectify the inner energies of the microcosm in the elemental domain.

Take your *mesa* crystals out of their bag and place them in groups of Earth, Water, Fire and Air to your right on a table, or on a rug. Lay a square piece of cloth in front of you. It can be specially selected for the purpose of laying the stones, or simply a piece of cotton or silk that you find suitable for this practice.

Begin by taking your Lemurian Jade in your hands and merging with its energy. When you feel deeply bonded with this piece and all it stands for, place it on the cloth. Then, take your Spirit Earth stone, Green Jade, and hold it. Meditate in the same way, and place it beside or on your Lemurian Jade.

Visualize the room you are in as a temple chamber, and see these two stones as being placed in the center of this temple space. You may want to imagine them being much larger than they are in actuality, or you may want to picture the cloth they are on as a square altar at the center of this room.

Next, meditate with your Yang Earth stone (Tiger's Eye) in the same way, and place it to the right of the Lemurian Jade and Green Jade. As you do this, visualize the colour, texture and energy of this stone filling the region of the ceiling of the temple room you are in, which is to say, it comes to occupy the region above you. The whole ceiling is composed of Tiger's Eye, and it is a complete energy field of Yang radiance.

Then, meditate with your Yin Earth stone (Petrified Wood) in the same way and place it to the left of the Lemurian Jade. Visualize this stone, its colour and energy becoming the floor of the room you are in.

At this point, you are meditating in a space where the Yang energies are above you and the Yin energies are below. See your spine as a column, or hollow tube, running up into the celestial energies, and down into the Yin Earth energies. Let these energies flow back and forth through your spine, and meditate until you feel aligned.

Next, take your Earthy Earth stone, either Red Jasper or Green Jasper, and try to feel its energies. Feel its quality and power entering your energy-field. Then, place it on the South side of the Lemurian Jade. See one wall of your temple room (in the South) as being entirely made of this stone. Meditate on the energy of this stone as filling the entire southern portion of this room, and being most strongly established in the solid wall you have visualized.

Then, take your Watery Earth stone, Malachite, and hold it in your hands, taking in its energy and noting how you feel about it. See the Western wall of your temple room being completely formed of this material, and place the stone to the West of the Lemurian Jade.

Continue in this way with Fire Agate in the East and Pyrite in the North.

When you have thus placed all the Earth stones in this configuration, and attuned to them, you have completed the work of rectifying your Earth energies by means of the Crystal Mesa. You may want to continue on with the other three groupings of crystals, or you may feel you have done enough work for now, and leave further attunements to another time.

Close the attunement by breathing in slowly and deeply, visualizing your physical body's Earth energies completely harmonized and balanced. Then, replace the stones in your *mesa* bag and conclude the session.

THE TENTH ATTUNEMENT: THE POWER OF THE WORD, PART II

Overview: Here the bardic element of Right Speech is applied to crystals. This activates the heart connection with your crystal, activates the crystal itself, develops bonding and enhances feeling-attunement.

Imagine yourself holding a Jade stone in your hands, and you can evoke even now the energy which makes magic possible. Imagine that you have a beautiful Jade of any shade you find especially attractive, a stone about the size of a pigeon's egg. Picture its colour and shape as you hold it in your hand. Or if you actually have a Jade in your *mesa*, use that. Then, with genuine feeling, say these words which I have used to express my own feeling for Jade; say them over and over. The feeling will grow as you do this. If you can feel, you can project feeling. And if you can project feeling into an imaginary stone in your hands, you can project it into a real one. If you can find stones which you consider beautiful, you will not have too much difficulty to express your feelings in speech. If you can create words of praise and admiration for each of the 33 stones in your *mesa*, you will have made a very good beginning of right relation and empowerment. Actually, your ruby, which is the Passion Stone, can help you put your heart into this practice of speaking to your stones.

(Building up a living relationship with your stones can be accomplished in a number of ways, but one of the best is by using the power of speech. For example, you can verbalize your admiration. Simply hold a stone in your hand, consider its beauty, and begin to speak: "I love you because...." Find as many reasons as you can why you feel that this crystal is loveable, beautiful, or significant and put each reason into words. Elizabeth Browning's poem, "Why do I love thee?" is a very good model for this kind of deeply appreciative speech, and the bonding it nurtures. Sit with your crystal and express your love with care and tenderness in the best words that come to you. Repeat the most beautiful phrases until there is such depth of feeling in your heart that tears come to your eyes. Not until you have let the salt tears of your love touch the crystal have you reached the depth of true sincerity, and if you cannot feel and express the deepest depth of your own passion, you cannot expect your crystals to give you their all in the power of the *mesa*. Write down your words and keep them as a formula to renew and intensify the feeling of relatedness that you have with your stone or stones.)

One of the most beautiful ancient sources for this kind of sacred speech is the Hymns of Orpheus. Many of these were found on small sheets of hammered gold buried with Orphic initiates in Crete and South Italy, others were written down and used in sacred rituals in ancient Greece. From the ancient Orphic poetry of the Greeks comes this piece in praise of the Moon:

> *Goddess of silver light,*
> *Horns of the divine bull,*
> *Searcher in the dark of night,*
> *We honour you.*
> *The stars honour you,*
> *They wait upon your orbit*
> *As you move like a torch*
> *Across the skies of night.*

You emanate rays of blue,
But your body is amber,
Beauteous in the black vast.
All-seeing eye,
Bejewelled with stars,
Bless your watchful devotees,
Preserve them from strife.
Guide us with intuitive light,
Lamp of beauty,
Companion of the night,
Goddess of the turning wheel of Fate.
Queen of the stars,
Artemis! Brilliant one!
Radiant lamplight veiled by darkness,
Shine down your blessed rays on us
And take with joy
Our words of praise.

Right speech is beautiful, pleasant, harmonious and musical. It soothes, elevates and harmonizes. The power of right speech can be used to suffuse the crystals of a *mesa* with active, unified, healing energy. Some people might call this 'programming' crystals, but the connotations of the word programming are problematic in many ways. This word does not imply respect, co-operation or any bond of sacred relationship. It is not a loving or a poetic word, and it does not resonate with the living spirit of Mother Earth and her crystalline children. The worker with crystal energies in a *mesa* configuration has undertaken to create *a symbolic microcosm of living energies* that function as a kind of *conscious spiritual battery*. Right speech in this context is a language of loving, respectful relationship, evocative of the inner power and descriptive of the inner beauty which the miniature *mesa*-cosmos embodies.

Hold a Sunstone in the palm of your hand and as you look into the depths of its golden warmth, feel that it is a crystallised portion of the body of a god, which indeed it is. Then, feel your way toward saying these ancient words of praise with deepest feeling. Repeat the words over and over. Slowly, slowly the key of magical empowerment turns in the lock of consciousness and the treasure chest of the great mystery yields its riches. When you integrate with Sunstone crystal in this way, you sing your own inner sun into life. A fragment of Sunstone from the macrocosm resonates in sympathetic accord with the inner sun which has been eclipsed by materialistic mental conditioning. By the power of right attunement, it can help you find a way to release the captive beams of your inner sun and bring light into the regions that have been darkened. In your body, gods are awakening and becoming conscious. Divine possibilities are finding their way into expression. Presences that never before sounded their existence are beginning to resonate. The crystal key of your cosmic *mesa* attune you to the light of liberation.

THE ELEVENTH ATTUNEMENT: RITUAL PART II

Overview: A more advanced and comprehensive placement exercise.

Take your *mesa* heartstone and hold it to your heart. Meditate with it, and feel its meaning and its power to actualize this meaning. Then, place it at the centre of your *mesa* cloth. Visualize a pillar of light flowing from the center of the sphere up into infinity, and down to the center of the Earth. Visualize it glowing with pure, radiant light.

Next, one by one, take and hold each of the crystal archetype stones, beginning with Lemurian Jade, the Mother, and moving on through Selenite, the Child, rutilated Citrine, the Hero, and Lapis Lazuli, the Sage. Hold each of them to your heart and meditate on the identity of each, one by one. Feel that each one embodies the potential of its archetype and is a home for the archetypal energy and consciousness. Place each one in turn in its place within the *mesa*.

Next, focus on the stones of Earth one by one. Begin with Jade, and move on to Tiger's Eye, petrified Wood, Pyrite, Fire Agate, Malachite and Jasper. Meditate with each one held close to the heart. Merge with its meaning and energy. Feel that each is a part of your own being. Feel that each is a god-energy. Feel that each one is coming to life in itself and inside your own being. Then, place each one in its correct position on the *mesa* cloth. Feel as you place each stone that you are placing that part of your being in right relationship to Source. Repeat the true name of the stone three times as you place it. For example, Spirit Earth, or Jade is the quality of the Heart Path. So you might repeat: Here is my heart path, connected to Source.

Then, for Yang Earth, Tiger's Eye, you might affirm: Here is Physical Mastery, connected to Source. Follow through along these lines with the words that come naturally to you. Be sure to do it with care and feeling, it is not an intellectual exercise but a matter of integral attunement.

Work through the stones for Water, Fire and Air in similar fashion. When the entire *mesa* has been laid out, meditate on it as a perfect expression of your unfolding wholeness and divinity.

THE TWELFTH ATTUNEMENT: RITUAL WITH AFFIRMATION

Overview: The use of affirmations with the Crystal Mesa.

For the purpose of aligning the body, vitality and mind with the light of the spirit, it can greatly help to affirm and re-affirm the core truths which, from the soul's point of view, express its reason for taking on a physical incarnation. In the following affirmations, the "I" is the soul, not the ego or the personality or the small self.

AFFIRMATIONS

1) The fullness of Truth is here now.

2) I am a centre of Its expression.

3) I manifest Its infinite Wisdom in my every thought, word and action.

4) I am guided moment by moment to become a fuller expression of this Divine Truth.

5) From the infinite supply of the Eternal Source, I draw all things necessary for my soul's work, both physical and spiritual.

6) I acknowledge and recognize the sustained action of a Supreme Providence in every aspect of my outer and inner life.

7) In all things, great and humble, I see the Beauty, Truth and Goodness of the Divine.

8) Aligned with the Divine Will, my life is a courageous self-giving to the ultimate victory of light, love and peace on Earth.

9) In the essence of my being, I am the Light of Truth, which will one day manifest in its completeness on Earth.

10) My physical existence is a microcosm, a temple, a crystal-resonance of the Supreme, Creative Word.

Read through these statements and settle on the one which you feel is most appropriate, or which you most need to re-affirm. Then, relax completely, and say it quietly to yourself with all the feeling and care of which you are capable. You can repeat the affirmation several times.

Then, pause, and hold your Source Stone next to your heart. Connect with this crystal with the intent of seeing and feeling as clearly as possible which stone or stones in your *mesa* will support you in this affirmation. When you feel the right stone or stones, pick them up and hold them with the Source stone.

Continue to repeat the affirmation while holding these stones until you feel some shift in your energy or consciousness. Be aware of the energy of the crystals and bring that feeling into the affirmation as you repeat the words slowly, clearly and silently to yourself over and over. You may want to visualize a light glowing in your heart each time you repeat the words, or you may inhale the energy of the crystals each time you breathe in.

A deep understanding of these truths puts the "sacred" into the process which is Earth. It is the nature of affirmations that, being often repeated with full attention, they become part of the core understanding from which we think, speak and act. It is in this way that focused attention and feeling can modify our consciousness and life-energy, ultimately effecting even a transformation of the cells.

THE THIRTEENTH ATTUNEMENT: PATHWORKING

Overview: A fully developed pathworking in the inner temple, applying skills learned through earlier attunement practice.

Take five or ten minutes to relax deeply. Breathe slowly and deeply, and relax each part of the body in turn. A guided relaxation exercise of this sort would be ideal. Also, suitable background music would be helpful for this visualization. You might like the pure sounds of crystal bowls, or Tibetan bowls, or chanting, or you might have other preferred music.

Begin by visualizing a set of stone steps leading downward into a stone grotto. The steps are fifteen in number. Step down onto each step in turn, breathing slowly and deeply at each step. When you have reached the bottom of the steps, you are facing the grotto-entrance to a cave-like tunnel.

You begin to walk down this tunnel, and after ten steps, you come to a torch which is attached to the stone walls on your right hand side. You continue another ten steps, and come to a torch similarly attached to the cave wall on your left side. Then, after ten more steps, you come to a circular staircase leading upward into a room filled with light.

You climb these steps slowly. There are fifteen steps. You mount the first step slowly and surely. Then the second. Then the third, and so on until you are standing in a room filled with light. The ceiling is a glowing white crystalline substance, opaline and radiant; the floor is of some dark crystalline substance. A circular opening in the dome of the ceiling allows a shaft of light to descend onto a large quartz sphere, perfect and clear, which is in the center of this hall, resting on a square altar, which is at the center of a square stone platform three steps high.

The room you are in has four sides, but each of these sides has a large, square portal opening into four further rooms. One of these smaller temple rooms is in the North, one is in the South, one in the East and one in the West. Thus, the layout of the temple as a whole is in the form of an Andean Cross, or *chakana.*

In each of the four corners of this room stands one of the archetypes. To the right of the Southern portal stands the Mother. To the right of the Western portal stands the Divine Child. To the right of the Eastern portal stands the Fiery Hero. And at the Northern opening stands the Sage. You gaze on each one in turn, slowly establishing a deep heart connection of love with each.

The Mother comes forward and takes your right hand. She takes you toward the square altar in the middle of this large chamber in which you are standing. You step up three steps with her, and you find yourself gazing into the center of the radiant, perfect quartz sphere. It is about a yard in diameter and perfect in every way. The light of this quartz sphere is beautifully radian. It draws your gaze into itself. You hear the Mother's voice:

Here, all that can be is alike in not having originated;
Here is the wonderment of pristine cognition, beyond duality;
Here is the dynamic range and reach of utter openess
and utter lucency;
Here is the unchanging continuum, the Ground of Being;
Here is the Primordial Enchantment, the consummate clearness;
Here, the mistaken presentations of your dreaming are no more.
Gaze deeply into this light.

As you gaze into the sphere of light, you enter deeper and deeper into its peace, stillness and blissful emptiness.

Allow this part of the visualization to deepen, and you may hold the clear quartz sphere from your *mesa* as you meditate in this way. Take as long as you like, and when you have finished, become aware once more of the Mother holding your hand.

When you are finished your silent meditation, the Mother takes you down the three steps, and over to the Sage. He holds your right hand as she backs away, and he speaks to you:

That which we call our 'reality' turns out to be only our intended meanings. They present themselves like a dream from nowhere, and out of nothing. And this alleged reality we weave from nothing is no more than a dream. It is we who have given it meaning and order. You have gazed into the infinite nowhere and nothing from which the elements of your dreaming arise. You have gazed into infinite consciousness, the Source from which the 'reality' you dream takes form, and to which it returns. Now, come with me into the temple of Air.

You pass between two pillars, one of dark blue Sodalite, and one of medium green Chrysoprase into a square chamber. In the center on a tripod is a large sphere of clear Apophyllite (or light blue Celestite, your choice). The ceiling is made of indigo-coloured Kyanite, and the floor of light Bluelace Agate. The Northern wall is of golden Fluorite; the Eastern wall is of clear, gold Citrine, and the Western wall is of dark blue Azurite.

The Sage guides you to the sphere of clear Apophyllite, and you put your two hands out to encompass it on both sides. First, you gaze through the clear crystal of Apophyllite at the wall of Golden Fluorite, ahead of you to the North, and assimilate the energies of Golden Fluorite and Apophyllite together. Then you gaze through the clear crystal of Apophyllite at the wall of golden coloured Citrine, taking in their two energies together, the energy of Citrine passing through the clear crystal into your hands and eyes. Then, you gaze at the Western wall and take in the energy of Azurite. Lastly, you choose one of the pillars, and gaze at it through the sphere, either Sodalite or Chrysoprase depending on which one you feel drawn to, taking in its energies and the Apophyllite together.

Remember while you practice this exercise that you can shift awareness into your subtle body as you learned to do in an earlier attunement exercise. Remember also that you can use your breathing to consciously inhale energies, and you can then visualize these energies being distributed through your entire being.

Finally, the Sage steps up and puts his hands on the sphere. You feel you have become the sphere and that you are being held in his hands. Feel that you are a clear crystal sphere, held in the hands of the Sage. Feel that your hands are his hands, and you are the sphere he is holding. The depths of his meditation becomes yours, and you merge in the most profound meditation. Some considerable amount of time passes, and when you open your eyes again, you are standing at the top of the stairs, ready to depart. You nod meaningfully to each of the archetypes, who are standing in their places, and then you descend the stairs, one by one. Slowly, step by step you retrace your way down the long corridor of stone, noting the torches to your right and left at ten step intervals. Then, you slowly climb the fifteen steps that lead up into the sunlight. Then, the attunement is over.

You may return to this inner temple, called the Imaginarium any time, and deepen your acquaintance with the various archetypes. You may invite any of them to take you into their temples, or you may ask any of them to take you up the three steps to meditate on the central crystal sphere. You may ask any of them for advice, help, or guidance. You may ask any of them to meditate with you or for you or on you. You may hold any of the *mesa* stones that are suitable to co-ordinate with inner work that you may choose to do in this temple. Because this is the Imaginarium, you should allow your heart to show you various ways of meditating and working with the various energies that are here. Or you can study the experience of primal Reality which the Source crystal embodies, entering into deeper and deeper states of silent meditation and ultimately the non-dual consciousness.

This is your inner temple, an astral temple corresponding to the physical temple symbolized by your *mesa* stones. This is the place where the crystal powers come alive and fully available to you on the subtle planes for the inner work you intend to do. These twelve attunement practices are an excellent foundation for the material in chapter 21, on using your *mesa*. With this foundation you will achieve better results. Be sure to work with these 12 attunements and develop your capacity to move forward in the practices in Chapter 21.

THE FOURTEENTH ATTUNEMENT: ACTIVATION

Overview: Imagination, feeling, speech and activation go together in this exercise, which you can do with any crystal from your *mesa* that you want to work with more fully.

The energies of light often flow through the veins of Mother Earth in a form traditionally referred to as dragons. A precious or semi-precious stone can be seen as a dragon's egg. Try holding a rounded stone from your *mesa* and thinking of it in this way. As the keeper of its energy, you may wish to incubate the crystal dragon-egg and re-lease the sleeping power that is inside it. The incubating is done with attention, feeling, speech, association, and most of all, with love. If you lavish these energies on your crystal dragon's egg, you can bring to life its inner spirit.

Not all dragons are alike. They have different colours and ener-gies. Be non-specific in your expectation until the energy involved reveals itself to you. You can visualize your seven Earth Stones as a nest of Earth-Dragon eggs, if you like, and it helps if they are a size and shape that makes it possible for you to really feel that there is a life within the stone that is waiting to be awakened. Holding a rounded crystal in the warmth of your hand will infuse it with your energy and consciousness, which is the catalyst of the awakening process. Or, you can hold all seven at once, as if the palms of your hands were a nest of love. Allow the love energy to flow into the eggs so that they will release their potential and come fully to life in service within the *mesa*. Again, you may wish to use words to convey the energy.

I am Black Jade,
The Matrix, the Wombstone,
Buried Gold of Life.
I have not found
The Phallus of Osiris;
My Child is bound.

High, higher, highest
In the sky of mind
The Eye of Horus soars,
Probing the azure blue;
My Hero, ascend!
On wings of will, transcend the empyrion.
Fly to the mind of Amun!
To the mountain of Rostau!
To the very heart of Ra!
To the gold beyond life,
The Immortal, the Pure.
Be Thou THAT in me,
The Word invoking thee,
The Bliss, the Sea,
The Ascension, the Tree,
The All, the Unknowable,
A crystal of the tears of Isis,
Undiscovered self-form
In the wastelands of destiny.

Roger Calverley, May 2006

INDEX

A

D

H

I

N

O

P

CDs by Calverley Available for Purchase

Crystal Yoga
Calverley & Margherita

Roger Calverley is the author of *Crystal Yoga One*, *The Crystal Mesa* as well as *The Healing Gems*, *The Language of Crystals* and *The Primal Runes*. The background music for this recording is from his most recent CD release, *Temple of Singing Bowls*, but his other albums include *Celitc Mysteries I and II*, *Avalon* and *Bard of Hearts*. He is the director of the Integral Yoga Meditation Centre in Lindsay. This recording was prepared with Margherita, a teacher of crystal healing and Genesa Crystal attunement.

The six exercises in attunement recorded here constitute the introductory practices of Crystal Yoga and are meant to be used in conjunction with training at workshops offered by Roger and Margherita.

Temple Of Singing Bowls

Writer, musician, meditation teacher Roger Calverley has combined his mystical vision and creativity with renowned composer and sound designer, Stephen Bacchus. Together they have created a sonic tour-de-force unlike any other previous Tibetan bowl album. This recording is an extended symphony of primal resonance using ancient bronze masterpieces from Nepal and Tibet as well as modern quartz crystal bowls. The Tibetan Bowls used in this recording are between fifty and two hundred years old, made in the time-honoured tradition with seven sacred metals, including gold, silver, copper, tin, mercury, and iron. Bowls fashioned in this way resonate the vibrations of the seven planets and create an echo of the music of the spheres. Combining various recordings of these rare bowls and then digitally editing and layering them, the artists were able to extract an elemental essence not attainable by playing of the bowls in real time. The resulting rich harmonics open up a truly remarkable world of inner experience which we hope will take you to new places in your inner journey.

For orders email: calverleyr@yahoo.com
CDs are $22.95USD including shipping.

Available from Lotus Press 1-800-824-6396

ANCIENT MYSTERIES TAROT BOOK

Roger Calverley

264 pages pb **Price: $17.95**

This book situates Tarot in its ancient roots, with particular emphasis on the tradition of the Mystery Schools. The first part of the book reviews the ancient sources of Tarot and the dynamics of the archetypes, with interesting side-lights on the author's personal experiences in this realm. Calverley uncovers evidence for the grounding of Tarot's internal structure in the esoteric wisdom of the ancient Mystery Schools. In the second part of the book, the writer follows The Fool on an adventure in which he experiences each of the figures of the Major Arcanum and arrives at the deeper wisdom of the Tarot. He is instructed by The Magician, The Priestess and The Hermit about the meanings and wisdom of Tarot, which he discovers to be a "Book of Truth."

ISBN 13: 978-0-9409-8572-8
ISBN 10: 0-9409-8572-1

THE PRIMAL RUNES
Archetypes of Invocation and Empowerment

Roger Calverley

352 pages pb **Price: $19.95**

Thousands of years before the Aryan invasion of Europe, in forested planes and valleys to the north of modern Greece, a civilization centred on the Great Mother came into existence. The people of Old Europe created sacred signs, the Primal Runes, and gave birth to our most ancient ancestral tradition of divination and magic. Based on the phases of the Moon, these archetypal rune-forms each have a sacred sound; they form a complete system of invocation and empowerment. Mother of all subsequent runes, lost to posterity before the dawn of recorded history, the Primal Runes reveal the hidden wisdom of early earth-mysteries. These ancient runes give direct access to the secret power and the timeless greatness of the Goddess herself.

ISBN 13: 978-0-9409-8583-4
ISBN 10: 0-9409-8583-7